# Adaptation to Chronic Childhood Illness

# Adaptation to Chronic Childhood Illness

Robert J. Thompson, Jr., and Kathryn E. Gustafson

AMERICAN PSYCHOLOGICAL ASSOCIATION
WASHINGTON, DC

Published by
American Psychological Association
750 First Street, NE
Washington, DC 20002

Copies may be ordered from
APA Order Department
P.O. Box 2710
Hyattsville, MD 20784

In the United Kingdom and Europe, copies may be ordered from
American Psychological Association
3 Henrietta Street
Covent Garden, London
WC2E 8LU England

Typeset in Goudy by PRO-IMAGE Corporation, Techna-Type Div., York, PA

Printer: Data Reproductions Corporation, Rochester Hills, MI
Jacket designer: Berg Design, Albany, NY
Technical/production editor: Valerie Montenegro

**Library of Congress Cataloging-in-Publication Data**
Thompson, Robert J. (Robert Joseph), 1945–
    Adaptation to chronic childhood illness / Robert J. Thompson, Jr.,
Kathryn E. Gustafson.
        p.   cm.
    Includes bibliographical references and index.
    ISBN 1-55798-327-5 (acid-free paper)
    1. Chronic diseases in children—Psychological aspects.
2. Adjustment (Psychology) in children.   3. Developmentally disabled
children—Psychology.   I. Gustafson, Kathryn E.   II. Title.
RJ380.T53   1995
618.92′0001′9—dc20                                                95-42008
                                                                              CIP

**British Library Cataloguing-in-Publication Data**
A CIP record is available from the British Library.

*Printed in the United States of America*
*First edition*

*To our families for their love and support:*
*Shirley, Christopher, Stephen, Paul, and Nicholas*
*and*
*Richard and Jeanne, Ron and Hallie*

# CONTENTS

# PREFACE

In caring for children with developmental problems and chronic illness, we have been impressed in three ways. First, we have been impressed by the impact on the life course of children and their parents of having to confront on a daily basis the challenges associated with developmental and health problems. Second, the arbitrariness of life's distribution of adversity is also impressive. Not only is there no customary or average share, but the range in the experiences of adversity accentuates the inequitable distribution. Third, we have been impressed by the amazing resiliency of children and parents in the face of adversity. The ways in which people confront the challenges and threats of suffering and loss with grace and dignity attest to the capabilities of the human spirit, which are truly inspiring. These impressions provide the motivation to determine the constellation of individual and social processes that are associated with adaptation in the face of adversity of chronic childhood illness.

This book is intended to be of interest to social scientists and health care professionals who are involved in caring for children with chronic childhood illness. We envision this book as more than a reference tool for those studying the process of adaptation. Our goal is to have an impact on both science and practice by providing an integrating, biopsychosocial framework that will influence the formulation of research questions, intervention efforts, and public policy. Furthermore, it is our hope that this book will serve to inspire others to seek the rewards of professional careers devoted to improving the quality of lives for these children and their parents. It is also our wish that this book, through its impact on care providers, researchers, and policy makers will contribute in some small way to the improvement of the quality of life of children with chronic illness and their parents.

We want to express our appreciation to our patients and their families, our students, and our colleagues, from whom we have learned much about the process of adaptation. We have been privileged to have been afforded relationships that inform and inspire. We also express our grateful appreciation to Rhonda Strickland for her preparation of this manuscript.

ROBERT J. THOMPSON, JR.
KATHRYN E. GUSTAFSON

# INTRODUCTION AND OVERVIEW

Advances in health care have prolonged and improved the lives of children with chronic illness. Correspondingly, attention is increasingly focused on enhancing the adaptation of children and their families to the stresses engendered by chronic childhood illness. Research in the field has moved to the analytic stage of formulating and evaluating multidimensional conceptual models of adaptation that include biomedical, psychological, and social–ecological parameters. The goal of this book is to use a biopsychosocial conceptual framework to integrate findings and to guide the development of intervention efforts to enhance adaptation. More specifically, the objectives are to delineate the following: (a) the types and frequencies of psychosocial adjustment problems demonstrated by children with chronic illness and their families; (b) the biomedical, psychological, and social–ecological processes associated with successful adaptation; (c) salient intervention targets; and (d) methods to enhance adaptation.

This introductory chapter provides an overview of chronic childhood illness, developmental issues, and systems-theory perspectives that provide the basis for the formulation of biopsychosocial conceptual frameworks that elucidate the process of adaptation. Then this framework is applied to intervention, research, and policy issues. The structure of this overview parallels that of the book and is organized into four sections.

# I. IMPACT OF CHRONIC CHILDHOOD ILLNESS

The purpose of the first section of the book is to portray the scope of chronic childhood illness and the impact on individuals and families. This is accomplished by reviewing what is known about the epidemiology of chronic childhood conditions and considering issues related to classification. Psychosocial adjustment is considered one manifestation of adaptation and a selective and illustrative review of psychosocial adjustment is undertaken, with an emphasis on integration of findings from conceptually driven empirical studies. This is followed by a consideration of theoretical perspectives on the processes that contribute to the adaptation of children and their families to the stresses associated with chronic illness.

## Increasing Prevalence

Children with developmental disorders and chronic illnesses and their families have been a relatively neglected group in our society (J. M. Perrin, 1985). One reason is the relative rarity of specific illnesses, which reflects the different epidemiologies of child and adult chronic illness. Adults face a relatively small number of chronic conditions, whereas children face a relatively large number of rare conditions (J. M. Perrin & MacLean, 1988b). However, as many as 1 million children in the United States have a severe chronic illness that may impair their daily functioning (J. M. Perrin & MacLean, 1988b), and an additional 10 million children have a less serious chronic illness (Haggerty, 1984). The estimates of the prevalence of chronic childhood illness vary widely because of differences in definitions, populations, and methods of study, but rates of 10% to 20% are frequently cited (Gortmaker & Sappenfield, 1984). The epidemiology of chronic childhood illness is addressed in chapter 1.

Although there is little evidence for significant change in the incidence of chronic childhood illness, the prevalence of children with chronic conditions has increased (Gortmaker & Sappenfield, 1984). From the 1960s to the 1980s, there was a doubling, from 1% to 2%, of children with a severe chronic health condition (Gortmaker, 1985).

Several factors contribute to the increase in prevalence. First, advances in health care reflected in improved early diagnosis and treatment have increased the life expectancy for many children who previously would have died in infancy or in early childhood. Increases in survival rates have occurred for many of the chronic childhood illnesses. For example, the median survival age for children with cystic fibrosis increased 2½-fold from 11 years in 1966 to 29.4 years in 1993 (Cystic Fibrosis Foundation, 1994). Acute lymphoblastic leukemia (ALL) was once almost uniformly fatal. In 1960, only 1% of patients with ALL survived to 5 years after diagnosis (Stehbens, 1988), but now 70% can be expected to remain disease free for

5 years (Friedman & Mulhern, 1992). Similarly, the median survival age for children with sickle-cell disease was reported to be about 14 years in 1960 (Diggs, 1973). In contrast, in the recent Cooperative Study of Sickle Cell Disease, the median age of death was 42 years for men and 48 years for women with sickle-cell anemia and 60 years for men and 68 years for women with sickle-cell hemoglobin C disease (Platt et al., 1994). Unfortunately, such dramatic increases in survival are not predicted to continue. It is estimated that 80% of the achievable improvements in mortality have occurred (Gortmaker, 1985).

A second contributor to the increased prevalence of chronic childhood conditions are the new survivors: infants surviving extreme prematurity or very low birth weight. Infants weighing 1,500 g or less constitute approximately 1% of all births (Kitchen et al., 1980). Before 1960, few of these very low birth weight infants survived. With the advances in neonatal intensive care over the last three decades, there has been a progressive decline in mortality for very low birth weight infants from 72% to 27% (McCormick, 1989). Survival rates range from 34% at less than 751 g to 93% at 1,251–1,500 g (Hack et al., 1991). However, the rate of moderate to severe handicaps in the survivors has remained relatively stable between 4.5% and 10.1%. Longer term outcome studies adopting a multidimensional approach reveal relatively high rates of respiratory and neurological morbidity, behavioral and learning problems (McCormick, 1989), and academic difficulties or special education class placement (Hunt, Cooper, & Tooley, 1988).

A third contributor to increased prevalence of chronic childhood conditions are new conditions, reflected in infants with prenatal drug exposure and children with AIDS. Each year an estimated 375,000 newborns are affected by drugs such as alcohol and cocaine that have known associations with neurodevelopmental problems (Chasnoff, 1989). The first case of AIDS in a child was diagnosed in 1982, and as of September 30, 1991, the Centers for Disease Control had reported a total of 3,312 cases (Fletcher et al., 1991). Although the majority of infants with perinatally acquired HIV infection appear normal at birth, HIV symptoms may develop within 6 months, and AIDS typically is evident within 24 months (Fletcher et al., 1991). The child's brain is a target site for HIV infection. Although many children function well for a number of years, by the end stage of their disease the majority develop characteristic progressive encephalopathy with resulting developmental delays, deterioration of motor skills and cognitive functioning, and loss of developmental milestones (Fahrner, 1992).

The increased prevalence of chronic childhood illness has had several major impacts on the health care and family systems. First, as acute diseases of childhood have declined, children with chronic conditions are an increasing proportion of the practice of primary care pediatricians. However, the range of disorders is large, with a small number of children in any one practice with any one disease. This makes it difficult for the pediatrician to keep abreast of advances in care and management. Second, children with chronic conditions use more and a wider array of health services than other children (Gortmaker & Sappenfield, 1984). Third, children and their families are, in increasing numbers, confronted with the task of coping with chronic illness over a substantial period of their lives (Thompson, 1985). This, in turn, has caused a concern about quality of life in general and psychosocial adjustment in particular.

## Classification

Chronic conditions of childhood include developmental illness, such as mental retardation, and chronic diseases, such as cystic fibrosis and sickle-cell disease. Although there can be some overlap, the primary focus of this book is on chronic childhood illness. "A chronic illness is one that lasts for a substantial period of time or that has sequelae that are debilitating for a long period of time" (J. M. Perrin, 1985, p. 2). Illnesses that persist for more than 3 months in a year or necessitate a period of continuous hospitalizations for more than a month are considered chronic (Pless & Pinkerton, 1975).

Chronic childhood illnesses differ in terms of the biomedical parameters of etiology, functional manifestations, course, and treatment regimens. Chronic childhood illness has been classified in two ways. The *categorical* approach typically groups chronic conditions in terms of specific diseases, such as diabetes and asthma, or body system impairment, such as metabolic illness and hearing disorders. The *noncategorical* approach to classification is based on the premise that regardless of the specific disease, children with chronic conditions, and their families, face common life experiences that are based on generic dimensions of their conditions (Stein & Jessop, 1982). These generic dimensions include whether the condition is visible or invisible, fatal or nonfatal, and stable or unpredictable; whether it impacts on the cognitive or sensorimotor system; whether it requires intrusive care; and age of onset (Stein & Jessop, 1982).

The categorical approach has fostered biomedical advances and the provision of treatment regimens that have improved the lives of children with chronic conditions. The noncategorical approach has fostered a recognition that children with chronic illnesses and their families have common challenges and needs that have implications for program development and public policy considerations. Rather than advocating an either–or approach to classification, we share the view that a partial (Pless & Perrin, 1985) or *modified* categorical approach that seeks to identify the common biomedical and therapeutic characteristics of groups of disorders can be beneficial to research, clinical practice, and policy formation. More specifically, we advocate that there are likely to be both illness-specific and generic processes of importance to adaptation of children and families to chronic illness and that it is premature for the field to adopt solely a categorical or noncategorical approach.

In keeping with our modified categorical approach, we develop a classification scheme, which is based on biomedical and psychosocial tasks, in chapter 1. These tasks are exemplified by a consideration of six disorders selected to be representative of the major dimensions of the classification schema: asthma, cancer, cystic fibrosis, diabetes, sickle-cell disease, and spina bifida.

## Psychosocial Adjustment

Chronic childhood illness is a well-recognized stressor for children and their families (J. M. Perrin & MacLean, 1988b). Although the findings of population studies and studies of specific disorders vary, it is estimated that children with chronic illness have a risk for adjustment problems that is 1.5 to 3 times as high as their healthy peers (Pless, 1984). Those at highest risk for adjustment difficulties appear to be those with poorly functioning families (Pless, Roghmann, & Haggerty, 1972). Whereas the risk of adjustment difficulties is not strongly related to illness severity, it is related to duration of the illness (Pless & Roghmann, 1971) and also to degree of functional impairment (Breslau, 1985).

There are a number of issues related to the assessment of psychosocial adjustment; these are addressed in chapter 2. It is useful to view *psychosocial adjustment* as an umbrella term that encompasses several dimensions: psychological adjustment, social adjustment, and school performance. We view the findings of empirical studies regarding the types and frequencies of psychosocial adjustment problems experienced by children with the six representative chronic disorders delineated above. Psychological adjustment, considered in terms of emotional and behavioral disorders and impact on self-esteem, is addressed in chapter 2. Social adjustment, peer relationships, and school performance are addressed in chapter 4. The increased risk for adjustment problems in children with chronic illness is clearly established, but the individual variability in adjustment is also apparent.

Chronic childhood conditions also increase the risk for parental adjustment difficulties. The emotional impact and the physical burden of the child's care fall primarily on the mother (Jessop, Riessman, & Stein, 1988), and increased levels of psychological distress have been reported for mothers of children with chronic disorders as compared with mothers of healthy children (Breslau, Staruch, & Mortimer, 1982). Moreover, there appears to be a direct relationship between the functional limitations of the child and the level of psychological distress of the mother (Jessop et al., 1988).

We review in chapter 6 the research findings regarding the psychological adjustment of parents and siblings of children with chronic illness. Research in the area of family adjustment has lagged behind that in the area of adjustment of children with chronic illness. Assessment methodologies need to be improved, developmental–longitudinal perspectives and designs need to be included, and studies need to be conceptually and theoretically driven. However, the evidence pointing to the role of maternal adjustment in the adjustment of children with chronic illness and their siblings is already sufficient to warrant the development of intervention efforts to enhance maternal adjustment.

Although there is an increased risk for adjustment difficulties, most children with chronic conditions, and their parents and siblings, demonstrate good adjustment. This variability in outcome has prompted the investigation of the processes associated with risk and resiliency in the face of the adversity of chronic childhood illness. The contribution of biomedical, psychological, and social–ecological parameters to psychosocial adjustment has been investigated in numerous studies, the findings of which are reviewed in chapter 3. It is now clear that there is no direct relationship between type of illness, or severity of illness, and psychosocial adjustment. Whereas some child and family characteristics have been associated with adjustment, the search for processes associated with adaptation has been hampered by a lack of theoretical or conceptual frameworks, which are necessary to guide research studies, integrate findings, and inform intervention efforts (Thompson, 1985). However, the situation is beginning to change. The advent of systems-theory perspectives to human development has provided the foundation for the formulation of models of adaptation that attempt to integrate empirical findings about the correlates of adjustment with theoretical perspectives to adaptation.

## Advent of Social–Ecological Perspectives

Concurrent with the advances in biomedical science and health care, there also have been advances in the behavioral and social sciences. First, the advances in computer technology have enabled increasingly sophisticated data-analytic methods, involving multiple variables. Second, conceptual models have been promulgated that seek to be inclusive, rather than reductionistic, in attending to the complexity and multiple determinants of human behavior. Important in this regard was the recognition of the need for a biopsychosocial model as a way to "broaden the approach to disease to include the psychosocial without sacrificing the enormous advantages of the biomedical approach" (Engel, 1977, p. 131). In particular, the emergence of multifaceted approaches to the pathogenesis of disease enabled linkage between the behavioral and biomedical sciences (Weiss, 1987). Also important were broader systems-theory perspectives that gave rise to specific models of how biological and psychosocial processes act together in human development across the life span.

The systems-theory perspective holds that all levels of an organization are linked to each other in a hierarchically arranged continuum, with more complex, larger units superordinate to the less complex, smaller units. Change at one level affects change in other levels as well. In terms of human development, the hierarchy progresses from the cell level through the organ systems level to the person level, which is at the highest level of the organism hierarchy. At the same time, the person level is the lowest unit of the social hierarchy, which progresses through the family and the community levels (Engel, 1980). A systems-theory perspective focuses on the accommodations that occur through the life span between the developing organism and his or her changing environment.

Viewing this progressive accommodation in systems-theory terms serves several useful purposes. First, it forces us to go beyond a single event, such as cystic fibrosis, sickle-cell disease, or cancer, to explore the multiple factors that mediate and moderate developmental outcome. Second, it forces us to assess the impact of experience on the developing person, or on other people and subsystems. Third, it forces us to focus on the continuous interaction of constitutional and environmental factors and processes over time.

In terms of our understanding of chronic childhood illness, the social–ecological systems-theory perspective of human development formulated by Bronfenbrenner (1977, 1979) has had the most impact. Social ecology is defined as "the study of the relation between the developing human being and the settings and contexts in which the person is actively involved" (Kazak, 1989, p. 26). The theory proposes a series of concentric circles that represent settings that have bidirectional influences on the child. The child is at the center. The closer concentric rings represent family and smaller settings such as school, whereas the more distant circles represent societal values and culture. Major tenets of social–ecological theory include (a) reciprocity, that is, not only does the environment affect the child, but the child also affects the environment; (b) interconnections and relations between settings, which influence the child's development; and (c) transitions, that is, successive shifts in role and setting across the life span have developmental significance (Bronfenbrenner, 1979).

Within a social–ecological perspective, the setting of immediate importance to the development of the child is the family system, in general, and the parent–child interaction, in particular. The transactional model of development (Sameroff & Chandler, 1975) called attention to the effect that children have on their environment through their characteristics and behaviors and to the bidirectional influence between the child and parents over time. The child is no longer viewed as the passive recipient of the socialization processes of the family and larger environment. The child is viewed as an active participant in shaping her or his environment. Subsequently, advances have been made in understanding the sociocultural, family, and individual parent and child processes that influence parent–child interactions and the processes whereby those interactions affect the child's cognitive and social development.

The impact of parents' child rearing behavior on their children's development is frequently investigated under the rubric of parenting. A body of information is accumulating regarding processes that affect parenting. Among these processes, attention has been directed to the role of maternal cognitions, such as beliefs, appraisals, expectations, and attributions, on parenting behaviors, which in turn affect children's development. Maternal cognitions about children's development reflects the influence of the sociocultural milieu (Miller, 1988) and guide mothers' proactive and reactive responses to their children's behavior (Mills & Rubin, 1990; Rubin, Mills, & Rose-Krasnor, 1989). Maternal stress and distress also influence maternal cognitive processes, such as appraisals and expectations of the children's behavior and development (Crnic & Greenberg, 1990; Patterson, 1983), and mothers' behavioral interactions with their children (Webster-Stratton, 1990). In particular, the stress of daily parenting hassles and maternal depression have been linked to less satisfactory parenting and to lower social (Crnic & Greenberg, 1990) and cognitive (Lyons-Ruth, Zoll, Connell, & Grunebaum, 1986) competencies in children.

Thus, systems-theory perspectives focus on the accommodations, that is, adaptations, that occur throughout the life span between the developing child and his or her environment and identify the crucial role of parenting, and the processes that influence it, in development. Chronic childhood illness presents substantial challenges to the process of adaptation.

### Chronic Childhood Illness as a Potential Stressor

Chronic childhood illness can be viewed as a potential stressor to which the individual and family systems endeavor to adapt. This enables the application of the considerable body of knowledge regarding stress and coping processes to the specific situation of fostering the adaptation of children and their families to chronic illness. In particular, three types of processes have been identified that are likely to influence adaptation to the stress of chronic illness and that also could serve as salient intervention targets: cognitive processes, social support, and coping methods.

Stress is not inherent in a situation or an event, such as chronic childhood illness, but arises from the person–environment transaction (Lazarus & Folkman, 1984). Psychological approaches to stress have emphasized the role of cognitive processes of appraisal and expectations. Stress is related to the individual's appraisal of the degree of threat in a situation in relation to the available environmental resources and individual coping capabilities. The links between the cognitive processes of appraisal and stress and distress have been well established (Lazarus & Folkman, 1984). *Expectations*, which refer to beliefs about control (Strickland, 1978) and self-efficacy (Bandura, 1977), have also been linked to adjustment.

There is also a substantial body of evidence that social support acts to prevent or mitigate the consequences of stress (Haggerty, 1980). Essential components of social support include consistent communication of what is expected, assistance with tasks, evaluation of performance, and provision of appropriate rewards (Thompson, 1985). In keeping with the focus on the family system of children with chronic disorders, social support is frequently assessed in terms of family functioning (Daniels, Moos, Billings, & Miller, 1987).

*Coping* is the multidimensional process that refers to the ways in which people deal with stress (Lazarus & Folkman, 1984). One function of coping is to be instrumental, that is, to alter the troubled transaction between person and environment through efforts directed at the environment or the self. This type of coping has been linked to the adaptive Piagetian processes of accommodation and assimilation (Lazarus & Launier, 1980) and is referred to as *adaptive–problem-focused* coping. Another function of coping is palliation, that is, to regulate emotional states that are associated with stress. This type of coping has been referred to as *palliative–emotion-focused*. These two types of coping come together in the situation of chronic childhood illness, which involves the threat of suffering and loss as well as specific tasks that need to be accomplished. These tasks include dealing with the symptoms and treatments, preserving parental and child emotional well-being, and preparing for an uncertain future (Moos & Tsu, 1977). The effectiveness of coping strategies depends on the degree of fit between characteristics of the stressor and the person's preferred style (Compas, Malcarne, & Fondacaro, 1988).

Consideration of chronic illness as a potential stressor not only has led to the identification of stress and coping processes as salient to adaptation but also has stimulated the application of two types of theories, cognitive–behavioral–social learning theories and family systems–social support theories, to the formulation of specific models. These specific models delineate the processes associated with adaptation to chronic childhood illness. They are discussed in chapter 5.

## Cognitive–Behavioral–Social Learning Theories

Social learning theories call attention to the role of learning through social interactions on cognitive and behavioral processes likely to influence adaptation. In an early effort at developing a model, Pless and Pinkerton (1975) proposed an integrated model in which adjustment was viewed as being multiply determined through a dynamic process of reciprocal transactions of the individual with his or her environment. This model emphasized the role of the child's self-concept and coping strategies as major determinants of the continuous process of adaptation over time to the stresses engendered by chronic illness. The treatment implications of the model include early intervention to enhance self-concept and coping methods and to influence the response of the family to the child's condition and coping efforts.

The model developed by Moos and Tsu (1977) viewed chronic illness as a life crisis. Illness, background, and environmental factors were seen as influencing the child's cognitive appraisal of the significance of the crisis, which set forth adaptive tasks to which coping skills could be applied. The focus on illness tasks enabled the application of the increasing body of information regarding the effectiveness of adaptive and palliative coping strategies to the situation of chronic childhood illness. The treatment implications of this model were an inclusion of cognitive processes of stress appraisal as well as coping methods as intervention targets.

Building on the efforts to delineate risk and protective factors for psychiatric disorders, Wallander and Varni (1992) formulated a disability–stress–coping model. Factors hypothesized to play a role in adjustment to chronic conditions were organized into a risk–resistance framework. Risk factors are aspects of the child's life and condition parameters that engender stress. Resistance factors are coping resources, including interpersonal characteristics; stress-processing factors, such as cognitive appraisal and coping behaviors; and family characteristics. Another aspect of this model is that adaptation is viewed multidimensionally and includes mental health, social functioning, and physical health. The treatment implications of this model are to reduce risk factors and increase resistance factors.

Although developed independently, our transactional stress and coping model (Thompson, Gil, Burbach, Keith, & Kinney, 1993a, 1993b; Thompson, Gustafson, Hamlett, & Spock, 1992a, 1992b) includes a similar focus on stress processing within an ecological–systems-theory perspective. Adaptation to chronic childhood illness is viewed as a function of the transaction of illness and demographic parameters and stress processing. In particular, cognitive process of appraisal and expectations, coping methods, and family functioning are hypothesized to mediate adaptation to chronic illness. Furthermore, child and parent adjustment are hypothesized to be mutually mediating. The treatment implications of this model are altering cognitive appraisals, coping methods, and family functioning to reduce stress related to illness tasks and environmental transactions. Adaptation is reflected in health and adherence as well as in psychosocial adjustment.

These cognitive–behavioral–social learning models have stimulated a considerable amount of research that is providing a foundation for intervention efforts, in terms of both prevention and treatment. These models are complex and difficult to test completely with any given sample. However, the stage is now set for evaluation of intervention programs that are based on these conceptual models.

### Family Systems Theories

Family systems theories call attention to the role of family interactions, in response to the stresses associated with chronic childhood illness, in adaptation. Research has focused on delineating dimensions of family structure and functioning that impact on adjustment.

The circumplex model of family systems (Olson, Sprenkle, & Russell, 1979) identified cohesion and adaptability as dimensions of family functioning that are important to adjustment. It is hypothesized that a balanced degree of family cohesion and adaptability is conducive to effective family and individual functioning.

Building on the extensive evidence that social networks serve to buffer and ameliorate the impact of stress, Kazak (1986) proposed a model of adaptation to chronic illness. The focus is on the child's and parent's social network structure as influencing the nature of social support available to the family. In addition, the parent's social network provides models for parenting strategies, which, in turn, influence adaptation.

Other investigators working within a family systems perspective have focused on other aspects of family functioning in addition to cohesion, adaptability, and social support. For example, Quittner and colleagues proposed a model that postulates that illness-specific and normal parenting tasks associated with developmental stages potentially alter the performance of key family roles (Quittner, DiGlirolamo, Michel, & Eigen, 1992). Alterations of family roles lead to increases in role strain and decreases in marital satisfaction, which, in turn, influence maternal adjustment.

The impact of a parent's child rearing strategies and behaviors on the child's cognitive and social development has been clearly demonstrated and serves as a basis for the development of models of determinants of parenting and of the role of parenting in promoting adaptation to chronic childhood illness. Belsky's (1984) process model views parenting as determined by parent characteristics, child characteristics, and contextual sources of stress and support. This model emphasizes that it is not the particular amount or type of these determinants that are important, but rather the goodness of fit among them, for example, the match between support desired and support received.

A number of investigators are also attempting to delineate the ways in which parenting influences the child's cognitive and social development as well as coping with stress. For example, several conceptual models emphasize the role of parental cognitions, beliefs, and causal attributions in child development (e.g., Dix, Ruble, Guisec, & Nixon, 1986; Miller, 1988; Mills & Rubin, 1990). Other conceptual models address the linkage between parental stress and distress, child rearing behaviors, and children's development. In particular, parental stress is associated with less optimal parent–child interactions and lower child's competence (Crnic & Greenberg, 1990). Maternal depression has been linked to perceptions of higher levels of a child's behavior problems (Webster-Stratton, 1990) and to lower child's competence.

The intervention implications of family and parenting theories are clear in targeting social support, parental stress and adjustment, and child rearing beliefs and practices as processes associated with child development and adaptation. In particular, these models call attention to promoting parent effectiveness by enhancing goodness of fit with the child's special characteristics and needs.

The stage is now set to attempt to integrate cognitive–behavioral–social learning theories and family systems theories. To this end, a hybrid stress-processing model of parenting is proposed, in chapter 5, to guide intervention efforts.

## II. DEVELOPMENTAL CHANGES

The purpose of the second section of the book is to make explicit that a developmental perspective is the necessary context for understanding and promoting adjustment to chronic childhood illness. An overview of Piagetian theory of cognitive development in chapter 7 provides a context within which to integrate findings regarding the development of children's conceptualizations related to health and illness. Developmental perspectives regarding cognitive processes and coping methods are addressed in chapters 8 and 9, respectively.

It is essential to recognize that the impact of chronic childhood illness is dynamic, not static, because it occurs within the context of ongoing developmental processes. Development can be viewed as occurring as a consequence of the transactions between innate qualities of the individual rooted in the biologic organism and life experiences occurring in a psychosocial context (Thompson, 1985). The transactional model of development focuses on the continuous and mutual influence of the child and his or her environment.

> The mechanism by which a child's physical illness may modify the expected developmental progression can be seen in the same light: the illness affects the child's interaction with the physical and social environment in which he or she lives, and aspects of the child's environment such as parents, peers, or school systems, are altered as a result of the illness. (E. C. Perrin & Gerrity, 1984, p. 19)

However, the implications of chronic disorder for a child's cognitive, social, and emotional development differ considerably depending on the child's developmental stage at its onset and the constraints of the disorder at each stage of development (E. C. Perrin & Gerrity, 1984).

### Direct and Indirect Effects

The child's interactions with the environment are affected by chronic illness in two ways. There can be a direct effect of biological processes on systems of the body that result in cognitive, motor, language, sensory, or other functional impairments. Developmental disorders, including mental retardation, cerebral palsy, and learning disabilities, constitute chronic disorders that affect the central nervous system (Thompson & O'Quinn, 1979). Other systems can also be affected and result in functional limitations. For example, cystic fibrosis affects the pulmonary systems and can result in susceptibility to fatigue. Some illnesses reflect a primary disorder in one system but also pose a risk to the central nervous system as a result of the illness itself or its treatment. For example, sickle-cell disease affects the blood system, but also poses risk to the central nervous system through stroke. Similarly, leukemia is another disorder that affects the blood system but its treatment with central nervous system irradiation and chemotherapy can also pose risks for the central nervous system (Madan-Swain & Brown, 1991).

The child's interaction with the environment can also be affected indirectly by chronic illness, through the impact on developmental tasks. The organism's biologically based drive toward growth combined with the demands, constraints, and opportunities provided by the social environment give rise to the concept of developmental or psychosocial tasks that must be accomplished during phases or stages of the life course. There are two principal sources of developmental tasks: (a) biological changes that present the individual with new opportunities, needs, and problems of adjustment; and (b) societal and personal expectations regarding social roles that change with age (Havinghurst, 1973). The expected socioemotional developmental stages and tasks have been described by Erikson (1964).

Erikson's theory of personality postulates eight stages of development; each stage is characterized by issues or conflicts that need to be resolved and constitute specific developmental tasks. The task to be accomplished during the first year of life is basic trust. During early childhood, the developmental task is autonomy. During adolescence, the developmental task is identity. Subsequently, other theorists have delineated developmental tasks of adulthood such as marriage, parenthood, and retirement. The indirect impact of chronic illness on the child's interaction with the environment, through the impact on developmental tasks of trust, autonomy, and identity, can readily be appreciated.

More complex developmental models are emerging to reflect the relationship among chronic illness and individual and family cycles. In one model (Rolland, 1987), chronic illnesses are characterized on the basis of the psychosocial demands on the ill individual and her or his family, in terms of two illness dimensions. The first dimension includes the illnesses' characteristics of onset (acute or gradual); course (progressive, constant, or relapsing–episodic); and outcome (fatal, life shortening, and nonfatal; and incapacitating and nonincapacitating). The second dimension includes three time phases of an illness: crisis, chronic, and terminal. The third dimension of this model reflects individual and family life cycles involving structure building or maintaining periods and transition periods. Within such a psychosocial developmental schema, the impact or potential stressfulness of chronic illness can be delineated in terms of the match or congruence of the illness-related psychosocial tasks with those of specific phases of individual and family life cycles.

Another avenue of indirect effect of chronic illness on the child's development is through responses elicited from parents and peers. There is a substantial body of information from the child development literature on the "stimulus value" of the infant as one mechanism of effect on his or her caregiver (M. Lewis & Rosenblum, 1974). The neurodevelopmental and temperamental consequences of developmental disorders impact on caretaker responses to the infant. For example, the neurobehavioral patterns of the premature infant can pose a substantial challenge to the efforts of the mother to interact in developmentally and mutually rewarding ways with her infant. Likewise, illness that is associated with visible impairments or that results in functional limitations of mobility contribute to the youngster's stimulus value and may evoke overprotection within the family and ridicule from peers.

Thus, chronic disorders have direct and indirect impact on children's transactions with their environment. Direct effects occur through biologically based functional impairments. Indirect effects occur through impact on accomplishment of psychosocial developmental tasks and the response of the environment to the characteristics and behavior of the child. It is the child's transactions with the environment that influences his or her development.

## Development of Children's Conceptualizations

There is a growing recognition that children's cognitive–developmental status plays a role in their knowledge, attitudes, and behaviors related to health and illness as well as in their emotional response. In particular, the child's developmental status has implications for compliance with therapeutic regimens, medical treatments, and psychosocial interventions (Garrison & McQuiston, 1989). One issue of concern is the relationship between the child's level of cognitive development and "his/her ability to process and benefit from the provision of health-related information" (Garrison & McQuiston, 1989, p. 76). Another issue is the impact of the child's ability to reason about causality on his or her perceptions of self-blame or responsibility for the disorder (E. C. Perrin & Gerrity, 1984) and in adherence to medical regimens. Finally, children's perceptions of the ability to control aspects of their health change developmentally. Health locus-of-control orientation may be related to adherence to medical regimens (Garrison & McQuiston, 1989), as well as to methods of coping with stress (Strickland, 1978). However, health knowledge and locus of control have been inconsistently linked to disease control and adherence (Garrison & McQuiston, 1989), pointing out the need for increased knowledge about the interaction of disease-specific biomedical and developmental tasks, child development, and child and family characteristics.

In addition to being important in eliciting children's adherence to medical regimens, the child's level of cognitive development is important in terms of the impact of his or her perceptions of illness on their emotional reaction and adjustment. Even though efforts are usually made to speak at the child's level, "there is little theoretical structure to guide the tasks of promoting explanations of illness which are both accurate and within the child's cognitive capacity for understanding" (Whitt, Dykstra, & Taylor, 1979, p. 331). Children frequently misconstrue fundamental elements of their disorder and its treatment. It has been postulated that children's conceptions of illness "follow a developmental progression which qualitatively parallels shifts in the child's cognitive processes [following Piaget's framework] changing from primitive, egocentric reasoning to more abstract and concretely logical views" (Whitt et al., 1979, p. 332). This framework can serve as a useful guide in efforts to provide information and explanations that are appropriately concrete for the child's level of cognitive development. Intervention efforts need to be developmentally appropriate, not only to promote adherence but also to facilitate the child's understanding and management of his or her feelings associated with the disorder and its treatments.

## III. ENHANCING ADAPTATION

The purpose of the third section of the book is to consider the implications of the biopsychosocial framework for intervention goals and effective intervention processes to foster the adaptation of children with chronic illness and their families. These general issues and objectives are considered in chapter 10. The specific issues of adherence and pain management are discussed in chapters 11 and 12, respectively.

## Intervention

The multidimensional biopsychosocial framework, which is the product of current models, serves to guide the development of comprehensive care programs for children with chronic illness and their families. The focus is on the continuous process of adaptation by the children and their families to the stresses associated with chronic illness. The goals of care are to diminish the impact of the illness and to prevent dysfunction (J. M. Perrin & MacLean, 1988b). More specifically, the objectives of care are to extend the life span and to improve the quality of life (Kaplan, 1990).

According to our framework, one way in which chronic childhood illness affects children and their families is through disruption of normal processes of child development and family functioning (J. M. Perrin & MacLean, 1988b). The various cognitive–behavioral and family systems models suggest that the impact can be lessened and adaptation promoted through stress reduction, enhancement of support-eliciting social problem-solving skills, and effective parenting.

One way to foster normalization is to lessen the impact of the children's illness on their social and academic performance in school. Frequently, chronic illness and its treatment can result in cognitive deficits, absenteeism, fatigue, and emotional distress, which disrupt academic and social performance. Individualized educational programming is frequently necessary to meet the educational needs of children with chronic illness, requiring cooperative efforts among health care providers, the child and family, and the school system. Specific school reintegration programs have been developed and their effectiveness demonstrated (Katz, Varni, Rubenstein, Blew, & Hubert, 1992).

Children with chronic illness are at high risk for peer difficulties because of physical changes and disruptions in social functioning. The particular importance of classmate social support for children's adjustment also has been documented. Given that the stress-buffering and mediating effects of social support have been well documented, several investigators have devised social skill enhancement programs that can be incorporated into school reintegration programs. Furthermore, researchers have begun to identify situation-specific social skills deficits (see Dodge, McClaskey, & Feldman, 1985) that will afford more specificity in treatment planning.

Based on these lines of research, Varni and Katz and their colleagues have devised a social skills training component and demonstrated its effectiveness in facilitating school reintegration with children with cancer (Varni, Katz, Colegrove, & Dolgin, 1993). At the 9-month follow-up evaluation, children who received the training programs had fewer reported behavior problems, greater classmate and teacher social support, and higher school competence than did children who received only the routine school reintegration services.

There have been few intervention programs that have specifically targeted improving parenting as a method of fostering adaptation to chronic childhood illness. However, the stage is set for major efforts in this area. The mental health and child development literature contains examples of parenting intervention programs that have proved to be effective in improving children's behavior problems (Forehand, 1993) and cognitive and social development (R. T. Gross, 1990). (Intervention programs that specifically target normalization and parenting processes are discussed in chap. 10.)

## Adherence

Concurrent with the advances in health care that have prolonged and improved the lives of children with chronic illness, parents have acquired case manager and nursing roles along with their parenting roles. This has resulted in a change in the goals and process of care. Intervention is now family centered, with goals based on the needs of the entire family (see Shelton & Stepanek, 1994). In terms of process, the prevailing model is one of a parent–professional collaborative relationship that supports parents in meeting their goals and "empowers" them by helping them to acquire the knowledge and skills needed to meet their child's special needs. One consequence of the change to a family-centered, parent–professional, collaborative model has been a change in view about compliance with medical regimens (discussed in chap. 11).

It has been well recognized that noncompliance with medical regimens is a relatively common occurrence, with an estimated median adherence rate of 50% for pediatric populations (Dunbar-Jacob, Dunning, Dwyer, 1993). Considerable research has been directed at identifying the biomedical, child, and social and ecological parameters that affect adherence. Furthermore, several multivariate models of adherence such as the health belief model (see Becker et al., 1979) have been formulated and are guiding research. Because of the particular importance of metabolic control in diabetes, adherence plays a central role in the treatment program, and diabetes has been a fertile ground for studies of adherence. Hanson (1992) developed a systems-theory approach to adaptation to diabetes, and she and her colleagues systematically assessed the role of key psychological processes in metabolic control, either directly or through adherence. One of the findings is that stress affects metabolic control directly, whereas positive family functioning is associated with improved adherence, which is associated with good metabolic control.

Congruent with the changes in the goals and processes of health care, a gradual change is taking place in how compliance is viewed. Traditionally, noncompliance was viewed as an indicator of irresponsibility, carelessness, or forgetfulness. However, the less than one-to-one correspondence between treatment and outcome and the emerging view of patient and family as decision makers have resulted in a more considered view in which noncompliance can be a well-reasoned, adaptive choice (Deaton, 1985). This changing view has led to changes in efforts to improve adherence to medical regimens (see L. H. Epstein & Cluss, 1982). In recognition of the patient and family as decision makers, the foci of adherence intervention efforts are the provision of knowledge, the acquisition of specific procedural skills, and "tailoring" a consensual, mutually negotiated regimen or management plan. That is, the management plan is tailored to the specific needs and life situation priorities and realities of the family.

### Pain Management

Pain is unavoidable in the course of children's daily lives and also is associated with illness and treatments. Pain involves both a sensory, nociceptive component and a response component that includes psychologic, physiologic, emotional, and behavioral responses to the nocioception. Approaches to pain management involve analgesics, behavioral interventions, and a combination of pharmacological and behavioral approaches. A consideration of pharmacological approaches is beyond the scope of this book. However, psychologically based approaches to helping children cope with the pain associated with medical procedures and illness-related pain are considered in chapter 12. Consistent with the transactional model of adaptation, the focus is on enhancing children's and parents' interactive coping skills. Furthermore, we advocate that the organic–psychogenic dichotomy viewpoint regarding pain etiology should be avoided. Instead, we posit that psychological and physiological processes interact in the phenomenological experience of pain and that the response of the socioecological environment can elicit, maintain, or decrease the expression of pain and coping behaviors.

Children with chronic illness may face two types of pain: pain associated with invasive medical procedures and the chronic and recurrent pain associated with illness such as sickle-cell disease and arthritis. The efficacy of cognitive–behavioral approaches for both types of pain is now well established. These cognitive–behavioral programs are multicomponent and focus on pain perception regulation and pain behavior modification. Pain perception regulation combines a number of self-regulatory techniques, including deep breathing, muscle relaxation, imagery, behavioral rehearsal (Dahlquist, 1992), distraction, and active coping attempts (Gil, Williams, Thompson, & Kinney, 1991; Varni, Walco, & Wilcox, 1990). Pain behavior modification techniques focus on identifying and modifying socioenvironmental factors that influence pain expression. Social learning theory calls attention to the role of the caregiver and selective reinforcement of behavioral expressions of pain. The role of the parent is to support his or her child's active coping efforts by coaching the use of distraction techniques, contingent praise, and active directives to cope along with the avoidance of the use of explanations and reassurance.

There has been a convergence of these lines of research with the development of cognitive–behavioral family intervention programs with the dual emphasis on teaching children pain coping skills and parent training. This approach is exemplified by the work of Sanders and colleagues with children with recurrent abdominal pain (Sanders, Shepherd, Gleghorn, & Woolford, 1994). The focus on coping skills helps children maintain the pleasures and joys afforded by their normal daily activities. Thus, efforts to promote active coping attempts are consistent with the overall approach of fostering adaptation to chronic childhood illness by minimizing the impact on everyday life experiences.


## IV. GOALS FOR PUBLIC POLICY AND RESEARCH

In this section, we consider the implications of biopsychosocial conceptual framework for policies regarding children with chronic illness and their families. We also identify future research goals appropriate to the stage of research in the area.


### Public Policy

Within American society, social policy is one method by which goals are formulated and resources allocated through a process of demonstrating needs and advocating that these needs be met. Although incomplete, the knowledge regarding children with chronic illness and their families is sufficient to guide policy development. Children with chronic illness and their families have the same health, welfare, and educational needs of any child and family, but they also have needs for specialized and integrated medical–surgical care and related support services. Our multifaceted biopsychosocial framework identifies preventing the disruption of the process of normal development and family functioning, particularly in terms of parenting, as primary mechanisms for promoting adaptation to the stresses associated with chronic childhood illness. Thus, this framework suggests that public policy objectives should include meeting the special needs of children with chronic illness and their families so as to maintain normal development and facilitate effective parenting through stress reduction and enhancing support.

Diversity and fragmentation of the organization and financing of services for children with chronic illness are major sources of stress. At a time when the health care system in the United States is undergoing unprecedented changes, it is imperative that the array of needed services be made available through a system of public and private financing in which there is a shared risk for the costs involved. Parent support policies (i.e., adequate day care and leave programs) are essential to enable parents to fulfill the case manager and nursing roles they have incurred along with their parenting roles.

Over several decades, federal policies have attempted to respond to the needs of children with special needs, most notably through legislation related to children with developmental disabilities and handicapping conditions. In chapter 13 we review the evolution and impact of this federal legislation. The common needs of children with diverse developmental, health, and educational needs have been identified; knowledge has been generated; training programs have been developed; and states have been stimulated to develop and finance service programs. Furthermore, these federal policies have specifically sought to involve and empower parents. For example, the Education for All Handicapped Children Act of 1975 requires a free, appropriate public education for children with disabilities and guarantees parents a role in the development of their child's individualized educational program.

Although not specific to children with chronic illness, these model federal policies do have provisions under which some of the needs of these children can be met. Equally important, however, is that these model federal policies demonstrate what can be accomplished over time, through the joint efforts of families and the scientific community, to enhance the well-being of children and families. Chronic childhood illness requires collaborative relationships among the family, health care, and educational systems. There is a need to support parents to enhance their success in promoting optimal development and adaptation of their children.

## Future Research Goals

The biopsychosocial framework that has guided this book has informed us about the process of adaptation to chronic childhood illness and the major conclusions are reviewed in chapter 14. This conceptual framework also delineates what is not yet known, which serves as the research agenda for future studies.

Almost all of the knowledge regarding adaptation of children with chronic childhood illness and their families is based on cross-sectional studies. There is a compelling need to determine how psychosocial adjustment, mediating and moderating adaptational processes, and their interrelationships change over time relative to individual and family developmental phases and illness course. Efficient and effective intervention efforts require the ability to identify high-risk individuals and opportunity for change.

The concept of "goodness of fit" needs to be extended beyond considerations of how coping methods have to match situational and individual characteristics. Now that researchers have some information about how adaptational processes such as cognitive processes, coping methods, and social support contribute to psychosocial adjustment, they need to determine how different patterns of interrelationships among these adaptational processes and adjustment occur for subgroups of individuals and families. Naturally occurring subgroups are those constituted on the basis of illness or condition type, gender, and racial–cultural groups. In this way, researchers will have a more refined appreciation of adaptive processes as a function of specific biomedical, individual, and social–ecological parameters.

Although current behavioral science knowledge is incomplete, it is sufficient to warrant moving to the next level of research, (i.e., the experimental level). Intervention studies are necessary to confirm knowledge about hypothesized adaptational processes and to further refine the biopsychosocial models that will guide subsequent research efforts. On the basis of the findings from the analytical level of research reflected in biopsychosocial models of adaptation, the stage is set for systematic treatment outcome studies using cognitive–behavioral–social learning theories and family systems methods and programs with well-established efficacy. Replication and integration across illnesses and conditions will serve to identify general and specific effective processes and program components. Through the progression of the research process, researchers will be able to generate the knowledge necessary to help children and their families adapt to the stresses associated with chronic childhood illness so as to enhance their quality of life.

# I

# IMPACT OF CHRONIC CHILDHOOD ILLNESS

# INTRODUCTION

# IMPACT OF CHRONIC CHILDHOOD ILLNESS

The impact of chronic childhood illness is obscured by the relative rarity of specific developmental and medical conditions. However, taken together, as many as 1 million children in the United States have a severe chronic condition that may impair their daily functioning, and an additional 10 million children have less serious chronic conditions.

In Section I, we delineate the impact of chronic conditions on children and their families. In chapter 1 we discuss epidemiology. Although there is little evidence of a significant change in the incidence of chronic illness, several factors that have contributed to an increase in prevalence are discussed. Consistent with the biopsychosocial conceptual framework that guides this book, a scheme for classifying chronic conditions is developed on the basis of biomedical and psychosocial tasks associated with specific conditions. These tasks are exemplified by a consideration of six illnesses selected to be representative of the major dimensions of the classification schema: asthma, cancer, cystic fibrosis, diabetes, sickle-cell disease, and spina bifida.

Impact also is manifested in terms of children's psychosocial adjustment. In chapter 2 we address the types and frequencies of psychological adjustment problems in terms of emotional and behavioral disorders and self-esteem problems revealed through empirical studies of children with the six representative illnesses. The increased risk for adjustment problems is established clearly, but the individual variability also is impressive and leads to an investigation of the correlates of psychological adjustment.

Consistent with our biopsychosocial framework, in chapter 3 we consider the evidence from clinical studies and meta-analyses regarding the role of illness parameters, child parameters, and social–ecological–family parameters in explaining the variability in adjustment. This consideration points to the need for theoretical studies to integrate findings and guide subsequent research efforts.

In chapter 4 we address children's psychosocial adjustment as manifested in social adjustment and school performance. Again, the increased risk and individual variability associated with these adjustment problems are clear. However, the search for correlates is just beginning to be undertaken.

In chapter 5 we examine prominent conceptual models that underlie empirical research programs directed at delineating the processes associated with adaptation to chronic childhood illness. These models fit well within an ecological systems-theory perspective and include cognitive–behavioral–social learning theories and family systems–social support theories. These models share a common view of chronic childhood illness as a potential stressor. A hybrid model is proposed that integrates stress processing and parenting components.

Chapter 6 concludes the section with a consideration of the impact on parents and siblings. Findings regarding psychological adjustment of parents and siblings of children with chronic illness are reviewed. Some information is available about the correlates of parental adjustment, but there is little information on the correlates of sibling adjustment.

# 1

# EPIDEMIOLOGY AND CLASSIFICATION

In this chapter we discuss the epidemiology of chronic childhood illness and provide a working definition of chronic illness. Facts regarding the incidence and prevalence of chronic childhood conditions in general are reviewed. We argue that whereas the incidence has remained relatively stable, a number of factors have resulted in an increased prevalence. We next consider classification in terms of biomedical and psychosocial dimensions. Issues related to categorical and noncategorical approaches to classification are reviewed. We present a psychosocial topology of classification in terms of biomedical parameters germane to psychosocial adaptation. This topology is a bridge to the biopsychosocial organization framework that serves as the matrix to integrate findings to guide efforts to foster adaptation. We conclude with a discussion of six specific illnesses chosen to be representative of patterns of manifestations along the biopsychosocial dimensions of the matrix.

## EPIDEMIOLOGY

### Definition of Chronic Illness

Advances in biomedical science and health care have prolonged the lives of many who previously would have died in infancy or childhood.

One consequence has been that many individuals are confronting the challenges of dealing with physical illness most of their lives (i.e., illness has become a chronic situation for many people).

There are many definitions of what constitutes a chronic illness. Mattsson (1972) defined chronic illness as

> a disorder with a protracted course which can be progressive and fatal, or associated with a relatively normal life span despite impaired physical or mental functioning. Such a disease frequently shows periods of acute exacerbation requiring medical attention. (p. 801)

The essence of this definition is an illness that has a protracted course. What constitutes a protracted course? Pless and Pinkerton (1975) defined a chronic illness as one in which the condition persists longer than 3 months in a given year or necessitates a period of continuous hospitalization of more than 1 month.

## Incidence and Prevalence

The epidemiology of childhood chronic illness is different from that of adult chronic illness (J. M. Perrin & MacLean, 1988b). Whereas adults face a relatively small number of common chronic conditions, children face a relatively large number of rare conditions. One consequence is that society and health service providers are more familiar with, and more used to accommodating, adult chronic conditions such as diabetes, osteoarthritis, and hypertension. The rarity of childhood chronic conditions results in a relative lack of community familiarity with and experience in dealing with these conditions (J. M. Perrin & MacLean, 1988a).

The rarity of childhood chronic illness also contributes to the difficulty in estimating population incidence and prevalence. *Incidence* is defined as the number of new occurrences of disease per unit of population during a specified period of time. *Prevalence* is defined as the number of new and continuing cases. Because most population health surveys contain data on less than 10,000 children (Gortmaker, 1985), few children with any one of the specific chronic conditions are likely to be included. Thus, knowledge about the incidence and prevalence of childhood chronic illness is necessarily based on estimates across studies in the United States and other countries, particularly the United Kingdom.

In the early 1970s, Pless and colleagues examined the data from three epidemiologic surveys on children's health and development (Pless & Roghmann, 1971). The National Survey of Health and Development comprises a representative sample of all children born in England, Wales, and Scotland between March 3 and March 9, 1946. Of the 15,130 children born then, more than 5,000 have been studied at repeated intervals (Pless & Douglas, 1971). The second study was a survey of educational, emotional, and physical disabilities in the total population of 9- to 11-year-old children ($N$ = 3,271) on the Isle of Wight (Rutter, Tizard, & Whitmore, 1970). The third study, the Rochester Child Health Survey, is a 1% probability sample of all children ($N$ = 1,756) under 18 years of age living in Monroe County, New York (Roghmann & Haggerty, 1970).

In reviewing these data, several conclusions were reached (Pless & Roghmann, 1971). The frequency of chronic illness varied from 5% to 20% depending on the definitions and methods used. In each of the three studies, the most prevalent condition was asthma, followed by other allergic disorders. Sensory disorder ranked second and nervous system disorders ranked third. At least one third of the chronic illnesses of childhood are likely to be permanent.

On the basis of reviews of a number of other studies, Gortmaker and Sappenfield (1984) arrived at a similar conclusion: that rates of children with any chronic disorder vary from 10% to 20%. Table 1.1 shows estimated prevalence data for a number of specific chronic childhood conditions for children (neonates to 20 years of age) in the United States using prevalence at birth and survival data or incidence and duration data (Gortmaker, 1985; Gortmaker & Sappenfield, 1984).

Similar to the earlier findings by Pless and Roghmann (1971), asthma was the most prevalent condition. Two other common chronic illness groups were neurological and developmental disabilities and behavioral disorders. All the other childhood chronic conditions occurred rarely: approximately 1 in 1,000 or less.

Overall, approximately 1% to 2% of children have severe physiological conditions that may regularly interfere with daily activities such as school attendance, play, and chores (J. M. Perrin & MacLean, 1988a). Thus, although specific conditions are rare, taken together approximately 2 out of every 100 children (i.e., more than 1 million children) have a severe chronic illness that may impair their daily functioning (J. M. Perrin & MacLean, 1988a).

There is relatively little variability in the incidence and prevalence of childhood chronic illness across social class and ethnic groups, but children from the lower socioeconomic status (SES) classes have more severe chronic illness (J. M. Perrin & MacLean, 1988a). There is some variability in specific conditions as a function of racial or ethnic descent. For example, cystic fibrosis primarily affects White people and sickle-cell disease primarily affects African American people.

## Changes in Incidence, Prevalence, and Impact

There is little evidence for significant changes in the incidence of childhood chronic illness. Gortmaker (1985) noted that changes in incidence during the past three decades are much smaller than changes in the

TABLE 1.1

Estimated Population Prevalence of Chronic Diseases and Conditions in Children, Aged 0–20, in the United States: 1980

| Disorder | Prevalence estimates per 100 | Maximum prevalence | % Surviving to age 20 |
|---|---|---|---|
| Arthritis | 2.2 | | |
| Asthma | 38.0 | | |
|    Moderate to severe | 10.0 | 10.20 | 98 |
| Autism | 0.44 | | |
| Central nervous system injury | | | |
|    Traumatic brain injury | 0.05 | | |
|    Paralysis | 2.1 | | |
| Cerebral palsy | 2.5 | | |
| Chronic renal failure | 0.080 | 0.19 | 25 |
|    Terminal | 0.010 | | |
|    Nonterminal | 0.070 | | |
| Cleft lip or palate | 1.5 | 1.62 | 92 |
| Congenital heart disease | 7.0 | 9.33 | 65 |
|    Severe congenital heart disease | 0.50 | | |
| Cystic fibrosis | 0.20 | 0.26 | 60 |
| Diabetes mellitus | 1.8 | 1.89 | 95 |
| Down's syndrome | 1.1 | | |
| Hearing impairment | 16.0 | | |
|    Deafness | 0.1 | | |
| Hemophilia | 0.15 | 0.16 | 90 |
| Leukemia | | | |
|    Acute lymphocytic leukemia | 0.11 | 0.22 | 40 |
| Mental retardation | 25.0 | | |
| Muscular dystrophy | 0.06 | 0.14 | 25 |
| Neural tube defect | 0.45 | | |
|    Spina bifida | 0.40 | 0.67 | 50 |
|    Encephalocele | 0.05 | | |
| Phenylketonuria | 0.10 | | |
| Sickle-cell disease | 0.46 | | |
|    Sickle-cell anemia | 0.28 | 0.29 | 90 |
| Seizure disorder | 3.5 | | |
| Visual impairment | 30.0 | | |
|    Impaired visual acuity | 20.0 | | |
|    Blind | 0.6 | | |

*Note.* From Gortmaker and Sappenfield (1984) and Gortmaker (1985). Adapted with permission.

size of birth cohorts. However, as discussed in the introduction, increases in the survival rates are substantial for several illnesses. For example, the median survival age for children with cystic fibrosis increased 2.5 times from 10.4 years in 1966 (Orenstein & Wachnowsky, 1985) to 29.4 years in 1993 (Cystic Fibrosis Foundation, 1994).

Table 1.1 also shows the estimated percentages of children with specific conditions surviving to 20 years of age and the estimated maximum prevalence if 100% of the patients survived to 20 years of age with constant incidence and age of onset. More than 80% of the maximum prevalence of these diseases has been reached. That is, "overall, only a 16 percent increase could be expected if survival among all these children were increased to 100 percent" (Gortmaker, 1985, p. 144).

These data suggest that a large increase in the prevalence of children with chronic illness is not expected. The prevalence of childhood chronic conditions is now primarily a function of survival rates, with little room for improvement overall, and cohort size, which is anticipated to remain relatively stable before rising again in the next century. As reviewed in the introduction, advances in the care of permaturely born children who have very low birth weight are resulting in "new survivors," and the impact of new illnesses such as AIDS also is apparent. Prevalence projections for educational and health care service planning are further complicated by the impact of increased ascertainment.

Data from the National Center for Health Statistics indicate that "both the number and proportions of children with activity-limiting chronic health conditions have been increasing for many years" (Newacheck, Budetti, & Halfon, 1986, p. 178). One primary data source is the National Health Interview Survey conducted by the Census Bureau for the National Center for Health Statistics. This is a continuing annual cross-sectional survey of 40,000 households, including 30,000 to 40,000 children. The survey classifies children into four categories of activity limitations on the basis of parental responses: (a) unable to carry on their major activity (i.e., play for preschool children and school attendance for school-age children); (b) limited in the amount or kind of major activity performed; (c) not limited in major activity but otherwise limited; and (d) not limited in activities.

Data from the National Health Interview Survey indicated that from 1960 to 1981, the prevalence of activity-limiting chronic conditions among children 17 years of age and younger doubled from 1.8% to 3.8% (Newacheck et al., 1986). Thus, more than 2 million children under the age of 17 now suffer some degree of limitation in their school, play, or other activities because of their chronic condition. Analysis of the factors contributing to this increase in the prevalence of activity limitations indicates that during the first decade of this period, most of the change was attributable to aging of the population and changes in questionnaire design. Changes in the second decade were more difficult to determine. Changes in prevalence were restricted to less severe levels of limitation, and the largest changes occurred for respiratory conditions, learning disabilities, and disorders of the mental and nervous systems. This suggests that increased reporting of childhood activity limitations is attributable, at least in part, to better ascertainment and increased concern of parents, educators, and health care providers. In this regard public laws, such as the Education of All Handicapped Children Act of 1975 (PL94-142), and efforts to mainstream children with disabilities called attention to the constellation of developmental, learning, and behavioral problems that have been termed the "new morbidity" (Haggerty, Roghmann, & Pless, 1975).


## CLASSIFICATION

The premise of the biopsychosocial framework that we are applying to the process of adaptation to chronic childhood illness is that a comprehensive view requires the confluence of biomedical, psychosocial, and developmental perspectives. We are conceptualizing chronic illness as a potential stressor to which the child and family systems need to adapt (Thompson, 1985). The term *adaptation*, in its original usage, referred to a change in structure or behavior that has survival value. Today, the term is used more generally to refer to any beneficial change to meet environmental demands (English & English, 1958).

The illness as a biomedical event has a dynamic impact on development through modifications of the child's interaction with his or her physical and social environments. This modification can be direct in terms of biological system dysfunctions, impairments, or limitations, indirect through psychosocial developmental tasks generated from normal child experiences and illness-specific tasks, or both direct and indirect.

### Biomedical and Psychosocial Dimensions

There is considerable diversity among the chronic illnesses of childhood in the biomedical dimensions of etiology and manifestations. There is a genetic component to many conditions "reflecting either a chromosome disorder or more subtle genetic defects that may affect the functioning of an enzyme important to a key biologic process" (J. M. Perrin & MacLean, 1988a, p. 15). Some conditions, such as hemophilia and muscular dystrophy, are sex-linked recessive illnesses in that asymptomic carrier females transmit the illness to their affected sons. More common are autosomal recessive patterns, such as those found in cystic fibrosis and sickle-cell disease, in which an affected child receives a disease-causing gene from each parent. For other chronic conditions, the etiology is less clear and may reflect a developmental phenomenon or a combination of environmental factors and genetic predispositions.

Other dimensions of chronic illness include structural and functional manifestations. For example, chronic conditions are frequently grouped into categories according to body systems using a classification system developed by the National Center for Health Statistics for the National Health Interview Survey discussed earlier (Newacheck et al., 1986). This classification scheme includes eight impairment categories such as impairment of vision, hearing, speech, special senses, intelligence, and extremity loss. Also included are 14 disease and injury categories such as infections; neoplasms; endocrine, metabolic, and blood disorders; and diseases of the respiratory, digestive, and musculoskeletal systems.

Another biomedical dimension is treatment regimen. The effectiveness of treatment for a chronic illness depends on the efficacy of the treatment and on the rate of adherence or compliance to the treatment (L. H. Epstein & Cluss, 1982). However, the overall adherence rate for pediatric populations is estimated to be 50% (Litt & Cuskey, 1980). Factors that influence adherence include the chronicity and complexity of the treatment regimen. Although health outcome and adherence are related, there is not a one-to-one correspondence between adherence and treatment outcome because of the considerable variability in regimen effectiveness. Furthermore, with many chronic illnesses, treatment regimens are only partially efficacious, and frequently there are negative side effects. Chronic childhood illnesses differ markedly in terms of the management requirements placed on the child and his or her family. Thus, one biomedical dimension of importance to adaptation to chronic childhood illness is the treatment regimen, both directly in terms of efficacy and indirectly through its impact on adherence.

Other methods for considering chronic illness from a functional perspective include both psychosocial and biomedical dimensions. For example, the National Health Interview Survey categorizes illnesses in terms of activity limitations. Moreover, other investigators have attempted to develop measures of functioning status to assess impairment according to how the illness affects the child's physical, psychological, and social functioning. For example, Stein and Jessop (1982) developed a measure of functional status in which child health was defined as the capacity to perform age-appropriate roles and tasks. Behavioral responses to illness that interfere with performance of normal social roles are measured for four age categories: infants, toddlers, preschoolers, and school-age children. Included in this framework are communication, mobility, mood, energy, sleeping, eating, and toileting patterns.

The life crisis model, developed by Moos and Tsu (1977), calls attention to adaptive tasks associated with chronic illness; in general, these tasks include dealing with symptoms and treatments as well as preserving emotional balance, self-image, and relationships with family and friends. These adaptive tasks can then be measured in terms of necessary coping skills. (This life crisis model is considered in more detail in chap. 5.) The important point is that chronic childhood illness can be considered a potential stressor with associated adaptive tasks.

The systems-theory approach to adaptation focuses on the ways in which biological and psychosocial processes influence each other. Each chronic illness is characterized by distinct biological processes involving etiology and manifestations and warrants a specific diagnosis. Subsequently, treatment and management are typically conducted in a condition-specific context such as clinics or units under the direction of specialty teams. For example, specialty clinics and teams typically care for children with cystic fibrosis, diabetes, sickle-cell disease, and cancer.

Biomedical research has resulted in tremendous advances in disease-specific therapies and is increasingly providing the basis for genuine cures. The biomedical system of classification of chronic illnesses has obvious utility in advancing knowledge and facilitating medical treatment. The distinctions between categories of illnesses also have suggested the potential for differential impact on adaptation.

The early history of the study of adaptation to chronic childhood illness was characterized by a search for illness-specific patterns of adjustment difficulties. However, what was learned was that there was as much variability in adjustment patterns within illness subgroups as there was between illness subgroups. Similarly, there was little correspondence between illness severity, measured objectively, and the quality of adjustment. There followed a period of active efforts to think about categorizing chronic childhood illness in terms of psychosocial adaptation. What was needed were conceptual frameworks to classify chronic illness in terms of meaningful biomedical parameters that dictate "significantly distinct psychosocial demands for the ill-individual and his or her family" (Rolland, 1987, p. 204).

## Commonalities of Chronic Conditions

Pless and Perrin (1985) advocated attending to dimensions that have implications for the delivery of services and public policy across chronic illnesses. They suggested a number of dimensions for categorizing and distinguishing among classes of chronic illnesses. One dimension is prevalence. As we discussed earlier, most chronic child illnesses, except perhaps asthma and allergies, are relatively rare. The more common the health problem, the more likely it can be managed by the primary care providers in the community and by the schools. However, both primary physicians and the school system are likely to have little experience and limited technical expertise to deal with illnesses that are more rare; therefore, collaboration with specialists will be needed.

A second dimension important in categorizing chronic illness is the age of onset. The age at which children and their families confront an illness interacts with developmental issues in determining service needs and challenges to adjustment. Dealing with a condition from birth is different from adapting to a condition after a period of normal development:

"Children who have once had a ability react to its loss differently from those who never had it" (Pless & Perrin, 1985, p. 47). The general view of the impact of age of onset was captured by Pless and Perrin (1985):

> Children born with a condition affecting their functioning appear to adjust to it more readily or to develop in the context of their illness in different ways from those able-bodied children who, having gone through typical developmental phases, develop permanent conditions later in childhood. (p. 47)

A third dimension of importance to service delivery and policies is mobility–activity. The extent to which the illness has a significant impact on mobility can affect access and participation in sports and other activities. It has been suggested that children at the margin (i.e., mildly or moderately affected) may have greater frustrations and psychological adjustment difficulties because of interference in their attempts to compete with their able-bodied peers than those who are more severely affected and consequently may feel less compelled to compete (Pless & Pinkerton, 1975).

A fourth dimension of importance to classification is the course of the illness. Static conditions are those in which the deficit is a relatively fixed event but the manifestations of the deficit can vary with developmental stages. Dynamic conditions are those in which the effects of the illness change over time. In turn, dynamic conditions can be further categorized in terms of fatality and predictability of improvement or decline. Cystic fibrosis is a classic example of a dynamic condition with progressive decline resulting in early death. Asthma is an example of an illness characterized by frequent crises and exacerbation but usually not progressive decline. Illness course, both in terms of trends and exacerbations, can have an impact on school attendance.

A fifth categorization dimension is the impact of the illness on cognitive functioning, sensory functioning, or both. Conditions directly impairing cognitive functioning or the ability of the child to communicate with his or her environment because of speech, hearing, or visual impairment have implications for service needs and patterns of psychosocial adjustment.

A sixth dimension of categorization is visibility. Some illnesses (e.g., myelodysplasia) are visible, whereas others (e.g., heart disease) are typically invisible. It has been thought for some time that visibility is particularly important in peer relations because how noticeably different a child is often affects the response of others. Somewhat paradoxically, there is some evidence that children with chronic illness whose appearance was normal had generally poorer adjustment (Pless & Nolan, 1991), perhaps because of the increased likelihood that a child with a visible disease may be forced to "accept" himself or herself as a person with a disability.

## The Noncategorical Approach

Researchers of psychosocial adjustment and adaptation to chronic childhood illness have moved away from contrasts between illnesses to a focus on commonalities confronting children and their families who are dealing with different chronic illnesses. In 1975, Pless and Pinkerton advocated that the chronicity of the illness and the impact on the family were likely to be more significant than the specific characteristics of the illness. This emphasis on similarities associated with chronic childhood illness as opposed to illness-specific characteristics became known as the *noncategorical approach*: "Thus, the essence of a non-categorical approach is that children face common life experiences and problems based on generic dimensions of their conditions rather than on idiosyncratic characteristics of any specific disease entity" (Stein & Jessop, 1982, p. 354).

Among the commonalities associated with chronic childhood illnesses, Stein and Jessop (1982) suggested common dimensions of particular importance to psychosocial adjustment around which specific illnesses vary: whether the condition is visible or invisible; whether the condition is life threatening, stable, or characterized by unpredictable crises; and whether it involves mental retardation, affects sensory or motor systems, has a cosmetic aspect, or requires an intrusive or demanding routine of care (Stein & Jessop, 1982). In terms of treatment, whereas there is a need for biomedically disease-specific therapies, children with chronic illness and their families have a number of common psychosocial rehabilitative needs.

## Psychosocial Topology of Chronic Illness

Rolland (1987) developed a conceptual framework to classify chronic illness in terms of meaningful biomedical parameters that are germane to psychosocial adaptation. One dimension in the development of the psychosocial topology of illness includes categories "hypothesized to be the most psychosocially significant at the interface of the illness and the family" (Rolland, 1987, p. 204). These categories include onset, course, outcome, and degree of incapacitation.

*Onset* can be divided into acute, such as stroke, or gradual, such as muscular dystrophy. The rate of change required within the family to cope with a gradual-onset disease is less than with acute conditions and enables a more protracted period of adjustment. The *course* of a disease can be constant or dynamic. A consistent course is one in which the biological aspects and functional limitations are stabilized. Dynamic courses can be progressive, in which symptomatic severity increases over time, with early death being the end point on the outcome continuum. Correspondingly, strain is constant and may increase, and adaptation and role change are continual. The illness course also can be relapsing or episodic, with alternation of stable periods of varying length with periods of symptomatic exacerbation. Illness also can be considered in terms of the degree of *incapacitation* in the child's cognitive capabilities, sensorimotor capabilities, or both. Combining onset, course, outcome, and incapacitation yields a topology with 32 potential psychosocial types of illness, presented in Table 1.2.

Rolland (1987) regarded the time phase of illness as another dimension that interacts with type of illness in forming specific psychosocial developmental tasks. Considering time phases facilitates an understanding of chronic illness as an ongoing process with landmark transitions and demands (Rolland, 1987). Three major phases of chronic illness reflect core psychosocial themes. The *crisis phase* ranges from prediagnostic symptoms through the strains of the initial diagnosis and treatment and adjustment. The *chronic phase* is one of day-to-day living in which efforts are made for the child and family to live as normal a life as possible. The *terminal phase* includes the period when the inevitability of death becomes apparent through death, grief, reduction, and resumption of normal family life beyond the loss (Rolland, 1987).

## Biopsychosocial Organizational Framework

This brief review indicates that chronic childhood illness can be categorized and organized along a number of biomedical and psychosocial dimensions. Biomedical advances, treatment regimens, and service delivery programs have developed from a categorical (i.e., a disease-specific) approach, typically organized by body system. Noncategorical approaches have categorized illnesses in terms of dimensions of importance for adaptation, service delivery programs, and public policy that cut across specific illnesses, such as age of onset, activity and functional limitations, visibility, and adaptive tasks including treatment-regimen-adherence requirements. The potential benefits for service program development and public policy considerations of development of a partial or modified categorical approach (i.e., one that explains some of the common biomedical and therapeutic characteristics of groups of illness) have been recognized (Pless & Perrin, 1985).

Table 1.3 represents an effort at such a modified categorical approach. Specific illnesses are organized in terms of biomedical and psychosocial dimensions thought to be relevant to patient and family adaptation. Organizing findings along these dimensions across studies or designing studies to include illness that enable a contrast among one or more dimensions should facilitate the accumulation of knowledge to promote adaptation to chronic illness. In this way, the problems associated with developing knowledge and expertise and public policy decisions on the basis of rare diseases can be addressed.

TABLE 1.2

Categorization of Chronic Illness by Psychosocial Type

| Type of illness | Incapacitating | | Nonincapacitating | |
|---|---|---|---|---|
| | Acute | Gradual | Acute | Gradual |
| **Fatal** | | | | |
| Progressive | | Lung cancer with CNS metastases<br>AIDS<br>Bone marrow failure<br>Amyotrophic lateral sclerosis | Acute leukemia<br>Pancreatic cancer<br>Metastatic breast cancer<br>Malignant melanoma<br>Lung cancer<br>Liver cancer, etc. | Cystic fibrosis[a] |
| Relapsing | | | Cancers in remission | |
| **Shortened life span** | | | | |
| Progressive | | Emphysema<br>Alzheimer's disease<br>Multi-infarct dementia<br>Multiple sclerosis (late)<br>Chronic alcoholism<br>Huntington's chorea<br>Scleroderma | | Juvenile diabetes[a]<br>Malignant hypertension<br>Insulin-dependent adult-onset diabetes |
| Relapsing | Angina | Early multiple sclerosis<br>Episodic alcoholism | Sickle-cell disease[a]<br>Hemophilia[a] | Systemic lupus erythematosis[a] |
| Constant | Stroke<br>Moderate-to-severe myocardial infarction | PKU and other inborn errors of metabolism | Mild myocardial infarction<br>Cardiac arrhythmia | Hemodialysis-treated renal disease<br>Hodgkin's disease |
| Progressive | | Parkinson's disease<br>Rheumatoid arthritis<br>Osteoarthritis | | Non-insulin-dependent adult-onset diabetes |

|  |  | Nonfatal |  |
| --- | --- | --- | --- |
| Relapsing | Lumbosacral disc disease |  | Kidney stones<br>Gout<br>Migraine<br>Seasonal allergy<br>Asthma<br>Epilepsy<br>Benign arrhythmia<br>Congenital heart disease | Peptic ulcer<br>Ulcerative colitis<br>Chronic bronchitis<br>Other inflammatory bowel diseases<br>Psoriasis<br>Malabsorption syndromes<br>Hyper- or hypothyroidism<br>Pernicious anemia<br>Controlled hypertension<br>Controlled glaucoma |
| Constant | Congenital malformations<br>Spinal cord injury<br>Acute blindness<br>Survived severe trauma and burns<br>Posthypoxic syndrome | Nonprogressive mental retardation<br>Cerebral palsy |  |  |

*Note.* CNS = central nervous system; PKU = phenylketonuria. From Rolland (1987). Reprinted with permission.
[a]Early.

# TABLE 1.3
## Biopsychosocial Organizational Framework

| Dimension | Chronic illness | | | | | |
|---|---|---|---|---|---|---|
| | Asthma | Cancer | CF | Diabetes | SCD | SB |
| Etiology | | | | | | |
|   Genetic | | | X | | X | |
|   Nongenetic | X | X | | X | | X |
| Age of onset | | | | | | |
|   Birth | | | X | | X | X |
|   Childhood | X | X | | X | | |
| Course | | | | | | |
|   Static | | | | | | X |
|   Episodic | X | | | | | |
|   Progressive | | | | X | X | |
|   Fatal | | ? | X | | | |
| Impairment | | | | | | |
|   Cognitive | | X | | ? | X | X |
|   Motor | | | | | X | X |
|   Sensory | | | | | | |
|   Visible | | X | X | | X | X |
| Medical regimen | | | | | | |
|   Pills | X | X | X | X | X | |
|   Injection | | X | | X | | |
|   Inhalants | X | | X | | | |
|   Physical therapy or exercise | | | X | X | | |
|   Diet | | | X | X | | |

Note. CF = cystic fibrosis; SCD = sickle-cell disease; SB = spina bifida.

In conducting such studies, in building the knowledge base, in developing service programs, and in formulating public policies, it is crucial to recognize that the biopsychosocial dimensions listed in Table 1.3 form one dimension of a two-dimensional matrix. The other dimension is the developmental phase. The level of the child's development, with associated normative developmental tasks, operates in a transactional way with these biopsychosocial dimensions of illness in the generation of adaptive tasks throughout the patient's and parents' respective life courses.

## REPRESENTATIVE CHRONIC CHILDHOOD ILLNESSES

Table 1.3 provides a visual depiction of six major chronic childhood illnesses in terms of biopsychosocial dimensions of postulated relevance for adaptation. Rather than reviewing what is known about adaptation with regard to all chronic childhood illnesses, we focus on these six specific illnesses, which we selected as being representative of patterns of manifestations along the dimensions of this modified categorical approach.

To provide a context for considering adaptation, each of these six illnesses is discussed in terms of etiology and description, manifestations and course, and treatment. The goal is to provide a synopsis of the illness and its treatment that will convey the nature of the adaptive illness-related tasks that confront the child and his or her family and how these illness-related tasks affect, and are affected by, developmental tasks.

## Asthma

### Etiology and Description

Asthma is one of the most common chronic illnesses affecting children. Depending on how asthma is defined, there are 2 to 5 million children with asthma in the United States (R. Evans et al., 1987). Asthma is more prevalent among boys than girls (R. Evans et al., 1987; Gergen, Mullally, & Evans, 1988). Moreover, African American children have a higher prevalence rate (Gergen et al., 1988) and mortality rate (R. Evans, et al., 1987) than White children. The morbidity and mortality of asthma in the United States have increased substantially since the 1970s (R. Evans et al., 1987). Although the reasons for the changing epidemiology of asthma are not clear, factors such as changes in the environment, changes in the diagnostic criteria, or changes in the natural history of the disease have been hypothesized (R. Evans et al., 1987).

Asthma has been difficult to define because no single definition has been acceptable to everyone (Creer, Renne, & Chai, 1982). However, asthma is a reactive airway disease that is "intermittent" in that attacks generally occur on an aperiodic basis, "variable" in that attacks range in severity from mild to status asthmaticus, and "reversible" in that the airways return to their previous condition spontaneously or following treatment (Creer et al., 1982).

Asthma may be precipitated by a variety of factors, including changes in air temperature or humidity, exposure to environmental allergens, exercise, upper respiratory infections, or emotional expression such as crying or laughing. The presenting symptoms are wheezing, dyspnea, and cough; additional symptoms, such as allergic reactions of the eyes, nose, or skin, may also be associated with asthma.

### Manifestations and Course

The diagnosis of asthma is often based on patient reports or clinical observations that the patient is experiencing symptoms thought to be asthma (Creer, Harm, & Marion, 1988). Provocation challenge testing also may be used in diagnosis. This involves pricking the patient's skin with a needle containing a small amount of a potential allergen or, more infrequently, having the patient inhale minute quantities of a stimulus thought to produce airway reactivity. Physical changes brought about by these challenges are assessed with pulmonary function testing (Creer et al., 1988).

Several pathophysiologic processes are evident in asthma, including bronchial obstruction, bronchial and pulmonary inflammation, and increased bronchial and pulmonary mucous secretions. The asthma response is composed of two phases: the early asthmatic response (EAR) and the late asthmatic response (LAR; Young, 1994). The EAR occurs within a few minutes of exposure to the precipitant, reaches a peak within approximately 30 min, and subsides in about 2 hr. The EAR is characterized by bronchospasm, edema, and increased mucous secretions. The LAR occurs 4 to 12 hr after exposure to the precipitant, reaches a peak within 4 to 8 hr, and may last for 24 hr or more. The LAR is characterized by an inflammatory reaction and lung tissue damage. The airways are hyperactive to allergic stimulation during this period, potentially resulting in further inflammation and bronchoconstriction.

The age of onset of symptoms may be somewhat earlier for boys than for girls. Approximately two thirds of boys and half of girls experience their first asthma episode by 3 years of age (Gergen et al., 1988). More than 90% of all children and adolescents with asthma have had their first episode of asthma by age 10 (Gergen et al., 1988).

The course of asthma varies considerably from patient to patient (Young, 1994). Most patients have discrete episodes of asthma with asymptomatic periods between episodes. Some patients, however, have more continuous symptoms, although the severity of symptoms may vary. A subset of patients has severe asthma that can be fatal secondary to acute asphyxial episodes (Young, 1994). Epidemiological data demonstrate that mortality from asthma is lowest in individuals under 14 years of age and that only about 100 children per year die from asthma (R. Evans et al., 1987).

The symptoms and severity of asthma also can vary with the season of the year, depending on the precipitant to which the individual is sensitive (Young, 1994). For example, one individual may experience the worst symptoms in the spring because of sensitivity to pollens, whereas another individual may experience the worst symptoms in the winter months secondary to airway reactivity to cold air.

Symptoms also may vary across the life span. There are conflicting data on the percentage of childhood asthma that persists beyond puberty, with figures ranging from 26% to 78% (Creer et al., 1982). Although improvement over time is expected in approximately 70% of asthmatic children, there also is the potential for redeveloping symptoms in adulthood (Young, 1994). In general, a better prognosis is associated with an earlier age of onset, except in those patients for whom disease onset occurred before 2 years of age (Slavin, 1977).

*Treatment*

The primary goals of treatment of asthma include both the prevention of attacks and management of the attacks when they occur. Treatment involves a combination of methods, including environmental control, pharmacologic management, behavioral interventions, and self-management.

A primary method for preventing attacks is to avoid precipitants associated with them. Environmental control methods are often recommended to patients with asthma and their families. These methods include installing special air-filtering systems in the home, limiting exposure to animal dander by not having pets, or decreasing exposure to dust and dust mites through regular and thorough housecleaning and encasing mattresses and pillows in plastic (Sandler, 1989).

Depending on the nature of an individual's symptoms, medications can be used both prophylactically to prevent attacks and to manage attacks when they do occur. Pharmacologic treatment typically involves three types of drugs: (a) bronchodilators, which relax and open the airways; (b) anti-inflammatory agents (corticosteroids), which decrease swelling and allergic reactions in the lungs; and (c) mast-cell stabilizers, which inhibit the production and release of substances that create allergic reactions in the lungs. Effective pharmacologic management depends on medication compliance and appropriate use of metered-dose inhalers.

Episodic asthma may be managed by intermittent bronchodilator medications administered either orally or through metered-dose inhalers. Bronchodilators or mast-cell stabilizer medications also may be used daily to treat recurrent acute attacks in order to maintain open airways and prevent attacks. Some of these medications are administered through daily home nebulizer treatments. For severe chronic asthma, corticosteroids are administered either through a metered-dose inhaler or orally. Severe acute asthma, or status asthmaticus, may be managed by injected or inhaled bronchodilators or with corticosteroids. If a patient is in respiratory failure, ventilatory assistance is necessary (Young, 1994).

Behavioral interventions and self-management programs also have played an important role in the treatment of asthma. Behavioral interventions include relaxation techniques to address the panic that is exhibited by some patients in response to asthma attacks, using contract negotiation and contingency management to enhance medication compliance, and decreasing hospital overuse by decreasing the reinforcing qualities of the hospital (Creer et al., 1988).

Education and self-management programs have been used to teach children and parents appropriate management of attacks. Although these programs vary in terms of aims and content, each of them is intended to teach children to become allies with their physicians in the control and management of asthma attacks (Creer et al., 1988). These programs typically include teaching children to (a) observe and record information related to their asthma, often using objective indexes such as peak flow meters to assess pulmonary functioning; (b) process this information, evaluate their condition, and make decisions regarding what steps they should take to maximize management of their symptoms; (c) instruct themselves to perform the steps necessary to bring the episode under control (e.g., reminding themselves to relax, removing themselves from a probable precipitant, or taking appropriate medications); and (d) reinforce themselves for steps taken in managing their symptoms (Creer et al., 1988).

## Cancer

### Etiology and Description

Cancer occurs in fewer than 1 in 600 children prior to 15 years of age (Cecalupa, 1994), but it is the most common cause of disease-related deaths in children (Friedman & Mulhern, 1992). The most common form of childhood cancer is acute lymphoblastic leukemia (ALL), followed by central nervous system tumors, various lymphomas, neuroblastomas, Wilms's tumor, bone tumors, and eye tumors. (For a description of various types of cancers, see Cecalupa, 1994.) In this chapter we address ALL and brain tumors, which account for 30% to 40% and 20% of pediatric tumors, respectively.

ALL is a group of heterogeneous diseases in which there is a malignancy of the bone marrow that produces blood cells. The etiology is unknown, but it is believed to be multifactorial, involving both genetic predisposing factors and environmental factors (Cecalupa, 1994). The bone marrow produces lymphoblasts (malignant cells that progressively replace normal bone marrow with fewer red blood cells and more white blood cells), which can cause anemia, infection, and hemorrhage (Friedman & Mulhern, 1992).

### Manifestations and Course

The clinical features include anemia, which causes pallor and fatigue, as well as neutropenia, which causes fever and infection. In addition, hemorrhage also occurs and is reflected in easy bruising or excessive bleeding. Enlargement of the liver, spleen, and lymph nodes also can occur (Lanzkowsky, 1995). Localized or diffuse bone pain, accompanied by limping, is a common initial symptom, as are nonspecific, systemic symptoms such as malaise, anorexia, weight loss, fatigue, or fever (Cecalupa, 1994; Friedman & Mulhern, 1992). On the basis of initial symptomatology, blood values, and age at diagnosis, patients are classified into low-, medium-, or high-risk categories, which determines the intensity of treatments (Cecalupa, 1994).

Childhood cancer used to be uniformly fatal. Advances in medical treatment have resulted in dramatic improvements in survival. In 1960, only 1% of patients with ALL survived to 5 years after diagnosis (Stehbens, 1988), but now 70% can expect to remain disease free for 5 years (Friedman & Mulhern, 1992).

Brain tumors are classified in terms of the location above or below the tentorium membrane, which separates the cerebellum and brain stem from the two hemispheres. Symptoms of infratentorial tumors, such as medulloblastoma, are related to intracranial pressure, including headaches, irritability, nausea and vomiting, increasing lethargy, drowsiness, or abnormalities of behavior. Symptoms of supratentorial tumors include hemiparesis, visual problems, seizures, or endocrine problems. The prognosis for brain tumors varies depending on the type and location and size of the tumor and the age at diagnosis.

*Treatments*

The treatment of ALL is typically conducted in three phases (Friedman & Mulhern, 1992). Remission induction consists of 4 to 6 weeks of intensive chemotherapy aimed at destroying all lymphoblasts (Friedman & Mulhern, 1992). The chemotherapy typically involves combinations of drugs, including Prednisone, Vincristine, and L-Asparaginase (Cecalupa, 1994). A complete remission is achieved in 95% of children (Friedman & Mulhern, 1992). The maintenance phase of chemotherapy uses a different set of drugs for approximately 2 to 3 years to maintain continuous complete remission (Friedman & Mulhern, 1992). The third phase—prophylactic central nervous system treatment—is used to decrease the risk of central nervous system relapse and consists of cranial irradiation, intrathecal chemotherapy (i.e., medications such as methotrexate are injected into the spinal canal; Friedman & Mulhern, 1992), or both. Because of the risk for long-term neurological effects, cranial irradiation is now used primarily with children who are at high risk for relapse (Friedman & Mulhern, 1992).

With regard to brain tumors, total or partial resection of the tumor followed by radiation therapy is the most common treatment (Friedman & Mulhern, 1992). However, chemotherapy is now being used more frequently to treat brain tumors. It is often used prior to or instead of irradiation with some types of tumors, particularly in young children in an effort to avoid the pronounced neurocognitive side effects associated with radiation therapy in young (less than 3 years old) children (Lanzkowsky, 1995).

Bone marrow transplantation is a treatment procedure that has been used increasingly for children who have not responded to conventional therapy or who have a very poor prognosis. High-dose, whole-body radiation and intensive chemotherapy are used to destroy ALL leukemic cells. Intravenous infusion of bone marrow from a related or unrelated donor or of one's own marrow (autologous) is accomplished. Because the radiation and chemotherapy destroy the immune system's defenses, the patient must be maintained in a germ-free environment until the new marrow successfully grafts (F. Johnson, 1990). Autologous bone marrow transplantation also is increasingly being used for treating pediatric brain tumors, particularly when a child is disease free after conventional therapy but is at risk for tumor recurrence.

Side effects of chemotherapy and radiation treatments include alopecia (hair loss), nausea, vomiting, diarrhea, skin and mucosal inflammation, and endocrine and growth retardation problems (Friedman & Mulhern, 1992).

Children and their families have to deal with this array of treatments and associated side effects over a 2- to 3-year period. Children also must cope with numerous painful medical procedures associated with the assessment and treatment, including venipuncture, insertion of intravenous lines for chemotherapy, bone marrow aspirations, and lumbar punctures. School absences are frequent during the acute phase of treatment, and school re-entry is often complicated by fatigue and hair loss and other side effects of treatment. Long-term complications may include recurrent malignancy, growth retardation, neuropsychological deficits, cataracts, and infertility (Friedman & Mulhern, 1992).

## Cystic Fibrosis

### Etiology and Description

Cystic fibrosis is the most common autosomal recessive disorder in the White population; it has an incidence of 1 in 2,000 live births and a carrier frequency of approximately 5% (Boat, Welsh, & Beaudet, 1989). Cystic fibrosis occurs only in about 1 in 17,000 births in the Black population and is virtually unheard of in Asian populations (Orenstein & Wachnowsky, 1985). In 1989, the cystic fibrosis gene was identified on chromosome 7, which accounts for approximately 70% of the cystic fibrosis mutations (Kerem et al., 1989). This discovery provides the basis for developing treatments to correct the basic defect, not just the symptoms, as is the case now.

Cystic fibrosis involves two primary problems. Mucous secretions in the ducts of the exocrine glands (sweat and salivary glands and the pancreas) are dehydrated, resulting in more viscous secretions than normal and the production of factors that prevent normal immunological mechanisms from clearing pathogens, both bacterial and fungal, from respiratory secretions (Lewiston, 1985). The outflow from the pancreas is blocked, and dehydrated mucus accumulates in the airways of the lungs (Levitan, 1989).

*Manifestations and Course*

Cystic fibrosis is diagnosed from evidence of an elevated sweat chloride or sweat sodium concentration and evidence of pulmonary, pancreatic, or liver disease (Lewiston, 1985). Since the advent of the sweat test in the early 1950s, the diagnosis of cystic fibrosis during infancy has been possible with a high degree (99%) of specificity (Lewiston, 1985). Cystic fibrosis is a progressive and fatal disease, but there have been dramatic increases in survival rates. In the early 1950s, the life expectancy of a child with cystic fibrosis was less than 6 months (Lewiston, 1985). Data from the Cystic Fibrosis Foundation patient registry indicated that the median survival from birth was 10.4 years in 1966 (Orenstein & Wachnowsky, 1985) and that it increased to 29.4 years in 1993 (Cystic Fibrosis Foundation, 1994).

Pulmonary involvement occurs because of the blockage of airways in the lungs by mucous. Pulmonary secretions become colonated with bacteria, and the resulting low-grade infection adds to the viscosity of the sputum. Patients are subjected to respiratory infection, pneumonia, and a gradual deterioration of pulmonary functioning.

Pancreatic involvement is estimated to occur in 85% of the patients with cystic fibrosis. This results in a digestive enzyme deficiency and a diminution or absence of gastric juice, resulting in failure to digest food, the passage of foul-smelling bulky stools, and poor absorption of undigested nutrients, especially fats (Matthews & Drotar, 1984). There also may be endocrine effects that result in insulin-dependent diabetes mellitus in 10% of patients with cystic fibrosis (Lewiston, 1985).

Reproductively, the majority of male patients with cystic fibrosis are sterile as a result of maldevelopment or obstruction of the epididymis, vas deferens, and seminal vesicles. Females with cystic fibrosis are believed to have slightly impaired fertility secondary to abnormally thick cervical mucus, plugging of the cervical canal, and primary and secondary amenorrhea attributable to poor lung function and nutritional status. Successful pregnancies have been achieved in some women with cystic fibrosis with little impact on pulmonary and nutritional status (Koch & Lanng, 1995). However, careful clinical evaluation of potential complicating factors that may cause risk to the mother or fetus, such as the risk of respiratory insufficiency or inadequate nutrition, must be assessed (Koch & Lanng, 1995).

*Treatment*

There are two foci for treatment: pulmonary disease and malnutrition (Lewiston, 1985). The goal of pulmonary treatment is to prevent or delay progression of deterioration of the lungs through relief of airway obstruction and control of infection (Orenstein & Wachnowsky, 1985). Chest physical therapy, involving postural drainage and clap percussion to loosen sputum and facilitate its expulsion through coughing, usually requires 45 min and is typically prescribed twice daily. Intermittent aerosols are used to deliver bronchodilating agents to increase air flow, deliver antibiotics or both. "There is general agreement that antibiotic treatment has probably been the single most important factor in the greatly improved prognosis in CF" (Orenstein & Wachnowsky, 1985, p. 17). If oral antibiotics are ineffective, patients are hospitalized for periods of 10 to 14 days to receive intravenous antibiotics. Exercise tolerance is diminished in proportion to the diminution of pulmonary functioning (Orenstein & Wachnowsky, 1985), and some patients require oxygen to engage in physical activities. Heart–lung transplantation is increasingly being used in the management of end-stage lung disease in children and adults with cystic fibrosis; organ rejection and infection are the main complications of transplantation (Sheppard, 1995).

Gastrointestinal therapy is aimed at establishing good nutrition through diet and replacement pancreatic enzyme preparations. Traditionally, high-calorie, low-fat diets have been prescribed for children with cystic fibrosis, but with adequate pancreatic enzyme supplementation, even very high-fat diets can be tolerated (Orenstein & Wachnowsky, 1985). An average of 4 to 10 capsules of replacement enzyme per meal is typical (Koocher, Gudas, & McGrath, 1992). Fat-soluble supplemental vitamins A, D, E, and K also are typically prescribed (Orenstein & Wachnowsky, 1985).

The usual treatment regimen for cystic fibrosis thus involves daily chest physical therapy, diet monitoring, taking multiple medications (often more than 40 pills per day; Koocher et al., 1992), frequent outpatient medical visits, and hospitalizations. Because the treatment regimen is arduous and difficult to implement and because the efficacy of treatment components is uncertain, adherence is a significant issue.

## Insulin-Dependent Diabetes Mellitus

### Etiology and Description

Insulin-dependent diabetes mellitus affects 1.6 per 1,000 school-age children and appears to affect boys and girls equally (Silverstein, 1994). Insulin-dependent diabetes mellitus is a disorder of the metabolic–endocrine system characterized by a defect in insulin secretion or action, elevation of blood glucose, and the development of long-term microvascular, macrovascular, and neuropathic changes (Arslanian, Becker, & Drash, 1995). Insulin-dependent diabetes mellitus is thought to result from autoimmune destruction of the beta cells (i.e., the insulin-producing cells) of the islets of Langerhans in the pancreas. The hypothesized pathogenesis for insulin-dependent diabetes mellitus is that a genetically susceptible person experiences multiple toxic or infectious insults to the beta cells. This causes an overreaction of the immune system, and antibodies cause destruction of beta cells, which results in insulin deficiency (Arslanian et al., 1995).

Insulin serves to lower blood glucose levels by making cell membranes permeable to glucose (Surwit, Feinglos, & Scovern, 1983). Because of the lack of insulin, glucose cannot enter the cells and accumulates in the blood stream, resulting in hyperglycemia. Because glucose cannot enter the appetite regulatory cells of the hypothalamus, the person tends to eat constantly but does not gain weight. Because glucose is not available, the cells metabolize glycogen, fat, and protein, thereby depleting the body's energy reserves (Surwit et al., 1983). As fat metabolism becomes excessive, the metabolic intermediates of fatty acid metabolism accumulate in the plasma in the form of ketone bodies (Maurer, 1979). The kidney eliminates these excessive amounts of glucose and ketone bodies through frequent urination. Ketones are excreted as sodium salts, which osmotically draw large volumes of water from the plasma, which will result in dehydration if unchecked. The loss of sodium disturbs the bicarbonate buffering system of the plasma and the blood becomes acidic, leading to ketoacidosis, coma, and ultimately death (Maurer, 1979).

*Manifestation and Course*

The diagnosis of insulin-dependent diabetes mellitus most often occurs in two age periods: 5 to 6 years and 11 to 13 years (S. B. Johnson, 1988). The majority of patients experience an acute onset of symptoms over several days or weeks, although a small proportion of patients experience intermittent or mild symptoms for several months (Arslanian et al., 1995). Onset symptoms include fatigue, thirst, hunger, frequent urination, and weight loss despite excessive eating. Insulin-dependent diabetes mellitus is a progressive disease. Chronic complications typically occur in young adulthood or beyond and include retinopathy, nephropathy, neuropathy, and accelerated cardiovascular disease (Arslanian et al., 1995). Diabetic nephropathy is evident in 50% of the patients with insulin-dependent diabetes mellitus 15 to 20 years after diagnosis. Up to 70% of the patients exhibit neuropathy and 40%–60% exhibit some degree of retinopathy 25 years after diagnosis. Life expectancy is one third less than that of the normal population (Silverstein, 1994). There also is evidence that onset of diabetes before 5 years of age may be associated with poorer cognitive performance (Rovet, Ehrlich, Czuchta, & Akler, 1993).

Whereas hyperglycemia can have short- and long-term complications, hypoglycemia (i.e., blood glucose levels that are too low because of an imbalance of glucose and insulin) can result in sweating, palpitations, tremor, and pallor, as well as neurological manifestations such as cognitive disorientation, seizures, coma, and even death (Arslanian et al., 1995). Furthermore, deterioration in cognitive functioning has been demonstrated during and subsequent to hypoglycemia, and severe hypoglycemic episodes are associated with neuropsychological impairment (Arslanian et al., 1995).

There appears to be a link between stress and metabolic control (Arslanian et al., 1995). The autonomic nervous system, particularly the sympathetic branch, is involved in the regulation of metabolism through direct neural innervation of the pancreas and liver and indirectly through hormones (i.e., the catecholamines epinephrine and norepinephrine, which serve to increase blood glucose levels). Under stress, the liver increases conversion of glycogen to blood glucose and the metabolism of fat to free fatty acids and ketoacids (Surwit et al., 1983).

### Treatment

The goal of treatment is to keep blood glucose levels as close to normal (80–120 mg per 100 mL before meals) as possible (Silverstein, 1994) through the exogenous administration of insulin. However, it is very difficult to mimic the normal pancreatic function of balancing insulin and glucose levels. The interactions among diet, exercise, illness, emotional state, and insulin make blood glucose regulation difficult. Daily treatment tasks include blood glucose monitoring, dietary constraints, injections of insulin, and learning how to balance energy demands and insulin needs. The lifestyle behavior changes required to manage diabetes are lifelong.

There are two types of insulin. Regular, or Semi-Lente, is short-acting. After injection, the onset of effect occurs in 30 to 60 min and maximal action in approximately 2 hr, with a duration of action of 4 to 6 hr. Intermediate-acting insulin, NPH or Lente, has an onset of effect of approximately 2 hr and maximal action in 8 to 12 hr, with a duration of action of 16 to 24 hr (Silverstein, 1994). The typical treatment regimen requires twice-daily injections of insulin that frequently is a combination of short- and intermediate-acting insulin.

Rather than relying on twice-daily injections, sometimes an insulin pump is used to deliver insulin continuously. An insulin pump is a battery-operated device of approximately $3 \times 4 \times 1$ in. ($7.62 \times 10.16 \times 2.54$ cm) that is worn externally and mechanically infuses insulin through a small plastic catheter that is attached to a needle inserted subcutaneously (S. B. Johnson, 1988). The infusion can be programmed to increase 20 to 30 min before a meal to handle the rise in glucose that occurs after eating. However, it is still difficult to achieve the moment-to-moment monitoring and balancing that is accomplished in an individual with a healthy pancreas, and the needle and catheter need to be changed every 48 hr to prevent infection (S. B. Johnson, 1988).

Because of the daily treatment tasks that must be accomplished and the difficulty maintaining metabolic control, adherence can be a major issue. In particular, adolescence is frequently a difficult period because of the impact that the illness has on self-esteem and social and educational experiences and because of the interaction between illness and developmental tasks. For example, having to adhere to the lifestyle changes required by insulin-dependent diabetes mellitus complicates accomplishing the developmental tasks of identity, competency, and autonomy.

## Sickle-Cell Disease

### Etiology and Description

Sickle-cell disease is a group of genetic disorders characterized by the predominance of the protein hemoglobin S (Hb S) in red blood cells. Hemoglobin carries oxygen to different parts of the body. Normal hemoglobin (Hb A) is composed of two alpha globulin chains and two beta globulin chains. In sickle hemoglobin (Hb S), the beta globulin differs from normal globulin by the substitution of valine or glutamic acid at the sixth position (Sickle Cell Disease Panel, 1993). This amino acid substitution results in polymerizations of the Hb S molecules on deoxygenation, which produces a change in the red cell shape from a biconcave disc to a crescent or sickle shape (Sickle Cell Disease Panel, 1993). On reoxygenation, the cell initially resumes a normal shape, but after repeated cycles the erythrocyte is damaged permanently and hemolyzes, thus causing anemia. All tissues are at risk for damage secondary to the obstruction of blood flow produced by the sickled red cells.

Sickle-cell disorders are found in people of African, Mediterranean, Indian, and Middle Eastern heritage (Charache, Lubin, & Reid, 1989). Sickle-cell disease affects approximately 1 of every 400 African Americans (Consensus Conference, 1987). In the United States, sickle-cell disease is "most commonly observed in blacks and Hispanics from the Caribbean, Central America, and parts of South America" (Charache et al., 1989, p. v).

A clear distinction must be made between sickle-cell disease and sickle-cell trait (Hb AS), in which individuals have a normal beta globin gene (BA) and a sickle beta globin gene (BS). With sickle-cell trait both Hb A and Hb S are produced, and there is a predominance of Hb A (Charache et al., 1989). Sickle-cell trait is not a disease.

The sickle-cell disorders are customarily classified by genotype. Each parent has two genes for hemoglobin but passes only one on to each child. Hemoglobin type is determined by two beta globin genes located on chromosome 11 and four alpha globin genes located on chromosome 16. Patients with sickle-cell anemia (Hb SS) are homozygous for the SB gene.

Individuals with Hb SC disease have two abnormal beta globin genes, BS and BC, resulting in two abnormal hemoglobin genes, Hb S and Hb C. Individuals with sickle beta thalassemia have a BS gene and a gene that produces one of two types of beta thalassemia. If some normal beta globin is produced by the thalassemia gene, it is referred to as Hb SB$^+$ thalassemia. If no normal beta globin is produced, it is referred to as Hb SB$^0$ thalassemia. The most common abnormality is the deletion of two of the alpha globin genes, which is termed *alpha thalassemia* (Charache et al., 1989).

*Manifestations and Course*

The two primary pathophysiologic characteristics of sickle-cell disease are chronic hemolytic anemia and vasocculusion resulting in ischemic tissue injury (Charache et al., 1989). Tissue injury results from hypoxia, which is secondary to obstruction of blood vessels brought about by an accumulation of sickled erythrocytes (Charache et al., 1989). The organs at greatest risk are the spleen, kidneys, bone marrow, eyes, and head of the femur (Charache et al., 1989). Symptoms associated with hypoxic injury can be acute or chronic.

Painful events occur as a result of ischemic tissue injury and can be precipitated by hypoxia, dehydration, and extreme cold. The frequency and severity of painful events are varied. Musculoskeletal pain is the most common, followed by abdominal pain and low back pain. Painful events typically last 4 to 6 days (Charache et al., 1989).

Acute chest syndrome involves chest pain, fever, prostration, and pneumonialike symptoms. Pulmonary infarction, caused by obstruction in the pulmonary vessels, is the typical cause. This acute illness can be self-limiting or can rapidly progress and may be fatal.

Between the ages of 5 months and 2 years, children with sickle-cell disease are at risk for sudden intrasplenic pooling of vast amounts of blood, which is known as "splenic sequestration crises." The hemoglobin level can drop precipitously, causing hypovolemic shock and death (Charache et al., 1989).

Stroke affects 6% to 12% of patients with sickle-cell disease (Charache et al., 1989). In children, the most common cause of stroke is cerebral infarction, and intracerebral hemorrhages become increasingly common with age. Recurrent stroke causes progressive impairment of cognitive functioning.

There are a number of other complications that frequently occur. Progressive kidney disease typically begins during the first decade of life and continues throughout the person's life. Priapism, which is a persistent painful penile erection, can occur in both children and adults. The reduced oxygen-carrying capacity associated with anemia increases the demand on the heart for increased cardiac output, which affects cardiac functioning over time. Leg ulcers typically appear between the ages of 10 and 50 years and occur in 10% to 20% of patients with sickle-cell disease, more frequently in males than females (Charache et al., 1989). Bone lesions are frequent, typically as a consequence of infarction, such as hand–foot syndrome in the young infant and child and aseptic necrosis of the femoral head in young and middle adulthood. Gallstones are common in patients with sickle-cell disease because of the increase in bilirubin production (Charache et al., 1989). The liver also can be affected in children and adults. Sickle-cell hemoglobinopathies also have the potential to cause ophthalmic complications that can affect vision, such as vascular occlusions and retinal hemorrhages. Retarded growth and delayed sexual development also occurs, but fertility remains intact (Charache et al., 1989).

Sickle-cell disease is progressive, but advances in the management of acute and chronic conditions have resulted in a more favorable prognosis. There are two peaks in mortality. The first occurs during the first 5 years of life as a result of infection. The second peak occurs in the 20- to 24-year-old age range (Serjeant, 1985) as a result of multiple organ-system failures.

The Cooperative Study of Sickle Cell Disease, a prospective study of the clinical course of sickle-cell disease in which more than 3,764 patients were enrolled from birth to 66 years of age at 23 clinical centers throughout the United States, provides information on mortality (Platt et al., 1994). Approximately 85% of the children with sickle-cell anemia and 95% of those with sickle cell-hemoglobin C disease (Hb SC) survived to 20 years of age (Leikin et al., 1989). Among patients younger than 20 years of age, mortality peaked between 1 and 3 years of age, with the primary cause of death being infection—predominantly streptococcus pneumonia sepsis (Platt et al., 1994).

In a recent study, Platt et al. (1994) found that the median age at death for children and adults with sickle-cell anemia was 42 years for males and 48 years for females. "This represents a decrease of roughly 25 to 30 years in life expectancy, as compared with that of the black American population in general" (Platt et al., 1994, p. 1642). For those with sickle cell-hemoglobin C disease, the median age at death was 60 years for males and 68 years for females. Among adults with sickle-cell disease, 33% were clinically free of organ failure but died during an acute episode of pain, chest syndrome, or stroke. Renal failure was the predominant cause of death due to organ failure.

*Treatment*

Screening programs for newborns have been instituted in many states as the first step in reducing morbidity and mortality caused by sickle-cell disease. Screening of newborns is essential because of the documented effectiveness of prophylactic penicillin and comprehensive care in reducing morbidity and mortality from pneumonial infections in infants with sickle-cell anemia and sickle beta thalassemia (Sickle Cell Disease Guideline Panel, 1993). Prophylactic penicillin is administered twice daily from 2 months to 5 years of age to reduce the risk of infection. Screening programs for newborns include medical follow-up and parent education and genetic counseling components as well as laboratory tests (Sickle Cell Disease Guideline Panel, 1993). Parents need to be educated about the importance of adhering to the prophylactic penicillin regimen and about recognition of early signs and management of specific complications such as fever, dehydration, and respiratory distress. Parents also should be provided with anticipatory guidance regarding psychosocial issues relevant to sickle-cell disease (Sickle Cell Disease Guideline Panel, 1993).

Subsequent medical management focuses on specific complications. Pain is treated with hydration and analgesics, but painful crises frequently require hospitalization and administration of parenteral narcotics. Transfusions are given to improve microvascular perfusion by decreasing the proportion of erythrocytes containing Hb S and to reduce the risk of recurrent stroke.

## Spina Bifida

### Etiology and Description

The incidence of spina bifida varies by geographic region and over time (Khoury, Erickson, & James, 1982). In the United States, the incidence is approximately 1 per 1,000 live births (Myers, 1984). It is the second most common birth defect after trisomy 21 and is the most frequent central nervous system malformation (Myers, 1984).

The normal spinal cord forms a straight column that is covered by membranes and then by a boney spine (Wolraich, 1983). In spina bifida there is a defect in the development of the neural tube, such that the membranes, spinal cord, or both do not form in a straight column but push out in a sac, with some or all of the spinal nerves below the sac not connected properly to the spinal cord (Wolraich, 1983). The etiology of spina bifida is not yet known and may result from a combination of causes (Wolraich, 1983).

There are two major types: spina bifida occulta and spina bifida manifesta. Spina bifida occulta is characterized by failure of the back of the vertebrae to form, but there are no abnormalities in the membranes, spinal cord, or skin (Wolraich, 1983). Spina bifida manifesta is the type associated with chronic impairments. In 4% of the cases, the neural tube defect does not involve the spinal cord, just the meninges, (i.e., the membranes covering the spinal cord), and is known as meningocele (Gordon, 1982). In the other 96% of cases, the neural tube defect involves the spinal cord and is known as myelodysplasia (Gordon, 1982).

*Manifestations and Course*

Myelomeningocele is a relatively static condition (i.e., there is no progression of the basic defect; Wolraich, 1983). However, secondary problems can worsen over time. Prior to the mid-1950s, fewer than 15% of infants with myelodysplasia survived longer than 1 year (M. M. Campbell, Hayden, & Davenport, 1977). Surgical advances, particularly cerebrospinal fluid shunting and computed tomography monitoring of hydrocephalus, improved survival rates: "With advances in biomechanics, pressure monitoring methods, intraventricular administration of antimicrobials, and the use of prophylactic antibiotics during back closure and insertion of shunts, 90% of these children are now expected to survive 10 or more years (Shurtleff, 1980)" (Thompson & Kronenberger, 1992, p. 90).

Myelomeningocele results in different degrees of motor and sensory paralysis. The higher up the defect is on the spinal cord, the greater the degree of paralysis (Wolraich, 1983). For example, if the defect occurs at thoracic level 12 or above, the child will not have leg movement (Wolraich, 1983).

There is marked individual variation in the specific muscles that are involved and in whether difficulties are manifested as spasticity or flaccidity: "Since the majority of myelomeningocele involve the mid-lumbar region, there are frequently normal or spastic abnormalities of muscles innervated by the upper lumbar cord and flaccidity or spasticity of those muscles innervated from lower" (Myers, 1984, p. 171). Imbalance between agonist and antagonist muscles can lead to progressive changes or deformities of the hips, knees, and ankles. Many children with myelodysplasia can walk with proper bracing. Poor muscle control, along with the spinal defect, can lead to curvature of the spine or scoliosis (Wolraich, 1983).

Most often, the spinal defects in myelomeningocele occur in the thoracic, lumbar, or sacral region (Wolraich, 1983). The nerves involved in bladder and bowel control come from the sacral region; therefore, most children with myelomeningocele have bladder and bowel control problems (Wolraich, 1983). This often results in incontinence and damage to the kidneys due to increased pressure, infections, or both.

The most common cause of death in older children with myelodysplasia is renal failure (Myers, 1984). Urologic problems arise from abnormal innervation of the bladder and include infection, incontinence, and retrograde high pressure (Myers, 1984). Intermittent clean catherization is a technique designed to ensure emptying of the bladder (Myers, 1984). In terms of sexual function, females are fertile but most males are sterile because of prostatitis and retrograde ejaculation (Myers, 1984). Although bowel control also varies depending on the degree of innervation of pelvic floor muscles, most children achieve some degree of bowel control (Myers, 1984).

Hydrocephalus is present in 80% of the patients with myelodysplasia (McLane, 1982). In hydrocephalus the cerebrospinal fluid is prevented from leaving the ventricles and being absorbed into the bloodstream (Wolraich, 1983). As a result, the ventricles enlarge and intracranial pressure builds up, which can cause brain damage. To prevent brain damage and mental retardation, a shunt is surgically placed, usually within the first 2 months of life (Wolraich, 1983). This involves placing a tube into the ventricles, which is then connected to a one-way valve that is connected to another tube that is placed under the skin into the abdominal cavity to allow the cerebrospinal fluid to be absorbed there. This type of system is referred to as a ventriculoperitoneal shunt. If the tube is threaded into the heart rather than the abdomen, this is called a ventriculoatrial shunt.

*Treatment*

The treatment regimen depends on the degree of sensory and motor impairment, which are a function of lesion level. The typical child with spina bifida is likely to have surgical intervention for closure of the spine early in the neonatal period, for placement of the shunt, and for periodic replacement. Bracing for ambulation and some type of bowel and bladder regimen, possibly with intermittent catheterization, are also likely.


# CONCLUSION

The modified categorical approach enables a consideration of illnesses in terms of biopsychosocial dimensions thought to be relevant to child and family adaptation. The modified categorical, biopsychosocial framework is also a useful way to conceptualize the potential stressors to which patients and their families must adapt in terms of illness-related tasks.

To provide a basis for efforts to foster quality of life, this biopsychosocial framework is used to integrate findings regarding the process of adaptation with six illnesses, selected to be representative of the range and patterns of symptoms, manifestations, and treatments confronted by patients and families. This framework provides a context for considering what is known about the adjustment of patients and their parents and siblings; the biomedical, psychological, and socioecological correlates of adjustment; and effective interventions designed to enhance adaptation.

# 2

# PSYCHOLOGICAL ADJUSTMENT OF CHILDREN WITH CHRONIC ILLNESS

One way in which the impact of chronic childhood illness is manifested is in psychosocial adjustment. We first provide an overview of assessment issues and then review the major findings from three types of studies: epidemiological, clinical, and meta-analytic. For clinical studies, we consider the findings in terms of psychological adjustment as reflected in emotional and behavioral disorders and self-esteem problems. The nature of the studies is discussed, and the findings on the frequency and types of problems and disorders are reviewed as a function of illness type, informant, and method. Psychosocial adjustment problems in terms of social adjustment and school performance are addressed in chapter 4.

## OVERVIEW OF ASSESSMENT ISSUES

The understanding and treatment of behavior problems and psychopathology in children have been hampered by the absence of an agreed-on, empirically based taxonomic classification system within which research findings could be integrated (Achenbach & Edelbrock, 1978). One reason is that children's psychological adjustment has been conceptualized and operationalized in numerous ways, ranging from self-esteem to specific symptoms and problems (e.g., anxiety, depression, and activity level), to behavioral and emotional behavior problem syndromes or patterns (e.g., internalizing or externalizing disorders), to psychiatric diagnoses (e.g., overanxious disorder, obsessive–compulsive disorder, oppositional disorder, and adjustment disorders).

Methods for assessing children's adjustment also have been diverse and include checklists and questionnaires and diagnostic clinical interviews completed by children (i.e., self-reports) or by adults about children. Classification systems for children's adjustment problems vary by assessment method.

Checklist-driven systems of classification rely on statistical techniques of grouping such as factor analysis or cluster analysis, whereas the psychiatric diagnostic systems rely on consensually generated categories. Typically, checklists yield standard scores on broadband dimensions of behavior (e.g., internalizing or externalizing) and narrow-band dimensions (e.g., somatization or anxiety) that are based on normal populations. The primary example is the Child Behavior Checklist (CBCL; Achenbach & Edelbrock, 1983). Other checklists also yield classifications of behavior problem patterns across a number of dimensions, such as internal or external behavior problems or poor social skills. An example is the Missouri Children's Behavior Checklist (MCBC; Sines, Pauker, Sines, & Owen, 1969).

The psychiatric diagnostic system currently in use is the fourth edition of the *Diagnostic and Statistical Manual of Mental Disorders* (DSM–IV; American Psychiatric Association, 1994). In addition, a child and adolescent version of the DSM–IV for use in the primary care setting is currently under development in collaboration with the American Academy of Pediatrics and with input from other professional organizations. Clearly, there are difficulties with both approaches to classification, and continued efforts will be necessary to derive an empirically based, clinically meaningful classification of children's adjustment.

The use of different informants raises the issues of validity and concordance. Research evidence indicates a relatively low level of agreement across reports of child adjustment from different informants such as parents, teachers, and the children themselves (Achenbach, McConaughy, & Howell, 1987). There also is a range in the level of agreement among alternative assessment strategies such as checklists and clinical diagnoses (Kazdin & Heidish, 1984; Steinhausen & Gobel, 1987). The lack of concordance between parent and child reports has been an area of particular focus. Low-to-moderate parent–child concordance on child symptoms has been found for rating scales and structured interviews (Edelbrock, Costello, Dulcan, Conover, & Kalas, 1986).

There are several factors that have been identified that influence the degree of concordance between parent and child assessments of children's adjustment. One factor is the child's age. Parent–child agreement has been found to be higher for adolescents than for children (Edelbrock et al.,

1986), which is partly attributable to the low reliability of young children's responses to structured interviews (Edelbrock, Costello, Dulcan, Kalas, & Conover, 1985).

The type of symptom the child has is another factor that affects concordance. In general, agreement is higher for overt symptoms than for nonovert symptoms (Edelbrock et al., 1986). Parents report more externalizing problems, such as conduct disorder and oppositional disorder, whereas children report more symptoms of internalizing difficulties, such as anxiety or depression (Hodges, Gordon, & Lennon, 1990). This pattern of differential concordance between parent (mother)-reported and child-reported child adjustment as a function of symptom type and child age is not limited to clinical samples. In our own work, low mother–child concordance for internalizing problems and moderate concordance for externalizing problems were found with nonreferred children (Thompson, Merritt, Keith, Murphy, & Johndrow, 1993). Furthermore, mother–child concordance also was found to be a function of the child's gender and age. Older children reported more symptoms, particularly related to mood, expression of anger, depression, and overanxiousness, than did younger children. Males reported more symptoms, particularly regarding attention deficit disorder and school, than did females. Mothers reported more externalizing symptoms of anger and oppositional disorder and internalizing symptoms of depression and dysthymia than their female and young children reported. Mothers also reported fewer internalizing symptoms of worries and separation anxiety than their older and male children reported (Thompson, Gil, Burbach, Keith, & Kinney, 1993b).

The impact of parental mental state on perceptions of child adjustment also has been identified as a factor that contributes to low agreement between parent and child reports (Angold et al., 1987). The research literature indicates that children's adjustment is related to parental stress and distress (Banez & Compas, 1990). In part, this relationship reflects the impact of stress and distress on the mother's perceptions of her children's behavior problems. The mother's level of psychological distress has been found to influence her *perception* of her children's behavior (Webster-Stratton, 1990). For example, mothers who experienced high negative life stress were also found to perceive their children's behavior as more deviant (Middlebrook & Forehand, 1985). However, our own work has shown that mothers' stress and distress is related not only to maternal reports of children's adjustment but also to children's self-reported symptoms. For example, in a nonreferred sample, maternal distress and stress were related to mother-reported externalizing behavior problems and total symptoms, respectively, and maternal daily stress was related to child-reported total symptoms (Thompson et al., 1993). With chronically ill children, maternal distress was found to be associated with total symptoms reported by children with cystic fibrosis (Thompson, Gustafson, Hamlett, & Spock, 1992a) but not with symptoms reported by children with sickle-cell disease (Thompson, Gil, Burbach, Keith, & Kinney, 1993b).

Thus, the evidence indicates that comprehensive assessment of the psychological adjustment of children requires multiple informants and measures. Correspondingly, the challenge has become how to integrate disparate data from multiple informants (Edelbrock et al., 1986).

There have been several hundred studies examining psychological adjustment in children with chronic illness and disability (Lavigne & Faier-Routman, 1992). These studies have primarily reflected two research strategies: large-scale epidemiological studies of a population of children in a particular region and clinical studies of a single condition or pooled disease groups (Wallander & Thompson, 1995).

## EPIDEMIOLOGICAL STUDIES

Pless and Roghmann (1971) reviewed three relevant epidemiological studies: the U.K. National Survey of Health and Development (Douglas & Bloomfield, 1958), the Isle of Wight study (Rutter, Tizard, & Whitmore, 1970), and the Rochester Child Health Survey (Roghmann & Haggerty, 1970). In addition to providing information on the total prevalence of chronic illness, as reviewed in chapter 1, each of these epidemiological studies also examined the psychological consequences of physical illness. The U.K. National Survey and the Isle of Wight study compared children with chronic illness with a random sample of healthy children, whereas the Rochester Child Health Study compared children with chronic illness with a matched control group of healthy children. Psychological functioning was assessed somewhat differently in each of the three studies. In the Isle of Wight study, each child was assessed by a psychiatrist, and parents and teachers completed rating scales. In the U.K. National Survey, parents, teachers, and children completed behavioral symptom questionnaires. In the Rochester Survey, information was obtained from parents, teachers, and peers; children completed a number of psychological tests.

Results of each of these epidemiological studies showed a higher proportion of psychological adjustment difficulties in the groups of children with chronic illness than in the groups of healthy control children. In the Isle of Wight study, the rate of psychiatric disorder was 17% in the children with chronic illness and only 7% in the healthy children. Parent and teacher questionnaires also revealed a higher rate of deviant scores among the children with chronic illness relative to the control children.

Findings from the U.K. National Survey revealed that 25% of the children with chronic illness had two or more behavioral symptoms compared with 17% of the healthy control children. Similarly, using teacher ratings of nervous or aggressive behavior, the percentages of deviant scores were 39% and 31% for the children with chronic illness and healthy children, respectively.

Results of the Rochester Child Health Survey indicated that for children with chronic illness, 23% of the children aged 6 to 10 and 30% of the children aged 11 to 15 had two or more abnormal behavioral symptoms. The comparable figures for the matched control group were 16% for the 6- to 10-year-old children and 13% for the 11- to 15-year-old children. In addition, the U.K. National Survey and the Rochester Child Health Survey revealed that children with chronic illness had more school difficulties and social adjustment problems than did the healthy children. In addition, they were more frequently truant, more often troublesome in school, more often socially isolated, and more frequently described by their teachers as having poor attitudes toward their academic work.

On the basis of their review of these three independently conducted epidemiological studies, Pless and Roghmann (1971) concluded that up to 30% of the children who experience a chronic illness by the age of 15 years may also be expected to be impaired by secondary psychological maladjustment.

A more recent large-scale epidemiological study, the Ontario Child Health Study (OCHS; Cadman, Boyle, Szatmari, & Offord, 1987), has provided further clarification regarding the relationship of chronic illness, medical conditions, and long-term disability to behavioral and emotional functioning and social adjustment in children. The OCHS included 3,294 children (aged 4 to 16 years) from 1,869 families living in Ontario. Complete physical and mental health data were available for more than 2,400 of the children.

A mental health survey was developed that incorporated items from the Behavior Problem and Social Competence scales of the CBCL (Achenbach & Edelbrock, 1983). The survey also included additional information to allow classification of children into psychiatric diagnostic categories from the third edition of the DSM (DSM–III), including conduct disorder, attention deficit hyperactivity disorder, and neurotic disorder (overanxious disorder, depression, or obsessive–compulsive disorder). For all children in the 4- to 16-year-old age range, the mental health survey was completed about each child by a parent, usually the mother. Teacher reports were obtained for children in the 4- to 11-year-old age range, and child self-reports were obtained for children aged 12 to 16 years.

Information also was obtained from parents regarding the presence at the time of the survey of various chronic physical illnesses and physical disability (i.e., limitations of normal functional abilities). The common but less serious conditions of hay fever and allergy were specifically excluded to avoid spuriously elevating the association between chronic physical illnesses and psychological adjustment difficulties. Children were classified into one of three levels of physical health: chronic illness with disability

($n = 110$), chronic illness without disability ($n = 418$), and physically healthy ($n = 2,360$).

Children with chronic illness with disability had a risk for psychiatric disorder that was 3.4 times that of healthy children, whereas children with chronic illness without disability had a risk for psychiatric disorder that was 2.1 times that of healthy children. The percentages of children with at least one psychiatric disorder was 31% for children with chronic illness and disability, 22% for children with chronic illness without disability, and 14% for healthy children. Neurotic disorders and attention deficit hyperactivity disorder were the most common, especially among children with chronic illness and disability. Social adjustment difficulties were also more prevalent among children with chronic illness and disability, whereas children with chronic illness without disability were only slightly more likely to have social adjustment problems than were healthy children. Children with chronic illness and disability also were at greater risk for school difficulties.

A subsequent epidemiological study used data from the 1981 National Health Survey and Child Health Supplement (National Center for Health Statistics, 1981) to examine the relation between chronic conditions and behavioral problems in children and adolescents (Gortmaker, Walker, Weitzman, & Sobol, 1990). Parents' reports of behavior problems and chronic childhood conditions were obtained from a nationally representative sample of 11,699 children and adolescents aged 4 to 17 in the United States. Chronic conditions were assessed using a 59-item checklist that yielded 19 chronic condition categories. Behavior problems were assessed by the Behavior Problem Index (J. L. Peterson & Zill, 1986), a brief measure adapted from the CBCL. The Behavior Problem Index yields an overall behavior problem score and contains several subscales (e.g., Antisocial Behavior, Anxious/Depressed). The results confirmed that chronic physical conditions were a significant risk factor for behavior problems, independent of socioeconomic status (SES). Behavior problems above the 90th percentile were 1.55 times higher among children with chronic illness than those without. Children with chronic illness primarily demonstrated internalizing problems (anxiety or depression) and social adjustment difficulties (peer conflict or social withdrawal). Chronic health conditions were also a risk factor for school problems in terms of placement in special educational classes and repeating a grade.

Thus, the findings of several large-scale epidemiological studies provide strong evidence that children with chronic physical illness are at increased risk for having secondary psychological adjustment difficulties. Risk for psychological adjustment difficulties in these children is apparent in three areas: (a) behavioral and emotional adjustment and self-esteem, (b) social adjustment and peer relationships, and (c) school adjustment and performance. We now review the findings of clinical studies for behavioral and emotional adjustment and self-esteem; the findings of the clinical studies for social adjustment and peer relationships and for school adjustment and performance will be discussed in chapter 4.

## CLINICAL STUDIES

There have been hundreds of studies of psychological adjustment in children and adolescents with chronic illness using clinic-based samples. Many of the early researchers of adjustment in children with chronic illness used small samples of questionable representativeness and clinical assessment with either nonstructured clinical interviews or psychological instruments with insufficient reliability and validity (e.g., Boyle, di Sant'Agnese, Sack, Millican, & Kulczycki, 1976; Pinkerton, 1967).

In response to these early efforts, subsequent researchers applied more rigorous scientific methods to the question of behavioral and emotional adjustment in children with chronic physical illness. Consequently, numerous between-group studies emerged in which a sample of patients with a single illness or a pooled illness group was compared with a control group composed of either healthy peers or psychiatrically ill peers or with normative data.

### Behavioral and Emotional Adjustment and Self-Esteem

In this section we review the findings of clinical studies of behavioral and emotional adjustment and self-esteem in children and adolescents with chronic physical illness using our biopsychosocial framework. Specifically, we address two questions: What are the types of adjustment problems? and What is the stability and change in adjustment problems over time? We reviewed findings on behavioral and emotional adjustment and self-esteem in children with chronic physical illness using the six representative illnesses discussed in chapter 1: asthma, cancer, cystic fibrosis, insulin-dependent diabetes mellitus, sickle-cell disease, and spina bifida, as well as studies of pooled illness samples. This review was not exhaustive. Instead, we included more rigorously designed studies in which relatively large samples and psychometrically sound instruments were used. Priority was given to studies that obtained data from multiple informants, used multiple measures, and assessed multiple dimensions of functioning or those that were driven by an underlying theoretical model of the contributions of biomedical, demographic, and psychosocial processes to adjustment. Table 2.1 lists the studies that were included in the review.

## TABLE 2.1
### Studies of Behavioral–Emotional and Social Adjustment

| Study | Age | N | Condition | Beh/Emot/SE adjustment dimension | Social adjustment dimension | Informant | Method |
|---|---|---|---|---|---|---|---|
| Breslau (1985) | 6–18 | 63<br>98<br>78<br>65<br>359 | SB<br>CP<br>MH<br>CF<br>Controls | Psy Symp | Isolation | M | Q |
| Breslau & Marshall (1985) | 11–23 | 50<br>82<br>67<br>56 | SB<br>CP<br>MH<br>CF<br>Controls | Psy Symp | Isolation | M | Q |
| R. T. Brown et al. (1991) | 6–16 | 28 | IDDM | Depression<br>Anxiety<br>Internal<br>External | | C, M, T | Q |
| R. T. Brown et al. (1992) | 2–17 | 55 | Cancer | Depression<br>Anxiety<br>Internal<br>External<br>Diagnoses | | C, M, T | Q, I |
| R. T. Brown, Kaslow, Doepke, et al. (1993) | 6–17 | 61<br>15 | SCD<br>Controls | Depression<br>Per Comp<br>Internal<br>External | | C, M, T | Q |
| Drotar et al. (1981) | M = 9 | 91<br>47<br>71<br>61 | CF<br>Asthma<br>Siblings<br>Healthy | Behavioral adaptation | Social withdrawal | P, T | Q |

| Study | Age | N | Sample | Behavioral adjustment | Peer relations | | |
|---|---|---|---|---|---|---|---|
| Eiser et al. (1992) | M = 9.4 | 144<br>53<br>35<br>17<br>16 | IDDM<br>Asthma<br>Epilepsy<br>Leukemia<br>Cardiac | | | M, F | Q |
| Graetz & Shute (1995) | 8–13 | 21<br>21 | Asthma<br>Controls | | Social Acc<br>Social Rep<br>Loneliness | C, Peer | Q |
| Greenberg et al. (1989) | 8–16 | 138<br>92 | Cancer<br>Controls | Depression<br>Self-concept | | C | Q |
| Howe et al. (1993) | 12–18 | 80<br>85<br>49 | Neurological<br>Nonneurological<br>Healthy | Internal<br>External<br>Psy Symp<br>Depression<br>Self-image | | P, A | Q, I |
| Hurtig & White (1986) | 8–16 | 50 | SCD | Internal<br>External | Social Comp | C, P | Q |
| Hurtig et al. (1989) | 8–16 | 70 | SCD | Self-esteem<br>Internal<br>External | Social Comp<br>Peer<br>relations | C, P, T | Q |
| Jacobson et al. (1986) | 9–15 | 64<br>68 | IDDM<br>Acute medical | Self-esteem<br>Per Comp<br>Internal<br>External<br>Total Beh Prob | Social Comp | C | Q |
| Kashani, Barbero, et al. (1988) | 7–17 | 30<br>30 | CF<br>Controls | Psy Symp<br>Diagnoses<br>Internal<br>External<br>Self-control<br>Hopelessness | Social Comp | C, P | Q, I |

*table continues*

TABLE 2.1 (Continued)

| Study | Age | N | Condition | Beh/Emot/SE adjustment dimension | Social adjustment dimension | Informant | Method |
|---|---|---|---|---|---|---|---|
| Kashani, Konig, et al. (1988) | 7–16 | 56<br>56 | Asthma<br>Controls | Psy Symp<br>Diagnoses<br>Internal<br>External<br>Self-control<br>Hopelessness | Social Comp | C, P | Q, I |
| Kazak (1989) | 10–15 | 35<br>13 | Cancer<br>Controls | Internal<br>External<br>Total Beh Prob<br>Self-concept | | C, M, F | Q |
| Kellerman et al. (1980) | $M = 15$ | 198<br>249 | Mixed<br>Healthy | Anxiety<br>Self-esteem | | A | Q |
| Kovacs et al. (1985) | 8–13 | 74 | IDDM | Diagnoses | | C, P | I |
| Kovacs et al. (1986) | 8–13 | 74 | IDDM | Anxiety<br>Depression<br>Self-esteem | | C | Q |
| Kovacs, Iyengar, Goldston, Stewart, et al. (1990) | 8–13 | 95 | IDDM | Anxiety<br>Depression<br>Self-esteem | | C | Q |
| La Greca (1992) | $M = 14.2$ | 74 | IDDM | | Social Supp | A | I |
| Lavigne, Nolan, & McLone (1988) | 3–8 | 34 | SB | Internal<br>External<br>Total Beh Prob | | M | Q |
| Lavigne et al. (1982) | 6–16 | 41<br>35<br>76 | IDDM<br>Controls<br>Siblings | Internal<br>External | Social Comp | P | Q |

| Study | Age | N | Group | Depression / Internal | Peer adjustment | Informant | Q |
|---|---|---|---|---|---|---|---|
| Lemanek et al. (1986) | 6–16 | 30 / 30 | SCD / Controls | Depression / Internal | | C, P | Q |
| MacLean et al. (1992) | 6–14 | 81 | Asthma | Internal / External / Total Beh Prob | Social Comp | M | Q |
| Morgan & Jackson (1986) | 12–17 | 24 / 24 | SCD / Controls | Depression / Anxiety / Body Satis | Social Comp | A, M | Q |
| Mulhern et al. (1989) | ≤15 | 183 | Cancer | Internal / External / Somatic | Social Comp | P | Q |
| Mulhern et al. (1992) | 8–16 | 99 | Cancer | Depression | | C, M, N | Q |
| Mulhern et al. (1993) | 4–16 | 81 / 31 | Brain tumor / Cancer | Internal / External / Total Beh Prob / Somatic | Social Comp | P | Q |
| Nassau & Drotar (1995) | 8–10 | 25 / 19 / 24 | IDDM / Asthma / Controls | | Social Adj / Social Comp / Social Perf / Social Skills | C, M, T | Q |
| Noll (1990) | 8–18 | 24 / 24 | Cancer / Controls | | Social Rep | T | Q |
| Noll (1991) | 8–18 | 24 / 24 | Cancer / Controls | | Social Rep | Peer | Q |
| Noll (1992) | 8–15 | 26 / 15 / 33 | Cancer / Brain tumor / SCD | | Social Rep | T | Q |
| Norrish et al. (1977) | 8–15 | 63 | Asthma | Emotion / Conduct / Mixed | | M, T | Q |
| Sanger et al. (1991) | 4–17 | 48 | Cancer | Personality | | M | Q |

table continues

TABLE 2.1 (Continued)

| Study | Age | N | Condition | Beh/Emot/SE adjustment dimension | Social adjustment dimension | Informant | Method |
|---|---|---|---|---|---|---|---|
| Sawyer et al. (1986) | 4–16 | 42<br>42<br>56 | Cancer<br>Controls<br>Siblings | Internal<br>External<br>Total Beh Prob | Social Comp | P, T | Q |
| Schoenherr et al. (1992) | 7–16 | 27<br>37<br>32 | IDDM<br>ALL<br>SCD | Internal<br>External<br>Depression | | C, M, T | Q |
| Simmons et al. (1985) | 12–15 | 62 | CF | Internal<br>External<br>Total Beh Prob<br>Self-esteem | Social Comp | C, P | Q |
| Simmons et al. (1987) | 6–11 | 108 | CF<br>Siblings | Internal<br>External<br>Total Beh Prob<br>Self-esteem | Social Comp | C, P | Q |
| Spaulding & Morgan (1986) | 5–15 | 19<br>19 | SB<br>Controls | Self-concept<br>Beh Adj | | C, M, F | Q |
| Spirito et al. (1990) | 5–12 | 56<br>52 | Cancer<br>Control | | Social Adj | T, P, C | Q, I |
| Tavormina et al. (1976) | 5–19 | 78<br>30<br>20<br>17 | IDDM<br>CF<br>Asthma<br>HI | Personality<br>Self-concept | Social alienation | C | Q |
| Thompson, Kronenberger, Johnson, et al. (1989) | 4–17 | 50 | SB | Internal<br>External<br>Mixed | Social skills | M | Q |

| Study | Age | N | Sample | Outcome | Construct | Source | Method |
|---|---|---|---|---|---|---|---|
| Thompson et al. (1990) | 6–17 | 43 43 43 | CF Psychiatric Nonreferred | Diagnoses Psy Symp | | C | I |
| Thompson et al. (1992a) | 7–12 | 45 | CF | Diagnoses Internal External Mixed | Social skills | M, C | Q, I |
| Thompson et al. (1993b) | 7–17 | 50 | SCD | Diagnoses Internal External Mixed | Social skills | M, C | Q, I |
| Thompson et al. (1995) | 13–17 | 37 35 | CF SCD | Diagnoses | | A | I |
| Thompson, Gustafson, et al. (1994) | 7–14 | 41 | CF | Diagnoses Internal External Mixed | Social skills | M, C | Q, I |
| Thompson, Gil, et al. (1994) | 7–14 | 35 | SCD | Diagnoses Internal External Mixed | Social skills | M, C | Q, I |
| Tin & Teasdale (1985) | 5–7 | 8 8 | SB Controls | | Social Adj | | Obs |
| Wallander, Feldman, & Varni (1989) | 4–16 | 61 | SB | Total Beh Prob Internal External | Social Comp | M | Q |
| Wallander, Varni, et al. (1988) | 4–16 | 270 | Mixed | Total Beh Prob Internal External | Social Comp | M | Q |

*table continues*

## TABLE 2.1  (Continued)

| Study | Age | N | Condition | Beh/Emot/SE adjustment dimension | Social adjustment dimension | Informant | Method |
|---|---|---|---|---|---|---|---|
| Wallander, Varni, Babani, Banis, DeHaan, et al. (1989) | 6–11 | 27 23 | CP SB | Total Beh Prob Internal External | Social Comp | M | Q |
| Wallander, Varni, Babani, Banis, & Wilcox (1989) | 4–16 | 153 | Mixed | Total Beh Prob Internal External | Social Comp | M | Q |
| Wertleib et al. (1986) | 9–16 | 46 | IDDM | Total Beh Prob Internal External | | M | Q |
| Worchel et al. (1988) | 7–18 | 76 42 304 | Cancer Psychiatric Healthy | Depression | | P, C, N | Q |

*Note.* Q = questionnaire; I = interview; Obs = observation; P = parent; M = mother; F = father; C = child; A = adolescent; T = teacher; SB = spina bifida; CP = cerebral palsy; MH = multiple handicaps; CF = cystic fibrosis; IDDM = insulin-dependent diabetes mellitus; SCD = sickle-cell disease; ALL = acute lymphocytic leukemia; HI = hearing impaired; Psy Symp = psychological symptoms; Total Beh Prob = total behavior problem; Beh Adj = behavioral adjustment; Per Comp = perceived compentency; Body Satis = body satisfaction; Beh/Emot/SE = behavioral/emotional/self-esteem; Social Comp = social competence; Social Rep = social reputation; Social Supp = social support; Social Perf = social performance; Social Adj = social adjustment; Social Acc = social acceptance.

*Nature of Studies*

Our review revealed several aspects of this literature that have limited the understanding of behavioral and emotional adjustment and self-esteem in children with chronic physical illness. First, researchers have typically compared illness groups against matched control or comparison groups or instrument norms by comparing group mean scores. The majority of researchers using group means for comparison purposes found no between-group differences (e.g., Kazak & Meadows, 1989; Spaulding & Morgan, 1986). Moreover, when between-group differences were found, they were often of questionable clinical significance because the mean scores for both groups were well within the normal range.

Comparing mean scores for groups masks the variability within the groups and fails to reveal that some proportion of children in the groups exhibit adjustment difficulties. Indeed, when score ranges are reported along with group mean scores, at least some of the children in the groups typically have significantly elevated scores on behavior problem scales (e.g., R. T. Brown, Kaslow, Sansbury, Meacham, & Culler, 1991). The question of interest is, What are the types of problems observed in that proportion of children with chronic illness who have clinically significant behavioral problems?

Second, most of the studies reviewed used parent-completed checklists (e.g., the CBCL; Achenbach & Edelbrock, 1983), which yield broadband factors such as Internalizing, Externalizing, or Total Behavior Problem scores. Use of total behavior problem scores provide information about rates of undifferentiated behavior problems but do not clarify the specific types of problems in these children.

Third, the rates of clinical elevations on these broadband factors and Total Behavior Problem scales vary considerably across studies. Some of the variability is attributable to different cutoff scores used in the different studies. For example, some researchers used the 90th percentile (a T score greater than or equal to 63) as the cutoff score (e.g., Simmons et al., 1987), whereas others used the 98th percentile (a T score greater than or equal to 70) as the cutoff score (e.g., MacLean, Perrin, Gortmaker, & Pierre, 1992; Wallander, Varni, Babani, Banis, & Wilcox, 1988).

Fourth, many researchers have not comprehensively studied the range of potential behavioral and emotional difficulties. Several researchers focused only on internalizing difficulties such as anxiety or depressive symptoms (e.g., Morgan & Jackson, 1986; Mulhern, Fairclough, Smith, & Douglas, 1992) or on self-esteem (e.g., Kellerman, Zeltzer, Ellenberg, Dash, & Rigler, 1980). Yet, there is evidence that when the range of difficulties was more comprehensively assessed, there was the potential for other difficulties, including externalizing problems, to emerge (Thompson, Gustafson,

& Gil, 1995; Thompson, Gustafson, Hamlett, & Spock, 1992a; Thompson, Hodges, & Hamlett, 1990).

Fifth, across all the studies reviewed, there was a small number of frequently used assessment instruments. Yet, the appropriateness of these measures to study children with chronic illness can be questioned because children with chronic illness are not usually included in the norms. Moreover, there are several other aspects of some of these instruments that limit their suitability to assess children with chronic illness. For example, although the CBCL reflected a major improvement in child assessment because it is an empirically derived, reliable, and valid instrument, its utility with children with chronic illness has been questioned on several grounds (E. C. Perrin, Stein, & Drotar, 1991). It is believed that the CBCL may not be sensitive to more subtle or milder forms of adjustment problems that may be present in children with chronic illness and that the inclusion of numerous somatic items on the CBCL can lead to scale elevations that reflect physical rather than psychological difficulties (E. C. Perrin et al., 1991). Moreover, cautions about the Children's Depression Inventory (Kovacs, 1983) have similarly been made (Worchel et al., 1988). Thus, the question remains as to what constitutes the most appropriate methods of assessing adjustment in general and in children with chronic illness in particular.

Sixth, relatively few researchers have assessed the prevalence of behavioral and emotional problems on the basis of diagnostic criteria such as the revised *DSM–III* (*DSM–III–R*; e.g., Kashani, Barbero, Wilfley, Morris, & Sheppard, 1988; Kashani, Konig, Sheppard, Wilfley, & Morris, 1988; Thompson et al., 1990; Thompson, Gustafson, Hamlett, & Spock, 1992a; Thompson, Gil, Burbach, Keith, & Kinney, 1993b). Understanding the types of adjustment problems in children with chronic physical illness requires the level of specificity inherent in diagnoses, because this will guide intervention efforts by enabling the field to draw on what has been learned about treatment and prevention efforts with other children with similar diagnoses.

*Frequencies and Types of Problems*

We now review findings on behavioral and emotional adjustment and self-esteem in children with chronic physical illness by discussing selected studies specific to each of the six representative illnesses.

*Asthma.* In an early descriptive study of 63 children with asthma, 44% were identified as being poorly adjusted by parents' reports, 28% were identified as being poorly adjusted by teachers' reports, and 17% were identified as being deviant by both parents and teachers (Norrish, Tooley, & Godfrey, 1977). Mothers were more likely to place their children in the "emotional" problem subgroup than in the "conduct" problem subgroup, whereas teachers placed the children equally in these subgroups.

In another study, mothers' reports of psychological adjustment of 81 children, as indicated by the mean score on the CBCL Total Behavior Problem scale, was significantly greater than that obtained by the CBCL normative group, with 11.5% of the children obtaining Total Behavior Problem scores greater than the 98th percentile (MacLean et al., 1992). The Internalizing scale mean score was significantly higher than the Externalizing scale mean score, and there was a slightly greater percentage of children with scores greater than the 98th percentile on the Internalizing scale (15%) than on the Externalizing scale (12%).

In a more comprehensive assessment of adjustment, 56 children with asthma were compared with 56 matched control children using structured diagnostic interviews and checklists completed by both the parent and the child (Kashani, Konig, et al., 1988). According to the children's reports, there were no significant between-group differences on total score on the interview, on type of diagnosis obtained, or on helplessness and self-concept. However, 63% of the children with asthma, compared with 48% of the control children, obtained a diagnosis. Parents of children with asthma reported a greater number of total symptoms, a greater number of overanxious and phobic symptoms, and more internalizing and externalizing behavior problems than did the parents of the control children.

Thus, children with asthma are at increased risk for psychological adjustment difficulties, with studies typically identifying internalizing-type problems or a combination of both internalizing and externalizing problems.

*Cancer.* Several descriptive studies have identified the frequencies and types of adjustment problems in children with cancer. In a study of 48 pediatric patients with cancer, 52% had personality scale profiles with two or more clinically significant elevations, although externalizing problems such as delinquency and hyperactivity were infrequent (Sanger, Copeland, & Davidson, 1991). Similarly, in another study, 73% of 81 children with recently diagnosed brain tumors and 77% of 31 children with recently diagnosed non-central-nervous-system malignancies had clinical elevations on one or more of the CBCL scales (Mulhern, Carpentieri, Shema, Stone, & Fairclough, 1993). Clinically significant scores on the Internalizing, Somatic Complaints, and Total scales of the Behavior Problems domain were obtained for both groups.

In addition to studies of broadband emotional and behavioral problems, several researchers have specifically examined depressive symptoms in pediatric patients with cancer. Worchel et al. (1988) compared 76 cancer patients actively in treatment, 42 child psychiatric inpatients, and 304 healthy schoolchildren on children's, parents', and nurses' ratings of depressive symptoms. Psychiatric patients had higher levels of self-reported depressive symptoms than did the children with cancer or the healthy children, and there was a trend toward higher scores among healthy children compared with children with cancer. Forty-eight percent of the psychiatric patients were considered depressed, whereas only 14% of the children with cancer and 22% of the healthy control children were considered depressed. In the children with cancer, parents' and nurses' ratings of depressive symptoms were related to each other but were unrelated to children's ratings. Parents tended to report higher levels of depressive symptoms in their children than did the children themselves.

Similarly, in another study of 99 children undergoing treatment for cancer, only 8 children had clinically significant scores on each of two self-report measures of depressive symptoms, and only 2 children had clinically significant scores on both measures (Mulhern et al., 1992).

Researchers who have examined psychological functioning in "survivors" of pediatric cancer have reported variable findings. Although limited by a small sample and low statistical power, Kazak and Meadows (1989) found few significant differences between long-term cancer survivors (i.e., disease free for 5 years) and control children on standardized instruments of psychiatric symptoms, perceived self-competence, and behavioral functioning, with scores generally within the normal range.

In another study, although 138 long-term survivors of cancer reported significantly poorer self-concepts than did 92 matched healthy comparison children, all of the survivors of cancer had self-concept scores that were within 1 SD of the mean (Greenberg, Kazak, & Meadows, 1989). Moreover, there were no significant between-group differences on the depression scale, with both groups reporting lower levels of depressive symptoms than the normative group of the depression measure.

Contrary to the benign findings in these studies, in another study of pediatric cancer patients who were disease free for at least 2 years, parent-reported behavior problems were found in 42% of the sample (Mulhern, Wasserman, Friedman, & Fairclough, 1989). Significant problems with internalizing and externalizing difficulties were noted in 20% and 17% of the sample, respectively.

In summary, descriptive studies of the types and frequencies of broad-band behavior problems in children with cancer have revealed that these children are at increased risk for behavior problems, although externalizing problems are rare. Moreover, studies that have specifically examined depressive symptoms have revealed that clinically significant symptoms of depression are relatively infrequent in children with cancer, at least according to self-reports. Finally, there are variable findings across studies on the adjustment of survivors of pediatric cancer, which may reflect differences in parents' versus children's reports of problems or variability in psychological problems as a function of length of time since illness.

*Cystic fibrosis.* In two related studies of 108 children (Simmons et al., 1987) and 62 adolescents (Simmons et al., 1985) with cystic fibrosis, adjustment was assessed with the CBCL for both males and females. Male children and adolescents had higher scores than did the CBCL normative group on the Internalizing, Externalizing, and Total Behavior Problem scales of the CBCL, whereas female children had higher scores on the Internalizing and Total Behavior Problem scales and female adolescents had higher scores on the Total Behavior Problem scale. The children with cystic fibrosis had higher self-esteem scores, whereas the adolescents with cystic fibrosis had self-esteem scores comparable to the normative group. Clinical elevations on the CBCL Internalizing scale were found for 48% of the male children and 25% of the female children, whereas clinical elevations on the CBCL Externalizing scale were found for 4% of the boys and 6% of the girls (Simmons et al., 1987).

In a controlled study, 30 children and adolescents with cystic fibrosis were compared with a matched sample of healthy children on self- and parent reports on a diagnostic interview, parent behavioral ratings, and self-esteem ratings (Kashani, Barbero, et al., 1988). There were no between-group differences in diagnoses on the basis of child or parent reports, although parents did report a greater number of overall symptoms for the children with cystic fibrosis than for the control children; this difference was primarily due to somatic symptoms in the children with cystic fibrosis. Moreover, parents of children with cystic fibrosis rated their children higher on the Internalizing and Externalizing scales of the CBCL than did the parents of the control children. No between-group differences in self-esteem were found.

In our own research program we have delineated the types of adjustment problems in children and adolescents with cystic fibrosis and their mothers in a series of studies. In using a structured clinical interview—the Child Assessment Schedule (CAS; Hodges, Kline, Stern, Cytryn, & McKnew, 1982)—children with cystic fibrosis were compared with psychiatrically referred and nonreferred children (Thompson et al., 1990). The criteria for a major *DSM–III* (American Psychiatric Association, 1980) diagnosis were met by 58% of the children with cystic fibrosis compared with 77% of the psychiatrically referred children and 23% of the nonreferred children. These results suggest a framework within which to reconcile previous disparate findings on the psychosocial adjustment of children with cystic fibrosis (see Lavigne, 1983). In general, school-age children with cystic fibrosis did not demonstrate more symptoms of behavioral disturbance than healthy children. It was only in terms of the internalizing problems of worries, self-image, and anxiety that the children with cystic fibrosis had symptom levels comparable to those of psychiatrically referred children. These findings suggest that children with cystic fibrosis are primarily at risk for internalizing as opposed to externalizing behavior problems.

In terms of specific diagnoses, 37% of the children were identified as having an anxiety disorder, whereas relatively few (2%) had a depressive disorder. Thus, the internalizing difficulties were primarily anxiety based, although depressive symptoms tended to increase with age. Moreover, although externalizing problems manifested in conduct disorder were relatively infrequent (12%), oppositional disorder reflected in disobedience, provocativeness, and stubbornness occurred frequently (23%), suggesting that when these children act out it is reflected in oppositional behavior rather than in severe conduct difficulties (Thompson et al., 1990).

In a second study both the CAS and the mother-completed MCBC (Sines et al., 1969) were used to assess the psychological adjustment of 45 children with cystic fibrosis (Thompson, Gustafson, Hamlett, & Spock, 1992a). Sixty percent of the children had a mother-reported behavior problem, 62% met the criteria for a *DSM–III* diagnosis based on their report on the CAS, and 44% met the criteria for poor adjustment on both measures. Again, children with cystic fibrosis were at risk for a constellation of anxiety-based internalizing problems and oppositional externalizing problems.

A third study examined the psychological adjustment of 13- to 17-year-old adolescents with cystic fibrosis using the CAS (Thompson et al., 1995). Fifty-one percent of the adolescents were found to be poorly adjusted, showing a mixture of internalizing and externalizing problems on the CAS. The most frequent specific diagnoses for the adolescents with cystic fibrosis were oppositional (30%), phobic (23%), and anxiety (14%) disorders. As with the child sample, conduct disorder was relatively infrequent (5%).

Thus, children and adolescents with cystic fibrosis are at increased risk for psychological adjustment problems. Studies using parent-completed checklists reveal increased risk for internalizing problems, alone or in combination with externalizing problems. When diagnostic interviews are used parents report increases in total symptoms, whereas children and adolescents report anxiety-based internalizing and oppositional-based externalizing problems. Depression and conduct disorder are infrequent.

*Insulin-dependent diabetes mellitus.* There have been many studies of the psychological adjustment of children with insulin-dependent diabetes mellitus. Representative are two studies in which comparisons were made with children with other medical problems or normative groups. Psychological adjustment in children with recent-onset insulin-dependent diabetes mellitus was compared with that of patients with recent acute medical problems (e.g., fractures, injuries, infections) that necessitated changes in daily activities (Jacobson et al., 1986). No significant between-group differences were found in self-esteem or self-reports of behavioral symptoms, although the patients with diabetes reported a lower sense of scholastic competence than did the patients with acute medical problems. Children with diabetes were rated by their mothers as having more internalizing symptoms than were the children with acute medical problems, although when SES was controlled, group differences on internalizing symptoms were no longer significant (Wertlieb, Hauser, & Jacobson, 1986).

Psychological functioning was examined in 28 children and adolescents with insulin-dependent diabetes mellitus in terms of children's reports of depressive and anxious symptoms, as well as mothers' and teachers' reports of behavioral symptoms (R. T. Brown et al., 1991). Group mean scores on these measures were generally within the normal range, although 29% of the children had clinically significant levels of externalizing symptoms according to teachers' reports.

Thus, cross-sectional, between-group studies have identified relatively few psychological adjustment difficulties in children with insulin-dependent diabetes mellitus, particularly in relation to normative groups and based on self- and parent reports. However, studies that have examined adjustment longitudinally or that have examined the biomedical and psychosocial correlates of adjustment have revealed patterns of adjustment difficulties. (Longitudinal studies are examined in a subsequent section, and correlates of adjustment are discussed in chapter 4.)

*Sickle-cell disease.* A number of controlled studies have been reported that have delineated the frequency and types of psychological adjustment problems. Compared with matched healthy adolescents, 24 adolescents with sickle-cell disease had significantly less body satisfaction and higher levels of depressive symptoms, even when somatic symptoms were controlled (Morgan & Jackson, 1986). Compared with sibling controls, 61 children with sickle-cell disease had more depressive symptoms based on self-reports, higher levels of internalizing symptoms based on mothers' reports, and higher levels of externalizing symptoms based on teachers' reports (R. T. Brown, Kaslow, Doepke, et al., 1993). Moreover, in a study of 50 children with sickle-cell disease, personality and behavioral adjustment difficulties were found to increase with age, and boys exhibited more difficulties than did girls; however, self-esteem was at or above the norm across age and gender groups (Hurtig & White, 1986).

One study of 30 children with sickle-cell disease and 30 control children of similar SES failed to show significant between-group differences on any of the psychological measures assessing behavior problems, self-esteem, and depressive symptoms (Lemanek, Moore, Gresham, Williamson, & Kelley, 1986). Although both the children with sickle-cell disease and the control children exhibited more internalizing behavior problems than did the children composing the psychological instrument normative sample, the authors concluded that these differences were likely attributable to the low SES of the participants rather than the illness.

In our own research program we have also examined patterns of adjustment in children and adolescents with sickle-cell disease. In a study of 50 children (aged 7 to 17 years) with sickle-cell disease, children's reports of symptoms using the CAS and mothers' reports of behavior problem types using the MCBC were obtained (Thompson, Gil, Burbach, Keith, & Kinney, 1993b). In terms of the CAS, 25 (50%) children met criteria for one or more *DSM–III* diagnoses and 25 (50%) children did not. Internalizing diagnoses including anxiety, phobic, and obsessive–compulsive were most frequent (38%), whereas externalizing problems including conduct disorder and oppositional disorder (6%) and combinations of internalizing and externalizing diagnoses (4%) were infrequent.

In terms of the mother-completed MCBC, 18 (36%) children had a problem-free (12%) or sociable (24%) profile, whereas 32 (64%) children had a behavior problem profile. The internal behavior problem profile (36%) was most frequent, whereas the mixed internal and external (14%), undifferentiated disturbance (8%), external (4%), and low social skills profiles (2%) were relatively infrequent.

In a subsequent study types of adjustment difficulties were examined in 35 adolescents (aged 13 to 17 years) with sickle-cell disease (Thompson et al., 1995). Fifty-one percent of the adolescents had at least one *DSM–III* diagnosis on the CAS. The most frequent specific diagnoses were anxiety disorders (26%), phobic disorder (23%), and oppositional disorder (14%).

Thus, most studies of children and adolescents with sickle-cell disease have revealed that these youngsters are at increased risk for psychological adjustment difficulties, with internalizing problems being the most frequently identified. Moreover, psychological adjustment problems, such as oppositional disorder, may increase with age.

*Spina bifida.* In a classic study (Breslau, 1985) of mother-reported psychological adjustment difficulties, children with spina bifida and other illnesses involving the brain (e.g., cerebral palsy and multiple physical or neurological impairments) were found to have a higher frequency of psychiatric impairment than children with illnesses not involving the brain (e.g., cystic fibrosis) and healthy children. Regarding types of difficulties, these children had higher levels of isolation and lower levels of aggression.

In addition, in our own research program we have found higher rates of internalizing than externalizing behavior problems in children and adolescents with spina bifida (Thompson, Kronenberger, Johnson, & Whiting, 1989). Using the MCBC behavior patterns, 50% of the children had a behavior problem profile and 2% had a low social skills profile, suggesting an overall behavior problem pattern rate of 52%. There was a high frequency of internalizing behavior problem profiles (26%) and a low frequency (2%) of externalizing behavior problem profiles. Similarly, a higher rate of internalizing problems (27%) than externalizing problems (6%) also has been found in preschool and early elementary school children with spina bifida (Lavigne, Nolan, & McLone, 1988).

However, another study showed more equivalent rates of internalizing and externalizing difficulties in 61 children and adolescents with spina bifida using the CBCL (Wallander, Feldman, & Varni, 1989). The percentage of children with behavior problems greater than the 90th percentile was 16% and 19% for internalizing and externalizing problems, respectively. Children with spina bifida also displayed more total behavior problems than did the non-clinic-referred normative sample but fewer behavior problems than did the mental-health-referred normative sample.

Thus, children with spina bifida are at risk for internalizing behavior problems, or perhaps a combination of both internalizing and externalizing problems.

A literature review on the psychosocial aspects of myelodysplasia identified seven studies that examined the impact of spina bifida on the child's self-perception or self-concept (Thompson & Kronenberger, 1992). The findings across studies indicated that children with spina bifida had self-concepts that were not lower than those of their siblings but that were lower than those of their peers.

## Findings as a Function of Illness Type

Our review revealed some evidence of differences in the type of behavioral and emotional problems as a function of illness group. For example, in their pooled illness samples, Wallander and colleagues (Wallander et al., 1988; Wallander, Varni, Babani, Banis, & Wilcox, 1989) found that children with juvenile rheumatoid arthritis had fewer externalizing difficulties than other illness groups. Breslau (1985) found that relative to healthy control children, children with chronic physical illness exhibited difficulties that included both internalizing- and externalizing-type problems. However, children with illnesses involving the brain had greater internalizing-type difficulties than did the children with illnesses not affecting the brain. Similarly, Howe and colleagues found that adolescents with neurological illnesses had more parent-reported behavior problems than did adolescents with nonneurological conditions (Howe, Feinstein, Reiss, Molock, & Berger, 1993).

In addition to pooled illness studies, differences by illness can be seen by comparing across studies using the same measures. For example, Thompson and colleagues found that mother-reported mixed internalizing and externalizing behavior patterns and children's reports of anxiety diagnoses and oppositional disorders were most frequent in children with cystic fibrosis (Thompson et al., 1992a), whereas mother-reported internalizing behavior patterns and child-reported anxiety diagnoses were most frequent in children with sickle-cell disease (Thompson et al., 1993b). This suggests that children with cystic fibrosis exhibit more externalizing problems and diagnoses than do children with sickle-cell disease. This finding is particularly striking because externalizing problems are typically elevated in situations characterized by lower SES, which is found among a disproportionate number of African Americans.

The question of differences in rates and types of behavioral problems as a function of illness type relates to the issue of noncategorical versus categorical models discussed in chapter 1. The evidence is considered in more detail in chapter 4, which addresses correlates of adjustment.

*Findings as a Function of Informant*

The majority of the studies of behavioral and emotional adjustment in children with chronic physical illness use parents' reports of problems. More specifically, mothers are the primary informants because they are the ones who usually bring their children to clinic appointments. Fathers are infrequently included and when they are, the responses of a small number of fathers are collapsed into the larger number of mother ratings; the ratings are then categorized as "parent reports." The practice of including a small number of fathers in a predominantly "mother sample" is questionable because fathers tend to report different (and usually lower) rates of adjustment problems (e.g., Kazak & Meadows, 1989; Eiser, Havermans, Pancer, & Eiser, 1992). Thus, what is known about parents' reports of behavioral problems in children with chronic illness primarily reflects the mothers' perceptions.

Moreover, as we have discussed previously in this chapter, there is evidence that the mother's own psychological adjustment affects her perceptions of her children's behavior (Angold et al., 1987; Mulhern et al., 1992; Webster-Stratton, 1990). Thus, when using only the mother's ratings, it is difficult to differentiate the impact of maternal adjustment on perceptions of child behavior and actual child behavior.

Studies of behavioral and emotional functioning in children with chronic illness that have used mothers' reports of adjustment problems have primarily identified group elevations in internalizing difficulties (e.g., Lemanek et al., 1986; Norrish et al., 1977; Simmons et al., 1987; Thompson, Kronenberger, Johnson, & Whiting, 1989; Wertlieb et al., 1986). However, other studies have revealed externalizing and internalizing difficulties (e.g., Kashani, Konig, et al., 1988; MacLean et al., 1992; Mulhern et al., 1989; Simmons et al., 1985; Wallander, Varni, et al., 1988; Wallander, Feldman, & Varni, 1989; Wallander, Varni, Babani, Banis, DeHaan, & Wilcox, 1989; Wallander, Varni, Babani, Banis, & Wilcox, 1989).

Thus, on the basis of mothers' reports, children with chronic physical illness exhibit internalizing difficulties alone or in combination with externalizing difficulties. Further evidence for this combination of internalizing and externalizing difficulties comes from assessment methods that allow researchers to obtain individual behavior problem profiles that include elevations on both internalizing and externalizing scales. For example, using a cluster analysis of the MCBC (Thompson, Kronenberger, & Curry, 1989), Thompson and colleagues found that the "mixed" internal–external profile occurred frequently (Thompson, Gustafson, George, & Spock, 1994; Thompson, Gustafson, Hamlett, & Spock, 1992a). For example, the mixed profile occurred in 22% of the children with cystic fibrosis (Thompson et al., 1992a; 1994) and in 14% of the children with sickle-cell disease (Thompson et al., 1993b).

Children's perceptions of their own emotional and behavioral functioning are also frequently assessed in studies of adjustment problems in children with chronic physical illness. However, when children's reports are obtained, they are assessed using measures that assess exclusively for internalizing difficulties such as anxiety or depressive symptoms (e.g., R. T. Brown et al., 1991; Greenberg et al., 1989; Kellerman et al., 1980; Kovacs, Brent, Steinberg, Paulauskas, & Reid, 1986; Kovaks et al., 1990; Lemanek et al., 1986; Morgan & Jackson, 1986; Mulhern et al., 1992; Worchel et al., 1988) or self-esteem (e.g., Greenberg et al., 1989; Hurtig & White, 1986; Kazak & Meadows, 1989; Kellerman et al., 1980; Kovacs et al., 1986, 1990; Lemanek et al., 1986; Morgan & Jackson, 1986; Simmons et al., 1985, 1987).

A few researchers have also assessed children's reports of adjustment using structured diagnostic interviews. These researchers have also identified both internalizing diagnoses and externalizing diagnoses in children with chronic illness. For example, anxiety diagnoses and oppositional disorder were most frequently found among children and adolescents with cystic fibrosis (Thompson et al., 1995; Thompson et al., 1992a; Thompson et al., 1990) and for adolescents with sickle-cell disease (Thompson et al., 1995).

Our literature review on adjustment in children with chronic physical illness indicated that other informants were used infrequently. Teachers were used as informants in a few studies; however, when they were used, they tended to identify externalizing difficulties (e.g., R. T. Brown et al., 1991; R. T. Brown, Kaslow, Doepke, et al., 1993) or both internalizing and externalizing difficulties (e.g., Norrish et al., 1977). Occasionally, nurses or physicians were used as informants, but only with nonstandardized instruments (e.g., Lemanek et al., 1986; Mulhern et al., 1992; Worchel et al., 1988).

When multiple informants are used within a single study, there is little agreement between informants. Even at the broadest level of categorization (i.e., the presence or absence of a clinical profile), relatively low rates of agreement between informants have been found. Thompson and colleagues found only a 44% congruence between mothers' and children's reports for children with cystic fibrosis (Thompson et al., 1992a) and only a 34% congruence between mothers' and children's reports for children with sickle-cell disease (Thompson et al., 1993b). In our review, we did not find any studies that addressed agreement between multiple informants at the level of diagnosis. However, in our work with physically healthy, nonreferred children, we found low agreement between mothers and children on CAS diagnosis (Thompson, Merritt, et al., 1993). For specific symptoms, such as depression, there also was low agreement between mothers and children (Mulhern et al., 1992; Worchel et al., 1977), between mothers and teachers (R. T. Brown et al., 1991; Norrish et al., 1977), and between mothers and fathers (Eiser et al., 1992). Given the low agreement between informants, it is likely that different individuals provide different information about different aspects of adjustment in children with chronic illness. That is, the differences are not merely "error." Thus, the importance of using multiple informants to assess adjustment comprehensively in these children can be appreciated.

*Findings as a Function of Method*

The types of behavior problems evident in children with chronic physical illness also seem to vary as a function of the method of assessment. Studies of children with chronic physical illness that use questionnaires and checklists have demonstrated elevations in broadband behavior problems, including both internalizing and externalizing problems. Interview methods provide more specificity in terms of diagnoses and typically have identified anxiety symptoms or disorders and milder externalizing problems such as oppositional disorder in some illness and age groups.

*Changes in Adjustment Over Time*

Cross-sectional studies predominate the literature on behavioral and emotional adjustment in children with chronic physical illness. However, these studies reflect only a single point in an ongoing process. To use a developmental perspective that considers change over time, longitudinal studies are necessary. Relatively few longitudinal studies have been conducted that have examined the change in frequency and types of adjustment problems over time.

In our own research program we have examined the stability over a 12-month period of mother-reported and child-reported adjustment in children with cystic fibrosis (Thompson, Gustafson, George, & Spock, 1994). Forty-one children (aged 7 to 14 years) and their mothers completed the protocol at the initial and follow-up assessment points. The rate of child-reported adjustment problems in terms of *DSM–III* diagnoses on the CAS was nearly identical at the initial (63%) and follow-up (61%) assessment points. However, there was significant change at the individual level. There were 20 (49%) children with stable poor adjustment, 10 (24%) children who had stable good adjustment, and 11 (27%) children who changed classification. The overall rate of stability of classification of adjustment was 73% and the kappa coefficient for the presence versus absence of any diagnosis at the initial and follow-up points was .43, indicating a relatively low level of agreement. The anxiety diagnoses and oppositional disorder were the most frequent at both Time 1 and Time 2. However, there was little congruence in specific diagnoses at Times 1 and 2.

In terms of mother-reported behavior problems on the MCBC, the frequency of occurrence of behavior problem profile was comparable at the initial (63%) and follow-up (58%) assessment points. The classification of individual children was relatively stable. There were 22 (54%) children who had stable poor adjustment, 13 (32%) children who had stable good adjustment, and 6 (15%) children who changed classification. The overall rate of stability of classification was 85% and the kappa coefficient for presence versus absence of a behavior problem at the initial and follow-up points was .69, indicating a relatively high level of agreement. At the initial assessment point, the most frequent behavior problem pattern was one reflecting a mixed internalizing and externalizing pattern. At the follow-up assessment, the internalizing profile was most frequent. There was a relatively low rate of congruence in specific behavior patterns across time.

Thus, stability in adjustment across time in children with cystic fibrosis was moderate, although there was more stability in mother-reported adjustment than in child-reported adjustment.

The stability of adjustment over time also was examined in 35 children (aged 7 to 14 years) with sickle-cell disease who completed the initial protocol and the follow-up protocol an average of 10 months later (Thompson, Gil, Keith, et al., 1994). Adjustment was again assessed using children's reports on the CAS and mothers' reports on the MCBC. The rate of diagnoses on the CAS was 49% at both Time 1 and Time 2. However, 14 children (40%) changed classification over the 10-month period. Ten children (29%) had stable poor adjustment and 11 children (31%) had stable good adjustment. The kappa coefficient was .20, indicating a very low level of agreement in classification across Time 1 and Time 2. Anxiety diagnoses were the most frequent at both Time 1 and Time 2. However, there was little congruence in specific diagnoses across Time 1 and Time 2.

In terms of mothers' reports of adjustment on the MCBC, 60% of the children at Time 1 and 69% of the children at Time 2 obtained a behavior problem profile. However, 11 children (31%) changed adjustment classification. A behavior problem profile emerged at both Times 1 and 2 for 17 children (49%) and a problem-free profile emerged at both Times 1 and 2 for 7 children (20%). The kappa coefficient was .32, indicating a low level of agreement in classification across Times 1 and 2. The internal behavior problem profile was most frequent at both Time 1 and Time 2. However, there was little congruence in specific behavior patterns at Time 1 and Time 2.

Thus, similar to the findings with children with cystic fibrosis, although the group data reflect consistency in the rate of adjustment problems on the CAS and MCBC, there were changes in the adjustment classification of individual children and in specific diagnoses and behavior patterns.

The course of psychological adjustment in children with diabetes was examined in a longitudinal, prospective study of children with newly diagnosed insulin-dependent diabetes mellitus (Kovacs et al., 1986). Thirty-six percent of the children met criteria for a psychiatric diagnosis within 3 months after their medical diagnosis. These psychiatric diagnoses were said to be reactive disorders and were not continuations or exacerbations of preexisting conditions. The phenomenological aspects of the adjustment disorders included depressed mood, anxious mood, and mixed emotional features. Longitudinal follow-up of these youngsters revealed a favorable prognosis, in that 93% had recovered from their psychiatric diagnosis by 9 months after their diagnosis of diabetes (Kovacs et al., 1986).

The interview responses of the other 64% of the children who did not receive a psychiatric diagnosis were examined to identify a "typical" initial psychological response to the diagnosis of insulin-dependent diabetes mellitus. Findings revealed five psychological variables with high initial ratings that improved over time that were believed to reflect the "typical" psychological response: depressed mood, feelings of friendlessness, irritability, social withdrawal, and general anxiety.

The findings across the first year after the diagnosis of insulin-dependent diabetes mellitus in terms of children's self-reports of psychological adjustment on several standardized self-report scales also have been reported (Kovacs et al., 1986). Children completed measures of anxiety, depressive symptoms, and self-esteem. At intake, the children's self-reports were consistent with, or in the direction of, greater psychological health relative to normative data. Over the course of the year, symptoms of depression and anxiety decreased and self-esteem increased, with the significant changes having already occurred by midyear. There was no relation between the children's self-reported psychological adjustment and the findings of the psychiatric diagnostic interview.

Long-term follow-up (M = 73 months) data have been reported for 89% of the children from the original sample (Kovacs, Iyengar, Goldston, Stewart, et al., 1990). Initial levels of depressive symptoms, anxiety, and self-esteem were predictors of subsequent levels. In general, anxiety and depression tended to increase over time, although group means were consistent with normative data and were not clinically significant. The level of anxiety increased over time for girls and decreased for boys.

Breslau and Marshall (1985) examined stability in adjustment as a function of illness type. They reported 5-year follow-up data on the stability of adjustment problems in their pooled illness sample, which included children aged 6 to 18 with cystic fibrosis, spina bifida, cerebral palsy, and multiple impairments. They reported high stability in the rate of severe impairment and in the types of problems initially observed in children with illnesses affecting the brain. However, in some areas improvement over time was noted in the children with cystic fibrosis.

## META-ANALYSES

Another way to examine the emotional and behavioral adjustment of children with chronic physical illness is to compare findings across a large number of studies using meta-analytic approaches. Lavigne and Faier-Routman (1992) conducted a meta-analytic review of studies that assessed psychological adjustment in terms of behavioral and emotional problems, psychopathology, or self-concept. Studies using other dimensions of adjustment were not included: School adjustment was excluded because it was beyond the scope of the review, and social functioning was excluded because there were not enough studies assessing this outcome dimension.

More than 700 studies were reviewed; of these, 87 met the criteria for inclusion in the meta-analysis. To be included, the studies had to (a) include a sample of children with a single physical condition or a pooled sample of several illnesses; (b) include a quantifiable outcome measure of adjustment such as an interview or behavioral measure; and (c) include data that allowed calculation of effect sizes through comparison with a control group or normative data. Results revealed effect sizes that were significantly different from zero, indicating higher levels of total adjustment problems and internalizing and externalizing difficulties and lower levels of self-esteem in children with chronic physical illness. Children with chronic physical illness were more likely to exhibit internalizing than externalizing difficulties. In studies using careful matching procedures or making comparisons with normative data, significantly lower levels of self-esteem in children with chronic illness were not observed.

Bennett (1994) reviewed 60 studies to specifically examine one type of internalizing problem: depressive symptoms and diagnoses among children and adolescents with chronic physical illness. Forty-six studies were included in a meta-analysis, which revealed that ratings of depressive symptoms in children with chronic medical conditions were approximately one fourth of 1 $SD$ above the mean score of control groups. Although there were a few studies on any one disorder, there was some evidence of a higher risk for depressive symptoms in some illnesses relative to others. For example, children with asthma and sickle-cell disease appeared to be more at risk for depressive symptoms than children with cancer, cystic fibrosis, and diabetes. There also was significant variability in depressive symptoms across children with the same illness.

Bennett (1994) also reviewed 18 studies that used diagnostic interviews to assess for depression (major depressive disorder or dysthymia) and found an average prevalence rate of 9%. However, there was considerable variability in prevalence rates across studies, with rates ranging from 0% to 38%.

## CONCLUSIONS

Children with chronic physical illness are at increased risk for behavioral and emotional difficulties. These children seem to be particularly at risk for internalizing difficulties or a combination of both internalizing and externalizing difficulties. More specifically, on the basis of structured diagnostic interviews, it appears that anxiety-based disorders are the most frequent, although milder forms of externalizing problems such as oppositional disorders are evident in some illnesses and age groups. Children with illnesses that affect the brain may be at particular risk for behavioral or emotional adjustment difficulties.

Given that there are low levels of agreement as a function of informant, different reporters are apparently attending to different aspects of adjustment. Therefore, a comprehensive assessment of behavioral and emotional adjustment in children with chronic physical illness requires using multiple informants.

Finally, there has been a paucity of research examining the stability of behavioral and emotional adjustment over time. However, existing longitudinal studies have demonstrated that stability in adjustment in children with chronic physical illness is only moderate; there is considerable change across time at the individual level in the presence or absence of a behavior problem or diagnosis, particularly in terms of specific diagnoses and behavior patterns. Future research should elucidate the factors that place children at risk for stable poor adjustment in the face of chronic illness. It is the children at risk for consistently poor adjustment who should be the focus of intervention efforts.

# 3

# CORRELATES OF PSYCHOSOCIAL ADJUSTMENT

We begin with general conclusions regarding the psychosocial adjustment of children with chronic illness that identify the need for a biopsychosocial framework to integrate findings on the correlates of adjustment. The method adopted for reviewing studies in this framework is then discussed. Finally, findings across studies are reviewed in terms of biomedical parameters, child parameters, and socioecological parameters.

## GENERAL CONCLUSIONS REGARDING ADJUSTMENT

Our review of the research literature on psychosocial adjustment to chronic illness yields three general conclusions. First, there is no direct relation between chronic conditions and psychosocial adjustment (Wallander & Thompson, 1995). Rather, there is a wide range of responses to the stress of chronic conditions. Second, although major psychiatric disturbance is not common, epidemiological and clinical studies across a number of illnesses indicate that children with chronic illness are at increased risk for psychosocial problems. Third, psychosocial problems fall into a broad general category that includes psychological adjustment—as manifested by behavioral and emotional problems, low self-esteem, and psychiatric disorders—social competence, and school performance.

The findings of considerable variability in the psychosocial adjustment of children with chronic illness have led to efforts to delineate the processes associated with good versus poor adjustment. This search for the correlates of adjustment is motivated not only by the need to acquire a better understanding of the processes of adaptation and adjustment but, more important to guide treatment and prevention efforts. There is substantial research literature on variables that mediate or moderate the psychosocial adjustment of children to the stress of chronic illness. However, there is considerable variability across studies in dimensions assessed, measures used, age ranges studied, and conditions considered. What is necessary is an organizational matrix that enables accumulation of findings on the specific correlates across studies. On the basis of empirical and conceptual perspectives, three broad dimensions emerge for such an organizational matrix: condition parameters, child parameters, and social–ecological parameters. This matrix serves as a framework for our discussion of the correlates of adjustment.

## METHOD

Our review extends the findings of the recent meta-analysis conducted by Lavigne and Faier-Routman (1993) of studies of variables associated with psychological adjustment to pediatric illness. Included in this meta-analysis were 38 studies that examined at least one risk or resistance factor in relation to a quantifiable measure of adjustment based on either an interview with a mental health professional or a broad-based questionnaire. We did not include self-concept as an indicator of adjustment, but we did consider it as one of the child parameters potentially related to adjustment. The findings of the meta-analysis provide evidence across studies about the contribution of dimensions of our organizational matrix to psychological adjustment to chronic childhood illness. Although pioneering and instructive, some concern can be raised about the relatively small number of studies on which the conclusions were based (Wallander & Thompson, 1995).

In addition, we reviewed studies not included in the meta-analysis that examined one or more potential correlates of empirically assessed adjustment. This review was not all-inclusive but focused on representative studies conducted within the past 10 years. The selection of studies was not limited to the six representative illnesses that are the focus of this book; we also included studies that examined other illnesses if the findings were particularly salient. In contrast to the meta-analysis, we included self-concept as both an aspect of adjustment and as a child parameter. Moreover, whereas the meta-analysis did not consider the interaction patterns among sets of correlates, this review included studies that addressed the interaction within and among sets of parameters.

Tables 3.1, 3.2, and 3.3 show the findings from these studies in terms of dimensions and component factors assessed in relation to specific manifestations of psychosocial adjustment: parent-reported behavior problems and social functioning; child-reported psychological adjustment such as depression, anxiety, self-concept; and adherence. The specific correlates of adjustment addressed in each study were identified and classified under one of three broad dimensions: condition parameters, child parameters, and social ecological parameters. Studies were then listed in the tables either as supporting (Y) or not supporting (N) the role of that factor in adjustment. Rather than reviewing each study presented in the tables, we summarize the findings and discuss issues and implications.


## BIOMEDICAL PARAMETERS

Whether psychosocial adjustment varies as a function of illness type has been controversial. A noncategorical approach has been advocated (Pless & Pinkerton, 1975; Stein & Jessop, 1982), in which adaptation is viewed as a function of dimensions that are common to all chronic physical illnesses rather than as a function of specific illnesses. These dimensions include visibility and social stigma, life-threatening potential, stability (vs. crises), need for intrusive or painful care, sensory or motor impairment, and mental retardation.

It is premature to adopt either an exclusively categorical or noncategorical approach. Specific illnesses clearly differ along a number of dimensions potentially important to adjustment, including illness tasks and the dimensions of the noncategorical model. Examining differences in adjustment as a function of illness type, considered in terms of illness tasks and underlying dimensions, offers the potential to develop a knowledge base that is applicable to enhancing adjustment to chronic illness in general while accumulating knowledge that is illness specific.

The findings of the meta-analysis (Lavigne & Faier-Routman, 1993) provided support for a significant contribution of condition parameters to child adjustment. Within this set of parameters, significant correlations with adjustment were obtained for the variables of severity, functional status (i.e., the degree to which the child could perform daily tasks at an age-appropriate level), and prognosis (i.e., a clinical opinion of the likely outcome of the disease, characterized as worsening or fatal vs. stable or improving). In addition to these variables, researchers also have addressed the contribution to adjustment of type of condition and duration.

## TABLE 3.1
### Correlates of Psychosocial Adjustment: Condition Characteristics

| Study | Age | N | Condition | Adjustment dimension | Type | Sev | Dur | Func Stat | Brain/IQ |
|---|---|---|---|---|---|---|---|---|---|
| Anderson et al. (1981) | 11–19 | 58 | IDDM | Self-esteem<br>Metabolic control | | Y | | | |
| Austin & Huberty (1993) | 9–12 | 136<br>133 | Epilepsy<br>Asthma | Self-Conc<br>Beh Prob<br>Depression | N<br>Y<br>Y | | | | |
| Barakat & Linney (1992) | 6–11 | 29<br>28 | SB<br>Controls | External<br>Internal<br>Self-Conc | | | | | |
| Breslau (1985) | 11–23 | 255 | Mixed | Regressive anxiety | Y | | | | |
| Carpentieri et al. (1993) | 4–16 | 40<br>40 | Br Tumor<br>Cancer | Soc Func<br>Internal | Y<br>Y | | | | |
| Daniels et al. (1987) | M = 10.8 | 93<br>72<br>93 | JRD<br>Sibs<br>Controls | Emotional and behavioral | | Y | Y | | |
| DeMaso et al. (1990) | 5–6 | 63<br>77<br>36 | TGA<br>TF<br>Controls | Global<br>Psychol<br>Funct | N | | | | Y |
| Hanson, Henggeler, et al. (1989) | M = 14.4 | 94 | IDDM | Metabolic control | | | Y | | |
| Hanson et al. (1990) | M = 14.5<br>M = 13.5 | 139<br>136<br>32 | IDDM<br>IDDM<br>Controls | Self-worth<br>Self-Perc<br>Athletic<br>Phy App | | | | | |
| Hanson, De Guire, et al. (1992) | 11–22<br>(M = 15.2) | 95 | IDDM | Self-esteem/<br>Beh Prob | | | | | |
| Hurtig et al. (1989) | 8–16<br>(M = 11.7) | 70 | SCD | Self-esteem<br>Personality<br>Beh Prob | N<br>N<br>N | | | | |

| Study | Age | N | Group | Measure | Result |
|---|---|---|---|---|---|
| Kovacs et al. (1986) | 8–13 | 74 | IDDM | Child Rep | |
| | | | | Anxiety | |
| | | | | Depression | |
| | | | | Self-esteem | |
| Kovacs, Iyengar, Goldston, Stewart, et al. (1990) | 8–13 (M = 11.1) | 95 | IDDM | Child Rep | |
| | | | | Anxiety | N |
| | | | | Depression | N |
| | | | | Self-esteem | Y |
| | | | | Metabolic control | |
| Kuttner et al. (1990) | 10–16 (M = 13.8) | 50 | IDDM | Child Rep | |
| | | | | Depression | N |
| Lavigne et al. (1988) | 3–8 | 34 | SB | Beh Prob | |
| | | | | Internal | |
| | | | | External | |
| | | | | Total | |
| MacLean et al. (1992) | 6–14 (M = 9.3) | 81 | Asthma | Beh Prob | |
| | | | | Internal | N |
| | | | | External | N |
| | | | | Total | N |
| | | | | Soc Func | Y |
| Murch & Cohen (1989) | 12–18 | 53 | SB | Child Rep | |
| | | | | Anxiety | |
| | | | | Depression | |
| | | | | Self-esteem | |
| J. M. Perrin et al. (1989) | 5–16 | 46 | Asthma | Soc Func | N |
| E. C. Perrin et al. (1993) | 7–18 | 91 / 96 | Mixed / Controls | Adjustment | |
| | | | | Child | N |
| | | | | Parent | Y |
| | | | | Teacher | Y |
| Ryan & Morrow (1986) | 10–19 | 125 / 82 | IDDM / Controls | Self-esteem | |
| | | | | Global | Y |
| | | | | Physical | Y |
| | | | | Anxiety | Y |

*table continues*

TABLE 3.1 (Continued)

| Study | Age | N | Condition | Adjustment dimension | Type | Sev | Dur | Func Stat | Brain/IQ |
|---|---|---|---|---|---|---|---|---|---|
| Rovet et al. (1987) | 6–13 (M = 9.8) | 51 30 | IDDM Sibs | Beh Prob Self-esteem | | | | | |
| Sanger et al. (1991) | 4–17 | 24 24 | Leukemia Lymphoma/ Solid Tum | Personality | N | | | | |
| Stein & Jessop (1984) | 5–10 | 81 | Mixed | Personal/role skills | | | | Y | |
| Thompson et al. (1992a) | 7–12 (M = 9.2) | 45 | CF | Beh Prob Child Rep Psy Symp | | N N | | | |
| Thompson, Gustafson, George, & Spock (1994) | 7–14 | 41 | CF | Beh Prob Child Rep Psy Symp | | | | | |
| Thompson et al. (1993b) | 7–12 | 50 | SCD | Beh Prob Child Rep Psy Symp | | | | | |
| Thompson, Gil, Gustafson, et al. (1994) | 7–14 | 30 | SCD | Beh Prob Child Rep Psy Symp | | | | | |
| Ungerer et al. (1988) | 7–31 | 363 | JA | Self-Conc | | Y | | | |
| Varni et al. (1989a) | 8–13 (M = 10.5) | 41 | Limb Defic | Child Rep Depression Self-esteem | | N N | | | |
| Varni & Setoguchi (1991) | 8–13 | 51 | Limb Defic | Child Rep Depression Anxiety Self-esteem Phy App | | N | | | |

| Study | Age | N | Group | Measure | | |
|---|---|---|---|---|---|---|
| L. S. Walker et al. (1989) | 8–19 | 95 | MR<br>CF<br>IDDM<br>Controls | Beh Prob | Y | Y |
| Wallander, Varni, et al. (1988) | 4–16 | 270 | Mixed | Beh Prob<br>Internal<br>External<br>Soc Func | | N<br>Y<br>Y |
| Wallander, Herbert, et al. (1988) | 6–11<br>(M = 7.9) | 27<br>23 | SB<br>CP | Beh Prob<br>Internal<br>External<br>Soc Func | | |
| Wallander, Feldman, & Varni (1989) | 4–16<br>(M = 9.3) | 61 | SB | Beh Prob<br>Internal<br>External<br>Soc Func | | N<br>N<br>N |
| Wallander, Varni, Babani, Banis, DeHaan, & Wilcox (1989) | 6–11 | 23<br>27 | SB<br>CP | Beh Prob<br>Internal<br>External<br>Soc Func | Y | N<br>N<br>N |
| Wallander, Varni, Babani, Banis, & Wilcox (1989) | 4–16 | 153 | Mixed | Beh Prob<br>Internal<br>External<br>Soc Func | Y | |
| Weist et al. (1993) | 8–19<br>(M = 13.3) | 56 | IDDM | Beh Prob<br>Child Rep<br>Anxiety | | N<br>N |
| Westbrook et al. (1992) | 16.1 | 64 | Epilepsy | Self-esteem | Y | Y |
| Wysocki (1993) | 11–18 | 115 | IDDM | Composite<br>Adj to diabetes | Y | |

*Note.* Sev = severity; Dur = duration; Func Sat = functional status; Temp = temperament; Cop Meth = coping method; HLOC = health locus of control; Self-Wor = self-worth; Ph App = physical appearance; Attit = attitude; Soc Sup = social support; Mar Rel = marital relationship; Self-Conf = self-confidence; Par Cop = parent coping; Par Adj = parent adjustment; Coh = cohesion; Exp = expressiveness; Sup = supportiveness; Conf = conflict; Con = control; Self-Conc = self-concept; Beh Prob = behavior problems; Soc Func = social function; Psychol = psychological; Funct = functioning; Self-Perc = self-perception; Child Rep = child reported; Psy Symp = psychological symptoms; Adj = adjustment; IDDM = insulin-dependent diabetes mellitus; SB = spina bifida; Br = brain; JRD = juvenile rheumatic disease; JA = juvenile arthritis; Sibs = siblings; TGA = transposition of the great arteries; TF = tetralogy of fallot; SCD = sickle-cell disease; Tum = tumor; CF = cystic fibrosis; Defic = deficiency; MR = mental retardation; CP = cerebral palsy; N = no; Y = yes.

ADAPTATION TO CHRONIC CHILDHOOD ILLNESS

TABLE 3.2
Correlates of Psychosocial Adjustment: Child Parameters

| Study | Age | N | Condition | Adjustment dimension | Gender | Age/ Onset | Temp | Cop Meth | HLOC | Self- worth | Stigma/ Ph App | Stress | Attit | Soc Sup |
|---|---|---|---|---|---|---|---|---|---|---|---|---|---|---|
| Anderson et al. (1981) | 11–19 | 58 | IDDM | Self-esteem | | | | | | Y | | | | |
| | | | | Metabolic control | | | | | | | | | | |
| Austin & Huberty (1993) | 9–12 | 136 133 | Epilepsy Asthma | Self-Conc | | | | | | | | | | Y |
| | | | | Beh Prob | | | | | | | | | | Y |
| | | | | Depression | | | | | | | | | | Y |
| Barakat & Linney (1992) | 6–11 | 29 28 | SB Controls | External | | | | | | | | | | |
| | | | | Internal | | | | | | | | | | |
| | | | | Self-Conc | | | | | | | | | | |
| Breslau (1985) | 11–23 | 255 | Mixed | Regressive anxiety | | | | | | | | | | |
| Carpentieri et al. (1993) | 4–16 | 40 40 | Br Tumor Cancer | Soc Func | | | | | | | | | | |
| | | | | Internal | | | | | | | | | | |
| Daniels et al. (1987) | M = 10.8 | 93 72 93 | JRD Sibs Controls | Emotional and behavioral | | | | | | | | | | |
| DeMaso et al. (1990) | 5–6 | 63 77 36 | TGA TF Controls | Global | | | | | | | | | | |
| | | | | Psychol | | | | | | | | | | |
| | | | | Funct | N | | | | | | | | | |
| Hanson, Henggeler, et al. (1989) | M = 14.4 | 94 | IDDM | Metabolic control | | | | | | | | | Y | |
| Hanson et al. (1990) | M = 14.5 M = 13.5 | 139 136 32 | IDDM IDDM Controls | Self-worth | | N | | | | | | | | |
| | | | | Self-Perc Athletic | Y | N | | | | | | | | |
| | | | | Phy App | Y | | | | | | | | | |
| Hanson, De Guire, et al. (1992) | 11–22 (M = 15.2) | 95 | IDDM | Self-esteem / Beh Prob | | | | | | | | | | |
| Hurtig et al. (1989) | 8–16 (M = 11.7) | 70 | SCD | Self-esteem | | N | | | | | | | | |
| | | | | Personality | | Y | | | | | | | | |
| | | | | Beh Prob | | N | | | | | | | | |

Cognitive processes

| Study | Age | N | Condition | Measure | Result |
|---|---|---|---|---|---|
| Kovacs et al. (1986) | 8–13 | 74 | IDDM | Child Rep | |
| | | | | Anxiety | N |
| | | | | Depression | N |
| | | | | Self-esteem | N   Y |
| Kovacs, Iyengar, Goldston, Stewart, et al. (1990) | 8–13 (M = 11.1) | 95 | IDDM | Child Rep | |
| | | | | Anxiety | N |
| | | | | Depression | N |
| | | | | Self-esteem | N |
| | | | | Metabolic Control | N |
| Kuttner et al. (1990) | 10–16 (M = 13.8) | 50 | IDDM | Child Rep | |
| | | | | Depression | |
| Lavigne et al. (1988) | 3–8 | 34 | SB | Beh Prob | |
| | | | | Internal | Y   Y |
| | | | | External | Y   Y |
| | | | | Total | Y   Y |
| MacLean et al. (1992) | 6–14 (M = 9.3) | 81 | Asthma | Beh Prob | |
| | | | | Internal | Y |
| | | | | External | N |
| | | | | Total | Y |
| | | | | Soc Func | N |
| Murch & Cohen (1989) | 12–18 | 53 | SB | Child Rep | |
| | | | | Anxiety | Y |
| | | | | Depression | Y |
| | | | | Self-esteem | Y |
| J. M. Perrin et al. (1989) | 5–16 | 46 | Asthma | Soc Func | |
| E. C. Perrin et al. (1993) | 7–18 | 91 / 96 | Mixed / Controls | Adjustment | |
| | | | | Child | N |
| | | | | Parent | N |
| | | | | Teacher | Y |
| Ryan & Morrow (1986) | 10–19 | 125 / 82 | IDDM / Controls | Self-esteem | |
| | | | | Global | N   N |
| | | | | Physical | Y   Y |
| | | | | Anxiety | Y   Y |

*table continues*

TABLE 3.2 (Continued)

| Study | Age | N | Condition | Adjustment dimension | Gender | Age/Onset | Temp | Cop Meth | HLOC | Self-worth | Stigma/Ph App | Stress | Attit | Soc Sup |
|---|---|---|---|---|---|---|---|---|---|---|---|---|---|---|
| Rovet et al. (1987) | 6–13 (M = 9.8) | 51 | IDDM | Beh Prob | Y | Y | | | | | | | | |
| | | 30 | Sibs | Self-esteem | N | N | | | | | | | | |
| Sanger et al. (1991) | 4–17 | 24 | Leukemia | Personality | Y | N | | | | | | | | |
| | | 24 | Lymphoma/ Solid Tum | | | | | | | | | | | |
| Stein & Jessop (1984) | 5–10 | 81 | Mixed | Personal/role skills | | | | | | | | | | |
| Thompson et al. (1992a) | 7–12 (M = 9.2) | 45 | CF | Beh Prob | N | | | | N | Y | | | | |
| | | | | Child Rep | | | | | | | | | | |
| | | | | Psy Symp | N | | | | N | Y | | | | |
| Thompson, Gustafson, George, & Spock (1994) | 7–14 | 41 | CF | Beh Prob | | | | | | | | | | |
| | | | | Child Rep | | | | | | | | | | |
| | | | | Psy Symp | | | | | | | | | | |
| Thompson et al. (1993b) | 7–12 | 50 | SCD | Beh Prob | | | | N | Y | | | | | |
| | | | | Child Rep | | | | | | | | | | |
| | | | | Psy Symp | | | | Y | N | | | | | |
| Thompson, Gil, Gustafson, et al. (1994) | 7–14 | 30 | SCD | Beh Prob | | | | | | | | | | |
| | | | | Child Rep | | | | | | | | | | |
| | | | | Psy Symp | | | | | | | | | | |
| Ungerer et al. (1988) | | 363 | JA | Self-Conc | | | | | | | | | | |
| Varni et al. (1989a) | 8–13 (M = 10.5) | 41 | Limb Defic | Child Rep | | | | | | Y | Y | | | N |
| | | | | Depression | | N | | | | N | Y | Y | | Y |
| | | | | Self-esteem | | N | | | | | | | | |
| Varni & Setoguchi (1991) | 8–13 | 51 | Limb Defic | Child Rep | | | | | | Y | Y | | | |
| | | | | Depression | | | | | | Y | Y | | | |
| | | | | Anxiety | | | | | | | Y | | | |
| | | | | Self-esteem | | | | | | | | Y | | |
| | | | | Phy App | | N | | | | | | | | Y |

| Study | Dur | N | Illness | Outcome | | |
|---|---|---|---|---|---|---|
| L. S. Walker et al. (1989) | 8–19 | 95 | MR CF IDDM Controls | Beh Prob | N | N |
| Wallander, Varni, et al. (1988) | 4–16 | 270 | Mixed | Beh Prob<br>Internal<br>External<br>Soc Func | N<br>Y<br>N | N<br>N<br>N |
| Wallander, Herbert, et al. (1988) | 6–11 (M = 7.9) | 27 SB<br>23 CP | Beh Prob<br>Internal<br>External<br>Soc Func | | Y<br>Y<br>N |
| Wallander, Feldman, & Varni (1989) | 4–16 (M = 9.3) | 61 SB | Beh Prob<br>Internal<br>External<br>Soc Func | | |
| Wallander, Varni, Babani, Banis, DeHaan, & Wilcox (1989) | 6–11 | 23 SB<br>27 CP | Beh Prob<br>Internal<br>External<br>Soc Func | | |
| Wallander, Varni, Babani, Banis, & Wilcox (1989) | 4–16 | 153 Mixed | Beh Prob<br>Internal<br>External<br>Sox Func | | |
| Weist et al. (1993) | 8–19 (M = 13.3) | 56 IDDM | Beh Prob<br>Child Rep<br>Anxiety | N<br><br>N | |
| Westbrook et al. (1992) | 16.1 | 64 Epilepsy | Self-esteem | N | Y |
| Wysocki (1993) | 11–18 | 115 IDDM | Composite Adj to diabetes | N | |

*Note.* Sev = severity; Dur = duration; Func Sat = functional status; Temp = temperament; Cop Meth = coping method; HLOC = health locus of control; Self-Wor = self-worth; Ph App = physical appearance; Attit = attitude; Soc Sup = social support; Mar Rel = marital relationship; Self-Conf = self-confidence; Par Cop = parent coping; Par Adj = parent adjustment; Coh = cohesion; Exp = expressiveness; Sup = supportiveness; Conf = conflict; Con = control; Self-Conc = self-concept; Beh Prob = behavior problems; Soc Func = social function; Psychol = psychological; Funct = functioning; Self-Perc = self-perception; Child Rep = child reported; Psy Symp = psychological symptoms; Adj = adjustment; IDDM = insulin-dependent diabetes mellitus; SB = spina bifida; Br = brain; JRD = juvenile rheumatic disease; JA = juvenile arthritis; Sibs = siblings; TGA = transposition of the great arteries; TF = tetralogy of fallot; SCD = sickle-cell disease; Tum = tumor; CF = cystic fibrosis; Defic = deficiency; MR = mental retardation; CP = cerebral palsy; N = no; Y = yes.

TABLE 3.3
Correlates of Psychosocial Adjustment: Social–Ecological Parameters

| Study | Age | N | Condition | Adjustment dimension | Parent processes | | | | | | | | Family functioning | | | | | |
|---|---|---|---|---|---|---|---|---|---|---|---|---|---|---|---|---|---|---|
| | | | | | SES | Mar Rel | Soc Sup | Self-Conf | Sev | Stress | Par Cop | Par Adj | Coh | Exp | Sup | Conf | Con | Other |
| Anderson et al. (1981) | 11–19 | 58 | IDDM | Self-esteem Metabolic control | | | | | | | | | Y | | | Y | | Y |
| Austin & Huberty (1993) | 9–12 | 136 133 | Epilepsy Asthma | Self-Conc Beh Prob Depression | | | | | | | | | | | | | | |
| Barakat & Linney (1992) | 6–11 | 29 28 | SB Controls | External Internal Self-Conc | | | Y N N | | | | | N N | | | | | | |
| Breslau (1985) | 11–23 | 255 | Mixed | Regressive anxiety | | | | | | | | | | | | | | |
| Carpentieri et al. (1993) | 4–16 | 40 40 | Br Tumor Cancer | Soc Func Internal | | | | | | | | | | | | | | |
| Daniels et al. (1987) | M = 10.8 | 93 72 93 | JRD Sibs Controls | Emotional and behavioral | | | Y | | | Y | | | N | N | | N | | |
| DeMaso et al. (1990) | 5–6 | 63 77 36 | TGA TF Controls | Global Psychol Funct | | | | | | | | | | | | | | |
| Hanson, Henggeler, et al. (1989) | M = 14.4 | 94 | IDDM | Metabolic control | | | | | | | | | Y | | | | | |
| Hanson et al. (1990) | M = 14.5 M = 13.5 | 139 136 32 | IDDM IDDM Controls | Self-worth Self-Perc Athletic Phy App | | | | | | | | | | | | | | |
| Hanson, De Guire, et al. (1992) | 11–22 (M = 15.2) | 95 | IDDM | Self-esteem / Beh Prob | | Y | Y | | | | | | | | | | | Y |
| Hurtig et al. (1989) | 8–16 (M = 11.7) | 70 | SCD | Self-esteem Personality Beh Prob | | | | | | | | | | | | | | |

| Study | Age | N | Group | Measure | | | | |
|---|---|---|---|---|---|---|---|---|
| Kovacs et al. (1986) | 8–13 | 74 | IDDM | Child Rep | | | N | |
| | | | | Anxiety | | | | |
| | | | | Depression | | | | |
| | | | | Self-esteem | | | | |
| Kovacs, Iyengar, Goldston, Stewart, et al. (1990) | 8–13 (M = 11.1) | 95 | IDDM | Child Rep | | | | |
| | | | | Anxiety | N | N | | |
| | | | | Depression | N | N | | |
| | | | | Self-esteem | Y | N | | |
| | | | | Metabolic Control | | | | |
| Kuttner et al. (1990) | 10–16 (M = 13.8) | 50 | IDDM | Child Rep | | | | |
| | | | | Depression | | | | |
| Lavigne et al. (1988) | 3–8 | 34 | SB | Beh Prob | | | | |
| | | | | Internal | N | | | |
| | | | | External | N | | | |
| | | | | Total | Y | | | |
| MacLean et al. (1992) | 6–14 (M = 9.3) | 81 | Asthma | Beh Prob | | | | |
| | | | | Internal | N | | | |
| | | | | External | N | | | |
| | | | | Total | Y | | | |
| | | | | Soc Func | Y | | | |
| Murch & Cohen (1989) | 12–18 | 53 | SB | Child Rep | N | N | Y | Y |
| | | | | Anxiety | Y | Y | Y | Y |
| | | | | Depression | Y | Y | N | Y |
| | | | | Self-esteem | Y | Y | N | Y |
| J. M. Perrin et al. (1989) | 5–16 | 46 | Asthma | Soc Func | Y | | | |
| E. C. Perrin et al. (1993) | 7–18 | 91 / 96 | Mixed / Controls | Adjustment | | | | |
| | | | | Child | N | N | | |
| | | | | Parent | N | N | | |
| | | | | Teacher | N | N | | |
| Ryan & Morrow (1986) | 10–19 | 125 / 82 | IDDM / Controls | Self-esteem | | | | |
| | | | | Global | Y | | | |
| | | | | Physical | Y | | | |
| | | | | Anxiety | Y | | | |

*table continues*

## TABLE 3.3 (Continued)

| Study | Age | N | Condition | Adjustment dimension | SES | Mar Rel | Soc Sup | Self-Conf | Sev | Stress | Par Cop | Par Adj | Coh | Exp | Sup | Conf | Con | Other |
|---|---|---|---|---|---|---|---|---|---|---|---|---|---|---|---|---|---|---|
| | | | | | | | | | | | | | Coh | Exp | Sup | Conf | Con | Other |
| Rovet et al. (1987) | 6–13 (M = 9.8) | 51 30 | IDDM Sibs | Beh Prob Self-esteem | | | | | | | | | | | | | | |
| Sanger et al. (1991) | 4–17 | 24 24 | Leukemia Lymphoma/ Solid Tum | Personality | | | | Y | | | | | | | | | | |
| Stein & Jessop (1984) | 5–10 | 81 | Mixed | Personal/role skills | | | | | | | | | | | | | | |
| Thompson et al. (1992a) | 7–12 (M = 9.2) | 45 | CF | Beh Prob Child Rep Psy Symp | | | | | | | | Y Y | | | | | | |
| Thompson, Gustafson, George, & Spock (1994) | 7–14 | 41 | CF | Beh Prob Child Rep Psy Symp | | | | | | | | N Y | | | | | | |
| Thompson et al. (1993b) | 7–12 | 50 | SCD | Beh Prob Child Rep Psy Symp | | | | | | | Y | N | | | | | | |
| Thompson, Gil, Gustafson, et al. (1994) | 7–14 | 30 | SCD | Beh Prob Child Rep Psy Symp | | | | | | | | N N | | | | | | |
| Ungerer et al. (1988) | | 363 | JA | Self-Conc | | | | | | | | | | | | | | |
| Varni et al. (1989a) | 8–13 (M = 10.5) | 41 | Limb Defic | Child Rep Depression Self-esteem | N N | | | | | N Y | | | | | | | | N Y |
| Varni & Setoguchi (1991) | 8–13 | 51 | Limb Defic | Child Rep Depression Anxiety Self-esteem Phy App | Y Y Y | | | | | | | | | | | | | Y |

| Study | Age | N | Group | Measure | Finding |
|---|---|---|---|---|---|
| L. S. Walker et al. (1989) | 8–19 | 95 | MR / CF / IDDM / Controls | Beh Prob | Y … Y |
| Wallander, Varni, et al. (1988) | 4–16 | 270 | Mixed | Beh Prob | |
| | | | | Internal | Y |
| | | | | External | Y |
| | | | | Soc Func | Y |
| Wallander, Herbert, et al. (1988) | 6–11 (M = 7.9) | 27 / 23 | SB / CP | Beh Prob | |
| | | | | Internal | Y |
| | | | | External | Y |
| | | | | Soc Func | Y |
| Wallander, Feldman, & Varni (1989) | 4–16 (M = 9.3) | 61 | SB | Beh Prob | |
| | | | | Internal | |
| | | | | External | |
| | | | | Soc Func | |
| Wallander, Varni, Babani, Banis, DeHaan, & Wilcox (1989) | 6–11 | 23 / 27 | SB / CP | Beh Prob | |
| | | | | Internal | N |
| | | | | External | N |
| | | | | Soc Func | Y |
| Wallander, Varni, Babani, Banis, & Wilcox (1989) | 4–16 | 153 | Mixed | Beh Prob | |
| | | | | Internal | Y |
| | | | | External | Y |
| | | | | Sox Func | Y |
| Weist et al. (1993) | 8–19 (M = 13.3) | 56 | IDDM | Beh Prob | Y |
| | | | | Child Rep | Y |
| | | | | Anxiety | Y |
| Westbrook et al. (1992) | 16.1 | 64 | Epilepsy | Self-esteem | |
| Wysocki (1993) | 11–18 | 115 | IDDM | Composite Adj to diabetes | Y |

*Note.* Sev = severity; Dur = duration; Func Sat = functional status; Temp = temperament; Cop Meth = coping method; HLOC = health locus of control; Self-Wor = self-worth; Ph App = physical appearance; Attit = attitude; Soc Sup = social support; Mar Rel = marital relationship; Self-Conf = self-confidence; Par Cop = parent coping; Par Adj = parent adjustment; Coh = cohesion; Exp = expressiveness; Conf = conflict; Con = control; Self-Conc = self-concept; Beh Prob = behavior problems; Soc Func = social function; Psychol = psychological; Funct = functioning; Self-Perc = self-perception; Child Rep = child reported; Psy Symp = psychological symptoms; Adj = adjustment; IDDM = insulin-dependent diabetes mellitus; SB = spina bifida; Br = brain; JRD = juvenile rheumatic disease; JA = juvenile arthritis; Sibs = siblings; TGA = transposition of the great arteries; TF = tetralogy of fallot; SCD = sickle-cell disease; Tum = tumor; CF = cystic fibrosis; Defic = deficiency; MR = mental retardation; CP = cerebral palsy; N = no; Y = yes.

## Condition Type

A number of researchers have assessed psychosocial adjustment as a function of medical condition or illness. The bases for selecting contrasts between and among illness conditions were not always clearly specified. At times condition contrasts appeared to be based on the prognosis, the visibility or appearance, or the central nervous system impairment dimensions of the noncategorical model (Stein & Jessop, 1982).

Contrasts among conditions that do not involve the brain, such as heart defects (e.g., DeMaso, Beardslee, Silbert, & Fyler, 1990) and types of cancer (e.g., Sanger, Copeland, & Davidson, 1991), generally do not yield significant differences in behavioral problems or social functioning. Studies that contrast multiple conditions tend to yield mixed findings that do not reflect a consistent pattern of psychological adjustment as a function of condition type (Wallander, Varni, Babani, Banis, DeHaan, & Wilcox, 1989; Wallander, Varni, Babani, Banis, & Wilcox, 1988). The most consistent finding is that children with conditions that involve the brain have more behavior problems and poorer social functioning than children with conditions that do not involve the brain. For example, across conditions, the level of intellectual functioning has been shown to make independent contributions to psychological adjustment (DeMaso et al., 1990). Furthermore, in a study of children with cerebral palsy, orthopedic problems, or seizure disorders and healthy control children, intellectual functioning was found to have a compensatory relationship with self-, parent-, and teacher-reported adjustment (E. C. Perrin, Ayoub, & Willett, 1993). Parents and teachers rated those with higher IQs as being better adjusted. High IQ had a compensatory relationship with children's self-reported adjustment among children with seizure disorders or orthopedic problems, but not among those with cerebral palsy or among healthy children (E. C. Perrin et al., 1993).

## Condition Severity

Except for one study, there was no evidence of a relation between behavioral problems and severity across a number of conditions including asthma (MacLean, Perrin, Gortmaker, & Pierre, 1992; J. M. Perrin, MacLean, & Perrin, 1989), sickle-cell disease (Hurtig, Koepke, & Park, 1989), cystic fibrosis (Thompson, Gustafson, Hamlett, & Spock, 1992a), spina bifida (Wallander, Feldman, & Varni, 1989; Wallander, Varni, Babani, Banis, DeHaan, & Wilcox, 1989), cerebral palsy (Wallander, Varni, Babani, Banis, DeHaan, & Wilcox, 1989), diabetes (Kuttner, Delamater, & Santiago, 1990; Weist, Finney, Barnar, David, & Ollendick,

1993), and limb deficiencies (Varni, Rubenfeld, Talbot, & Setoguchi, 1989b). The one exception was a reported relation between increased disease severity in children with juvenile rheumatoid arthritis and increased psychological adjustment problems (Daniels, Moos, Billings, & Miller, 1987). By contrast, the findings of the meta-analysis (Lavigne & Faier-Routman, 1993) provided support for the contribution of severity to adjustment. However, the findings across studies may reflect a confounding of severity with condition type.

In terms of self-esteem or self-worth, the evidence is inconclusive. For example, a direct (i.e., positive) relationship between metabolic control, an index of severity in diabetes, and self-esteem was found in one study (Anderson, Miller, Auslander, & Santiago, 1981) but not in another (Kovacs, Ivengar, Goldston, Stewart, Obrosky, & Marsh, 1990). Similarly, self-concept was negatively related to the severity of juvenile rheumatoid arthritis for primary- and high-school-age children but not for young adults (Ungerer, Horgan, Chaitow, & Champion, 1988). The findings for social competence also have been inconsistent, such as in studies of children with asthma (MacLean et al., 1992; J. M. Perrin et al., 1989) and children with spina bifida (Wallander, Varni, Babani, Banis, DeHaan, & Wilcox, 1989; Wallander, Varni, Babani, DeHaan, Wilcox, & Banis, 1989).

## Functional Status

Rather than assessing medical severity per se, several investigators have examined the relationship of children's functional status to psychosocial adjustment. For example, in a study of children with multiple physical conditions, psychological adjustment problems were significantly positively related to poor functional status, defined as the capacity to perform age-appropriate roles and tasks (Stein & Jessop, 1984). In another study of children with physical limitations, poor social functioning was positively associated with teachers' assessments of children's adaptive functioning as poor, defined in terms of personal self-sufficiency, community self-sufficiency, and personal social responsibility, (Wallander, Varni, Babani, Banis, DeHaan, & Wilcox, 1989).

Conceptualizing the degree of condition-related impairment in terms of functional status is potentially a useful way to operationalize severity, particularly as a common unit to be used across different illnesses. However, these measures need to be based on biomedical parameters such as the degree of ambulation, pulmonary functioning, or metabolic control and objective measures of competency in relation to age expectations. This is necessary to keep this dimension distinct from psychological adjustment and other potentially mediating or moderating variables such as *perceived severity*.

## Duration

Although early epidemiological studies have suggested that psychological adjustment is related to the duration of chronic conditions (Pless & Roghmann, 1971), surprisingly few studies have examined the relation between duration and adjustment. In a cross-sectional study of children with juvenile rheumatoid arthritis, longer disease duration was positively related to more psychological adjustment problems (Daniels et al., 1987). In a longitudinal study, the stability and change in adjustment of children over the first 6 years of their diabetes (Kovacs, Iyengar, Goldston, Obrosky, et al., 1990) was examined. Over time, children appraised their diabetes as being more stressful and management as being more difficult. The ratings of boys and girls with initially high levels of depression or anxiety remained high, whereas those whose ratings were initially low became somewhat more symptomatic. Over time, both boys and girls exhibited a mild increase in depressive symptoms. Girls exhibited an increase in anxiety and boys a decrease. Self-esteem remained stable over time, with the initial level strongly predictive of subsequent self-esteem.

The impact of duration has also been examined in children with insulin-dependent diabetes mellitus not on psychological adjustment but on metabolic control. The findings are of interest because they demonstrate the value of developmental studies in identifying the emergence of relationships among variables as the illness continued. With increased duration, metabolic control decreased and duration attenuated the relationship of marital satisfaction, family adaptation, and family cohesion to metabolic control such that only under the condition of long duration were these variables associated with metabolic control (Hanson, Henggeler, Harris, Burghen, & Moore, 1989). Similarly, in another study of children with insulin-dependent diabetes mellitus, duration interacted with family adaptability to influence children's coping such that under long duration and low family adaptability, there was a high use of ventilation and avoidance coping in contrast to low levels of these coping methods under long duration and high family adaptability (Hanson, Cigrang, et al., 1989). The results of these studies suggest the possibility that the relationship of other variables to psychological adjustment also could be moderated by duration.

If researchers are to incorporate a developmental perspective it is essential to investigate duration as one of the variables that can mediate or moderate adjustment. Furthermore, longitudinal studies are needed to determine how condition parameters interact over time with child characteristics and social–ecological parameters to influence psychosocial adjustment.

# CHILD PARAMETERS

In Lavigne and Faier-Routman's (1993) meta-analysis, the set of variables addressing child characteristics was more significantly positively associated with child adjustment than was the set of condition variables. Within the set of child characteristics, self-concept, poor coping, and low IQ, but not temperament and distractibility, were significantly and positively related to adjustment. Age and gender were not included in this set, but they were significantly positively associated with child adjustment, with older children and boys demonstrating more adjustment problems. In addition to these variables, researchers have also studied the contribution to adjustment of various cognitive processes, including appraisal of stress, attitude toward the illness, perceived physical appearance, perceived social support, and health locus of control.

## Gender

The evidence regarding the contribution of gender to children's psychological adjustment varies depending on the dimension of adjustment considered and who is doing the reporting. The evidence was mixed on parent- and teacher-reported behavior problems. Some studies showed no differences as a function of gender. When differences in adjustment were found, boys had more reported behavior problems than girls (E. C. Perrin et al., 1993; Rovet, Ehrlich, & Hoppe, 1987; Wallander, Varni, et al., 1988). When adjustment was assessed through child-reported symptoms, girls reported more symptoms of distress than did boys. For example, girls with diabetes reported higher levels of anxiety and more negative perceptions of physical appearance (Ryan & Morrow, 1986) and girls with cystic fibrosis reported symptoms that more frequently met the criteria for a diagnosis from the third edition of the *Diagnostic and Statistical Manual of Mental Disorders* (*DSM–III*) than did boys with these respective conditions (Thompson et al., 1992a). Most studies indicated a significant relationship between gender and self-esteem (e.g., Thompson et al., 1992a; L. S. Walker, Ortiz-Valdes, & Newbrough, 1989). It may be that girls are more willing to acknowledge and report problems than are boys.

## Age and Age of Onset

The studies reviewed were consistent in the lack of an age effect on behavior and emotional problems and self-esteem. By contrast, the findings on age of onset were mixed. For example, boys who developed diabetes after age 4 had more parent-reported behavior problems than did boys with early onset and girls with both early and late onset (Rovet et al., 1987). However, the age of onset was not related to self-reported symptoms of psychological distress (Kovacs, Iyengar, Goldston, Stewart, et al., 1990). There was no age-of-onset effect in terms of self-esteem in two studies (Hanson et al., 1990; Rovet et al., 1987), but in another study girls with early onset reported poorer self-concept than did boys with early onset (Ryan & Morrow, 1986).

Thus, age generally does not appear to be a variable that, by itself, is related to adjustment of children with chronic illness. The age of onset may be a variable with regard to diabetes. To our knowledge, however, age has not been investigated longitudinally. Similar to duration, the influence of age of onset on psychosocial adjustment of children with chronic illness needs to be investigated longitudinally. This would require repeated assessment of adjustment at different points, perhaps during periods of developmental transition such as school entry, movement to junior high, and graduation from high school. In this way, the influence of age could be assessed developmentally rather than cross sectionally and its interactions with other dimensions could be investigated.

## Temperament

We could find only two studies in which temperament was investigated. In a study of children with spina bifida (Lavigne, Nolan, & McLone, 1988), mother-reported behavior problems were positively associated with greater temperamental difficulty and lower distractibility. In another study of children with spina bifida or cerebral palsy, mother-reported child activity level and child-reactivity were positively related to mother-reported internalizing and externalizing behavior problems (Wallander, Hubert, & Varni, 1988).

## Child Coping Methods

Although there is substantial theoretical and empirical support for the role of coping methods in the adjustment of adults (Lazarus & Folkman, 1984), there have been few studies that directly examined the relationship between children's coping methods and adjustment. No significant relationship was found between palliative or instrumental coping methods and self-reported symptoms of psychological distress in children with diabetes (Kovacs, Brent, Steinberg, Paulauskas, & Reid, 1986). However, adaptive coping, measured in terms of one's ability to manage internal feelings, was inversely related to mother-reported external and total behavior problems in children with spina bifida (Lavigne et al., 1988).

In a study of children with sickle-cell disease (Thompson et al., 1993b), the children's pain coping strategies did not contribute to mother-reported behavior problems. However, the children's pain coping strategies characterized by negative thinking accounted for a significant increment in child-reported psychological symptoms over and above that accounted for by illness and demographic parameters. That is, with the influence of illness and demographic parameters controlled, higher levels of negative thinking were associated with higher levels of self-reported distress. These findings suggest that psychological adjustment could be enhanced by teaching children with sickle-cell disease to replace negative thinking patterns of pain coping strategies, such as catastrophizing and self-statements of fear, with active cognitive–behavioral pain coping strategies, such as diverting attention and calming self-statements (Gil, Williams, Thompson, & Kinney, 1991).

This area of investigation has been hampered by the lack of good measures of children's coping, which reflects the need for conceptual clarity on what constitutes coping by children and how coping changes developmentally (cf. Compas, 1987).

### Cognitive Processes

The contribution of an array of cognitive processes to children's adjustment has been examined. Although there have been relatively few studies of each variable, information is emerging on several processes, including perceptions of stress, illness, appearance, social support, and self-worth.

Perceived stress, measured in terms of negative life events and daily hassles, has been related to behavior problems, self-esteem, and self-reported symptoms, such that the higher the perceived stress, the higher the levels and frequencies of adjustment problems. For example, poor psychological adjustment of children with asthma (MacLean et al., 1992) and spina bifida (Murch & Cohen, 1989) was positively related to high levels of perceived stress of negative life events. Children's perceptions of daily stress were significantly inversely related to general self-worth (Varni, Rubenfeld, Talbot, & Setoguchi, 1989a) and perceived physical appearance (Varni & Setoguchi, 1991) in children with limb deficiencies. In a study of children with diabetes, appraisal of the stress associated with diabetes management was positively related to self-reported levels of anxiety and depression (Kovacs, Iyengar, Goldston, Obrosky, et al., 1990).

Perceived stigma was inversely related to self-esteem in children with seizure disorders (Westbrook, Bauman, & Shinnar, 1992), and self-perceptions of physical appearance were inversely associated with self-worth (Varni et al., 1989a; Varni & Setoguchi, 1991), depressive symptoms, and trait anxiety (Varni & Setoguchi, 1991) in children with limb deficiencies. Children's perceptions of social support—measured as the degree to which children perceived that parents, teachers, classmates, and close friends cared for them, listened to them, and generally treated them as a person who mattered—were significantly positively correlated with general self-worth in children with limb deficiencies (Varni et al., 1989a).

The role of children's perceptions about their illness has been examined by several researchers. The attitudes of children with epilepsy and asthma toward their illness (i.e., how favorably they felt about having a chronic illness) were negatively correlated with mother-reported total behavior problems and depression and positively correlated with self-concept (Austin & Huberty, 1993). The perceptions of health locus of control in children with cystic fibrosis were not significantly related to child adjustment in terms of mother-reported behavior problems, child-reported symptoms, or both (Thompson et al., 1992a). However, with illness and demographic parameters controlled, low levels of powerful-other health locus of control perceptions of children with sickle-cell disease were associated with higher levels of mother-reported internalizing behavior problems (Thompson et al., 1993b).

Whereas perceptions of stress, physical appearance, stigma, and social support have been related to general self-worth, perceptions of self-esteem have also been related to other dimensions of psychological adjustment. For example, perceptions of self-worth were inversely related to depressive symptomatology in children with limb deficiencies (Varni et al., 1989a) and to mother-reported internalizing and externalizing behavior problems and child-reported symptoms in children with cystic fibrosis (Thompson et al., 1992a).

Although there have been relatively few studies of cognitive variables, the evidence across variables attests to the role of cognitive processes in children's adjustment. As the contributions of specific processes are replicated, the foundation will be laid for identifying these cognitive processes as salient targets for intervention efforts to enhance the psychosocial adjustment of children with chronic illness.


## SOCIAL–ECOLOGICAL PARAMETERS

The meta-analysis conducted by Lavigne and Faier-Routman (1993) included two sets of variables that fall within this dimension of the organizational matrix. One set included parents' ratings of life stressors and socioeconomic status (SES). Only the component variable of increased life stress was significantly positively correlated with child adjustment. Another set included the family and parent variables of maternal and paternal adjustment, marital–family adjustment or conflict, and family support or cohesiveness. As with child parameters, this set of variables also was more strongly associated with child adjustment than were the illness–disability variables. Furthermore, all of the component variables in the set, except for paternal adjustment, were significantly positively correlated with child adjustment.

In addition to the variables included in the meta-analysis, researchers have also studied coping method or temperament style and parental perceptions of stress, social support, and condition severity.

## Socioeconomic Status

A consistent finding in the mental health literature is that lower SES is associated with an increased rate of psychological adjustment problems. However, the direct contribution of SES to adjustment is infrequently assessed. In some studies, SES is used as a control variable for group comparability. Also, there has been no consistently used measure of SES. Consequently, it is not surprising that the findings on the role of SES in child adjustment are mixed. Even within some studies, SES was related to one dimension of child adjustment but not another (e.g., MacLean et al., 1992).

Perhaps what these studies indicate most strongly is the need to seriously consider SES as a potential contributor to the adjustment of children with chronic illness. That is, there needs to be conceptual clarity about what aspects of the social–ecological environment are being reflected in various measures of SES and how these aspects are hypothesized to affect child adjustment directly or in interaction with other hypothesized adaptational processes. For example, perhaps perceptions of stress, family functioning, or coping methods vary as a function of SES. This type of knowledge would appear to be essential to the development of intervention strategies to foster adjustment of children from different social–ecological backgrounds.

## Family Functioning

Family functioning was the most frequently investigated dimension in the studies reviewed. Conceptually, the role of the family frequently is measured in terms of the dimensions of cohesion, expressiveness, organization, independence, and control identified by Moos and Moos (1981) and the adaptability and cohesion dimensions identified by the circumplex model of Olson, Sprenkle, and Russell (1979). These dimensions of family functioning were developed for observation of families in general but may not be fully generalizable to families with children with chronic physical illness.

The findings of the studies reviewed provide strong support for the role of family functioning in children's psychological adjustment. Some researchers investigated a single dimension of family functioning. For example, cohesion was related to the adjustment of children with myelo-meningocele (Lavigne, Nolan, & McLone, 1988). Other investigators examined more than one dimension. For example, Wallander, Varni, Babani, Banis, and Wilcox (1989) formulated a measure of family psychological resources based on five subscales of the Family Environment Scale (Moos & Moos, 1981): Cohesion, Expressiveness, Conflict, Organization, and Control. Low levels of these family psychological resources accounted for a significant increment in variance in mother-reported children's internalizing and externalizing behavior problems and social functioning over and above the contribution of utilitarian resources reflected in family income and maternal education. Family cohesion made a particularly significant positive contribution to social functioning.

Dimensions of family functioning not only have been shown to have direct associations with adjustment, but interaction effects with other potential correlates of adjustment also have been demonstrated. In a study of children with spina bifida (Murch & Cohen, 1989), low conflict, low control, and high cohesion served to buffer depression in uncontrollable life stress, whereas high independence exacerbated depression and anxiety in controllable life stress. This type of study portends a new level of research into the correlates of adjustment that considers the ways in which sets of correlates act together. The contribution of family functioning may vary not only in relation to perceptions of stress but also in terms of SES, coping methods, and child characteristics. In particular, patterns of family functioning conducive to adjustment may vary with the child's developmental level.

## Marital Adjustment

The role of marital adjustment, as distinct from family functioning, in the adjustment of children with chronic illness has received little attention. Only one of the studies reviewed investigated this variable; it was found that higher maternal and paternal perceived marital discord was positively associated with lower perceptions of physical appearance in children with limb deficiencies (Varni & Setoguchi, 1991).

The field has clearly moved to a focus on the role of family functioning in adjustment of children with chronic illness, and it can be argued that marital discord is subsumed within the conflict dimension of family functioning. However, the role of marital adjustment warrants investigation because of its potential as a salient intervention target.

## Parental Social Support

There have been few studies that have included an assessment of the impact of parental social support, other than as reflected in family functioning, on child adjustment, and the findings are mixed. In a study of children with spina bifida (Barakat & Linney, 1992), the greater the social support reported by mothers, the fewer externalizing behavior problems they reported for their child. However, in a study that included children with different types of illnesses (E. C. Perrin et al., 1993), maternal social network size did not significantly contribute to child adjustment. Considering the extensive evidence in the literature of the direct and stress-buffering effects of social support in psychological adjustment, more systematic assessment of the contribution of social support, other than in terms of family functioning, to the adjustment of children with chronic illness appears warranted.

### Parental Adjustment

The mental health research literature also supports a relationship between children's adjustment and parental stress and distress (Banez & Compas, 1990). Parental adjustment, particularly maternal adjustment, is beginning to be included among the variables considered as potential correlates of the adjustment of children with chronic illness. Concurrently, as discussed in chapter 2, it is increasingly recognized that there is a need to assess child adjustment through both children's and mothers' reports to differentiate the impact of maternal adjustment on child adjustment from that on maternal perceptions of her child's behavior (Thompson, Merritt, Keith, Murphy, & Johndrow, 1993).

Although there have been some negative findings (e.g., Kovacs et al., 1986), several studies have shown a positive relationship between parental depression and mother-reported child adjustment. For example, in a study that included children with mental retardation, cystic fibrosis, and diabetes and healthy control children, mothers who were more depressed reported more behavior problems in their children (L. S. Walker et al., 1989).

Assessing the contribution of maternal adjustment to child adjustment has been a component of our series of longitudinal studies of children with chronic illness. These research studies assessed children's adjustment in terms of mother-reported behavior problems using the Missouri Children's Behavior Checklist (MCBC; Sines, Pauker, Sines, & Owen, 1969) and child-reported symptoms using the Child Assessment Schedule (CAS; Hodges, Kline, Stern, Cytryn, & McKnew, 1982), which yields DSM–III diagnoses and a total symptom score. Maternal adjustment was assessed relative to anxiety, depression, and the Global Severity Index of the SCL-90-R (Derogatis, 1983). In a study of children with cystic fibrosis (Thompson et al., 1992a), with demographic parameters and illness severity controlled, high levels of maternal anxiety accounted for a significant increment in the variance in mother-reported children's behavior problems and child-reported symptoms. Moreover, with initial levels of psychological symptoms controlled, higher levels of maternal distress at follow-up 12 months later accounted for a significant increment in the variance in the overall child-reported symptoms at follow-up (Thompson, Gustafson, George, & Spock, 1994).

In a study of children with sickle-cell disease (Thompson et al., 1993b), with illness and demographic variables controlled, higher levels of maternal anxiety accounted for significant increments in the variance in mother-reported internalizing and externalizing behavior problems, respectively. By contrast, maternal distress did not account for a significant increment in the child-reported symptoms. In the follow-up study 10 months later (Thompson, Gil, Gustafson, et al., 1994), with initial level of child adjustment controlled, maternal anxiety did not account for a significant increment in mother-reported behavior problems or child-reported symptoms.

Thus, there is considerable support for the association of parental adjustment, particularly maternal depression, with mother-reported adjustment of children with chronic illness. Although it is possible that this relationship reflects maternal report bias, other studies indicate that the mother's reports of her child's behavior is influenced by child behavior as well as by the mother's own mood (L. S. Walker et al., 1989). Furthermore, in the study of children with cystic fibrosis reported earlier (Thompson et al., 1993), child-reported symptoms were found to be positively related to maternal anxiety. Thus, evidence indicates that child adjustment is positively related to maternal adjustment and that it is not just an artifact of the impact of maternal stress and distress on the mother's perceptions of her child's behavior and adjustment. However, researchers who examine correlates of adjustment will need to include both child-reported and mother-reported measures of adjustment.

## Parental Cognitive Processes

Several researchers have investigated variables that can be considered to reflect parental processes, such as perceived social support, self-concept, health locus of control, perceived illness severity, and coping style. For example, parental perceptions of low social support were related to parent-reported behavior problems (Barakat & Linney, 1992; Daniels et al., 1987) but not to adjustment as rated by the child, parent, or teacher (E. C. Perrin et al., 1993). The findings were mixed in terms of self-esteem (Hanson, DeGuire, Schinkel, Henggeler, & Burghen, 1992a; E. C. Perrin et al., 1993). There was a lack of support for the association of maternal health locus of control beliefs and maternal self-concept with parent-reported child adjustment (E. C. Perrin et al., 1993). For parents' perceptions of severity, children who were perceived as having either mild or severe asthma were rated significantly lower in social functioning than those rated as having moderately severe asthma (J. M. Perrin et al., 1989). In a study of children with cancer (Sanger et al., 1991), parent coping, characterized by a focus on maintaining family integration and a sense of optimism about the illness, was positively related to good child adjustment according to parental reports.

Investigation of the role of parental cognitive processes in the adjustment of children with chronic conditions is just beginning to emerge. These processes may serve to moderate or mediate the effects of other sets of parameters such as family functioning or disease and disability parameters. It will also be important to assess whether these parental processes have their effect through their relationship to parental adjustment.

## CONCLUSIONS

Tables 3.1, 3.2, and 3.3 show the current status of the search for correlates of psychological adjustment of children with chronic illness. The focal points have been illness parameters and family functioning. Although a number of child and social–ecological parameters have been investigated, these sections of the tables have too many blank spaces. Moreover, too often the correlates have been investigated in only one study. When correlates have been addressed in more than one study, findings have been inconsistent across studies relative to one or more measures of children's adjustment. Thus, in spite of the efforts to date, the knowledge base is limited. Currently, there is support for brain involvement, perceptions of high levels of stress and low levels of self-esteem, family functioning characterized as low in cohesion and supportiveness, and high levels of maternal distress as correlates of poor adjustment in children with chronic illness.

In the next steps in this research process, researchers need to determine whether positive and negative findings can be replicated. Moreover, the role of child parameters in general and, more specifically, the interrelationships among condition, child, and social–ecological parameters in children's adjustment need to be studied. Longitudinal studies are needed to determine how the relationships among and between parameters and adjustment change as a function of development. These efforts need to be conceptually and theoretically driven to provide a sound basis for the pattern of variables investigated and to integrate findings across studies.

# 4

# SOCIAL ADJUSTMENT, PEER RELATIONSHIPS, AND SCHOOL PERFORMANCE

Psychosocial adjustment is manifested not only by psychological adjustment but also through social adjustment and peer relationships and school performance. In this chapter, we follow a format similar to that used in chapter 2 to discuss psychological adjustment. We first review the nature of the studies. Because of the paucity of studies, we did not find it useful to examine the findings of studies in terms of the six representative illnesses. However, the frequencies and types of problems are considered as a function of illness type, informant, and method. In addition, we discuss the correlates (i.e., the factors and processes) that have been found to be associated with adjustment.

## SOCIAL ADJUSTMENT AND PEER RELATIONSHIPS

Achieving adequate social adjustment and peer relationships represents a major developmental task of childhood. As noted by Hartup (1989),

> a child's effectiveness in dealing with the social world emerges largely
> from experience in close relationships. In these contexts language
> emerges; so does a repertoire for coordinating one's actions with those
> of others, one's knowledge of oneself, and much of one's knowledge
> about the world. (p. 120)

Early peer relationships also are important for later functioning. Social rejection in early life has been found to be associated with adjustment problems in adulthood (Cowen, Pederson, Babigian, Izzo, & Trost, 1973; Parker & Asher, 1987).

As identified by epidemiological researchers (Cadman, Boyle, Szatmari, & Offord, 1987; Rutter, Tizard, & Whitmore, 1970), social adjustment and peer relationships constitute an additional domain of psychosocial functioning in which children with chronic physical illness are at increased risk for adjustment difficulties. Chronic physical illness can potentially interfere with opportunities for normal socioemotional development by limiting age-appropriate independence from parents, exposure to same-age healthy peers, participation in childhood activities, and development of a sense of self-efficacy and self-definition.

Despite this increased risk, there has been little systematic research on social adjustment and peer relationships in youngsters with chronic illness (La Greca, 1990, 1992). We conducted a literature review on social adjustment and peer relationships in children with the six representative illnesses as well as on studies of pooled illness samples. We focused this review on recent studies demonstrating more robust methodology. Although there were several studies in which peer relationships in children with chronic illness were studied using projective techniques (e.g., Straker & Kuttner, 1980) or nonstructured interviews (e.g., Boyle, di Sant'Agnese, Sack, Millican, & Kulczycki, 1976), we did not include those studies in this review. Table 2.1 includes a listing of the studies included in our review.

## Nature of Studies

In addition to the paucity of studies of social adjustment and peer relationships in children with chronic physical illness, the studies that have been conducted have suffered from several methodological shortcomings. As a result relatively little is known about this aspect of psychosocial adjustment in children with chronic illness.

First, social adjustment infrequently has been the primary focus of the studies; most researchers investigated more global constructs such as psychosocial adjustment (Spirito, DeLawyer, & Stark, 1991). As a result, social adjustment is typically not conceptualized or assessed adequately (Nassau & Drotar, 1995).

Second, in the majority of the studies a between-group design was used, with the chronically ill group being compared with a healthy control or comparison group or with instrument norms. Variable findings across these studies are evident, with some studies indicating between-group differences (e.g., Kashani, Barbero, et al., 1988; Morgan & Jackson, 1986; Wallander, Feldman, & Varni, 1989; Wallander, Varni, Babani, Banis, &

Wilcox, 1988a) and others indicating no such differences (e.g., Graetz & Shute, 1995; Jacobson et al., 1986; Kashani, Konig, et al., 1988; Lavigne, Traisman, Marr, & Chasnoff, 1982; Nassau & Drotar, 1995). Moreover, these between-group studies provide little information about variables that differentiate the children with chronic illness who have good versus poor social adjustment or peer relationships. Within-group studies are necessary to delineate the relevant variables that increase the risk for poor outcome in the social adjustment domain.

Third, there have been only a few studies in which multiple informants were used to assess social adjustment (e.g., Nassau & Drotar, 1995), yet the importance of using multiple informants because of low agreement between raters has been well documented (Achenbach, McConaughy, & Howell, 1987). Most studies are based solely on parental ratings, most typically mothers (e.g., Kashani, Barbero, et al., 1988; Kashani, Konig, et al., 1988; Wallander, Varni, Babani, Banis, & Wilcox, 1988; Wallander, Varni, Babani, Banis, DeHaan, et al., 1989; Wallander, Varni, Babani, Banis, & Wilcox, 1989). Teacher ratings also have been used somewhat frequently (e.g., Drotar et al., 1981; Noll, Bukowski, Rogosch, Le Roy, & Kulkarni, 1990; Noll, Ris, Davies, Bukowski, & Koontz, 1992; Spirito et al., 1990). Children's self-reports (e.g., Graetz & Shute, 1995; Jacobson et al., 1986; La Greca, 1992; Nassau & Drotar, 1995; Spirito et al., 1990) and peer reports (e.g., Graetz & Shute, 1995; Noll et al., 1991) have been used infrequently despite the importance of self- and peer perceptions of social acceptance and functioning.

Fourth, only a few researchers have used multiple methods of assessment (e.g., Hurtig & White, 1986; Spirito et al., 1990). Because we specifically excluded studies in which only projective techniques or nonstructured interviews were used in favor of studies using more reliable and valid methods of assessment, questionnaires were by far the most frequently used assessment method. Direct assessment of actual peer relationships is rare. Only one study used direct observation of interaction with peers (Tin & Teasdale, 1985), although this study had a small sample.

The social competence domain of the Child Behavior Checklist (CBCL) has been the most frequently used questionnaire; it was used by the researchers in 17 out of 36 of the studies. However, cautions about the use of the CBCL with patients with chronic illness have been raised given the incomplete and potentially misleading assessment of social competence (E. C. Perrin, Stein, & Drotar, 1991).

The social competence domain of the CBCL contains questions about school, activities, and social performance, and it yields T-scores for each of these areas as well as a Total Social Competence T-score, which is a composite of these three areas. An examination of the items that make up these scales suggests that the Total Social Competence score is not likely a valid measure of "social competence," to the extent that social competence is defined as competence in social interactions. Only two or three items in the CBCL social competence domain are directly related to peer relationships; these questions assess the number of friends and the frequency of peer contacts. A child who demonstrates skill in social situations may nonetheless score in the clinical range on the Social Competence scale. In children with chronic illness, the CBCL social competence domain may reflect the impact of the illness on children's ability to participate fully in social activities rather than their social competence.

Moreover, the inclusion of items related to school performance in the social competence domain further complicates interpretation of clinical evaluations on this scale in children with chronic illness. For example, based on school problems such as placement in a special class in school, poor grades, or repeating a grade, a child may obtain a low score in the social competence domain, but the problems may reflect direct effects of the illness on neurocognitive functioning or the indirect effects of the illness in terms of school absences rather than deficits per se in social competence.

Fifth, all the studies reviewed have been cross sectional in nature; none have examined social adjustment and peer relationships over time. Longitudinal studies are necessary to appreciate developmental changes in social adjustment and peer relationships. As previously reviewed, longitudinal studies of emotional and behavioral adjustment have demonstrated moderate-to-low levels of stability over time in both child- and parent-reported behavioral problems (e.g., Thompson, Gil, Keith, et al., 1994; Thompson, Gustafson, George, & Spock, 1994). However, the patterns of stability or change, as well as the correlates of change in social adjustment difficulties in children with chronic physical illness, have not yet been demonstrated. Such findings would have implications for interventions with children who have social adjustment and peer relationship problems. Although there has been a relative paucity of studies and methodological weaknesses are apparent, some information has emerged about frequencies and types of adjustment problems and correlates of adjustment.

### Frequencies and Types of Problems

Several of the clinical studies reviewed identified rates of social adjustment and peer relationship difficulties in children with chronic illness. However, there is tremendous variability in rates reported across studies, probably as a result of the use of different measures and cutoff scores.

Researchers using the CBCL have reported scores below the 2nd percentile on the Social Competence scale in 5% of a sample of patients with asthma (MacLean, Perrin, Gortmaker, & Pierre, 1992), 20% of a pooled sample with multiple illnesses (Wallander, Varni, Babani, Banis, & Wilcox, 1988), and 52% of a sample of patients with cerebral palsy and spina bifida

(Wallander, Varni, Babani, Banis, DeHaan, et al., 1989). Mulhern, Wasserman, Friedman, and Fairclough (1989) reported that 54% of their sample of long-term survivors of cancer had one or more abnormally low scores on the Social Competence scale.

The percentages of children with social adjustment problems are more similar across illnesses in studies using the Missouri Child Behavior Checklist (MCBC; Sines, Pauker, Sines, & Owen, 1969) to assess behavior problem patterns. In addition to behavior problem patterns such as internal or external problems, the MCBC yields profiles that can be differentiated on the basis of the degree of sociability. For example, a low social skills profile reflects an absence of behavior problems but a deficit in social relationship skills (Thompson, Kronenberger, & Curry, 1989). Thompson and colleagues found parent-reported low social skills profiles in 2% of the patients with spina bifida (Thompson, Kronenberger, Johnson, & Whiting, 1989), 4% of the patients with cystic fibrosis (Thompson, Gustafson, Hamlett, & Spock, 1992a), and 2% of the patients with sickle-cell disease (Thompson, Gil, Burbach, et al., 1993b).

### Findings as a Function of Illness Type

Given the relative paucity of studies of social adjustment and peer relationships in children with chronic physical illness, it is difficult to determine whether differences exist as a function of type of illness. Although additional research is necessary, the researchers who included groups with various illnesses found that increased social adjustment problems were evident in children with illnesses primarily affecting the central nervous system (CNS).

Wallander and colleagues compared groups with various illnesses including spina bifida, cerebral palsy, juvenile rheumatoid arthritis, diabetes, obesity, and hemophilia, on parents' ratings on the CBCL social competence domain (Wallander, Varni, Babani, Banis, & Wilcox, 1988; Wallander, Varni, Babani, Banis, & Wilcox, 1989). Although all illness groups had a significantly lower Total Social Competence score than did the CBCL nonclinic normative sample, the children with cerebral palsy scored lower than each of the other illness groups.

Similarly, Breslau (1985) compared children with cystic fibrosis, cerebral palsy, spina bifida, and multiple handicaps with healthy control children and found that although all groups with chronic illness scored lower than the control children on a measure of social isolation, the patients with conditions affecting the brain (i.e., cerebral palsy, spina bifida, multiple handicaps) were more socially isolated than the patients with a condition not affecting the brain (i.e., cystic fibrosis).

Moreover, in two studies in which children with brain tumors were included, there were greater difficulties in social adjustment and peer relationships among the children with brain tumors than among children with other illnesses such as non-CNS cancer or sickle-cell disease. Mulhern, Carpentieri, Shema, Stone, and Fairclough (1993) found that although children with brain tumors and children with non-CNS cancer had higher scores than did the CBCL normative group in the CBCL behavior problem domain, only the children with brain tumors had lower scores than the CBCL normative group in the CBCL social competence domain, including the Social and Activities subscales and Total Score.

Similarly, Noll et al. (1992) compared children with brain tumors, non-CNS cancer, and sickle-cell disease with matched control children on teachers' ratings on the Revised Class Play (Masten, Morison, & Pelligrini, 1985). The children with brain tumors scored higher on the sensitive–isolated dimension than did control children, whereas children with sickle-cell disease were similar to control children, and children with non-CNS cancer actually had higher scores than control children on the sociability–leadership dimension and lower scores than control children on the aggressive–disruptive dimension.

Eiser, Havermans, Pancer, and Eiser (1992) compared children with diabetes, asthma, epilepsy, leukemia, and cardiac disease on mothers' ratings on the Child and Adolescent Adjustment Profile (Ellsworth, 1979). They found that the children with epilepsy were the least well adjusted based on Peer Relations scale scores, followed by children with asthma. Fewer peer problems were identified in children with diabetes, leukemia, and cardiac disease. Eiser et al. (1992) hypothesized that the unpredictable episodes that characterize epilepsy and asthma may negatively affect peer relations because these episodes cause anxiety in peers.

*Findings as a Function of Informant*

As noted earlier, parents and teachers are the most frequent informants about social adjustment and peer relationships in children with chronic illness, and the findings are variable across studies. Few researchers have used both parents and teachers as informants within the same study. The researchers who have used both types of informants have generally found significant differences between children with illness and control children based only on parents' reports (e.g., Drotar et al., 1981; Sawyer, Crettendon, & Toogood, 1986). These findings suggest that parents and teachers are likely attending to different aspects of social adjustment and peer relationships, which provides further support for the need for multiple informants.

*Findings as a Function of Method*

Because almost all of the researchers in our review used questionnaires, differences as a function of type of method are not apparent. However, as noted previously, differences in the rate of social adjustment problems are apparent across different questionnaires such as the CBCL and the MCBC. Given that different measures assess different aspects of social adjustment and peer relationships, these differences are not surprising.

## Correlates of Adjustment

The variables that differentiate children with good versus poor social adjustment are important for identifying which children are most at risk and in greatest need of intervention, as well as for suggesting potential intervention targets. Although some mediational–moderational variables were apparent in our review, caution must be used in interpreting the results because of the limited number of studies of social adjustment and peer relationships.

Because chronic illness results in lifestyle interruptions that limit opportunities for social interaction (La Greca, 1990), illness severity or the extent of lifestyle disruption may affect social adjustment outcome. Indeed, at least one study (Graetz & Shute, 1995) indicated that of children with moderate-to-severe asthma, those with more hospitalizations were less preferred as playmates, were perceived by their peers as being more sensitive and isolated, and felt more lonely.

Results of a few studies suggested that boys may be at greater risk for social adjustment difficulties than girls. In a study of 81 children (aged 6 to 14 years) with asthma, only the 6- to 11-year-old boys had lower scores than the normative group on the CBCL Social Competence scale (MacLean et al., 1992). Similarly, in a study of preschool children with cystic fibrosis, girls had scores similar to the normative group on the CBCL Social Competence scale, whereas boys had significantly lower scores than the normative group (Simmons et al., 1985). Differences as a function of age are also apparent; older boys with sickle-cell disease (Hurtig & White, 1986) and younger boys with asthma (MacLean et al., 1992) were found to be most at risk for social adjustment difficulties as measured by the CBCL.

There also is some indication that family variables may be associated with social adjustment. For example, in their pooled illness sample of 153 children, Wallander and colleagues found that family psychological resources (e.g., cohesion, expressiveness, and conflict) as well as family utilitarian resources (e.g., income and maternal education) contributed significantly and independently to the variance in CBCL Social Competence scale scores in the expected direction (Wallander, Varni, Babani, Banis, & Wilcox, 1989).

# SCHOOL ADJUSTMENT AND PERFORMANCE

School adjustment and performance represent the third domain in which children and adolescents with chronic physical illness are at increased risk for adjustment difficulties. This increased risk can be a function of direct (primary) effects of the illness or treatment in terms of associated CNS sequelae or a function of indirect (secondary) consequences of the illness such as fatigue, absenteeism, or psychological stress.

## Frequencies and Types of Problems

An increased risk for school performance difficulties in children with chronic illness has been well documented. The Isle of Wight study (Rutter et al., 1970) represents one of the most comprehensive studies of the educational consequences of physical illnesses in school-age children. Two groups of children were included: those with and without conditions that involved the brain. Rutter et al. (1970) assumed that by comparing these two groups, the direct and indirect consequences of illness could be differentiated. That is, the school performance difficulties of children with brain-related illnesses were thought to be direct consequences of the illness, whereas the school performance difficulties of children with non-brain-related illnesses were thought to be indirect consequences of the illness (e.g., absenteeism) or, alternatively, independent of the physical condition.

Children with physical non-brain-related illnesses tended to have normal educational placements and intellectual functioning that was normally distributed and similar to that of children in the general population. However, considerable problems were evident in reading, with reading achievement, on average, 6 to 9 months behind chronological age norms. Fourteen percent were reading at a level at least 28 months below chronological age norms, whereas only 5.4% of children in the general population exhibited delays of this magnitude. Thus, these school problems were most likely a function of indirect effects of the illness given the absence of direct brain-related effects of the illnesses.

Of the children with brain-related illnesses, only half had normal educational placements and the other half were either in special educational placements or were not attending school. Intellectual functioning was well below that of the general population, with nonverbal functioning being significantly lower than verbal functioning. The children's reading achievement was, on average, 2 years behind their chronological age. This achievement delay was not simply a function of their lower intelligence, in that 27% were functioning at least 28 months behind chronological age, and at a level significantly below that which would be predicted based on their level of intellectual functioning.

The Ontario Child Health Study also examined school performance in children with chronic illness (Cadman et al., 1987). Cadman et al., however, did not examine objective indexes of school performance such as grades, achievement test scores, or educational placement. Instead, parents' reports of school problems were obtained. Parents were asked whether the children had repeated a grade, whether the children were using remedial educational services, and whether the children were performing poorly in school.

Children with chronic illness with disabilities that interfered with normal functioning were compared with children with chronic illness without disabilities and with healthy children. Unlike the Isle of Wight study (Rutter et al., 1970), the degree of brain involvement was not ascertained. Findings revealed that school problems were evident for children with illness and disability, although children with illness but no disability were not at increased risk relative to physically healthy children. Forty-two percent of children with illness and disability had repeated a grade or were receiving remedial educational services compared with 15% of children with chronic illness without disability and 12% of healthy children. Eighteen percent of children with illness and disability were not performing well in school compared with 5% and 4% of children with illness without disability and healthy children, respectively.

A subsequent epidemiological study used the U.S. National Health Survey data (National Center for Health Statistics, 1981) to examine psychosocial risk in children with chronic physical illness (Gortmaker, Walker, Weitzman, & Sobel, 1990). Information on school placement and functioning was based on parental responses to questions about special educational placement, having to repeat a grade, and suspension or expulsion from school. Children with chronic health conditions demonstrated a significantly higher risk for special educational placement and repeating a grade than did healthy children. However, children with chronic illness did not demonstrate an increased risk for suspension or expulsion.

Although the aforementioned studies examined school problems in pooled samples of children with illness, there also have been epidemiological studies of school problems in children with specific illnesses. For example, using the 1988 U.S. National Health Interview Survey on Child Health, Fowler, Davenport, and Garg (1992) examined school functioning in children with asthma. Among the 10,362 1st- through 12th-grade children, 536 (4.9%) were reported to have asthma. As with the study of chronic illness in general (Gortmaker et al., 1990), objective indexes of school performance were not obtained and the findings were based on parental reports. Parents were asked whether their children had ever repeated a grade, ever had a learning disability, or ever been suspended or expelled from school. The number of days absent during the previous 12 months also was obtained from parents.

Children with asthma were reported to have slightly higher rates of grade failure but similar rates of suspension or expulsion. Moreover, children with asthma were rated by their parents as having twice the rate of learning disabilities (9%) compared with healthy children (5%). Differences in risk for school problems emerged as a function of demographic and illness variables. Among families with incomes below $20,000, children with asthma had twice the risk for grade failure than did healthy children. Moreover, after controlling for demographic variables, children with parent-reported fair-to-poor health were twice as likely to have a learning disability than were children in good-to-excellent health. Overall, these national data demonstrate a moderately increased risk for school problems in children with asthma compared with healthy children.

These epidemiological studies demonstrate that children with chronic illness are at increased risk for school problems. This risk is particularly apparent in children with chronic illnesses that affect the brain or who have physical disability along with their illness.

Clinic-based studies have also examined school performance in children with chronic illness. For example, Howe, Feinstein, Reiss, Molock, and Berger (1993) examined school functioning in 165 adolescents with chronic physical illness and 49 healthy adolescents. In light of the findings of the Isle of Wight study (Rutter et al., 1970), adolescents with brain-related illnesses (e.g., cerebral palsy) were compared with adolescents with non-brain-related illnesses (e.g., cystic fibrosis). School functioning was assessed using standard achievement tests.

Results showed that both groups of adolescents scored significantly below the healthy control group on school achievement. However, the adolescents with brain-related illnesses scored significantly lower than the healthy control adolescents in math, reading, and general knowledge, whereas the adolescents with non-brain-related illnesses scored significantly lower than the healthy control adolescents only in math.

Fowler, Johnson, and Atkinson (1985) examined school functioning in 270 children with 11 different chronic health conditions. Data were obtained from the children's schools, including information on achievement scores from statewide standardized testing. Children with chronic health conditions scored significantly lower than their healthy peers, although their scores were within the average range. Thirty percent of the children with chronic illness had repeated a grade, and 34% were receiving special educational services. Considerable variability in achievement in the children with chronic illness was accounted for by race and socioeconomic status (SES). Children with epilepsy, sickle-cell disease, and spina bifida were particularly at risk for special educational services, repeating a grade, and poor scores on standardized achievement tests.

## Correlates of Adjustment

Given the considerable evidence of increased risk for school problems in children with chronic illness, we now examine the factors that contribute to this increased risk. First, we examine the direct (primary) effects of illness on school functioning: neurocognitive sequelae of the illness and the iatrogenic CNS effects of treatment. Second, we examine the indirect (secondary) consequences of illness on school functioning: absenteeism and psychological factors such as stress and distress.

### Neurocognitive Sequelae of Illness

The six representative illnesses discussed in chapter 2 differ in terms of their impact on the CNS. Given the evidence reviewed earlier for increased risk for school problems in children with brain-related illnesses, we review the evidence for direct CNS effects in three of the six representative illnesses that are believed to have differing levels of CNS involvement.

Given that spina bifida is a malformation of the CNS, there is potential risk for neurocognitive sequelae in these children. A recent comprehensive review of the neuropsychological functioning of children with spina bifida, hydrocephalus, or both revealed the following:

> Their verbal abilities, especially more "crystallized" aspects of language, and their memory capacities are usually intact. However, they are likely to have difficulties with visuospatial and tactile perception tasks; tasks involving rapid, precise, or sequenced movement; arithmetic calculation, spelling, and reading comprehension; and tasks that involve "executive control" functions governing the ability to establish and sustain one's focus of concentration, to inhibit inappropriate or irrelevant behaviors, and to shift flexibly among responses or modulate one's behavior according to situational demands. (Wills, 1993, p. 260)

There is increasing evidence that children with sickle-cell disease are at risk for school problems secondary to CNS effects of the illness itself (R. T. Brown, Armstrong, & Eckman, 1993). Researchers have found lower intellectual functioning and greater neuropsychological deficits in patients with sickle-cell disease compared with sibling controls (e.g., R. T. Brown, Buchanan, et al., 1993; Swift et al., 1989; Wasserman, Wilimas, Fairclough, Mulhern, & Wang, 1991). R. T. Brown, Buchanan, et al. (1993) found associations among neuropsychological functioning and SES and hemoglobin, suggesting that deficits in cognitive functioning may be attributable partly to social class and to possible etiological effects of chronically reduced oxygen delivery.

Although these studies provide a beginning in terms of the understanding of the neurocognitive effects of sickle-cell disease, several multisite collaborative studies are under way and should provide more conclusive information about the neurocognitive performance of patients with sickle-cell disease.

Similarly, there has been a recent increase in research designed to examine the neurocognitive aspects of diabetes. Evidence suggests that children with insulin-dependent diabetes mellitus may indeed be at risk for neuropsychological impairment that would have a potential impact on school performance and achievement. A recent review of the literature by Rovet, Ehrlich, Czuchta, and Akler (1993) revealed that children with a disease onset before age 5, children who experience severe hypo- or hyperglycemia, or children who have frequent episodes of mild-to-moderate hypoglycemia may be at particular risk for neurocognitive effects. Although there is little consensus in terms of the specific types of deficits observed in these children, there does seem to be an association between visuospatial deficits and earlier diabetes onset, and possibly between verbal deficits and later disease onset, suggesting that different brain regions may have different critical periods of vulnerability to the neurological effects of diabetes (Rovet et al., 1993).

*Iatrogenic Effects of Treatments*

Children with chronic illness may also require treatments that affect school functioning in that the treatments required for their illnesses may have iatrogenic effects on cognitive functioning. Iatrogenic effects may range from mental changes associated with particular pharmacological agents to neurocognitive sequelae of cranial–spinal radiation or intrathecal chemotherapy.

There has been considerable debate in both the scientific literature and the popular press about the effects on cognitive functioning and learning of medications used to treat asthma. Theophylline, a bronchodilator that has been used widely for the treatment of asthma, has been the subject of numerous studies examining its effects on learning and attention (for reviews, see Creer & Gustafson, 1989; Creer et al., 1988). In general, the findings of iatrogenic effects of theophylline on learning in children with asthma are ambiguous and lacking in consistency. However, there does seem to be a subset of children who have a heightened CNS response to this caffeinelike substance and who warrant careful monitoring by their physicians (Creer & Gustafson, 1989; Creer et al., 1988).

Similarly, corticosteroids that are used to treat asthma also have been criticized on the grounds that they affect learning, mood, and behavior, although such studies have had methodological limitations (Celano & Geller, 1993; Satel, 1990). However, there appears to be some evidence for subtle, reversible, dose-dependent effects on memory and recall (Bender, Lerner, & Kollasch, 1988; Suess, Stump, Chai, & Kalisker, 1986).

There also has been considerable evidence for iatrogenic effects of treatment for childhood cancer. Children with leukemia receive CNS prophylactic treatment to prevent leukemic infiltration of the CNS. Although this practice has increased survival, it has had deleterious effects on neurocognitive functioning. CNS prophylaxis in patients with leukemia has included cranial radiation and intrathecal chemotherapy (usually methotrexate, a known neurotoxic agent).

Several reviews of existing studies showed evidence for iatrogenic effects of CNS prophylaxis, particularly cranial irradiation, in patients with leukemia (Cousens, Said, Waters, & Stevens, 1988; Fletcher & Copeland, 1988; Madan-Swain & Brown, 1991). Although there is preliminary evidence that intrathecal chemotherapy may have deleterious effects in the absence of radiation therapy (Madan-Swain & Brown, 1991), additional research examining children who receive only prophylactic chemotherapy is necessary to differentiate the effects of chemotherapy from radiation (Cousens, Ungerer, Crawford, & Stevens, 1991).

Children with brain tumors are also treated with cranial irradiation and chemotherapy, and similar deleterious CNS effects have been identified (Glauser & Packer, 1991). Moreover, the combination of radiotherapy and methotrexate chemotherapy significantly elevates the incidence of encephalopathy in these children (Glauser & Packer, 1991).

The deleterious effects of radiation therapy in children with leukemia or brain tumors appear to be particularly pronounced in younger children (Fletcher & Copeland, 1988; Glauser & Packer, 1991; Madan-Swain & Brown, 1991), and the deficits increase with the length of time since treatment (Cousens et al., 1988). Moreover, there is some evidence that the extent of radiation therapy (focal vs. whole brain) in patients with brain tumors may be related to the extent of neurocognitive difficulties (Kun, Mulhern, & Crisco, 1983).

Despite serious methodological shortcomings in this literature (Butler & Copeland, 1993), some patterns have emerged on the extent of cognitive impact and the specific types of deficits. A meta-analysis identified a mean decline of 10 IQ points in studies of the iatrogenic effects of leukemic CNS prophylaxis (Cousens et al., 1988). The most common neurocognitive sequelae appear to be in nonverbal abilities and with attention or concentration functions (Fletcher & Copeland, 1988), as well as in short-term memory, speed of processing, visuomotor coordination, and sequencing ability (Cousens et al., 1991).

## Absenteeism

Attending school is important to children's academic, social, and emotional development. Yet, children and adolescents with chronic illness can potentially miss large amounts of school because of illness-related factors such as illness exacerbation, minor illnesses or health problems, treatment side effects, hospitalizations, and outpatient clinic appointments. Even in healthy children, school attendance has been found to be inversely associated with the number of physical symptoms (Kidwell, Riley, Finney, & Wilkerson, 1992) and health care utilization (Diaz et al., 1986).

Studies of children and adolescents with chronic illness have consistently shown higher rates of school absence than in children without chronic illness. Results of a community survey of parents' reports of their children's school attendance indicated that children with a wide range of chronic health impairments missed an average of 8.7 days compared with 5.8 days for their healthy peers (Weitzman, Walker, & Gortmaker, 1986). Examination of the school records of children followed through pediatric subspecialty clinics in a tertiary care medical center indicated that children with chronic illness averaged 16 days absent compared with the national norm of 5.7 days (Fowler et al., 1985). A similar school absence rate was found among chronically ill, Medicaid-eligible children, with 10.4% of the children missing more than 20% of the school year (Cook, Schaller, & Krischer, 1985). There was considerable range in the number of days absent across these studies: 0 to more than 150 days.

There seems to be some variability in the rates and patterns of absenteeism across illnesses that likely reflects the variable manifestations and courses of these illnesses. Asthma has been identified as the leading cause of school absences among chronic illnesses (Dorland, 1977). Children with asthma have significantly higher absenteeism rates than their healthy peers, although this trend seems to diminish with increased age (Parcel, Gilman, Nader, & Bunce, 1979). School attendance in children with asthma is characterized by frequent, brief absences (Creer & Yoches, 1971).

Rates of absenteeism that are four times higher than that of the general school-age population have been found for children with cancer (Stehbens, Kisker, & Wilson, 1983). In a large prospective study of absenteeism rates over a 5-year period, absenteeism rates were significantly higher among 239 children being treated for cancer than among their fellow students (Lansky, Cairns, & Zwartjes, 1983). The highest rates of nonattendance occurred during the first year after diagnosis, with an average of 43 days missed. Although attendance rates improved gradually in subsequent years, the high rates of absence continued even through 3 years postdiagnosis, when children missed an average of 21 days. The pattern of school attendance in children with cancer is characterized by one long period of absence at the time of diagnosis and treatment initiation, followed by regular short absences for follow-up treatment or monitoring of progress (Charlton et al., 1991).

Absenteeism rates for children with cystic fibrosis and sickle-cell disease have been among the highest of patients with chronic illness, with these children missing 23 to 25 days per year (Fowler et al., 1985). Even among children with sickle-cell disease with a low frequency of hospitalization for pain crises, absence rates are high (Eaton, Hayes, Armstrong, Pegelow, & Thomas, 1991). Although children with insulin-dependent diabetes mellitus have fewer absences than many children with other chronic illnesses (Fowler et al., 1985), they do have more absences than their healthy peers (Ryan, Longstreet, & Morrow, 1985).

Numerous factors have been associated with absenteeism in children with chronic illness. Medical factors that are associated with absenteeism include the type of illness, the degree of physical restrictions (Fowler et al., 1985), eventually succumbing to the illness, and the type of treatment (e.g., CNS chemotherapy) (Cairns, Klopovich, Hearne, & Lansky, 1982). Demographic factors also have been associated with lower rates of school attendance, such as lower parental education level (Cook et al., 1985; Charlton et al., 1991), being female (Cairns et al., 1982; Charlton et al., 1991; Fowler et al., 1985), having a hometown population greater than 100,000, and having a later birth position (Cairns et al., 1982).

*Psychological Effects*

Psychosocial and emotional factors also can play an important role in school functioning in children with chronic illness by affecting attendance and influencing the child's ability to effectively engage in the academic process or social milieu while at school. Illness-related stress, psychological distress, concerns about peer reactions to physical changes, and lack of confidence in ability all may contribute to the child's willingness to attend school and his or her engagement or performance when in school.

There is a significant positive relationship between psychological adjustment and school attendance in children with chronic illness (Stein & Jessop, 1984). More specifically, children with chronic illness and parent-reported psychosocial adjustment problems have lower attendance rates than do children with chronic illness without adjustment problems (Weitzman et al., 1986). Moreover, concurrent school phobia has been described in several case studies of children with cancer (Futterman & Hoffman, 1970; Lansky, Lowman, Vats, & Gyulay, 1975).

Some children with chronic illness miss more school than appears warranted given their illness or functional limitations (Weitzman, 1986). Nonspecific physical complaints may be presented as the reasons for absence, but these complaints may actually represent inappropriate health beliefs; an increased sense of child vulnerability on the child's or parent's part; child psychological adjustment problems such as depression or anxiety; or parental psychological adjustment problems, altered expectations, or discipline strategies (Weitzman, 1986).

# CONCLUSIONS

As reviewed in this chapter, children with chronic physical illness are at increased risk for difficulties in social adjustment and peer relationships as well as school adjustment and performance. These difficulties may vary as a function of illness type, with children with illnesses that affect the CNS being at particular risk.

Risk for social adjustment difficulties also may vary as a function of demographic or psychosocial or family variables. However, it is difficult to draw firm conclusions given the lack of studies and the conceptual and methodological limitations that characterize this literature. Additional research that more adequately conceptualizes and assesses social adjustment, uses multiple informants and methods, examines the within-group processes that differentiate between those with good versus poor adjustment, and longitudinally examines patterns of social adjustment is necessary to design interventions for children with chronic illnesses who have stable social adjustment difficulties.

Difficulties in school adjustment and performance appear to reflect both the primary effects of the illness or treatment on the CNS as well as the secondary effects of the illness in terms of absenteeism or psychological stress or distress. However, current research precludes partialing out the independent contribution of primary and secondary effects on school performance, which is necessary to design appropriate interventions for children with chronic illness. Additional research is necessary to determine whether there are more academic difficulties among children with conditions or treatments affecting the brain than in those without, with secondary effects such as absenteeism and psychological factors controlled. Moreover, future research should determine whether the degree of academic difficulties varies as a function of degree of illness- or treatment-related CNS impairment as reflected by neurocognitive or neuroimaging findings.

# 5

# MODELS OF ADAPTATION

The review in chapter 3 of the findings on processes contributing to the variability in psychosocial adjustment to chronic illness indicates that a wide array of processes have been investigated. However, there is little converging evidence that any of these processes account for a major portion of the variance in adjustment. This points out the need for conceptually and theoretically based studies to guide future research and clinical practice. The basic questions to be addressed in this chapter are as follows: How do biological, psychological, and social–ecological processes act together in contributing to the variability in the process of adaptation? Of the contributing processes, which are likely to be salient intervention targets for prevention and treatment services?

We begin with a consideration of the customary progression of research through the exploratory, descriptive, analytical, and experimental stages. This discussion provides the foundation for a review of analytic-level studies of specific models of adaptation to chronic illness.

These models share a common view of chronic illness as a potential stressor. More recent models also include a family perspective. We then present a hybrid model that combines stress processing and parenting components.

# RESEARCH: A PROGRESSIVE PROCESS

Research generally proceeds in stages (Starfield, 1985). The initial stage of research is usually exploratory: "The aim is to develop insights that allow a potentially unlimited range of characteristics to be narrowed sufficiently to make it possible to observe them" (Starfield, 1985, p. 110). The second stage is descriptive research in which events are unplanned but systematically observed. Variables are specified but there are no specific hypotheses. The third stage is analytical research. There are specific hypotheses about interrelationships among observed, but unplanned, events or characteristics. The fourth stage is experimental research. The knowledge gained in prior stages leads to the formulation of a theoretical framework within which events are manipulated to test specific hypotheses about the interrelationship among variables. In experimental-level research, the independent variable is manipulated by the researcher, and there is random assignment of participants to conditions. *Quasi-experimental research* is the term used to describe experimental-level research without random assignment to conditions.

A theory is an explanatory, rather than descriptive, statement about the interrelationship of variables, events, or characteristics. Thus, theories are conceptualized to delineate mechanisms of effect for the relationship under consideration. A theory also provides a frame of reference for organizing and explaining phenomena and the variability in phenomena that leads to testable hypotheses (Wallander, 1992). Theory-driven research has been defined as

> that conducted from a conceptual base consisting of some statements as to what relevant variables mean, why they are important, and how they are related to one another. . . . This theoretical structure should lead to a set of hypotheses clearly identifying the relationships which are to be studied and what the expected outcome will be. (Wallander, 1992, p. 552)

A theory provides a specifically articulated rationale for choices about participant selection, identifying which variables to include and how these are to be measured, study design, and strategies for analyzing data. Theory-driven research not only helps to organize findings but also to make the inquiry a systematic process. Theory-driven research leads to specific studies that systematically address critical gaps in knowledge and thereby yield a significant increment in that knowledge. It is inefficient and wasteful of precious resources to be asking study questions that are redundant and do not yield new information. Just as it is critical to determine questions that need to be addressed, it is equally critical to identify questions that no longer need to be addressed. Thus, theory-driven research is essential to the cumulative process, across many investigators, of building a knowledge base on the relationships and mechanisms of effect that can serve to guide intervention efforts.

## MODELS OF ADAPTATION TO CHRONIC ILLNESS

For adaptation to chronic illness, reaching the level of theory-driven research has been a slow process. The field is beginning to see the first wave of this type of research, and several theoretical models are emerging. What these models share is a common conceptual basis for viewing chronic illness as a potential stressor and viewing adaptation in systems-theory terms, as outlined in chapter 1.

The remainder of this chapter focuses on a selective review of several influential models, both in the initial shaping of approaches to the field and in more current conceptualizations. Most of these models can be considered descriptive and illustrative of variables and processes found, or hypothesized, to affect adaptation to the stress of chronic illness. That is, these models are not yet at the explanatory level. However, models at the descriptive level do serve the heuristic value of integrating findings across a range of investigators and studies that serves to guide both subsequent investigative efforts and initial intervention efforts to enhance adaptation.

### The Integrated Model

One of the first comprehensive models to emphasize the role of psychological processes in adjustment to chronic illness was formulated by Pless and Pinkerton (1975). Several conceptual aspects of this model, depicted in Figure 5.1, made an important contribution at the time to viewing chronic childhood illness in ways that provided a strategic basis for therapeutic intervention. Furthermore, these conceptual aspects have served as a foundation for subsequent models.

One conceptual aspect was viewing adjustment as being multiply determined by the individual's transactions with his or her environment. Pless and Pinkerton (1975) postulated the presence of "cybernetic circuits between family attitudes, other social factors, the child's own basic attributes and his response to illness" (p. 30). The transactional nature of this process is reflected in the concept of "feedback loops," such "that current functioning influences the response of others, which in turn, reciprocally influence future functioning" (Pless & Pinkerton, 1975, p. 30). A related conceptual premise is that adjustment changes over time and that at any given moment psychological functioning will reflect the cumulative product of earlier transactions. Thus, it is postulated that functioning in early childhood is at least partly predictive of later functioning during adolescence and adult life.

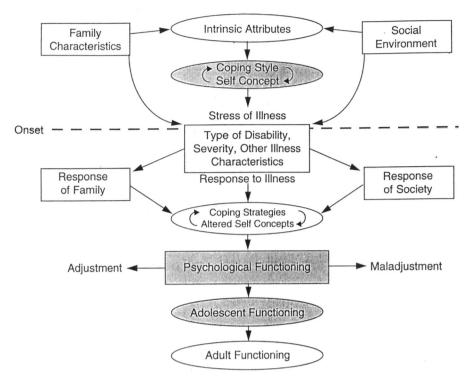

*Figure 5.1.* Integrated model of adjustment to chronic illness. From Pless and Pinkerton (1975). Reprinted with permission of the author.

Pless and Pinkerton's (1975) model emphasizes the role of two psychological processes—self-concept and coping style—in psychological adjustment to chronic illness. Self-concept and coping style are thought to be determined by the child's intrinsic attributes, such as temperament, personality, and intelligence, which are influenced by genetic, family, and social processes. Self-concept and coping strategies are major determinants of the response to stress engendered by chronic illness. However, the response is also influenced by the nature of the physical condition and by the way in which family, peers, teachers, and significant others react to the condition and the behavior of the child in response to his or her condition. This emphasis reflects the linking of evidence existing at that time about the importance of these psychological processes to adjustment. This linking of streams of evidence serves an integrative heuristic function and is one of the major benefits of model building.

Pless and Pinkerton's (1975) model provided a guide to therapeutic interventions. Because adaptation is viewed as a continuous process, early intervention was advocated to promote effective adjustment and to prevent maladjustment. Another implication was that "efforts to predict the response to stress engendered by chronic illness must take cognizance of the premorbid profile" (Pless & Pinkerton, 1975, p. 30). This profile included intrinsic attributes, family characteristics, and the social environment. Thus, treatment targets would include self-concept and coping style as well as the responses of family and of society to the condition and to the child's responses.

In particular, there are three conceptual components of Pless and Pinkerton's (1975) model that have proved to be seminal for subsequent efforts. First, chronic illness is conceptualized as a stressor. Second, adaptation is viewed as a continuous process over time. Third, the importance of coping methods in the process of adaptation is emphasized.

During this period, major advances were being made in the conceptualizations of stress and coping. In the psychological and medical literature, the term *stress* is a broad concept that has been used to refer to a stimulus, a response, or an interaction. There has been a tendency to distinguish three types of stress (Monat & Lazarus, 1977): physiological, psychological, and social. Physiological stress is concerned with the disturbance of tissue; psychological stress is concerned with the interchange between person and environment and emphasizes the role of mediation and cognition; and social stress is concerned with the disruption of a social system (Thompson, 1985). Correspondingly, stress was broadly defined as any situation "in which environmental demands, internal demands, or both tax or exceed the adaptive resources of an individual, social system, or tissue system" (Monat & Lazarus, 1977, p. 3).

A major focus of research on stress became the delineation of factors that contributed to the marked inter- and intraindividual variability that was observed in the experience of stress. In particular, it was recognized that there were marked individual differences in perceptions of situations as being stressful. Furthermore, the perception of the stressfulness of the same situation also could vary over time. Psychological approaches to understanding the variability in the experience of stress have emphasized the role of cognitive processes, including appraisals, expectations of efficacy and control, and causal attributions.

## The Life Crisis Model

The conceptual model developed by Moos and Tsu (1977) incorporated psychological approaches to stress and viewed chronic illness as a life crisis. This model, depicted in Figure 5.2, emphasizes the individual's cognitive appraisal of the significance of the crisis, which sets forth adaptive tasks to which coping skills can be applied. The processes of cognitive appraisal, perceptions of the tasks involved, and the selection of relevant coping skills are postulated to be influenced by three factors: background and personal characteristics; illness-related factors; and features of the physical and sociocultural environment. According to this model, the crisis not

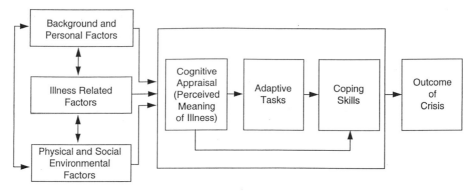

*Figure 5.2.* Life crisis model of adjustment to chronic illness. From Moos and Tsu (1977). Reprinted with permission.

only affects the person with the illness but also family and friends who encounter some of the same adaptive tasks.

Moos and Tsu (1977) delineated seven general categories of adaptive tasks related to physical illness. Three of the adaptive tasks are illness related and four are related to general life crises. Illness related tasks include (a) dealing with the symptoms of the condition, including pain, discomfort, and incapacitation; (b) dealing with the stress associated with treatment procedures and environments, including medical and surgical procedures and their concomitant side effects, and the separation frequently associated with hospitalization; and (c) developing and maintaining an adequate relationship with the health care team, which customarily includes a number of providers from a number of disciplines with the attendant problems of communication, coordination, and divergent opinions.

General adaptive tasks include (a) preserving a reasonable emotional balance by managing upsetting feelings engendered by the condition, including anger, anxiety, alienation, and isolation, and by maintaining hope; (b) preserving a satisfactory self-image, maintaining a sense of competence and mastery, and readjusting goals and expectations in the face of changes in functioning or appearance; (c) preserving relationships with family and friends, which are often challenged by the sense of alienation and physical separations associated with illness; and (d) preparing for an uncertain future, in which there is the threat of significant losses, while maintaining hope.

The relative importance of adaptive tasks varies depending on the characteristics of the individual, the nature of the illness or condition, and the person's environmental strains and resources. The delineation of illness-related tasks and general adaptive tasks by Moos and Tsu (1977) established a basis for addressing the issue of specificity versus generality. Currently, there is controversy about categorical versus noncategorical approaches to psychological adjustment to chronic illness. It can be postulated that characteristics of the illness affect the three illness adaptive tasks in a specific way but that effectiveness in dealing with the general adaptive tasks is a common contribution to psychological adjustment across illness types.

One of the intrapersonal resources that affects the accomplishment of these illness and general adaptive tasks is coping skills. The term *coping* refers to the process of an individual's struggle to adapt in the face of adversity. Mattsson (1972) defined coping as "all the adaptational techniques used by an individual to master a major psychological threat and its attendant negative feelings in order to allow him to achieve personal and social goals" (p. 805).

There are two functions to coping: defensive and problem solving. The defensive aspect of coping involves protecting oneself from threat. Included are the mechanisms that serve to avoid, minimize, relieve, and distract potentially threatening situations or thoughts and feelings, such as avoidance and wishful thinking. The problem-solving aspect of coping involves the application of knowledge, skills, and techniques to meeting demands and goals. These two aspects of coping can be complementary in dealing with chronic illness:

> Physical illness or disability can be conceived of as a form of psychological stress involving threat of suffering and losses that impose tasks to be dealt with and impair to some degree the person's capacity to meet life demands and goals. (Lipowski, 1970, p. 92)

Moos and Tsu (1977) described a number of coping skills or strategies that are commonly used, singly or in combination, to deal with the adaptive tasks associated with illness. Whereas the term *task* refers to the requirements for adaption in a particular situation, the term *strategy* refers to the ways in which these requirements may be met (Hamburg, 1974). Specific coping techniques are not inherently adaptive or maladaptive, but effectiveness depends on the match with the requirements of the situation over time.

One set of coping skills involves denying or minimizing the seriousness of the situation. This is a defense mechanism because the individual is being self-protective, is keeping himself or herself from being overwhelmed, and is buying time to garner other resources. Another set of coping skills involves seeking information or social support. Seeking information is a coping skill that is necessary for developing appropriate expectations and can be instrumental in relieving anxiety associated with uncertainty or misconceptions. In light of the considerable evidence that social support serves to moderate the impact of stressful situations, skills involved in requesting reassurance and emotional support also are important coping resources.

A third set of coping skills involves learning general problem-solving skills and specific illness-related procedures. Problem-solving skills involve setting concrete limited goals; breaking seemingly overwhelming problems into smaller, manageable bits; and rehearsing alternative outcomes through mental preparation and discussion with family and friends. Learning specific illness-related procedures is necessary for effectively adhering to medical regimens and allows one to develop feelings of independence and mastery.

A fourth set of coping skills involves finding a general purpose or meaning in one's illness. This often manifests itself in religious beliefs, but it also can be manifested in aspects of a person's identity (e.g., as a fighter or as a role model for others).

In an effort to account for variability in response to the stress associated with illness, Moos and Tsu (1977) proposed a conceptual framework with three major categories of determinants. *Background and personal characteristics* include age, intelligence, cognitive and emotional development, philosophical or religious beliefs, and previous coping experiences. These characteristics determine the meaning that the illness has for the individual and the cognitive and psychological resources available to deal with the condition. The timing of the condition in the individual's life cycle is important in this regard. *Illness-related factors* include the type of condition and the type and location of symptoms, rate of onset and progression, and prognosis. *Physical and sociocultural environmental factors* include aspects that can contribute to stress or can serve as resources for help and support. These three factors influence each other. However, their relationship to outcome is mediated by the process of cognitive appraisal, adaptive tasks, and coping skills, which also are mutually influencing.

This conceptual framework has implications for intervention. Caregivers can attend to the needs of patients and family members for information and emotional support. Caregivers can promote adjustment by informing patients and families about the usual responses to a given situation, the major tasks to be confronted, and typical coping strategies. Attention can be given to moderating the stress and enhancing the coping resources in the patient's environment. Awareness of adaptive tasks, necessary coping skills, and contributing factors can provide a basis for formulating individual intervention strategies. It is therefore important to recognize and communicate that the process of coping with stress has the dual function of problem-solving efforts to alter the threatening situation and emotional palliation (i.e., regulation of emotional distress). Furthermore, the effectiveness of coping methods is likely to vary as a function of individual characteristics. Thus, coping effectiveness becomes a "goodness-of-fit" process that is aptly reflected in the Serenity Prayer used by many Twelve Step groups:

God grant me the serenity to accept the things I cannot change; courage to change the things I can; and wisdom to know the difference.

## Risk and Resiliency

Conceptualizing chronic illness as a potential stressor enabled the application of research findings from mental health studies regarding risk factors for psychiatric disorder in childhood and adult life. These studies examined the processes involved in the marked individual variation in people's responses to stress and adversity. This research has focused on vulnerability (i.e., risk factors for psychological adjustment difficulties) and resiliency (i.e., protective factors).

There is extensive research literature that supports the relation between life event stress, that associated with major events and with daily hassles, and psychiatric illnesses. However, Rutter (1983) cautioned that

> if the concept of stress is to take us beyond the banal conclusion that bad experiences may have bad effects, we need to undertake a more searching analysis that would implicate three factors: (1) which features of life events may predispose to (2) which types of disorder (3) by which underlying processes or mechanisms. (p. 6)

Whereas studies of specific acute and chronic stressors such as loss of a parent, hospitalization, and parental divorce have been linked to psychological disorders in children, "in considering all types of stimuli, individual differences in responsiveness are crucial" (Rutter, 1983, p. 33). Also crucial is the effect of stress events on the developmental process and on subsequent functioning. Stressful events are inevitable, and "one of the developmental tasks is to learn how to deal with them successfully when they occur" (Rutter, 1983, p. 31). This is one way in which early experiences might be linked to subsequent illnesses. Early experiences may alter sensitivities to stress, either through sensitization or steeling effects, and may modify styles of coping that can predispose an individual toward, or protect against, illnesses in the presence of subsequent stress events. The recognition that the majority of children exposed to stressful situations do not develop illnesses leads to a focus on the invulnerability of stress-resistant children (Garmezy, 1981):

> If we can study the forces and attributes that seemingly move such children to survival and adaptation, then society may derive benefits far more significant than our current efforts to construct primary prevention models designed to curtail the rising tide of vulnerable high-risk children. (p. 217)

Subsequently, Rutter (1987) advocated that researchers go beyond identifying robust predictors of resiliency in the face of adversity (i.e., protective factors) to delineating protective mechanisms and processes. Rutter also argued that the defining feature of a focus on protective mechanisms is that which serves to modify the person's response to the risk situation either by intensifying (vulnerability) or ameliorating (protection). It is a catalytic process that changes the effect of another variable (i.e., an interaction effect): "The vulnerability or protective effect is evident only in combination with the risk variable" (Rutter, 1987, p. 317). Risk mechanisms lead directly, either strongly or weakly, to illness. Vulnerability or protective processes operate indirectly in their interaction with the risk variable. For example, many vulnerability or protective processes involve key turning points in people's lives. The way in which the person deals with the event determines the direction or trajectory of his or her life course for years to follow (e.g., the decision to stay in school or the way in which an unplanned pregnancy is handled).

Rutter (1987) identified several processes that may protect people against the psychological risks associated with adversity. One way is to alter the meaning or danger of the risk variable for the child or alter the exposure of the child to the risk. Considering that stress is inevitable, protection may lie in the "steeling" qualities gained from exposure to stress that the child can manage successfully. Physical and emotional distancing also can be effective. Another way is to reduce the negative chain reactions that follow, and serve to perpetuate, the risk effects. Finally, having feelings of self-esteem and self-efficacy (i.e., feelings of one's own self-worth and the belief that one can successfully cope with life's challenges) can serve protective functions. It appears that secure love relationships and successfully accomplishing tasks that are important to the person influence the development and maintenance of these protective processes. Turning points provide opportunities for successful coping with new challenges, which may take the form of personal relationships or task accomplishments that may place the person's life course on a more adaptive trajectory.

## The Disability–Stress–Coping Model

A new conceptual model, derived from the stress and coping perspective, has been developed: the disability–stress–coping model (Wallander & Varni, 1992; Wallander, Varni, Babani, Banis, & Wilcox, 1989; see Figure 5.3). In this model, the various factors hypothesized to play a role in adjusting to chronic conditions are organized into a risk–resistance framework. Adaptation is viewed multidimensionally and includes mental health, social functioning, and physical health. The factor hypothesized to be primarily responsible for elevating the risk for developing psychosocial problems in children with chronic conditions is stress. There are several sources of stress. The disease or condition parameters and the associated functional limitations are sources of stress that emanate from the condition.

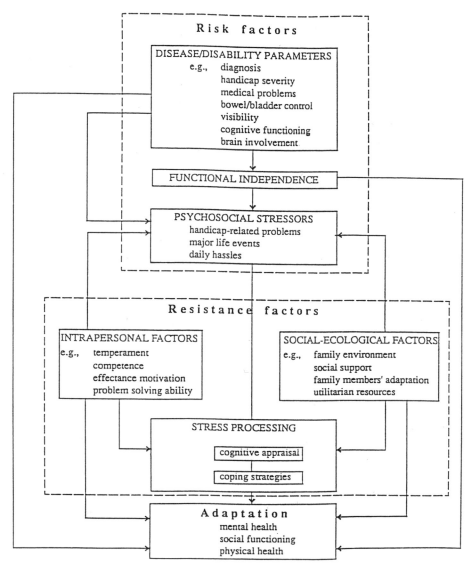

*Figure 5.3.* Disability–stress–coping model of adjustment to chronic illness. From Wallander, Varni, Babani, Banis, & Wilcox (1989). Reprinted with permission.

In addition, stress also emanates from the course of children's lives, such as stresses associated with major life events, daily hassles, or transitions. The condition parameters sometimes may serve to exacerbate the stresses associated with daily living, such as the start of school.

Three broad types of resistance factors are also hypothesized to be important and are subsumed under the rubric of coping resources. *Intrapersonal factors* include relatively stable factors such as temperament, competence, effectance motivation, and problem-solving ability. *Stress process-*

*ing factors* include cognitive appraisal and coping behaviors. *Social ecological factors* include family resources, such as the family's characteristic mode of perceiving and interacting with the social world and practical resources available to deal with acute and chronic problems and issues (Wallander, Varni, Babani, Banis, & Wilcox, 1989).

Wallander and Varni's (1992) risk–resistance model is comprehensive and sophisticated, and testing the entire model in one study is difficult. However, the previous chapter on correlates of adjustment attests to the impact this model has had on identifying processes associated with psychological adjustment to chronic conditions. For the most part, condition type and severity have been found to have little impact on adjustment. By contrast, child temperament, socioeconomic status (SES), parent coping, and various aspects of family functioning have been shown to influence psychological adjustment and social functioning of children with physical conditions.

## The Transactional Stress and Coping Model

The transactional stress and coping model, developed by Thompson and colleagues (Thompson, Gil, Burbach, Keith, & Kinney, 1993a, 1993b; Thompson, Gustafson, Hamlett, & Spock, 1992a, 1992b), is set within ecological-systems theory (Bronfrenbrenner, 1977). In this model, shown in Figure 5.4, chronic illness is viewed as a potential stressor to which the

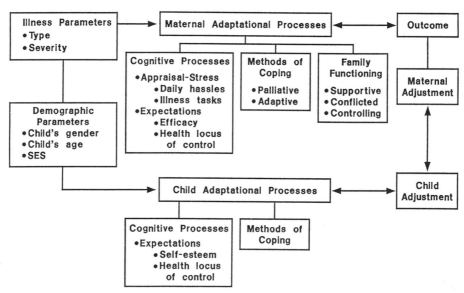

*Figure 5.4.* Transactional stress and coping model of adjustment to chronic illness. From Thompson, Gustafson, George, and Spock (1994). Reprinted with permission.

individual and family systems endeavor to adapt. The illness–outcome relationship is hypothesized to be a function of the transactions among biomedical, developmental, and psychosocial processes. Illness parameters are those that reflect the type of illness and its severity. Demographic parameters include gender, age, and SES. However, the model's focus is on patient and family processes that are hypothesized to further mediate the illness–outcome relationship over and above the contributions of illness and demographic parameters.

Guided by the cognitive stress and coping model of Lazarus and Folkman (1984), the choice of psychosocial mediational processes to be included in the model was based on two criteria: empirical evidence that the process served to reduce the impact of stress and saliency as a potential intervention target. Within an ecological-systems theory perspective, it is hypothesized that the psychological adjustment of children is affected by levels of stress and symptoms experienced by other family members. Thus, adjustment is considered in terms of both maternal adjustment and child adjustment and their interrelationship.

Three types of psychosocial mediational processes have been included in the model to account for psychological adjustment of adults with chronic illness and of mothers of children with chronic illness: the cognitive processes of appraisals of stress (Lazarus & Folkman, 1984) and expectations of locus of control (Strickland, 1978) and efficacy (Bandura, 1977); coping methods (Folkman & Lazarus, 1980); and family functioning (Kronenberger & Thompson, 1990; Moos & Moos, 1981).

The hypothesized adaptational processes included in the model to account for psychological adjustment of children with chronic illness are the cognitive processes of expectations about self-esteem and health locus of control and methods of coping. More specifically, children's pain-coping strategies have been investigated among children with sickle-cell disease. The model is currently being expanded to include children's appraisals of stress and social support.

A number of studies have been conducted to test this model among children with cystic fibrosis, sickle-cell disease, and spina bifida as well as the mothers of children with sickle-cell disease and cystic fibrosis. This model is explicitly developmental. Studies are investigating the stability and change in adjustment, hypothesized maternal and child and family mediational processes, and their interrelationships over time.

Support has been found in a number of cross-sectional and longitudinal studies for the hypothesized role of maternal and child adaptational processes in both maternal and child psychological adjustment to chronic illness. For example, in the cross-sectional study of children with cystic fibrosis (Thompson, Gustafson, Hamlett, & Spock, 1992a), illness parameters accounted for 9% of the variance in mother-reported internalizing behavior problems, 1% of the variance in mother-reported externalizing behavior problems, and 3% of the variance in child-reported symptoms. Demographic parameters accounted for another 9% to 11% of the variance in both mother-reported and child-reported problems. However, with illness and demographic parameters controlled, child self-worth accounted for significant increments in the variance in mother-reported internalizing (11%) and externalizing (14%) behavior problems and child-reported symptoms (44%). Maternal anxiety also accounted for a significant increment in internalizing (10%) and externalizing (16%) behavior problems and child-reported symptoms (6%). Together, the transactional stress and coping model accounted for a substantial portion of the variance in mother-reported internalizing (39%) and externalizing (43%) behavior problems and child-reported symptoms (68%).

In a subsequent longitudinal study (Thompson, Gustafson, George, & Spock, 1994), with initial levels of internalizing behavior problems controlled, child self-worth accounted for an 8% increment in maternal-reported internalizing behavior problems. Child self-worth accounted for a 38% increment, and maternal distress accounted for another 6% increment in child-reported symptoms. Moreover, lower levels of child self-worth differentiated stable poor from stable good adjustment, as determined by children's and mother's reports, and higher levels of maternal stress differentiated stable poor from stable good child-reported adjustment.

In the cross-sectional study of children with sickle-cell disease (Thompson, Gil, Burbach, Keith, & Kinney, 1993b), illness parameters accounted for 4% of the variance in mother-reported externalizing behavior problems, 17% of the variance in internalizing behavior problems, and only 3% of the variance in child-reported symptoms. Demographic parameters accounted for 6% to 8% of the variance in mother- and child-reported adjustment. With these parameters controlled, parental anxiety accounted for 16% and 33% of the variance in mother-reported internalizing and externalizing behavior problems, respectively. However, maternal distress did not account for a significant increment in child-reported symptoms. Children's pain-coping strategies characterized by negative thinking accounted for a 20% increment. Together, the variables of the transactional stress and coping model accounted for 30% of the variance in child-reported symptoms and 45% to 49% of the variance in mother-reported behavior problems.

In the longitudinal study of the stability and change in the psychological adjustment of children with sickle-cell disease over a 10-month period (Thompson, Gil, Keith, et al., 1994), with initial levels of adjustment controlled, children's pain-coping strategies accounted for a significant increment in child-reported symptoms (19%) and mother-reported internalizing behavior problems (8%). However, support was not provided for the hypothesis that maternal anxiety would contribute to mother-reported behavioral problems. These findings suggest that efforts to promote the adjustment of children with sickle-cell disease might be directed at decreasing pain-coping strategies characterized by negative thinking and increasing strategies characterized by coping attempts.

In the cross-sectional study of the adjustment of mothers of children with cystic fibrosis (Thompson et al., 1992b), children's health status accounted for 3% to 4% of the variance in maternal-reported distress and demographic variables accounted for another 10% to 11% of the variance. With illness and demographic variables controlled, maternal daily stress accounted for a 30% increment in variance in maternal-reported depression and a 22% increment in maternal-reported anxiety. Together, the variables of the model accounted for 53% and 50% of the variance in maternal depression and anxiety symptoms, respectively.

Similarly, in the cross-sectional study of the psychological adjustment of mothers of children and adolescents with sickle-cell disease (Thompson, Gil, Burbach, Keith, & Kinney, 1993a), illness parameters accounted for 7% of the variance and demographic parameters accounted for 2% of the variance in maternal distress. With illness and demographic parameters controlled, significant increments in variance were accounted for by palliative coping ratio (30%), stress of daily hassles (13%), and emphasis on control in the family (3%). Together, the variables of the model accounted for 55% of the variance in maternal distress, of which 46% was accounted for by psychosocial and mediational processes.

The results of the longitudinal study of stability and change in the psychological adjustment of mothers of children and adolescents with cystic fibrosis and sickle-cell disease (Thompson, Gil, Gustafson, et al., 1994) indicated that for both illness groups, persistent poor maternal adjustment was associated with higher levels of daily stress, a greater use of palliative coping, and lower levels of family supportiveness. There also were illness-specific markers: higher levels of illness-related stress and family conflict in the mothers of children with cystic fibrosis and a higher palliative coping ratio in the mothers of children with sickle-cell disease. The hypothesis that child adjustment will contribute to maternal adjustment was supported only for the mothers of children with cystic fibrosis.

Across these studies of children with cystic fibrosis and sickle-cell disease, considerable support was provided for the role of the hypothesized adaptational processes in both maternal and child adjustment. Together the variables of the model accounted for 30% to 68% of the variance in adjustment; illness and demographic parameters together accounted for only a small portion of this variance (up to 20%). Furthermore, illness-specific findings on the patterns of relationships of adaptational processes to both maternal and child adjustment emerged. Even though substantial portions of variance were accounted for, there were major portions of variance that were not. This indicates that there is a need to incorporate other potential adaptational processes into models that attempt to account for the psychosocial adjustment component of children's adaptation to chronic illness. For example, researchers could examine how the social ecological context is manifested through the family in general and through the processes of caretaking and child rearing more specifically. These processes, subsumed under the concept of parenting, affect not only the parents' and child's psychological adjustment but also the cognitive and social–emotional development of the child.

### Family-Systems and Social Support Theories

The confluence of social ecological systems theory (Bronfenbrenner, 1977) and the transactional model of development (Sameroff & Chandler, 1975) provides a framework for conceptualizing and describing the nested hierarchy of family and societal contexts within which to consider adaptation to chronic illness. There are reciprocal, mutually influencing effects among the proximal (i.e., parents and family) and more distal (i.e., cultural) environments in which the child is embedded. Outcome at any one time is a function of the complex interplay among components of the system over time.

There have been two broad perspectives on the role of the family in children's health (Fiese & Sameroff, 1992). One perspective is the impact of childhood illness on the family. The second perspective is the impact of the family in changing health behaviors and in maintaining illness systems.

A family-systems perspective emphasizes the role of family dynamics or interactions in response to the stress associated with the child's illness. Not only is the family the primary vehicle for the delivery of health services to children, it also is the primary unit of influence on the child's cognitive and social development. In turn, family interaction patterns become potential treatment targets for enhancing adaptation.

The concept of the family is not static but continues to evolve. The so-called "nuclear" family, comprised of a mother as full-time homemaker, a father as the breadwinner, and two children, is not the norm anymore. There are many alternative family structures and styles. What is common is the element of mutual obligations to one another (see Roberts & Wallander, 1992). These societal changes in family characteristics affect clinical and research efforts. The family becomes a rubric or a context. Membership and roles vary not only across families but within families over time. As Roberts and Wallander (1992) suggested, "family research or intervention does not mean all members of a family as a total unit are involved every time. Indeed, individuals or subunits (siblings, parents, all combinations, and interactions) may be considered within the rubric" (p. 4).

A commonality among various family-systems theories is an emphasis on the dynamics of the whole family (i.e., on relationships or interactions among family members). Whereas the importance of the family in children with chronic illness is recognized, Roberts and Wallander (1992) noted that family-systems notions are used in discussing results after the fact rather than to guide investigations. Thus, family-systems models of adaptation to chronic childhood illness reflect the stage of research in which models have primary heuristic value to organize findings rather than to explain processes.

Similar to stress and coping theories, one way in which family-systems models and theories are important to the study of adaptation to chronic childhood illness is in elucidating processes within one component of the entire system. For example, understanding adaptation to chronic childhood illness is enhanced through an understanding of stress processing. If the case for a role of stress processing in adaptation to chronic childhood illness can be made, then intervention programs with demonstrated effectiveness (e.g., cognitive–behavioral stress management techniques) become potentially applicable to enhancing adaptation to chronic childhood illness. Similarly, various family-systems theories elucidate the role of dimensions of family structure and functioning in the well-being of family members. In particular, we briefly review two lines of research that focus on different dimensions of family structure or functioning that elucidate processes in which the family affects adaptation to chronic childhood illness.

*The Circumplex Model of Family Systems*

In constructing this model, Olson, Sprenkle, and Russell (1979) identified, through an inductive conceptual clustering, two dimensions of marital and family dynamics that appeared to underlie the array of concepts in the field of family studies: cohesion and adaptability.

The term *cohesion* refers to "the emotional bonding members have with one another and the degree of individual autonomy a person experiences in the family system" (Olson et al., 1979, p. 5). This dimension is viewed as a continuum ranging from enmeshment (i.e., an overidentification within the family resulting in extreme bonding and limited individual autonomy), through connected and separated, to disengagement (i.e., low bonding and a high degree of individual autonomy).

The term *adaptability* refers to "the ability of a marital/family system to change its power structure, role relationships, and relationships rules in response to situational and developmental stress" (Olson et al., 1979, p. 12). This dimension also is continuous, ranging from chaotic, excessive change, through flexible and structured, to rigid, excessive stability. It is hypothesized that a balanced degree of family cohesion and adaptability is the most conductive to effective family and individual functioning.

These dimensions of cohesion and adaptability were placed within a circumplex model, which yielded a 4 × 4 matrix involving 16 types of marital and family systems. The four types in the center of the model—flexible separateness, flexible connectedness, structured connectedness, and structured separateness—are hypothesized to be the most functional, whereas the four types on the extreme—chaotically disengaged, chaotically enmeshed, rigidly enmeshed, and rigidly disengaged—are hypothesized to be the most dysfunctional.

This model (Olson et al., 1979) has been useful not only in delineating the underlying dimensions of cohesion and adaptability but also in stimulating a consideration of how these dimensions interact with each other in family functioning. The findings on the correlates of adjustment reviewed in chapter 3 indicate that support is building for the contribution of family cohesion, in particular to adaptation to chronic childhood illness. However, the results of some studies also suggest differences in findings on the role of these dimensions on the basis of the measurement methods associated with circumplex models.

*Social Support and Parental Roles*

Kazak (1986) proposed a model of adaptation to chronic childhood illness that integrates family-systems theory and social ecology. The family is viewed as the key link in the child's social support network. This model builds on the extensive evidence that social support serves to buffer or ameliorate stress (see Cohen & Wills, 1985). Kazak advocated social network analysis as a means to assess social support (Kazak, Reber, & Carter, 1988). The characteristics of the child's and parents' social network structure are analyzed in terms of size and density; the extent to which members know one another independent of the focal person; and qualitative dimensions such as dimensionality (i.e., the number of functions served by relationships) and reciprocity (i.e., the extent of aid given and received). In general, larger networks and those with lower diversity are associated with more positive adjustment (Kazak et al., 1988). Compared with families without children with physical impairments, families with children with spina bifida, phenylketonuria, and mental retardation were found to have higher levels of parenting stress but generally normative levels of marital satisfaction (Kazak, 1992). These findings suggest that much of the distress stemmed from the impact of the condition on parenting demands. Furthermore, there was a tendency for higher network density in families of children with disabilities, and higher network density was linked to higher levels of parenting stress.

Important for our considerations on model building is Kazak's (1986, 1989) application of the concepts presented by Cochran and Brassard (1979) on the impact of the social network on parenting roles and, as a consequence, on child development. Parental social networks can influence parenting roles by providing support and material assistance, advocating, and serving as role models for specific child-rearing strategies.

Parenting roles also have been identified as an area of impact of chronic childhood illness (Quittner, DiGirolamo, Michel, & Eigen, 1992). Illness-specific and normal parenting tasks can interact with family phase (Rolland, 1987) to cause role strain in social and parenting roles. In turn, the stress of role strain is related to parental adjustment. Not only is there an association between parental adjustment and child adjustment, but changes in parenting roles also can affect child cognitive and social development.

It is well recognized that parent–child interactions are key to child development. In addition to parenting roles, these interactions have been studied in terms of caregiving behaviors and child-rearing behaviors subsumed under the general rubric of parenting. Parenting can be viewed as one common pathway through which the influence of the larger social ecological context within which the child is embedded affects his or her development.

## Parenting

There is a considerable body of information on the impact of parents' child-rearing strategies and behaviors on their children's development. Belsky (1984) suggested that research indicates that across childhood, "parenting that is *sensitively* attuned to children's capabilities and to the developmental tasks they face promotes a variety of highly valued developmental outcomes, including emotional security, behavioral independence, social competence, and intellectual achievement (Belsky, Lerner, & Spanier, 1984)" (p. 85; emphasis in the original). The child's socioemotional development and cognitive–motivational competence are promoted by attentive, warm, stimulating, responsive, and nonrestrictive caregiving (Belsky, Lerner, et al., 1984). Use of induction or reasoning, consistent discipline, and expression of warmth relate positively to self-esteem, internalized locus of control, prosocial orientation, and intellectual achievement (Belsky, 1984). Attention is now being given to understanding the processes by which this effect occurs. Beyond social class and cross-cultural comparisons of the effect of the child on parenting behavior, less attention has been directed at understanding the processes that influence the way in which parents parent (Belsky, 1984).

### The Process Model of Parenting

Belsky (1984) formulated a process model of parenting that includes three domains of determinants: parent personality, child characteristics, and contextual sources of stress and support. These three determinants are viewed as directly influencing parenting, as depicted in Figure 5.5.

The parents' contribution involves their psychological well-being and personality, which is viewed as a product, at least in part, of their developmental history. Belsky (1984) reviewed findings from the literature on child abuse, depression, and fathering to marshall support for this view that developmental history shapes personality and psychological well-being, which in turn influences parental functioning.

The child's contribution has received the most attention and includes an array of characteristics. Belsky (1984) pointed in particular to characteristics of the child that make him or her more or less difficult to care for as important in "shaping the quantity and quality of parental care [he or she] receive[s]" (p. 86). It is not the child characteristics per se that are the determinants but the goodness of fit between the child and parent characteristics that determines the development of parent–child relations (Lerner & Lerner, 1983).

This process model of parenting also addresses the larger social–ecological context in which the child and parents are embedded. This context is considered in terms of sources of stress and support. In addition to the extensive evidence of the overall general benefit of social support on both psychological and physical health, Belsky (1984) reviewed the evidence showing that, more specifically, parental functioning is also positively related to support. The influence of social support on parenting is viewed as being both direct and indirect through three functions: emotional support (love and interpersonal acceptance), instrumental assistance, and social expectations.

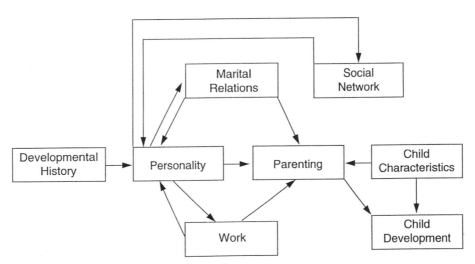

*Figure 5.5.* Process model of parenting. From Belsky (1984). Reprinted with permission.

The model also identifies three sources of stress and support. Marital relations have been shown to influence parenting directly and possibly indirectly through their impact on the general psychological well-being of the parents. Similarly, the parents' social network also has direct and indirect effects on parenting. It is not so much the absolute number of people or contacts in the social network that is important but the goodness of fit in terms of the match between support desired and support received (Belsky, 1984). Parents' work also is a source of stress or support that can affect parenting directly or indirectly through processes such as the relationship of work absorption to irritability in interactions and job satisfaction to self-esteem and tolerance. In terms of the relative importance of these contextual sources of stress and support, Belsky (1984) argued that the marital relationship is primary, followed by the social network.

In this process model, parenting is multiply determined and the parenting system is therefore buffered against threats to its integrity that derive from weakness in any single source (Belsky, Robins, & Gamble, 1984). Because of the value of personal psychological resources in promoting sensitive involvement in child interactions and in recruiting contextual support, it is regarded as the most influential determinant of parenting (Belsky, 1984). The child's characteristics are considered the least influential determinants because problematic parental functioning in the face of difficult child characteristics is not found in the absence of at-risk subsystems of support or personal resources (Belsky, 1984).

## Cognitive Processing and Parenting

Belsky's (1984) process model of parenting includes the broad processes of personality and psychological well-being within the parental determinants of parenting. However, other lines of research are also identifying other parental processes that can affect parenting. One line of research concerns parent stress processing, which we considered previously. Another line of research is addressing how parental cognitions affect the child's development (Miller, 1988).

The possibility that parents' beliefs about children may mediate parenting and child development has been referred to as the "missing link in accounts of parent-child relationships" (Goodnow, 1984, p. 193). Furthermore, studies of parental cognitions on child rearing may illuminate the effects of the social–ecological milieu about child development (Miller, 1986). There is growing evidence that socioecological factors influence parental values, attitudes, and expectations about children and the quality of parent–child interactions (Rubin, Mills, & Rose-Krasnor, 1989). In addition, several conceptual models have been offered on the role of parental cognition, and its determinants, in child development. Mills and Rubin (1990) described an information-processing model of parental behavior in which parental beliefs guide the parents' proactive and reactive responses in parent–child interactions. Several lines of evidence are emerging on the hypothesized links among parenting, social–ecological milieu, and children's cognitive and social development.

First, a review of the research literature (Miller, 1988) indicates that parents do have beliefs about development and that there is considerable variability in beliefs even within fairly homogeneous cultural settings. Most parents hold interactionist views about hereditary versus environmental determinants of development, and their beliefs can be ordered in terms of the degree to which the child is regarded as an active constructivist in his or her development (Miller, 1988).

A second line of evidence pertains to the link between parental beliefs and child development, either directly or through parenting and child-rearing practices. The evidence reviewed by Miller (1988) supports a "modest" link between parental beliefs, in terms of both the process of development and specific abilities, and child development: "More adaptive child rearing behaviors are associated with either relatively sophisticated belief systems about development or relatively accurate conceptions of children's ability" (Miller, 1988, p. 277). Evidence also supports a modest relationship between parental beliefs about development and the quality of the child's intellectual functioning. A relationship also was found between mother's accuracy regarding her child's ability and the child's competence. In general, mothers underestimate their children's abilities in the early years and overestimate their abilities in later years (Miller, 1986).

Regarding social development, the work of Rubin et al. (1989) suggested that maternal tendencies to attribute social skills and difficulties to causes within the child rather than to external causes appears to be associated with both maternal stress and poor social adjustment of the child. Parents' causal attributions about why their child behaved in a certain way influence parents' affective reactions and their choices of socialization strategies (Dix & Grusec, 1985; Dix, Ruble, Grusec, & Nixon, 1986; Dix, Ruble, & Zambarano, 1989). Parental assessment focuses on intentionality and control. Parents' negative reactions and choice of power-assertive socialization strategies have been found to be related to their appraisals of children's control and intentionality (Dix et al., 1986, 1989). It also has been found that parents think that children's behavior becomes increasingly intentional with age (Dix & Grusec, 1985). Thus, parental causal attributions reflect parental beliefs about developmental processes and abilities.

A third line of evidence addresses the determinants of parental beliefs about development. In particular, effects of social class or ethnic status have been found. Parents with a higher SES are more likely to espouse concepts of the child as an active processor than are parents with a lower SES, and these beliefs relate to both positive behaviors in the parent and to positive child outcomes (Miller, 1988). In general, "there is a positive relationship between various demographic indicators of social class and the nurturant, non-coercive, or supportive behaviors of parents that are typically associated with positive socialization outcomes" (Conger, McCarty, Yang, Lahey, & Kropp, 1984, p. 2234).

### Stress, Distress, and Parenting

Another line of research has addressed the linkages among parental stress and distress, child-rearing practices, and child cognitive and social development. It is recognized that stress has direct and indirect effects on child development: "Greater stress is associated with less optimal parent and family functioning, less optimal parent-child interactions, and lower child developmental competence" (Crnic & Greenberg, 1990, p. 1628).

Conger et al. (1984) examined three hypothesized links among stressful environmental conditions and parental actions in child development: maternal distress, child-rearing values, and maternal evaluative judgments. These psychological variables partially mediated the influence of stressful life conditions on the positive and negative behaviors of mothers toward their children. More specifically, chronic stress had direct influences on maternal behavior and also was partially mediated by mothers' emotional distress, authoritarian values, and negative perceptions of their children.

Crnic and Greenberg (1990), in a study involving both premature and full-term children, found that various indexes of stress, particularly the stress of daily parenting hassles, were related to maternal-reported behavior problems and lower social competencies in children at 5 years of age as well as to greater maternal distress, less satisfactory parenting, and less functional family status. Although there were no main effects for social support or stress on maternal behaviors, under high levels of stress mothers with greater support satisfaction had more positive behaviors than did mothers with low support.

Stress also has been found to influence parental perceptions of child behavior. Patterson (1983) found that minor daily hassles experienced by mothers were related to irritable responding to their children, which in turn increased the likelihood of aggressive responses from the children. Middlebrook and Forehand (1985) found that mothers who experienced high negative life stress perceived their children's behavior as being more deviant and used more controlling, abusive, and punitive parenting behaviors than did low-stress mothers.

In addition to the influences of maternal stress, there is considerable evidence that the mother's level of psychological functioning influences her perception of and behavioral interactions with her children (Webster-Stratton, 1990). In particular, the mother's depressive mood has been shown to influence perceptions of child maladjustment and her responses to her children, such as increased levels of vague or interrupting commands to which children cannot comply (Forehand, Lautenschlager, Faust, & Graziano, 1986). Maternal depression also has been related to infant withdrawal and avoidance behavioral patterns (Cohn & Tronick, 1983; Field et al., 1988), as well as to lower child cognitive functioning at 1 year of age (Lyons-Ruth, Zoll, Connell, & Grunebaum, 1986). In general, infants of depressed mothers are thought to experience more negative interactions and fewer opportunities to learn (Cohn, Matias, Tronick, Lyons-Ruth, & Connell, 1986), as well as less facilitation of their goal-directed behavior (Tronick, 1989).

### A Cognitive and Stress Processing Model of Parenting

The following hybrid model, shown in Figure 5.6, reflects an integration of cognitive processes regarding child development and stress processing components of cognitive processes and coping methods into the process model of parenting.

The utility of this hybrid model lies in depicting the established and predicted determinants of parenting that could be salient intervention targets. That is, if parenting is the primary mechanism for reflecting the social–ecological effects on children's development, then enhancing parenting effectiveness in terms of the goodness of fit with the child's special characteristics and needs would be instrumental in enhancing adaptation. In turn, parents' psychological functioning and child-rearing knowledge

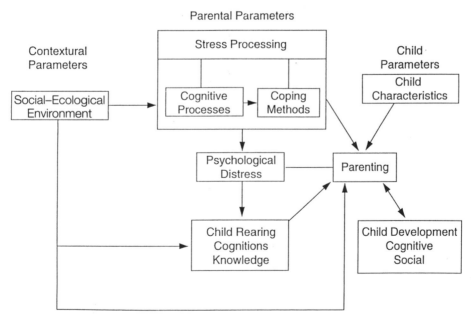

*Figure 5.6.* Cognitive and stress processing model of parenting.

would be major influences on parenting and become salient intervention targets through education, stress processing and management training, and enhancing family support.

*The Transactional Model of Family Functioning*

Fiese and Sameroff (1992) formulated a transactional model of family functioning that has direct implications for intervention. The model is based on the view that child development is the result of a three-part process: child behavior, the parents' interpretations of the child's behavior, and the parents' responses. For families with caretaking disruption, intervention strategies are targeted at one of these three parts. Interventions are designed to improve parent–child interactions by changing (a) the child's behavior, (b) the parents' interpretations of the child's behavior, or (c) the parents' responses to the child.

The strategy of remediation involves changing the child's behavior such that routine caretaking can proceed. For example, modifying feeding problems or the use of psychostimulants to reduce hyperactive behavior can have positive effects on parent–child interactions. The strategy of re-definition is useful when the child's behavior cannot be changed and is not viewed as being consistent with the family code on the expected behavior of the child and family. The family code incorporates the family's general view of the world, the definition of itself as distinct from other families, and the structure of daily routines (Fiese & Sameroff, 1992). In the case of children with chronic illness, family codes may have to be redefined to enable the child to be appropriately included. Similarly, the family's beliefs about health behaviors, passed down through generations, also may have to be redefined. The strategy of reeducation, in terms of the family code and child-raising skills, is likely to be necessary in all families who have children with illness. The specifics will necessarily vary as a function of the specific illness-related tasks associated with illness conditions. The specific strategies of redefinition and reeducation are methods of enhancing the effectiveness of parenting with children with chronic conditions.

## CONCLUSIONS

The movement toward the analytical level of research on adaptation to chronic childhood illness has yielded several conceptual models that are based on social learning and family-systems theories. In turn, the findings of studies guided by these models are providing information about two basic questions.

With regard to how biomedical, psychological, and social–ecological processes act together in contributing to the process of adaptation, understanding has been enhanced by the convergence of models in viewing chronic childhood illness as a potential stressor. This has led to a focus on the interrelationships of cognitive processes of stress appraisal, social support, and coping methods with illness-related and developmental tasks. Social ecological processes and social networks not only provide support and material assistance but also influence specific child-rearing strategies that affect children's development and adjustment. It is becoming clear that adjustment is a function of the goodness of fit (i.e., the match between parenting style and child characteristics and between tasks demands and coping methods).

Regarding which of these contributing processes is likely to be a salient intervention target, each model has specific intervention implications. However, across these models, it is useful to think about targeting risk and resilience factors and processes for intervention and prevention efforts. In general, these biopsychosocial models suggest that stress processing, social support, and parenting are currently the most promising intervention targets. However, intervention efforts also need to be informed by understanding of the effects of chronic childhood illness on parents and siblings.

# 6

# PSYCHOLOGICAL ADJUSTMENT OF PARENTS AND SIBLINGS

This chapter concludes the section on the impact of chronic childhood illness with a consideration of psychological adjustment of parents and siblings of children with chronic conditions. Parents' adjustment is considered first. Frequencies and types of adjustment problems are reviewed in general and as a function of illness type. Next, changes in parental adjustment over time and correlates of parental adjustment are reviewed. This is followed by an in-depth consideration of our studies of maternal adjustment at Duke University.

Psychological adjustment of siblings is considered next. The frequencies of sibling adjustment problems, changes in adjustment over time, and correlates of adjustment are reviewed. We conclude with a discussion of future research directions for this area of sibling adjustment, which has lagged behind the study of children with chronic illness and their parents.

## PSYCHOLOGICAL ADJUSTMENT OF PARENTS

The psychological adjustment of parents of children with chronic illness is important in itself but also because of the role of parental adjustment in the adjustment of children with chronic illness. However, the investigation of the psychological adjustment of parents of children with chronic illness has lagged behind that of the children themselves.

Many of the research questions and issues discussed in chapter 2 on the psychological adjustment of children also apply to parental adjustment. Five general research questions can be identified in the literature: (a) Do parents of children with chronic illness have higher rates or levels of psychological distress, symptoms, and disorders than do parents of healthy children? (b) Do mothers and fathers differ in psychological adjustment? (c) Are there illness-specific patterns of parental distress? (d) How does parental adjustment change over time? (e) What are the correlates of parental psychological adjustment?

The methods typically used to study parental adjustment rely on self-report measures of psychological distress assessed in terms of both overall distress and specific symptom dimensions, particularly depression and to a lesser extent anxiety. Participants studied are overwhelmingly mothers. Group scores frequently are compared with instrument norms or with scores from comparison groups of parents of healthy children. Rates of distress in the clinical range sometimes are calculated and compared. The search for correlates of maternal adjustment is just beginning to be guided by conceptual models such as the risk–resistance model, developed by Wallander and Varni (1992), and the transactional stress and coping model, developed by Thompson and colleagues (Thompson, Gil, Burbach, Keith, & Kinney, 1993b; Thompson, Gustafson, Hamlett, & Spock, 1992a, 1992b; see chapter 5).

As with the consideration in chapters 2 and 4 of child adjustment, the review of studies here is not intended to be exhaustive. Studies were selected to be representative of the six illnesses of focus, with an emphasis on studies that were conceptually driven. The findings are organized in three primary areas of focus: parental adjustment, changes in adjustment over time, and correlates of adjustment.

## Frequencies and Types of Adjustment Problems

One of the major epidemiological studies of chronic illness, the Isle of Wight study (Rutter, Tizard, & Whitmore, 1970), included an assessment of maternal mental health through completion of a 24-item malaise inventory on a subgroup of mothers of children with physical ($n = 153$) or psychiatric ($n = 107$) illnesses. No data were provided on the rates or types of psychological adjustment difficulties experienced by the mothers of children with physical impairments. However, comparisons were made among the types of child physical impairment and between mothers of children with physical and psychiatric illnesses. There were no significant differences in the mean scores of mothers of children with different types of physical impairments. However, mothers of children with physical impairments had significantly lower mean malaise scores than did mothers of children with diagnosed psychiatric illnesses.

To our knowledge, there has been only one major epidemiological study of the psychological adjustment of parents of children with chronic illness reported in the literature. Data from the Ontario Child Health Study (OCHS) were used to compare the demographic features, individual parent mental health factors, and family functioning of families with a child with chronic health problems with those of families of well children (Cadman, Rosenbaum, Boyle, & Offord, 1991). The OCHS included 1,869 randomly selected families with 3,294 children aged 4 to 16 years. Respondents were almost always mothers. The General Functioning scale of the Family Assessment Device (N. Epstein, Baldwin, & Bishop, 1983) was used to assess family functioning. The General Functioning scale contains two items for each of six domains: problem solving, communication, roles, affective responsiveness, affective involvement, and behavior control. Parental psychological adjustment was assessed with the Bradburn Affect Balance Scale (Bradburn, 1969), which consists of five negatively and five positively worded descriptions of recent feeling states. Respondents indicated the frequency of experiencing these states.

The findings indicated significantly higher maternal negative affective scores among parents of children with a chronic health problem. Rates of parent-reported mental health treatment for "nerves" among both mothers (29%) and fathers (8%) of children with chronic illness were a significant 2 to 3 times higher than the rates reported by parents of well children. However, there were no significant differences between groups in increases in single-parent families, social isolation, or alcohol problems. The authors concluded that "contrary to some clinical opinion, we found no evidence in this general community sample to support the belief that the families of children with chronic health problems function any differently than families in the general population" (Cadman et al., 1991, p. 886). However, they did note the limitations of their study, which involved the use of survey measures to assess adjustment and family functioning.

Most information about parental adjustment comes from studies with samples comprised of one specific chronic illness or pooled samples of several illnesses. Many of these studies assess adjustment at a single point in time. Only occasionally is the assessment point selected relative to a phase of illness or treatment stage.

In one of the earliest studies, personality functioning was assessed in a study of mothers ($n = 43$) and fathers ($n = 29$) of children (aged 5 to 18 years) with cystic fibrosis (Gayton, Friedman, Tavormina, & Tucker, 1977). The findings indicated that 32% of the fathers and 22% of the mothers had one or more scale scores on the Minnesota Multiphasic Personality Inventory (MMPI) in the clinical range (i.e., a score greater than 2 $SD$s above the mean). Compared with parents ($n = 50$) of normal pre-adolescent boys, mothers of children with cystic fibrosis were found to have significantly higher scores on the Depression and Masculinity–Femininity scales and fathers of children with cystic fibrosis had significantly higher scores on the Lie, Hypochondriasis, Hysteria, and Psychopathic Deviate scales. Thus, there was some evidence that mothers of children with cystic fibrosis manifested less personality disturbance than fathers.

In an early study in which children with spina bifida and no retardation ($n = 19$) were compared with healthy children ($n = 19$) matched on sex and age, (range $= 5$ to 15 years, M $= 8.7$ years), no significant differences between groups were found in parenting attitudes, marital adjustment, perceptions of child behavior, child self-concept, stress, and overall functioning (Spaulding & Morgan, 1986). Mothers and fathers of the children with spina bifida did not differ significantly in perceived stress and impact of the child with a physical impairment on areas of family life, including personal strain.

In a study ($n = 50$) of children with physical impairments aged 6 to 11 years (M $= 8.0$ years) with spina bifida (54%) or cerebral palsy (46%) and their mothers, maternal adaptation was assessed in terms of physical, emotional, and social functioning (Wallander, Varni, Babani, Banis, DeHaan, & Wilcox, 1989). Because of its use in epidemiological research, the malaise inventory (Rutter et al., 1970) was used as a self-report measure of mental and physical health symptoms and complaints. The findings indicated that mothers of children with physical impairments reported significantly more symptoms than did the mothers in the Isle of Wight epidemiological study and a level of symptoms similar to that reported by mothers of children with psychiatric illness (Rutter et al., 1970).

Some studies have shown increased but subclinical levels of self-reported symptoms of psychological distress compared with normative groups. For example, mothers of children with cystic fibrosis (Mullins et al., 1991) reported higher levels of depression, anxiety, and hostility symptoms and a higher Global Severity Index score than the normative group on the Brief Symptom Index (Derogatis & Spencer, 1982). A study of marital distress in parents of children ($n = 134$) with newly diagnosed cancer (aged 1 to 17 years, M $= 6.9$ years) examined rates of self-reported symptoms in the clinical range as well as group means in relation to norms (Dahlquist et al., 1993). Both mothers' and fathers' State Anxiety scale scores and mothers' Trait Anxiety scale scores on the State-Trait Anxiety Inventory (STAI; Spielberger, Gorsuch, Lunshene, Vagg, & Jacobs, 1970) were slightly but significantly higher than norms for nonclinical adults. Rates of T-scores of 70 or greater (i.e., $\geq$ 90th percentile) were obtained by 13% of the mothers and 12% of the fathers for state anxiety and 12% of the mothers and 3% of the fathers for trait anxiety. Approximately 13% of the mothers and 8% of the fathers reported clinically elevated levels of depression on the Beck Depression Inventory (BDI; i.e., a score ≥16; Beck, Ward, Mendelson, Mock, & Erbaugh, 1961).

Maternal depression was assessed in a study of mothers ($n = 95$) of children with diabetes ($n = 24$), cystic fibrosis ($n = 23$) and mental retardation ($n = 24$) and of healthy children ($n = 24$; L. S. Walker, Ortiz-Valdes, & Newbrough, 1989). The children were aged 8 to 19 years. Mothers completed the Center for Epidemiological Studies Depression Scale (CES-D; Radloff, 1977). The results indicated that the level of self-reported depression was not significantly higher for mothers of children with chronic conditions than for mothers of well children. Controlling for socioeconomic status (SES) and child illness, lack of employment outside the home was associated with higher maternal depression.

Maternal depression, as reflected by scores on the CES-D, also was assessed in another study of mothers of children ($n = 32$) with cystic fibrosis and mothers of healthy children ($n = 32$; L. S. Walker, Ford, & Donald, 1987). Four age groups were included: preschool (4 to 5 years), school age (8 to 9 years), young adolescent (11 to 14 years), and late adolescent (15 to 19 years). Compared with mothers of healthy children, mothers of children with cystic fibrosis did not report significantly higher levels of stress, but mothers of preschoolers and early adolescent youngsters reported higher levels of depression. Among mothers of children with cystic fibrosis, the mother's subjective ratings of her child's illness was a stronger indicator of maternal stress, particularly that related to the caretaking role, than was the child's clinical severity, as reflected in the Shwachman score. Maternal depression was not significantly associated with either measure of the child's illness severity.

In another study of the adjustment of parents ($n = 37$) of children (aged 18 months to 12 years) with cystic fibrosis, mothers reported significantly higher levels of distress and lower feelings of well-being than the norms on a mental health inventory (Nagy & Ungerer, 1990). Fathers' reports did not differ from the normative population. On the STAI, mothers reported significantly greater trait anxiety and fathers reported significantly lower state anxiety than did the normative samples. Only one significant difference was found between mothers and fathers of children with cystic fibrosis. Mothers reported significantly less emotional and behavioral control than did fathers. Mothers and fathers did not differ significantly in their perceptions of the stresses associated with rearing a child with cystic fibrosis or in the total amount of support or distress associated with social networks. Mothers reported significantly more instrumental support from their social networks and higher ratings of support received from friends than fathers reported. Mothers also spent significantly more time than fathers in household tasks, child-rearing activities, and providing physical therapy. Mothers' mental health was related to perceptions of support from their husbands but not to husbands' actual involvement in household or child-rearing tasks.

In a study of mothers ($n = 61$) of children (aged 2 to 17 years, $M = 7$ years 1 month) with acute lymphocytic leukemia (R. T. Brown et al., 1993), maternal psychiatric symptomatology was assessed using the Structured Clinical Interview for DSM-III-R (SCID; Williams & Gibbons, 1987), a semistructured interview that yields diagnoses from the revised third edition of the *Diagnostic and Statistical Manual of Mental Disorders* (*DSM–III–R*; American Psychiatric Association, 1987). Mothers also completed the BDI (Beck, Steer, & Garbin, 1988), a self-report measure of depression. The findings indicated that 34% of the mothers met *DSM–III–R* criteria for two or more disorders. The most frequent diagnoses included major depressive disorder (21.3%), generalized anxiety disorder (18%), dysthymic disorder (8.2%), and panic disorder (8.2%). Mean BDI depression scores were within the normal range.

## Parental Adjustment as a Function of Illness Type

One of the earliest investigations of psychological distress in mothers of children with disabilities as a function of illness type compared 369 mothers of children with cystic fibrosis, cerebral palsy, myelodysplasia, or multiple handicaps with 456 mothers from a randomly selected sample of families (Breslau, Staruch, & Mortimer, 1982). Compared with mothers in the control sample, mothers of children with disabilities had significantly higher mean scores on a depression–anxiety scale and on a measure of distress. Types of disability did not have a significant effect on either maternal depression–anxiety or maternal distress. However, there was a significant impact of the extent of the child's dependence in activities of daily living on both maternal depression–anxiety and maternal distress.

Surprisingly, there has been a lack of subsequent investigations of maternal adjustment as a function of illness type. For example, the previously reported study of mothers of children with mental retardation, diabetes, cystic fibrosis, and healthy children (L. S. Walker et al., 1989) did not show significant differences in maternal depression between mothers of children with chronic conditions and mothers of healthy children, but Walker et al. apparently did not test differences among illness subgroups. One exception is the previously described study of mothers of children with physical impairments (Wallander, Varni, Babani, Banis, DeHaan, & Wilcox, 1989). No significant differences were found in the adjustment of mothers of children with spina bifida and cerebral palsy.

## Changes in Parental Adjustment Over Time

Kupst and her colleagues conducted one of the first longitudinal studies of the adjustment of families to childhood leukemia. Sixty-four families were randomly assigned to intervention and control groups that differed in the degree of outreach and the frequency of contact (Kupst, Tylke, et al., 1983). Subsequent follow-up occurred at 1 year (Kupst et al., 1982), 2 years (Kupst et al., 1984) and 6–8 years (Kupst & Schulman, 1988) after diagnosis. Intervention had been found to be effective in fostering maternal adjustment in the early outpatient phase (Kupst, Schulman, et al., 1983), but not in the later phases of the illness. Of the original sample of 64 families, 43 participated in the follow-up study 6–8 years post diagnosis (Kupst & Schulman, 1988). Of the 43 children in these families, 1 had relapsed, 27 were in remission, and 15 had died. Both staff ratings and parent self-reports tended to reflect an improvement in the adjustment of both mothers and fathers over time.

The psychological adjustment of parents of children with acute lymphocytic leukemia was assessed, in a cross-sectional design, at three points in time: diagnosis ($n = 23$), 1 year postdiagnosis (i.e., consolidation; $n = 22$), and 1 year after completion of chemotherapy (i.e., off therapy; $n = 10$; R. T. Brown et al., 1992). Parental adjustment was assessed with the BDI (Beck et al., 1988) and the SCID (Spitzer et al., 1987), which yields *DSM–III–R*-compatible diagnoses. The findings indicated that 34% of the mothers in the 1-year postdiagnosis group were classified as overanxious. Mothers in the newly diagnosed group and the 1-year postdiagnosis group reported significantly more depressive symptoms on the BDI than did the mothers in the off-therapy group, but the mean scores for all three groups were not indicative of clinical depression. For fathers, 17% in the 1-year postdiagnosis group were classified as having had a major depression according to their wife's report on the SCID.

The family's adaptation to childhood leukemia throughout the first year of the illness was also examined in a study ($n = 34$) of children (aged 22 months to 16 years, $M = 6.3$ years) who were newly diagnosed with acute lymphocytic leukemia (Fife, Norton, & Groom, 1987). Parents' adjustment was assessed with the STAI (Spielberger, 1977) the first week following diagnosis, during radiation treatment (state only), and at the 6th, 9th, and 12th months after diagnosis. MMPI scores were obtained at the 3rd and 12th months after diagnosis. For both mothers ($n = 33$) and fathers ($n = 27$), there was a significant continuous decrease in the level of situational (i.e., state) anxiety, with the largest decline occurring in the first 2 months after diagnosis. There were no significant changes over time in trait anxiety. On the Anxiety scale of the MMPI scores were low, with only 8% of the mothers and 15% of the fathers registering moderate (T-scores = 60 to 70) or higher elevations of conscious anxiety, and there was little change between the 3rd and 12th months following diagnosis. On the Psychasthenia scale, which measures long-term anxiety, 21.4% of the fathers and 28.6% of the mothers had at least moderate elevations at 3 months, with the percentage for mothers dropping to 23.8% and fathers easing to 35.7% at the 12th month. On the Depression scale, 33.3% the mothers and 21.4% of the fathers had at least a moderate degree of elevation at the 3rd month, which dropped for mothers to 19% and increased for fathers to 28.6% at the 12th month. On the Hypochondriasis scale, the percentage of at least moderate elevations increased slightly for mothers from 14.3% at the 3rd month to 19% at the 12th month, but the percentage increased markedly for fathers from 14.3% to 42.9%.

Several dimensions of parental adjustment were assessed in a longitudinal study of 159 mothers and fathers of children with juvenile rheumatic disease (mean age = 9.4 years) at Time 1 and of 111 of these couples at Time 2 follow-up 1 year later (Timko, Stovel, & Moos, 1992). At Times 1 and 2, mothers reported higher levels of depressed mood than did fathers. However, both mothers and fathers had considerably lower scores than did a sample of clinically depressed adults (Moos, Cronkite, & Finney, 1990). Mothers' and fathers' functioning in terms of depression, personal strain, social activities, and mastery were highly stable over time.

### Correlates of Parental Adjustment

In her longitudinal studies of family adjustment to childhood leukemia, Kupst (Kupst & Schulman, 1988) found a consistent pattern of correlates of parental adjustment. Whereas the child's medical status and duration of illness were not significantly related to parental adjustment, those who adjusted poorly tended to have fewer supports, more marital problems, less open family communication, and more concurrent stress, especially financial stress.

The study of parents of children with juvenile rheumatoid arthritis (Timko et al., 1992) also investigated concurrent and predictive correlates of parental adaptation. The child's functional disability and pain, spouse dysfunction, illness-related avoidance coping, and fewer family resources were related to poor parental functioning. In terms of longitudinal determinants of functioning, mothers' and fathers' reliance on avoidance coping and spouse dysfunction were related to poorer parental adaptation concurrently and 1 year later. The mothers' adjustment was predicted by the child's prior and current dysfunction, suggesting that over time the child's poor disease-related functioning may be more of a risk factor for mothers' adjustment than for fathers' adjustment.

In a study of 107 parents of children with cancer, parental adjustment was found to vary as a function of social support, parental age, and treatment stage (Morrow, Hoagland, & Carnrike, 1981). Psychosocial adjustment was assessed with the parent-completed Psychosocial Adjustment to Illness Scale (Derogatis, 1975). Parents under 30 years of age and parents whose children had died, compared with those whose child was still in treatment or who had completed treatment, had significantly more impaired adjustment; parents whose children were in treatment seemed to benefit more from social support than parents of children who had died or who had completed treatment.

The relationship of coping method to maternal adjustment was examined in a study of 46 mothers of children (aged 3 to 18 years, M = 9.43 years) with cancer (Baskin, Forehand, & Saylor, 1986). Psychological adjustment was assessed with the Global Severity Index and the SCL-90-R (Derogatis, 1977). The findings indicated that emotion-focused coping, as assessed with the Ways of Coping Scale (Folkman & Lazarus, 1980), was related to maternal maladjustment, accounting for 17% of the variance in Global Severity Index scores. Lower SES and less use of problem-focused coping also accounted for a significant amount of the variance in maternal adjustment. However, together, the model accounted for only 2% to 4% of the variance in maternal adjustment.

In the study of children with physical impairments (spina bifida = 54%, cerebral palsy = 46%) and their mothers (described previously), the risk–resistance conceptual model developed by Wallander and colleagues was used to guide the search for correlates of maternal adjustment (Wallander, Varni, Babani, DeHaan, Wilcox, & Banis, 1989; Wallander, Varni, Babani, Banis, DeHaan, & Wilcox, 1989). Mothers' adaptation, as reflected in reports of mental and physical symptoms and complaints on the malaise inventory (Rutter et al., 1970), was not significantly related to the degree of the child's physical impairments, as rated on the basis of mother interviews and interactions with the child, or to chronic strain in terms of the child's functional status, as assessed by teacher reports (Wallander, Varni, Babani, DeHaan, Wilcox, & Banis, 1989). However, parameters of the social environment were strongly associated with mother's adaptation in terms of mental symptoms and social functioning, accounting for 57% to 68% of the variance in these domains (Wallander, Varni, Babani, DeHaan, Wilcox, & Banis, 1989). Utilitarian resources (i.e., structural characteristics of the family) accounted for significant proportions of variance in mothers' social functioning, in that a longer marriage and having a larger family and a child older than the child with the physical impairment were predictive of poorer social functioning. Child adjustment, measured in terms of mother-reported behavior problems on the Child Behavior Checklist (Achenbach & Edelbrock, 1983), was significantly related to mothers' physical health but did not add a significant increment in variance in mothers' mental, physical, or social adaptation. Psychosocial family resources (i.e., the family's characteristic mode of receiving and interacting with the social world) accounted for significant and sizable increments in the variance in all three domains of maternal adaptation over and above the contribution by utilitarian resources and child adjustment. Better marital satisfaction reported by mothers was associated with better mental health and social functioning. Better family support and a larger social network was associated with better physical health. Better marital satisfaction, a larger support group, but less family support was associated with better social functioning (Wallander, Varni, Babani, DeHaan, Wilcox, & Banis, 1989).

The risk–resistance model was evaluated in another study of the adaptation of mothers of children (n = 35; aged 1 to 16 years, M = 8.1 years) with cystic fibrosis (Mullins et al., 1991). Maternal adaptation was assessed with the Brief Symptom Inventory (Derogatis & Spencer, 1982), a shorter version of the SCL-90-R, in terms of the Global Severity Index and the Depression, Anxiety, and Hostility symptom scales. After controlling for income and physicians' ratings of disease severity, which did not account for significant portions of variance in maternal adjustment (the Global Severity Index), the presence of high levels of family life stress in the past year and a coping style involving escape–avoidance were significantly associated with maternal distress. Family adaptability and cohesion did not contribute significantly to maternal adjustment. The overall model accounted for 57% of the variance in maternal adaptation. Some differences in contributions occurred as a function of the measure of adjustment. Family life stress was a significant predictor of maternal anxiety and hostility, but not depression. The escape–avoidance dimension of coping was a significant predictor of depression and anxiety, but not hostility. Of the variables evaluated, family life stress during the past year, as assessed with the 71-item Family Inventory of Life Events (McCubbin, Patterson, & Wilson, 1985), appeared to exert the most influence on maternal adaptation.

Another study based on Lazarus and Folkman's (1984) stress and coping model examined the psychological adjustment of 29 parents of children (aged 6 to 11 years) with myelomeningocele and 28 parents of healthy children (Barakat & Linney, 1992). There was no significant difference between groups in maternal psychological adjustment as measured by the General Severity Index of the Brief Symptom Inventory. However, psychological adjustment of mothers of children with myelomeningocele was related to the size of the support network, the proportion of family members in the network, and the satisfaction with received support.

## Duke Studies

Our research program has investigated the type and frequency of adjustment problems in mothers of children with chronic illness; the correlates and adaptational process associated with maternal adjustment; and the changes in adjustment, adaptational processes, and their interrelationship over time. The delineation of adaptational processes has been guided by the transactional stress and coping model discussed in chapter 5.

Psychological adjustment of mothers has been assessed with the SCL-90-R (Derogatis, 1977), which is a 90-item self-report measure of psychological distress along nine symptom dimensions: depression, anxiety, somatization, obsessive–compulsive, interpersonal sensitivity, hostility, phobic anxiety, paranoid ideation, and psychoticism. The Global Severity Index combines information on numbers of symptoms and intensity of distress and is used as a measure of the overall level of psychological distress. Raw scores on the nine symptom dimensions and the Global Severity Index are converted to T-scores using nonpatient norms for females; T-scores greater than or equal to 63 (i.e., above the 90th percentile) are considered in the clinical range. Overall poor adjustment is determined in accordance with the established criteria for "caseness" (i.e., T-scores $\geq$ 63 on the Global Severity Index or any two of the nine symptom dimensions).

In a study of children ($n = 35$; aged 4.5 to 14 years, M = 12 years) with Duchenne muscular dystrophy, parents (32 mothers and 3 fathers) were found to have relatively high levels of psychological distress (Thompson, Zeman, Fanurik, & Sirotkin-Roses, 1992). Whereas 43% of the parents demonstrated good adjustment on the SCL-90-R, 57% met case criteria for poor adjustment. Elevations into the clinical range of distress occurred for 37% of the parents on the Global Severity Index and 29% and 20% of the parents on the symptom dimensions of depression and anxiety, respectively. In terms of adaptational processes, compared with parents with poor adjustment, parents with good adjustment had (a) lower levels of illness-related stress; (b) less use of palliative coping methods and a lower ratio of use of palliative coping methods to adaptive coping methods; and (c) family functioning characterized by higher levels of family supportiveness and lower levels of conflict. These three sets of variables accounted for 58% of the variance in global distress, 50% of the variance in depressive symptoms, and 31% of the variance in anxiety symptoms, respectively.

The role of family functioning in maternal psychological adjustment was also the focus of a study of 66 mothers of children (aged 2 months to 18 years, M = 7 years 7 months) with spina bifida. Mothers' scores on the depression, anxiety, and somatization symptom dimensions and on the Global Severity Index were significantly higher (5 to 7 points) than scale norms, and 44% of the mothers met case criteria on the SCL-90-R for poor adjustment (Kronenberger & Thompson, 1992). Correlational analysis revealed that family functioning characterized by high levels of supportiveness and low levels of emphasis on control and conflict and marital quality or support were related to maternal adjustment. With demographic and illness parameters controlled, marital quality or support and family functioning characterized by an emphasis on control accounted for a 27% increment in the variance in maternal distress (Global Severity Index).

Additional components of the transactional stress and coping model were investigated in our studies of the psychological adjustment of mothers of children and adolescents with cystic fibrosis. In a cross-sectional study (*n* = 68) of children and adolescents (aged 7 to 17 years), 66% of the mothers had good adjustment, but 34% met case criteria for poor adjustment on the SCL-90-R (Thompson, Gustafson, Hamlett, & Spock, 1992b). Elevations into the clinical range of distress occurred for 21% and 18% of the mothers on the symptom dimensions of depression and anxiety, respectively. Compared with mothers with poor adjustment, mothers with good adjustment had significantly lower levels of stress related to daily hassles and to illness tasks, higher efficacy expectations regarding illness tasks, lower levels of use of palliative coping methods, and higher levels of family supportiveness and lower family conflict. There were no significant differences between maternal adjustment subgroups in severity of their children's illness or in maternal health locus of control expectations. With illness and demographic parameters controlled, maternal perceptions of higher levels of daily stress, lower levels of family supportiveness, and higher levels of palliative coping accounted for a 40% increment in the variance in maternal depression. Perceptions of higher levels of daily stress, lower levels of efficacy about preserving their children's emotional well-being, and higher levels of emphasis on family control accounted for a 35% increment in the variance in maternal anxiety.

In a subsequent longitudinal study, 57 mothers of the original study sample completed the follow-up assessment 9 to 19 months later (M = 12.33 months) (Thompson, Gil, Gustafson, et al., 1994). There were no significant changes in illness parameters on any of the adaptational processes over time. Adjustment, as measured by the Global Severity Index, was highly correlated across time (*r* = .66, *p* < .001). The level of distress decreased significantly. Furthermore, the rate of poor adjustment decreased from 30% at the initial evaluation to 19% at the follow-up evaluations. Across both assessment points, 14% of the mothers met case criteria for poor adjustment, 65% of the mothers met the criteria for good adjustment, and 21% of the mothers changed adjustment classification. Mothers with stable good adjustment differed from those with stable poor adjustment in that they had lower ratings of daily stress, less use of palliative coping methods, and lower levels of family conflict. In terms of adjustment at follow-up, with initial levels of adjustment and demographic parameters controlled, follow-up levels of illness severity (5%), child adjustment (5%), maternal perceptions of daily stress (6%), and family conflict (4%) accounted for significant increments in maternal adjustment.

The transactional stress and coping model also has been used to study adaptation to sickle-cell disease. The psychological adjustment of mothers of children and adolescents with sickle-cell disease (*n* = 78; aged 7 to 17 years) was assessed in a cross-sectional study (Thompson, Gil, Burbach,

Keith, & Kinney, 1993a). Whereas 64% of the mothers reported good adjustment, 36% of the mothers met case criteria for poor adjustment on the SCL-90-R. The maternal adjustment subgroups did not differ significantly on any of the illness or demographic variables. Compared with mothers with poor adjustment, mothers with good adjustment had significantly lower levels of daily stress, less use of palliative coping, a lower ratio of palliative-to-adaptive coping, and higher levels of family supportiveness. With illness (7%) and demographic parameters (2%) controlled, significant increments in variance in maternal distress (Global Severity Index) were accounted for by palliative coping ratio (30%), stress of daily hassles (13%), and emphasis on control in the family (3%). Together, the variables of the model accounted for 55% of the variance in maternal distress, of which 46% was accounted for by the psychosocial adaptational processes.

In a subsequent longitudinal study, 60 mothers of the original study sample completed the follow-up assessment 8 to 16 months (M = 10.03 months) later (Thompson, Gil, Gustafson, et al., 1994). There were no significant changes in illness parameters or adaptational processes over time. Maternal adjustment, as measured by the Global Severity Index, was highly correlated ($r = .75$, $p < .0001$) and did not change significantly over time. However, the rate of poor adjustment decreased from 37% initially to 28% at follow-up. Poor adjustment at both assessment points was found in 20% of the mothers, and good adjustment at both assessment points was found in 55% of the mothers. A change in adjustment classification occurred for 25% of mothers. Compared with mothers with stable poor adjustment, mothers with stable good adjustment had significantly lower ratings of daily stress and illness stress, less use of palliative coping methods (and in relation to the use of adaptive coping methods), and higher levels of family supportiveness. In terms of adjustment at follow-up, with initial level of adjustment and demographic variables controlled, a significant 15% increment in variance was accounted for by follow-up levels of maternal perceptions of daily stress.

This series of studies indicates that the rates of poor maternal adjustment varied somewhat across illness groups: Duchenne muscular dystrophy (57%), spina bifida (44%), cystic fibrosis (34%), and sickle-cell disease (36%). The longitudinal studies of mothers of children and adolescents with cystic fibrosis and sickle-cell disease indicate moderate stability in the individual classification of maternal adjustment ($\kappa = .44$ for both groups) across an 8- to 19-month period. A change in classification was found in 21% of the mothers with children with cystic fibrosis and 25% of the mothers with children with sickle-cell disease.

Considerable support has been provided for the role of the adaptational processes of the transactional stress and coping model in maternal adjustment. More specifically, persistently good maternal adjustment was associated with lower levels of appraisals of daily stress, less use of palliative coping methods, and higher levels of family supportiveness. There were also some illness-specific findings. For example, the hypothesis that child psychological adjustment would contribute to maternal adjustment was supported in the cystic fibrosis study but not in the sickle-cell disease study. For the most part, illness severity did not make a substantial contribution to the variance in maternal adjustment. Although the variables of the transactional stress and coping model accounted for significant portions of the variance in the psychological adjustment of mothers of children with chronic illness, a considerable amount of variance was not accounted for. This suggests that other variables need to be added to the model. The risk–resistance model developed by Wallander and colleagues calls attention to the other variables that also are related to maternal adjustment, such as a functional care strain (Wallander, Varni, Babani, DeHaan, et al., 1989) and psychological and utilitarian family resources (Wallander, Varni, Babani, Banis, et al., 1989).

## PSYCHOLOGICAL ADJUSTMENT OF SIBLINGS

Consistent with social–ecological theoretical perspectives and the family-centered focus of pediatric health care, attention has been focused on the effects of chronic disease and disability on children's sibling relationships. Although the number of studies has been relatively small, there have been several excellent reviews of this research (Drotar & Crawford, 1985; Lobato, 1983; Lobato, Faust, & Spirito, 1988; McKeever, 1983; Rodger, 1985; Simeonsson & McHale, 1981).

It has been argued that the sibling relationships of children with chronic illness need to be considered within the context of research findings on normal sibling relationships (Lobato et al., 1988). However, although the literature on normal child development conceptualizes outcome multidimensionally as the result of interacting systems of child, family, situational, and cultural variables, the research focus on siblings of children with developmental and medical problems is narrow (Lobato et al., 1988). Furthermore, there have been few controlled investigations, and, although many articles purport to assess the impact on families, siblings have been excluded from much of this research (Lobato et al., 1988).

In a review of conceptual and methodological issues, Senapati and Hayes (1988) contrasted the characteristics of research on the sibling relationships of children with handicaps with those on healthy siblings. Research on the siblings of children with handicaps has focused on negative effects under a unidirectional model. For the most part, the impact of the child with a handicap on healthy siblings has been the focal point. Only a few studies have addressed the impact of the healthy child on the sibling with an impairment. By contrast, studies of healthy sibling relationships are characterized by a focus on multidirectional positive and negative effects and mediational processes. Although studies of siblings with handicaps have focused on the mediational role of relatively static structural factors such as age, gender, and birth order, studies of healthy siblings have focused on the role of mediational processes. Furthermore, in contrast to the absence of theoretical bases for research on sibling relationships of children with handicaps, research on healthy sibling relationships has been guided by contemporary theoretical approaches including attachment, social mediational, and family-systems approaches (Senapati & Hayes, 1988).

## Frequencies of Sibling Adjustment Problems

The most frequently addressed question has been the extent of maladjustment among healthy siblings of children with developmental or medical problems. This reflects the common belief that children with a chronic condition have a harmful effect on siblings, resulting in healthy siblings having a higher rate of adjustment problems. Dyson (1989) pointed out that this belief in harmful effects is based on reasonable considerations such as the effects of increased parental stress related to caring for the child with a disability, decreased parental attention to the healthy child, decreased family resources, and pathological identification with the child with a disability. Group research generally does not support this popular belief that siblings of children with disabilities or chronic illness exhibit poorer psychological adjustment than do siblings of healthy children (Lobato et al., 1988). However, research also has demonstrated that adverse psychological outcomes do occur.

A review of early studies (Drotar & Crawford, 1985) pointed out the wide variability in findings on the frequency of sibling adaptational problems. For example, Tew and Lawrence (1973) reported a frequency of maladjustment among siblings of children with spina bifida that was 4 times that of siblings of normal control children. Ferrari (1987) reported that well siblings of children with diabetes reported significantly lower self-concept scores compared with matched control children. However, Breslau, Weitzman, and Messenger (1981) found that siblings of children with cystic fibrosis, cerebral palsy, myelodysplasia, and multiple handicaps did not have higher rates of serious mental disorders or greater overall symptomatology than a normative sample; however, they did score higher on interpersonal aggression with peers and within the school system. Dyson (1989) reported no significant differences between siblings of children with disabilities and matched siblings of healthy children in self-concept, behavior problems, and social competence. Finally, some studies indicate that siblings may actually benefit from their experiences with a sibling who is disabled (see McHale & Gamble, 1989). These diverse findings have led to efforts to delineate processes associated with good and poor sibling adjustment.

### Changes in Sibling Adjustment Over Time

In spite of the obvious need for longitudinal studies of how siblings' adjustment changes over time, we could find only one longitudinal study in the literature. Breslau and Prabucki (1987) conducted a 5-year follow-up study of 192 siblings of children with disabilities and a geographically based probability sample of 284 children. The children were aged 6 to 18 years at the initial assessment (Time 1) and 11 to 23 years at follow-up (Time 2). The children with disabilities included those with cystic fibrosis, cerebral palsy, myelodysplasia, or multiple handicaps. Psychological disturbance was assessed at Times 1 and 2 with the mother-completed Psychiatric Screening Inventory. At Time 2, children's psychopathology was assessed with the National Institute of Mental Health Diagnostic Interview Schedule for Children (Costello, Edelbrock, Dulcan, Kalas, & Klaric, 1984), which yields *DSM–III* diagnoses and scores on symptom scales.

The findings indicated that at Time 1, the siblings and control children had comparable rates of severe psychiatric impairment according to mothers' reports: 15% and 11%, respectively. However, similar to the initial report (Breslau et al., 1981), siblings of children with disabilities were reported to have significantly more aggressive behaviors. At the 5-year follow-up, the rate of severe psychiatric impairment rose to 18% for the subgroup of siblings of children with disabilities, which was significantly higher than the rate for the control group, which remained constant at 11%. Over the 5-year period, the siblings showed increases in depressive affect and social isolation compared with the control children, who showed no significant change in these domains.

In terms of the diagnostic interview at Time 2, the rate of major depression was 19.7% in the siblings of children with disabilities, which was not significantly higher than the 17.5% in the control children. However, the siblings scored significantly higher than the control children on the Depression scale. Thus, the siblings' psychiatric functioning had deteriorated, relative to control children, over the 5-year period. Exploratory analysis suggested that mothers' psychological distress might be one of the mechanisms linking chronic stress to children's problems.

Longitudinal research is necessary to inform us about the stability of sibling adjustment and the effects of chronic stress over time and about changes in adjustment as a function of developmental period. Longitudinal research is needed to delineate how illness characteristics, individual parameters including developmental level, and characteristics of family functioning interact to produce high-risk situations for adjustment difficulties. This level of specificity is needed to guide prevention efforts.

### Correlates of Sibling Adjustment

Investigations of the correlates of maladjustment have focused on sibling constellation variables such as gender, birth order, and age spacing (Lobato et al., 1988). In general, closer age spacing is associated with increased risk for sibling adjustment problems, and older sisters and younger brothers, in relation to the child with a disability, show higher rates of behavioral problems as reported by mothers and teachers (Lobato et al., 1988). Well-controlled studies have not shown a one-to-one correspondence between illness or disability and adverse psychological outcome among siblings. This has led to the conceptualization of childhood developmental or medical problems as a risk factor for sibling adjustment, which is mediated by individual and family characteristics (Lobato et al., 1988).

In commenting on this research, Lobato et al. (1988) noted that although there is no direct relationship between the presence of illness and sibling functioning, "this does not preclude the possibility that certain disease and disabilities, with their idiosyncratic sequelae, may create common stresses, complaints, or rewards for siblings" (p. 402). Drotar and Crawford (1985) postulated that sibling adaptation "may depend less upon illness-related stress per se than upon how the family manages communication, problem-solving, and the relationships among physically healthy and ill siblings" (p. 358). In particular, there is a need to understand sibling relationships throughout the life span and the relevance of these relationships to psychological development.

Studies that address potentially mediating processes are beginning to emerge. For example, C. A. Evans, Stevens, Cushway, and Houghton (1992) investigated the effect of sibling knowledge about cancer on their psychological adjustment, as reflected in parent-reported behavior problems and level of social competence. The study included 16 siblings (aged 6 to 16 years) of children diagnosed and treated for cancer 6 to 18 months previously. The findings indicated that the siblings' Behavior Problem and Social Competency scores on the Child Behavior Checklist were within normal limits. Level of sibling knowledge about cancer was related to parent-reported social competence but not to behavior problems.

Although it has been more than a decade since there was recognition of the need to study the contribution of healthy siblings to the adjustment of the child with chronic illness (Simeonsson & McHale, 1981), few studies have addressed this question. Hanson and colleagues evaluated the extent to which sibling relations contributed to the illness-specific and general psychosocial adaptation of youths ($n = 66$) with insulin-dependent diabetes mellitus (Hanson, Henggeler, Harris, et al., 1992). Study inclusion criteria were (a) having both parents in the home, (b) having a child with insulin-dependent diabetes mellitus who is 12 or older, and (c) having a sibling 12 years or older who is within 3 years of the age of the child with insulin-dependent diabetes mellitus. The quality of sibling relations was assessed with the Sibling Relationship Questionnaire, which includes 15 three-item scales that tap four dimensions: warmth and closeness, relative status and power, conflict, and rivalry (Furman & Buhrmester, 1985).

The findings indicated that sibling relations, especially sibling conflict, contributed an independent source of variance beyond that accounted for by demographics, sibling gender and age, and family relations and stress to illness-specific and general psychosocial adaptation of children with insulin-dependent diabetes mellitus. Sibling relations contributed an additional 8% variance to acceptance of illness, 12% to general self-esteem, 11% to internalizing behaviors, and 14% to externalizing behaviors. Sibling conflict contributed to externalizing behaviors, self-esteem, and adjustment to illness. High sibling status and power contributed to internalizing problems in children with insulin-dependent diabetes mellitus, indicating that having an older sibling attenuated internalizing problems. Sibling relations were not associated with metabolic control or adherence. The findings support a social–ecological perspective to child adaptation, with parent–child dyads and sibling dyads being interrelated and independent subsystems, both of which may influence psychosocial functioning of youths.

This type of study is an important step in the progression of research on siblings of children with chronic illness to the stage based on transactional models. Thus, the recognition of the mutual influence on adjustment of children with chronic illness and their parents is now extended to children with chronic illness and their siblings. Parent–child dyads and sibling dyads can be viewed as interrelated subsystems within the family. The unique and combined contribution of each of these subsystems in the adjustment of the child with chronic illness, his or her parents, and his or her siblings can be investigated.

Another important step is direct investigation of the impact of chronic illness on siblings' daily functioning and interactions. McHale and Gamble (1989) maintained that little is known about the daily activities of children who have siblings with disabilities that presumably give rise to emotional or behavioral problems. They addressed these issues in a study of 62 youngsters (aged 8 to 14 years) who had at least one sibling with a disability and their mothers. In half of these families the younger sibling had mental retardation. The findings indicated that children who had a sibling with mental retardation had poorer adjustment than did children with healthy siblings as measured in terms of depression, anxiety, perceived social acceptance, and perceived conflict. Girls who had siblings with disabilities exhibited the lowest global self-esteem. Children in both groups reported that they engaged in approximately five activities per day with their siblings totaling 2.5 to 3 hours. Children who had siblings with disabilities recalled spending about twice as much time in caregiving activities than did those with healthy siblings. There were no group differences in positive or negative sibling interactions. Girls recalled more involvement in household tasks than boys and more frequent negative interactions with their siblings. Boys who had siblings with disabilities provided as much caregiving as did girls with healthy siblings. There were no direct connections between characteristics of the siblings with disabilities and their healthy siblings' well-being. Family process variables, measured in terms of negative interactions with their mothers and siblings, were associated with children's depression, anxiety, and low self-esteem.

**Future Directions**

These findings on sibling adjustment and its correlates have led to a reframing of the question about the effects of chronic illness on the adjustment of physically healthy siblings: "Under what circumstances, and by what processes, does the experience of living with a chronically ill sibling effect various psychological outcomes?" (Droter & Crawford, 1985, p. 360). The next wave of research will involve the application of theoretical and conceptually driven models and longitudinal designs to address this question.

## CONCLUSIONS

The major questions that have been addressed concerning the adjustment of parents and siblings of children with chronic illness are similar to those that have been addressed regarding the adjustment of children with chronic illness themselves: What are the types and frequencies of adjustment problems? What are the correlates of good and poor adjustment? However, the level of research on the adjustment of parents and siblings has lagged behind that of children with chronic illness.

There have been few studies of parental adjustment in which structured diagnostic interviews have been used. For the most part, information about parental adjustment is based on self-reports obtained with questionnaires and inventories. Although multiple methods and informants are now the accepted methods for assessing children's adjustment, including children with chronic illness, there is still a relative absence of these methods in the assessment of the adjustment of siblings. Thus, it can be argued that more appropriate assessment methods need to be applied to the question of adjustment difficulties in parents and siblings of children with chronic illness. However, it can also be argued that this type of question is losing its importance. That is, it is now known that parents and siblings, as well as the children with chronic illness themselves, have increased risks for adjustment difficulties. It is also known that good adaptation and adjustment also are possible. Thus, what is most impressive are individual differences in adjustment. Consequently, the question of interest becomes delineating the processes that are differentially associated with adjustment.

Parent and sibling adjustment also lags behind on this question of the correlates of adjustment. The field is only beginning to benefit from the application of theoretical models to the delineation of parent adjustment. The lag in theoretically driven models involving siblings is even greater.

Research on the correlates of parental and sibling adjustment needs to incorporate a developmental perspective. Longitudinal research is necessary not only to establish the stability of adjustment but also to determine how adjustment varies as a function of developmental stage of family members. There also needs to be a more specific investigation of the variability in adjustment in relation to phase of illness, stage of treatment, or both.

In addition to including longitudinal–developmental perspectives, the search for correlates needs to examine the role of functional behaviors and relationships. For example, the impact of illness needs to be assessed in terms of illness tasks, household tasks, parenting, and family relationships. This focus on daily functioning and interactions and how these vary over time will enable greater specificity in intervention efforts.

Although there is still much to learn about the correlates of adjustment, the knowledge base is sufficient to move to the experimental stage of clinical research (Thompson, Gil, Gustafson, et al., 1994). Intervention studies need to be developed and their effectiveness evaluated. This process will confirm the role of hypothesized mediational processes that have been delineated thus far. For example, the research findings on maternal adjustment suggest that intervention programs should be designed to reduce appraisals of daily stress, decrease the use of palliative coping in relation to adaptive coping methods, increase family supportiveness, and decrease family conflict. In particular, a combination of stress management and family-systems intervention components appear warranted.

The focus on maternal adjustment as a target for intervention studies would appear to be particularly salient. Not only would this serve to alleviate parental stress and foster adjustment, which are important goals in their own right, but improvements in maternal adjustment also would seem to offer the possibility of thereby improving the adjustment of children with chronic illness and their siblings. From the clinical and research perspectives, the stage is set for clinical intervention studies directed at fostering maternal adjustment in the face of the stresses associated with chronic childhood illness.

# II

# DEVELOPMENTAL CHANGES

# INTRODUCTION

# DEVELOPMENTAL CHANGES

Psychologists and other health professionals are recognizing, more than ever, that children's cognitive development plays a role in their knowledge, attitudes, and behaviors related to health and illness, as well as in their psychological adjustment to illness. This section addresses developmental changes as a necessary context for understanding and promoting adjustment to chronic childhood conditions. The impact of chronic childhood illnesses, delineated in section I in terms of our biopsychosocial conceptual framework, is dynamic because it transacts with developmental process; childhood illness affects children's interactions with their social–cological environments.

Developmental changes in children's cognitive processes are thought to impact the child's physical status by influencing preventive and adherence behaviors and to impact the child's psychological adjustment by influencing coping methods. Furthermore, children's cognitive developmental status affects parental expectations and parenting behaviors, which in turn can influence the psychological adjustment of the child. We will argue that efforts to enhance adjustment necessarily will need to vary as a function of children's cognitive–developmental status.

In chapter 7, we will review what is known about developmental changes in conceptualizations of health, illness, pain, and death. In chapter 8, we will review what is known about developmental changes in cognitive process, which may serve to mediate or moderate the stresses associated with chronic conditions. More specifically, we will review studies regarding the emergence and change over time of the cognitive processes of stress appraisal, causal attributions, expectations of self-control, and self-esteem. In chapter 9, we will consider developmental changes in children's methods of coping.

# 7

# DEVELOPMENTAL CHANGES IN CONCEPTUALIZATIONS OF HEALTH, ILLNESS, PAIN, AND DEATH

To provide a context for considering developmental changes in cognitions related to health and illness and to the specific events of pain and death, this chapter begins with an overview of Jean Piaget's theory of cognitive development. We then review studies that address the impact of experiences with health-related matters on conceptual development and of the differential impact, as a function of cognitive development, on children's comprehension of providing information about these experiences. We conclude by discussing the implications of these findings for health care providers and parents in their efforts to allay children's fears and to elicit adherence to medical regimens.

## PIAGET'S THEORY OF COGNITIVE DEVELOPMENT

Piaget's theory of cognitive development has been the most frequently used conceptual framework in psychology, reflecting the influence of biological perspectives regarding the development of adaptive structures (Baldwin, 1967). In biology, *structures* adapt to changed circumstances or environmental demands, and in turn structures modify environmental demands (Baldwin, 1967). In Piagetian theory, *schema*, "a complex concept encompassing both overt motor behavior patterns and internalized thought processes" (Baldwin, 1967, p. 175), is the behavioral parallel of *structure*.

Schemas adapt through the complementary processes of assimilation and accommodation. *Assimilation* is the process whereby physical and social environmental stimuli or challenges are modified to conform to existing schemas (Simeonsson, 1992). *Accommodation* is the process whereby environmental events result in children changing or restructuring their schemas or cognitive frameworks to fit new experiences (Simeonsson, 1992). Assimilation refers to the situation in which the child's schemas are sufficient to handle what is presented; accommodation is the process of changing schemas to handle situations that are initially too difficult to tackle (Baldwin, 1967).

Adapting schemas to environmental demands "involves the active construction of reality in which the child both influences and is influenced by experiences" (Simeonsson, 1992, p. 30). Successive adaption results in qualitatively different stages of reality construction or thought. The sequence of qualitatively different stages is viewed as invariate, but the rate of development, or movement within and across qualitative stages, may vary depending on "genetic endowment as well as the range and intensity of available environmental stimulation" (Simeonsson, 1992, p. 31). Movement from one stage to another requires that the child have opportunities to act on, structure, and restructure reality (Simeonsson, 1992).

Piaget described four main stages of development. The *sensorimotor period* extends from birth to about 2 years of age, during which time the child develops schemas to organize and integrate information from various sensory modalities. Intentional goal-directed behavior emerges during this stage.

The *preoperational period* extends from about 2 to 7 years of age, during which time the child's internal cognitive schemas gradually emerge. Thinking in the preoperational stage is characterized by concreteness, irreversibility, egocentrism, centering, and transducive reasoning (Bibace & Walsh, 1979). *Concreteness* is a preoccupation with external perceptual events, and *centering* is focusing on a part of the event to the exclusion of the whole. *Egocentrism* is viewing the world exclusively from one's own perspective and is manifested in children's difficulty understanding the distinctions between reality and its representation—in other words, their own perceptions—and between the self and the world. Children also have difficulty anticipating how an object will look from another point of view or that another's view of an event may differ from theirs (Baldwin, 1967). *Transducive reasoning* is thinking "that proceeds from one particular to another, rather than from particular to general or vice versa" (Bibace & Walsh, 1979, p. 290).

The *concrete operational period* extends from about 7 to 11 years of age, during which time the child acquires the ability to think logically.

The child in this stage has cognitive schema that reflect an understanding of concepts of time, space, and number. *Decentering* describes the process of developing schemas necessary to move beyond focusing on momentary perceptions to thinking that includes multiple aspects of the situation, temporal elements, and the viewpoint of another person. The child's thinking in the concrete operational period is less egocentric than that of the preoperational child, and the child is able to differentiate between the self and the world. The child is able to conceptualize the reversal of processes—for example, becoming sick and getting well—but is not yet able to accommodate to hypothetical events.

The *formal operational period* occurs in late childhood and is characterized by thinking that reflects an understanding of basic principles of cause and effect. Children demonstrate deductive and inductive thinking and the ability to "engage in hypothetical, abstract, and propositional thinking" (Simeonsson, 1992, p. 31).

## CHILDREN'S UNDERSTANDING OF HEALTH, ILLNESS, AND DEATH

The findings of a review of 11 studies that examined healthy or hospitalized children's illness concepts as a function of cognitive–developmental level indicated that children's concepts of illness do evolve in a systematic and predictable sequence consistent with Piaget's theory of cognitive development (Burbach & Peterson, 1986). However, the variations in understanding, particularly as a function of experiences, have important implications for efforts to foster adherence to medical regimens and emotional adjustment.

### Conceptual Stages Regarding Health and Illness

Bibace and Walsh (1979) have addressed the ways in which children assimilate the particular phenomena of health and illness to their general schema. In a pilot study ($N = 180$) of children age 3 to 13 years and a subsequent study ($N = 72$) of children ages 4, 7, and 11, Bibace and Walsh assessed children's conceptualizations about health and illness. The protocol included 12 sets of questions, including "What happens to people when they are sick?" and "Where does a cold come from?"

The findings indicated that children's responses could be classified in terms of Piaget's three broad categories of cognitive development. Furthermore, the children's responses could be differentiated into two subcategories within each stage: phenomenism and contagion within the preoperational stage; contamination and internalization within the concrete operational stage; and physiological and psychophysiological within the formal operational stage. Table 7.1 presents the findings from this study and shows the conceptual stages of thinking regarding health and illness demonstrated by percentages of children within each age group.

As expected, the type of explanation varied as a function of the children's developmental status. Within the preoperational period, at the *phenomenism level*, children defined illness in terms of sensory phenomena that the child, through experience, associated with an illness. These children articulated the causal link between the external source of illness and the body only in terms of magic or co-occurrence. Centering and egocentrism characteristic of the preoperational period were evident. Children's thinking at the *contagion level* reflected a restructuring of vulnerability. The child described the source of illness as located spatially near to the body and temporally prior to the illness.

Within the concrete operational period, at the *contamination level*, children located the source of illness as external to the body and the causal link in concretized terms of germs, dirt, or bad behavior transmitted through contact or participation in activities. Children at this stage often conceptualized cures as involving medicines that are rubbed on the surface of the body. The child perceived some control over cause and cure by avoiding or engaging in contact with objects or specific behaviors. At the *internalization level*, children described external causes or cures through processes such as swallowing or inhaling, which were seen as directly affecting internal organs. Children began to appreciate the healing power of the body. Within the period of concrete operations, children demonstrated the schema for reversibility: People who are sick can become well, and those who are well can become sick.

TABLE 7.1
Percentage of Children by Age Demonstrating Conceptual Stages of
Illness Explanation

| Conceptual Stage | Age (years) | | |
| --- | --- | --- | --- |
| | 4 | 7 | 11 |
| Preoperational | | | |
| Phenomenism | 12.5 | — | — |
| Contagion | 70.8 | 16.7 | — |
| Concrete operational | | | |
| Contamination | 16.7 | 75.0 | — |
| Internalization | — | 8.3 | 25.0 |
| Formal operational | | | |
| Physiological | — | — | 70.8 |
| Psychophysiological | — | — | 4.2 |

*Note.* From Bibace and Walsh (1979). Adapted with permission.

Within the formal operational period, at the *physiological level*, children defined illness in terms of internal body organs and functions that are not visible. They perceived multiple efficient and final causes and cures, and there was an increasing sense that personal actions can influence illness and recovery. Children demonstrated thinking at the *psychophysiological level* when they became able to differentiate between the physical and psychological domains within the self and were aware that thoughts or feelings can affect how the body functions. Bibace and Walsh (1979) noted that "psychological causes appear to be invoked earlier than psychological cures" (p. 296).

Other studies also have demonstrated that there is a systematic progression of children's understanding of illness and health that corresponds to Piaget's framework of cognitive development. In a study ($N = 128$) of healthy children from kindergarten, second, fourth, sixth, and eighth grades, E. C. Perrin and Gerrity (1981) demonstrated that the growth of children's conceptualizations of illness paralleled, but lagged behind, conceptual development of physical causality. The finding of variability of levels of conceptual thinking within the health and illness content areas was of particular importance. For example, the concept of preventing illness was especially difficult for children to understand.

The relationship between age, illness conception, and accuracy of children's understanding about their illness was addressed in a study ($N = 54$) of children 6 to 17 years of age with juvenile arthritis (Berry, Hayford, Ross, Pachman, Lavigne, 1993). They assessed conceptions of illness in terms of the categories developed by Bibace and Walsh (1979). Although there was a developmental progression in children's understanding, most subjects answered questions at the concrete operational stage of development. The 7- to 10-year-olds rarely demonstrated a formal operational understanding of their illness, and 22% to 28% demonstrated prelogical levels of understanding. A proportionately greater number of older children and adolescents demonstrated an understanding at the formal operational level. Cognitive development was a better predictor of understanding than was age. However, across questions, children demonstrated variability in their level of understanding. Misconceptions and inaccuracies in the children's descriptions were striking.

The lag between conceptualizations of health and general conceptual development has been found in other studies. For example, in a study ($N = 60$) of hospitalized children, only 6% of 7- and 9-year-olds demonstrated an understanding of illness in terms of generalized, relative, or abstract notions (Simeonsson, Buckley, & Monson, 1979).

Specific to children's conceptualizations of health and illness is the extent to which young children consider illness a punishment for misbehavior. The belief that negative consequences automatically result from misbehavior is an example of *immanent justice*. A number of studies have provided evidence for such misconceptions, but recent work in cognitive development using different methodologies reveals relatively little acceptance of immanent justice among young children (Springer & Ruckel, 1992). For example, a study of 17 preschoolers (4- to 5-year-olds) with cancer and 17 healthy preschoolers (Springer, 1994) demonstrated that most preschoolers rejected the possibility that misbehavior will cause illness. Most of the preschoolers, both those who were healthy and those with cancer, believed that contamination causes illness.

Children 9 to 13 years old were found to be able to discriminate between medical disorders, which were seen as caused by physically based factors, and psychological disorders, which were seen as caused by environmental factors (such as too much television) (Roberts, Beidleman, & Wurtele, 1981). Physical problems were viewed as curable by medical personnel and treatable by mental health professionals, but psychological problems were viewed as best handled by teachers and ministers and not mental health professionals (Roberts et al., 1981).

## Conceptualizations of Pain

Pain is both a normative experience of everyday life and an integral component of illness and health care. Pain management is one of the major tasks associated with chronic illness. The International Association for the Study of Pain has defined pain as an unpleasant sensory and emotional experience associated with actual or potential tissue damage (Schechter, Berde, & Yaster, 1993). This definition reflects that pain has at least two major components: *nociception*, a sensory component, and the response to nociception (P. J. McGrath et al., 1990). Pain "is always a complex matrix of biologic, psychologic, and social interactions" (P. J. McGrath & McAlpine, 1993, p. s.2).

Over the past several decades, the view of the nociceptive system as a passive relay mechanism has changed to one of an active integrative mechanism that has considerable plasticity as reflected in different responses to equal amounts of tissue damage (P. A. McGrath, 1993). Children's pain perceptions are the result of complex neural interactions that reflect the impact of interpersonal and sociocultural factors. Pain is both an abstract concept and a concrete experience (Harbeck & Peterson, 1992). Thus, children's perceptions and understanding of pain, and their ability to communicate about it, depend on their levels of development as well as on their frames of reference formed through previous pain experiences (P. A. McGrath, 1993).

*Types and Categories of Pediatric Pain*

There are three types of pain: acute, chronic, and recurrent. *Acute pain* is a warning signal that directs attention to an injured part and stimulates escape or avoidance, for example, pain from touching a hot stove. Acute pain has adaptive value and is rarely seen as psychogenic. In a similar way, from a disease perspective, acute pain signals the need for diagnosing the underlying pathological process that is causing the pain (Varni, Katz, & Dash, 1982). The experience of acute pain can be seen as made up of two components: the sensation and the reaction to the sensation (Varni et al., 1982). An anxious or fearful response to the pain sensation often intensifies the reaction to it.

*Chronic pain* is associated with a constellation of reactive features such as compensatory posturing, depressed mood, and inactivity or restrictions in daily activities. These chronic pain behaviors may be reinforced by socioenvironmental influences and can be maintained independently of the original nociceptive component (Varni et al., 1982). In contrast to acute pain, chronic pain is not conceptualized in terms of adaptive value (Bush & Harkins, 1991). In addition, the anxious or fearful reaction is lacking or greatly diminished (Varni et al., 1982). Whereas chronic pain does not have the adaptive value of acute pain, it can be associated with secondary gain by eliciting nurturance and attention from others or providing a basis for avoiding challenging or threatening expectations or responsibilities.

*Recurrent pain* contains elements of both acute and chronic pain. Repetitive painful episodes alternate with pain-free periods. Recurrent pain is associated with chronic illness in terms of recurrent medical procedures and disease processes that give rise to episodes of pain, such as with arthritis, hemophilia, and sickle-cell disease.

Varni and colleagues (1982) have delineated four categories of pediatric pain:

1. observable physical injury or trauma, such as burns, laceration, and fractures;
2. disease states, such as hemophilia, arthritis, and sickle-cell disease;
3. medical or dental procedures, such as injections, lumbar punctures, and bone marrow aspirations;
4. idiopathic, that is, unknown etiology, such as recurrent abdominal pain or headache.

Because pain is a frequent concomitant of children's health care, it is essential that effective pain-management strategies be developed. However, the scientific study of children's pain has lagged behind the study of adults' pain. This lag has been attributed to a number of erroneous assumptions about children's pain that have persisted in spite of evidence to the contrary (Ross & Ross, 1984). For example, infants were thought not to experience pain at all, and children were believed to be less sensitive to pain than adults and to lack memory of pain. Because of the dearth of study, little is known about the prevalence of pain and the biological and psychosocial processes that contribute to individual differences in children's responses to pain. Lack of knowledge, erroneous beliefs, and the concern that use of potent analgesics will lead to addiction, have resulted in undertreatment of children's pain. The report of the Consensus Conference on the Management of Pain in Childhood Cancer (Schechter, Altman, & Weisman, 1990) indicates that there is no basis for the concerns about physical dependency and addiction with opioid administration. Physical dependence is common in patients receiving opioids for pain, but it can be handled through gradual tapering (Berde et al., 1990). Addiction is a behavioral/psychological syndrome and is not caused by the administration of opioids (Berde et al., 1990).

Research in the past few years has begun to address critical questions regarding children's pain, such as what and how children learn about pain and the source of their learning (P. J. McGrath & McAlpine, 1993). It is now recognized that a developmental perspective to the issue of children's pain is necessary in terms of children's cognitive development and the extent to which children's conceptualizations of pain are influenced by their families (Harbeck & Peterson, 1992).

*Stages of Children's Conceptualization of Pain*

In considering children's pain, Gaffney (1993) advocated caution: "The conceptualization of pain should not be equated with the experience of pain; conceptualization refers to children's ability to objectify and express elements of their experience. . . ." (p. 81). From a developmental perspective, understanding of children's experience of pain is influenced by children's changing abilities to communicate and understand cause–effect relationships. Psychologists and physicians now recognize that children who are 18 months of age can express and localize pain and recognize it in another individual. By 3 years of age, children can give a gross indication of pain intensity (P. J. McGrath & McAlpine, 1993).

Since children's concepts of illness have been found to develop in a systematic way consonant with Piaget's theory of cognitive development, many have hypothesized that children's understanding of pain is also likely to progress through a similar sequence. However, the evidence is equivocal. Ross and Ross (1984) did not find evidence of clearly defined age trends (or gender differences) in the understanding of pain in their large sample ($N = 994$) of children between the ages of 5 and 12 years old. In contrast,

Gaffney and Dunne (1986) examined definitions of pain used by 680 Irish schoolchildren aged 5 to 15 years old and found developmental patterns consistent with Piagetian theory. Gaffney and Dunne formed three age groups that correspond to the preoperational (5 to 7 years), concrete operational (8 to 10 years), and formal operational (11 to 14 years) stages of cognitive development, and they analyzed differences in responses to 10 sentence-completion items. Definition of pain shifted with increasing age from perceptually dominated to more abstract and psychologically oriented responses. The mention of objective physical and psychological causes of pain increased with age, which reflected "an increasing understanding with age of the biological purpose of pain and its causal relationship with illness and trauma, and a developing awareness of the more abstract psychological and psychosocial aspects of pain" (Gaffney & Dunne, 1986, p. 113). The gradual emergence of more advanced understanding is reflected in the finding of the coexistence of both less and more sophisticated definitions. It is also important to note that 44% of subjects cited one or more elements of transgression or self-causality (Gaffney & Dunne, 1987). (With this in mind, it is interesting to note that the word *pain* derives from the Latin *poena*, which means *punishment*.)

Based on these findings, Gaffney (1993) summarized ways of thinking about pain typical of cognitive stages. During the preoperational stage, pain is understood as a physical entity that is unpleasant and aversive. Children in this stage are more familiar with words such as *hurt* and *sore* than with *pain*. Children are unaware of the relationship between pain and negative affect. Some children may attribute pain to punishment for transgressions. Perceptual cues dominate children's thinking, and their concept of internal pain is limited. "Up to about six years of age, children's descriptions of pain appear to be limited to simple sensory aspects" (Gaffney, 1993, p. 82). Their attitude toward pain is passive, and they perceive a lack of control. Children in this stage are aware only of concrete, passive methods of pain relief, such as tablets, medicine, or food, and to cope with pain they tend to rely on parental support. Diverting the children's attention and enabling the presence of parents are likely to be useful in managing pain of children at this stage.

During the concrete operational stage, children's understanding of pain broadens to include an awareness of the negative affect associated with pain, as well as the physical. Toward the end of this stage, children develop an awareness of the quantitative and qualitative variability of pain, the uncertainty of duration, and the unpredictability of pain onset. "A more active attitude toward pain, as something you feel rather than something you have, develops" (Gaffney, 1993, p. 83). Attributions of self-causality may still exist in combination with more objective explanations. Pain is understood to occur within the body, and localization is more differentiated. Effective coping methods are also more active and include physical activity, such as exercise, and cognitive strategies, such as talking with friends.

During the period of formal operational thinking, children's conceptualizations of pain reflect the capacities for abstraction and introspection. They view pain as involving physical and mental suffering and recognize the utility of pain as a warning signal. There is a decreased emphasis on the physical aspects of pain and an increasing emphasis on the psychological aspects, which expand to include psychosocial factors such as the impact of pain on relationships. Children recognize the subjectivity of pain, and that their anxiety about the significance of pain in terms of future disability may exacerbate the experience of pain. At the formal operational stage, cognitive–behavioral strategies to manage pain can be used.

Harbeck and Peterson (1992) sought to create an empirically derived developmental continuum of children's understanding of pain. In a study of children and young adults 3 to 23 years of age, subjects were interviewed about three different sources of pain: an injury (skinned knee), a medical procedure (injection), and an illness (headache). Subjects were asked to describe each pain, tell why the pain hurt, and state the value of the pain. Their answers were categorized and ordered developmentally by experts in pediatric pain. The researchers formed five age subgroups: (a) preschool (ages 3 to 4), (b) first grade (ages 6 to 7), (c) third grade (ages 8 to 10), (d) sixth grade (ages 11 to 12), and (e) college freshmen (ages 18 to 23).

There were no gender effects. Also, there were no significant differences in the relationship of variables with age and the relationship of variables with developmental level, so age was used as the index of developmental level. Age probably captured both cognitive–development level and experience with pain, both in terms of types and frequency.

Across the three questions, age differences varied by type of pain, indicating that pain understanding does not develop as a unitary construct. Rather, "understanding of different aspects of pain occurs at different age levels" (Harbeck & Peterson, 1992, p. 147). With increasing age, pain descriptions became more complex, and understanding of the value of pain increased. Understanding of why pain hurts—that is, pain causality—also followed a developmental progression from inability to verbalize a reason, to verbalizing a general external cause, to including physiological or psychological causes. The percentage of children reporting no pain value decreased from 91% of preschoolers, to 45% of sixth graders, to 25% of college-aged young adults. Type of pain affected ratings of pain value. Most children best understood the value of an injection and least understood the value of a headache. The relationship of children's reports of the pain their parents experience and their own pain was moderately strong and attests to the importance of studying contextual aspects of pain.

**Conceptualizations of Death**

Developing conceptualizations about death has been shown to follow the Piagetian conceptual framework also. In a study of children ($N = 75$) from 6 to 15 years of age (Koocher, 1973), children at the concrete and formal operational periods differed significantly from those at the preoperational period in response to the question "What makes things die?" Those at the concrete and formal operational period provided significantly more abstract and generalized reasons that reflected a view of death as a consequence of natural processes, physical deterioration, and accidents. One hundred percent of the children in the formal operational stage gave an abstract or generalized reason compared to 66% of the children in the concrete operational stage and only 17% of the preoperational group. Forty percent (8 of 20) of the children at the preoperational level thought that a revival of dead things was possible.

In a study ($N = 42$) of children from 6 to 12 years of age, Cotton and Range (1990) examined four components of death concepts as a function of age, cognitive functioning, experience, and affect: (a) irreversibility; (b) finality or cessation of function of all bodily functions; (c) inevitability of death for all living things, including oneself; and (d) causality. The findings indicated that conservation ability, as a marker of cognitive development, was related more strongly to accurate death concepts than was age. However, past experience with death was correlated negatively with accurate death concepts, particularly with the components of causality and inevitability. Feelings of hopelessness were not significantly related to accuracy of death concepts, but fear of death interfered with the child's developing an understanding of death, particularly with the subcomponent of finality. One implication of these findings is that previous experience with death of a loved one does not ensure accurate understanding of death concepts and again signals the need to match explanations to the child's cognitive–developmental level.

## IMPACT OF EXPERIENCE ON CONCEPTUAL DEVELOPMENT

The variability of cognitive development within age groups points to the fallacy of equating stage of cognitive development with age (Bibace & Walsh, 1979) and the corresponding necessity of determining stage of cognitive development, and it also prompts research on how cognitive development varies as a function of experience. In addition to delineating the developmental progression in children's conceptions of health and illness, a few studies have addressed the premise of Piagetian theory that cognitive development varies as a function of experience. E. C. Perrin and Gerrity (1981) maintain the following:

> The finding that children hold relatively less sophisticated notions about illness as compared to their notions about phenomenon of the physical world is consistent with Piaget's observation that development proceeds at variable rates dependent on both the child's experience with the phenomenon and the affect connected with it. (p. 848)

Several researchers have investigated whether extensive contact with illness, such as that experienced by children with chronic illness, results in a more sophisticated understanding of the related concepts, or whether the heightened affect as a consequence of these experiences interferes with cognitive development. A review of studies that have addressed the question of the impact of illness or hospitalizations on children's illness concepts presented mixed findings. Children who experienced hospitalization demonstrated less, equally, and more mature illness concepts (Burbach & Peterson, 1986) compared with those who had not been hospitalized.

Several studies have compared the development of children's understanding of their own illness with their understanding of illness in general and other phenomena. The findings are mixed. In terms of the categories developed by Bibace and Walsh (1980), children with spina bifida ($N = 40$) developed conceptualizations of health and illness that followed a similar developmental sequence as that of their general cognitive development (Feldman & Varni, 1985). However, the findings did not support the predictions that the stresses of dealing with a chronic condition would result in lower levels of conceptual development regarding health and illness. The children's mean scores on health and illness concepts were generally higher for spina bifida than for health and illness in general, which were also higher than those for general cognitive development. The researchers suggested that the relative differences in sophistication of understanding reflected the impact of restricting experience with the environment that is associated with spina bifida and a desensitization to stress through repeated exposure to illness and medically related procedures.

In contrast, children's ($N = 50$) conceptualization of seizures was found to parallel, but consistently lag behind, their conceptualization of physical causality, general illness causality, and brain functioning (Sanger, Perrin, & Sandler, 1993). Only 40% of children in Grades 3 through 5 and 36% of children in Grades 6 through 8 reported the brain as the locus of dysfunction. Two themes were evident in causal explanations of seizures. One theme was to infer the cause of the seizures to the time when they occurred—for example, attributing the cause to too much exercise or overexcitement. The second theme was to portray convulsions as the body's way of releasing built-up energy.

Children's ($N = 30$) concepts of hospitals, medical personnel, and operations, as well as illness, also have been found to be related to their level of cognitive development (Redpath & Rogers, 1984). In addition, previous hospitalization experience improved the hospital concepts of second-grade students but not of preschoolers.

Beales, Keen, and Holt (1983) have addressed the role of affective impact in children's understanding of illness. In a study of children ($N = 39$) with juvenile chronic arthritis, children 6 to 11 years of age reported lower levels of pain than children 12 to 17 years of age. The differences were not attributable to differences in pain thresholds, as reported by parents. The "affective coloring" of the sensations varied between the age groups, and it was this affective component that was thought to account for greater severity in pain reported by older children. "The more the child associates internally originating sensations with internal pathology and serious consequences for activities and ambitions, the more likely he might be therefore to experience the sensations as 'unpleasant' in their own right, i.e., as constituting pain" (p. 61). Although the researchers did not directly assess the stage of cognitive development, they hypothesized that the closer the child comes to an adult's appreciation of the significance and implications of sensations occurring in his or her joints, the more the level of pain experienced is similar to that reported by adult patients. The children who were 6 to 11 years of age did not perceive the sensations from their affected joints as representing any particular pathology. However, the children who were 12 to 17 years of age unanimously reported that the sensations they experienced were associated with the unpleasant implications of their arthritis in terms of increasing or continued pathology or limitations on activities.

Studies are beginning to address other factors, in addition to experience and affective impact, which also may influence the development of conceptualizations regarding health and illness. In a study ($N = 264$) of children 6 to 12 years of age who were short-term ($Mdn = 5$ days) patients in a pediatric hospital, children's conceptualizations of illness were compared to their mother's conceptualizations (J. D. Campbell, 1975). The findings indicated that children and their mothers had similar themes but mothers' explanations had greater definitional sophistication. Older children's patterns were more similar to their mothers' than were those of younger children. Older children moved away from definitions based on feelings to more precision and recognition of role performance and psychosocial dispositions. However, there was not a great degree of agreement of children's explanations with those of their mothers either at the level of specific thematic content or in terms of conceptual sophistication. Age-linked intellectual development and health experiences, as moderated by age, affected conceptual sophistication, indicating that children profited from experience, but the extent to which they profited varied as a function of their level of development. The study showed a link between hospital experiences and the children's level of emotionality, but there was no indication of concomitant disruption of conceptual sophistication by level of emotionality.

## IMPACT OF INFORMATION AS A FUNCTION OF COGNITIVE DEVELOPMENT

In a study ($N = 112$) of children in first, third, and fourth grades, Potter and Roberts (1984) demonstrated that the type of illness information and cognitive stage of the child affected children's comprehension of the illness and perceptions of vulnerability to the illness, but not perceptions of illness severity. Children in both the preoperational and concrete operational stages of cognitive development were found to be capable of increased understanding of illness when information was provided. However, children in the concrete operational stage comprehended and retained more specific information than the children in the preoperational stage. Regardless of their cognitive maturity, children receiving explanations of the illness demonstrated more comprehension than did children receiving only descriptions of symptoms. Both those who were less informed and those less cognitively mature perceived themselves as more vulnerable to the illness.

## CONCLUSION

The relationship between cognitive level and perceptions of control are critical regarding the efforts of health care providers and parents to allay children's fears and to elicit adherence to medical regimens. The degree of personal control that children perceive regarding their illness is related directly to their cognitive–developmental status (Bibace & Walsh, 1980). Bibace and Walsh (1979) emphasized that "the child's conceptions of health and illness are correlated with marked differences in degree of personal control over the cause and alleviation of illness" (p. 298). Important in this regard is that children at the phenomenistic level of thinking experience vulnerability to events that are remote in time or space. At the contagion level, the vulnerability is limited to events that are near the body, and limited further at the contamination stage to events at the surface of the body. Greater control is appreciated in terms of avoiding contact with the contaminated world or by applying medicines. It is only at the internalizing level of thinking that children believe that they can maintain health through their behavior—for example, through their eating habits.

Recognizing the multiplicity of causes and cures characteristic of the physiological and psychophysiological levels make it possible to recognize the multiple ways the person can influence health and illness.

Determining the child's level of conceptualization can help health care providers and parents to understand, and deal more effectively with, what might appear to be irrational fears. That is, rather than dismissing the child's fears, health care providers could determine that these fears are normal for a particular stage of cognitive development and address them by providing explanations that are consistent with the child's level of understanding (Bibace & Walsh, 1980). In interpreting illness phenomena and treatments to children and in eliciting their adherence, caregivers must explain the illness in ways appropriate to the child's level of conceptual understanding. In particular, it is important to avoid explanations that may have an unintended secondary meaning that would evoke fear and to provide concrete, perceptually based reference or metaphors appropriate to the stage of the child's cognitive development to describe symptoms, underlying processes, and interventions (Whitt, Dykstra, & Taylor, 1979).

# 8

# DEVELOPMENTAL CHANGES IN COGNITIVE PROCESSES

This chapter addresses developmental changes in cognitive processes identified through the biopsychosocial framework that may serve to mediate and/or moderate the relationship between the stress of chronic childhood illness and adjustment. We will review the nature of stress, the cognitive theory of stress, and major related themes, as derived from the literature on adult studies. Then we will address the development of children's conceptualization of stress in terms of Piagetian stages of cognitive development. We will continue by considering the applicability of major findings from the adult literature to children and adolescents. We will seek to determine whether children's perceptions of the stressfulness of daily and major events are associated with adjustment and whether there is a reciprocal relationship between stress, social support, and distress in general and in terms of vulnerability engendered by developmental transitions in particular.

We will then address developmental changes in two other cognitive processes—perceptions of control and causal attributions—and review the evidence regarding control as a moderator of the stress–adjustment relationship and the applicability of the goodness-of-fit concept with children. We will consider the findings regarding the effects of experience with chronic illness on children's perceptions of control and discuss the findings regarding the role of causal attributions in adjustment and the implications in terms of intervention efforts to rectify children's maladaptive attributional styles.

We will conclude by considering self-concept as another cognitive process of potential importance to adjustment. We will address changes in the content and structure of the self-concept with development, the association of self-concept with performance, and the implications of efforts to enhance children's sense of self-worth.

## STRESS

The literature on adult stress is extensive and yields conceptualizations and findings that serve to guide research on children's stress. From this literature we understand many issues. Stress involves both biological reactions to stimuli as well as subjective experiences. *Potentially stressful situations* are those that give rise to demand characteristics to respond or adapt. Current conceptualizations of psychological stress illustrate that stress is not an inherent characteristic of an event or a situation but rather arises out of the transactions of individuals with their environments (Lazarus & Folkman, 1984). There are both situational and individual characteristics that influence stress. The demands on an individual vary with the stage of the event and the adequacy of the resources available to deal with it. Potentially stressful situations also vary in duration or chronicity from daily hassles, to acute events, to chronic situations such as illness. The ways in which individuals think about and respond to situations shape their subjective experiences. In particular, researchers have focused on the role of cognitive processes of appraisal, expectations of control, and causal attributions in influencing the perceived stressfulness of events. "Both theory and data imply that the potential for an external event to generate affect is a function of the cognitive interpretation imposed by the person" (Kagan, 1983, p. 212). Researchers also have focused on the role of these cognitive processes in influencing a person's response to events—that is, on their methods of coping. There is a strong association between level of stress and psychological distress or adjustment. Social support serves to moderate the relationship between stress and adjustment. Psychological distress varies as a function of the goodness of fit between cognitive appraisal, particularly with regard to controllability and to coping methods (Lazarus & Folkman, 1984).

### Cognitive Theory of Stress

In the transactional view of stress, developed by Lazarus and Folkman (1984), stress is not a property of the person or of the environment. Stress is not a stimulus or a response but instead arises out of the transaction—that is, bidirectional interaction—between the individuals and their environments. Because individuals are active participants in these transactions and not passive recipients, the ways in which individuals think about the situation and themselves will influence their responses and subjective experiences. The ways in which people think about a situation constitute cognitive processes that include appraisals or judgments, expectations or beliefs, and attributions of meaning and cause. Each of these cognitive processes have been shown to have a role in influencing the stressfulness of a situation, methods of coping with the situation, and psychological adjustment to the situation.

One class of cognitive processes are appraisals or judgments about the significance or the meaning of the event to the individual. Lazarus and Folkman (1984) distinguished two types of appraisals⁻ that converge to shape the meaning of an encounter: primary appraisal and secondary appraisal.

*Primary appraisal* involves evaluating the significance of a transaction with respect to personal well-being. People can appraise transactions as irrelevant, benign–positive, or stressful. Folkman (1984) postulated three types of stressful appraisals. *Harm/loss* refers to damage already done. *Threat* refers to a potential for harm or loss. *Challenge* refers to an opportunity for gain, growth, or mastery. Appraisals of harm/loss and threat are associated with negative emotions, whereas appraisals of challenge are associated with positive emotions such as excitement (Folkman, 1984).

Personal factors and situational factors influence appraisals. Included among the personal factors are other cognitive processes such as expectations and commitments (Folkman, 1984). *Expectations* are beliefs that can influence the ways in which people view situations. Religious beliefs and beliefs about control are expectations that have received considerable attention. *Commitments* range from values and ideals to specific goals, and they define what is important to the person and thus what is at stake in a specific transaction (Folkman, 1984).

*Secondary appraisal* involves evaluating coping resources and options with respect to the demands of the situation. Coping resources include physical, social, psychological, and material assets (Folkman, 1984). Secondary appraisal includes judgment regarding control and efficacy. Appraisals of control involve evaluating the degree to which the outcome of an event or transaction is under one's control, some other person's control, or is a matter of chance (Rotter, 1966). If a situation is perceived to be under one's own control, then appraisals are made of personal efficacy—that is, whether one perceives that one can execute successfully the strategy required to produce the desired outcome (Bandura, 1977).

The processes of appraisals of control and efficacy are related to broader cognitive processes involving both generalized and situational-specific expectations and attributions that, although related to appraisal of stress, need to be considered on their own. Subsequent sections will address changes in these cognitive processes with cognitive development.

Five specific questions are being addressed within the literature on children's stress: (a) Do children's conceptualizations of stress vary as a function of cognitive development? (b) What is the relationship between children's stress and adjustment? (c) Does social support moderate the relationship between stress and children's adjustment? (d) Are developmental transitions periods of increased vulnerability to stress? and (e) Does the goodness-of-fit relationship between cognitive processes and coping methods apply to children?

## Conceptualizations of Stress

The findings that the degree of stressfulness of a situation is related to the cognitive processes of appraisals, expectations, and attributions makes it possible to recognize that children's experience of stress is likely to be different as a function of their level of cognitive development. More specifically, researchers have focused on evolving conceptualizations of stress related to the changes in sensitivity to potentially stressful situations associated with the various stages of cognitive development.

> The emphasis on the child's interpretation of events that might be potential stressors implies that there should be, across developmental stages, differential receptivity to specific events because of the lawful changes in cognitive function that occur over the first dozen years of life. (Kagan, 1983, p. 209)

During the first year of life, infants show increasing sensitivity to events that conflict with existing schema. Their inability to resolve discrepancies leads to distress. For example, because of enhanced cognitive ability, the infant becomes vulnerable to the stresses of separation from the caretaker and exposure to unfamiliar adults (Kagan, 1983).

By the end of the second year, children develop an appreciation of right and wrong. Two- and 3-year-old children show awareness of themselves as agents who can affect others and who can empathize (Kagan, 1983). In this way, children become vulnerable to distress that follows their violations of standards. By 4 years of age, this distress can constitute guilt (Kagan, 1983).

Five- to 7-year-old children can evaluate their competencies in comparison with that of others on culturally valued qualities (Kagan, 1983). Furthermore, with advancing age, children make increasing use of social comparison and reaction of others in evaluating themselves. These comparisons and peer reactions give rise to another source of subjective stress.

At the stage of formal operational thinking, adolescents acquire the ability to deal with hypothetical premises, which can subject them to new vulnerabilities. Along with increases in problem-solving capabilities, there is more awareness of possible risks that can be foreseen but perhaps not protected against.

During late childhood and early adolescence, youngsters' self-concepts are progressively defined in terms of aspirations, ideals, and competencies, and these commitments make them vulnerable to stress. "Failure in an uninvested area is not especially distressing; failure in an activity which has become part of one's self-definition is" (Maccoby, 1983, p. 226).

This dovetailing of increasing capabilities and competencies and increasing vulnerabilities to stress has been captured well by Maccoby (1983).

> We cannot be upset by events whose power to harm we do not understand; we cannot be humiliated by failure to handle problems whose solutions are someone else's responsibility; we cannot be distressed by anticipating others' contemptuous or critical reactions to our weaknesses if we are not aware of others' probable reactions and if our egos are not yet invested in appearing strong and competent. (p. 219)

In an effort to address the lack of an operational definition of stress from the child's perspective, C. E. Lewis, Siegel, and Lewis (1984) asked fifth- and sixth-grade children to generate a response to the question "What happens that makes you feel bad, nervous or worry?" They then administered the resulting list of 20 items to more than 2,400 fifth graders. Factor analysis of frequency and intensity ratings revealed three dimensions: (a) anxieties surrounding conflict with parents, (b) self-image and peer-group relationships, and (c) geographic mobility. Only 5 of 20 items reflected discrete events, whereas 15 items reflected chronic role strains such as being pressured to get good grades. Although girls and boys differed in the magnitude of ratings and there were some racial differences, the rank order of ratings were highly correlated. These data suggest that "the principal sources of children's distress are more often problems of an enduring nature" (p. 120) and that "the life events approach may not be the most appropriate way to study distress in children" (p. 120).

Through a series of studies, Compas and colleagues endeavored to delineate the types of life events that children and adolescents 12 to 20 years of age experience as stressful and the mechanisms through which life events impact individuals. They focused on delineating the contribution of the objective characteristics of events and subjective appraisals of stress.

Compas, Davis, and Forsythe (1985) found the valence or desirability of events varied as a function of age, gender, and cognitive appraisal processes. The children reported daily events as negative more frequently than they did major events, and the number of daily events reported increased with age. Girls reported more negative than positive daily events, whereas boys reported more positive than negative daily events. Early adolescent males (ages 12 to 14) and older adolescent females (age 18 to 20) reported positive and negative daily events with equal frequency.

Overall, these children and adolescents were not plagued by expected aversive experiences. They perceived their recent past and their immediate future to be characterized by positive experiences. The higher frequency of negative than positive events reported by early- and middle-adolescent females (12 to 18 years of age) suggest that they may be more vulnerable to adverse consequences of events during this period. In addition to positive or negative valence, the researchers also investigated perceptions of type of event (daily or major) and domain or content (Compas, Davis, & Forsythe, 1985). In contrast to perceptions of valence, the findings suggested that perceptions of type and content were not inherent or objective characteristics within an event.

Researchers also have assessed the changes in the nature of cognitive appraisals of major and daily stressful events during adolescence (Compas, Davis, Forsythe, & Wagner, 1987; Davis & Compas, 1986). The studies found cognitive complexity of stress appraisal ($N = 36$) to increase from early- (12 to 14 years of age) to middle- (15 to 17 years of age) and late- (18 to 20 years of age) adolescence. Early adolescents distinguished events on the basis of the single dimension of desirability. It was not until middle- and late-adolescence that children made judgments based on the dimensions of the amount of *impact* the event would have on their lives and the *generality* of cause of the event—that is, the degree to which the cause of an event precipitates other events, as well as the event's desirability.

The literature on adults indicates that daily stress accounts for approximately twice as much of the variance in psychological distress as do major events (Wagner, Compas, & Howell, 1988). However, the relationship between major events and daily events is not clear. Major events could serve to make daily events more stressful, or major events—such as divorce or death of a loved one—could have their effect through daily hassles.

A study addressed the relative contribution of daily stress and major stressful life events to psychological adjustment of children and young adolescents ($N = 211$) from 10 to 14 years of age ($M = 12.01$ years) (Compas, Howell, Phares, Williams, & Ledoux, 1989). The findings indicated that the relationship between major life events and psychological distress was mediated by the level of daily stress. These findings extended those of a study ($N = 58$) of older adolescents (17.5 to 18.8 years old) who were making the transition from high school to college (Wagner et al., 1988) in showing a general lack of a significant independent relationship between the stress of major events and psychological distress, but a significant relationship between major events and daily stress, which in turn was significantly associated with psychological symptoms. In other words, the effects of major life events on psychological distress were mediated by negative daily events. However, major events also have a role: "to an important extent, the daily stress that leads to symptoms is caused by major events" (Wagner et al., 1988, p. 201). Daily events, then, are simultaneously dependent and independent variables.

## Relationship Between Children's Stress and Adjustment

The literature on adult stress has established a strong relationship between the stress of major life events, chronic stress, and daily stress and poor psychological adjustment. There has been a corresponding effort to determine whether these relationships also pertain to children.

A study ($N = 159$) of children 6 to 9 years of age ($M = 96.4$ months) and their mothers through a health maintenance organization demonstrated a relationship between children's stress and adjustment as reported by mothers (Wertlieb, Weigel, & Feldstein, 1987). The study revealed a relationship between children's undesirable life events and the intensity of daily hassles. The higher the stress, the more behavior symptoms reported. There was also a significant main effect for social support. The less the social support, the greater the behavior problems.

It has been well established that children's psychological dysfunction is related to their parents'—particularly their mother's—stress and distress (Banez & Compas, 1990). Furthermore, it has been established that a mother's distress affects her perceptions of her children's behavior (see Thompson, Merritt, Keith, Murphy, & Johndrow, 1993). However, children's perceptions of stress are related to child-reported distress over and above the effects of parental stress and distress.

Banez and Compas (1990) addressed this issue in terms of children's daily stress. The participants of their study included 75 children from 9 to 11 years of age and their parents. The researchers assessed the children's experiences of daily stress in terms of their ratings of "How much fun" each of a list of 155 daily events and activities were for them. Children's emotional–behavioral problems were assessed with two self-report measures: The Children's Depression Inventory (Kovacs, 1980–1981; 1983) and the Revised Children's Manifest Anxiety Scale (Reynolds & Richmond, 1985). Mothers' and fathers' reports of their children's emotional–behavioral problems were obtained with the Child Behavior Checklist (Achenbach & Edelbrock, 1983). Parental stress was assessed with a revised form of the Hassles and Uplifts Scale (DeLongis, Folkman, & Lazarus, 1988), and parental distress was assessed with the Symptom Checklist–90–Revised (Derogatis, 1983). Mothers' and fathers' reports of their children's internalizing behavior problems correlated significantly with mothers' and fathers' daily stress and distress. Furthermore, parents' level of daily stress was related significantly to their children's self-reported anxiety. With parents' levels of distress controlled, children's reports of negative daily events were associated significantly with their self-reported symptoms of depression but not significantly related to children's self-reported anxiety.

Our own unpublished pilot studies with children with chronic illness also have demonstrated that perceived stress is related to self-reported emotional–behavioral problems. In children 7 to 12 years of age with sickle-cell disease ($n = 49$) or cystic fibrosis ($n = 43$), stress correlated with self-reported total symptoms score ($r = .36$, $p < .01$, and $r = .50$, $p < .0007$, respectively).

## Reciprocal Influences and Transitional Vulnerability

Compas, Wagner, Slavin, and Vannatta (1986) studied life events, perceived social support, and psychological symptoms among older adolescents ($N = 64$, $M = 18.4$ years) during the transition from high school to college. Across three assessment points and over a 6-month period, the findings indicated that these variables were related reciprocally and the pattern of relationships changed during a major life transition. The relationship between prior life events and psychological distress was highest during the time of transition. The reciprocal relationship of stress, support, and distress also indicates that during a transition, perceptions of low levels of social support could increase vulnerability to stressful events, and in turn, distress could interfere with generating a new, satisfying sense of support. The findings also have implications for intervention:

> Because life events and satisfaction with social support accounted for separate and significant portions of the variance in symptomatology beyond that explained by prior symptoms, the enhancement of coping with stressful life events as well as fostering the development of satisfying social networks both represent appropriate targets for prevention efforts. (Compas et al., 1986, p. 253)

## PERCEPTIONS OF CONTROL

Beliefs about control—that is, the extent to which one believes that one can control outcomes of importance—are relevant to both primary and secondary appraisal. In terms of a generalized belief, Rotter (1966) formulated the concept of locus of control. An *internal locus of control* is the belief that events are contingent on one's own behavior. An *external locus of control* is the belief that events are not contingent on one's actions but on chance, fate, or powerful others. The concept of locus of control has spawned considerable research that in general shows that those with an internal locus of control have better psychological, vocational, and health outcomes than do those with an external locus of control (see Strickland, 1978, for a review). In general, the perception that one is in control of a situation tends to reduce stress levels (Neufield & Paterson, 1989). However, perceptions of control also can heighten appraisals of threat in situations in which control exacts cost in other areas or is antagonistic to a preferred style of interacting with others or dealing with situations (Folkman, 1984).

Perceptions of control can influence appraisals of stress and also influence coping methods. Both generalized expectancies of internal control and *efficacy expectations* (Bandura, 1977)—that is, situational appraisals of control—are associated with the use of problem-focused coping methods (Strickland, 1978). The effectiveness of coping efforts is related to the match between the person's appraisal of controllability of the situation and the extent to which the outcome is actually controllable (Folkman, 1984). Inaccurate perceptions regarding personal control have been seen as central components of an array of adjustment problems and underachievement (Weisz & Stipek, 1982).

## Developmental Changes in Perceptions of Control

The theories and evidence regarding how perceptions of control change with development are mixed. Some theorists and researchers view perceived internal control as increasing with development. In contrast, those following a Piagetian viewpoint see a decline in perceived internal control as children mature. The Piagetian view is based on the evidence that young children have considerable difficulty recognizing the inherent uncontrollability of noncontingent events (Weisz & Stipek, 1982).

Weisz and Stipek (1982) reviewed the evidence from 33 studies that examined changes in perceptions of locus of control with age. Across these developmental studies, 12 different scales to measure locus of control were used. The method of assessing locus of control involved questionnaires (agree/disagree) that generally reflected models of perceived control that emphasized cross-situational generality of beliefs or choice of attribution scales that reflected models that emphasized situational variations in perceived control or causality. The studies using the questionnaires generally showed significant developmental increments in internality, whereas the studies using the choice of attribution measures typically showed no developmental increase in internality.

The measures used to assess locus of control failed to distinguish between two dimensions of perceived control: contingency of outcomes and competence of self, which may show quite different patterns of developmental change. Weisz and Stipek (1982) pointed out that two conditions are necessary for actual control over a given outcome. First, there must be contingency—the outcome must be causally dependent on variations in behavior. A noncontingent outcome is inherently uncontrollable. Second, there must be the personal competence to produce the behavior on which the desired outcome is contingent. If either condition is absent, control is not possible.

Although the question of how notions of contingency and competence vary with developmental level has not yet been answered definitively, Weisz and Stipek (1982) argued that there is reason to believe that these two dimensions can operate differently in shaping developmentally significant changes in perceived control. In general, there is evidence that perceptions of competence increase developmentally in relation to cognitive, motor, and social skill development. There is also evidence that perception of contingency declines with developmental level, particularly in relation to what has been termed *illusory contingency*. The evidence regarding the development of causal reasoning indicates that young children overestimate contingency between outcomes and individuals' behaviors, and this illusory contingency declines with maturation (Weisz, 1980). For example, children's awareness of noncontingency was found to change between kindergarten and fourth grade in accordance with Piagetian theory (Weisz, 1980).

Jean Piaget illustrated that children younger than 6 or 7 years of age have primitive understanding of causality and overestimate the degree of influence of their thoughts and desires, and those of others, on physical events. They also tend to see misfortune as a consequence of violation of moral precepts or social norms—that is, immanent justice—and perceive chance outcomes as contingent on behavior (Weisz, Yeates, Robertson, & Bekham, 1982). Piagetian theory portrays illusory contingency in causality, moral reasoning, and chance as declining with cognitive development (Weisz et al., 1982).

Weisz and colleagues (1982) investigated age differences in recognizing contingency between chance activities and skilled–controlled activities in a study ($N = 92$) of kindergarten-age, fourth-grade, eighth-grade, and college-age students. Two developmental trends were evident. With increasing age, there was a decrease in expectation that age, intelligence, effort, and practice would influence both chance and skilled tasks; and older children were more adept at distinguishing between skill and chance tasks. Kindergarten-age children were not able to make the skilled–chance distinction. Fourth-grade students were aware of this distinction but not of some important logical implications. For example, they illogically expected that variations in the contingency of intelligence, age, practice, and effort would influence the chance outcomes. Eighth-grade and college-age students were aware of the skilled–chance distinction and most of the logical implications but still believed that chance outcomes could be influenced slightly by variations in peoples' attitudes and behaviors. Thus, traces of illusory contingency persisted into young adulthood, with more than 45% of the college-age students predicting that at least one of the contingency factors would influence outcomes on a chance task.

## Control as a Moderator of Stress–Adjustment Relationships in Children

Studies support the two-dimensional model of control—perceived contingency and perceived competency—in moderating the stress–behavior symptom relationship in children. In a study ($N = 154$) of children 6 to 9 years of age, Weigel, Wertlieb, and Feldstein (1989) assessed stress in relation to life events and behavioral symptoms in terms of the internalizing and externalizing dimensions of the Child Behavior Checklist (Achenbach & Edelbrock, 1983). Either of the more differentiated perceived competence or perceived control scores was a better predictor of behavioral symptoms than was the more generalized measure of externality typically used in locus of control studies. Furthermore, perceived control was a significant moderator of the stress–symptom relationship. Also of interest was the finding that with age, willingness to admit lack of knowledge about the sources of control increased, which indirectly provides support for the illusory control beliefs of younger children. In addition, children who were less willing to acknowledge lack of control over events were perceived by their mothers to have higher levels of total behavior problems. There is some indirect evidence, then, for associating illusory control with negative consequences in terms of maternal perceptions of behavior.

A study ($N = 238$) that included children from 8 to 16 years of age ($M = 11.28$ years) who had experienced a parental divorce ($n = 85$), had chronic asthma ($n = 88$), or were part of a nonstress comparison group ($n = 65$) found no significant group differences in negative life events, locus of control, or self-esteem (Kliewer & Sandler, 1992). However, internal expectations of locus of control buffered the effects of negative life events across ages and gender. High self-esteem buffered the effects of stress only for girls; girls without an internal locus of control and without high self-esteem were most vulnerable to psychological maladjustment.

Another study ($N = 100$) involving second- and fifth-grade students (Kliewer, 1991) addressed the influence of children's cognition on the process of coping with everyday stressful events. Teacher-rated social competence was related to greater use of avoidant behaviors and cognitive avoidance. Children with internal locus of control beliefs reported using more cognitive avoidance. Use of these coping strategies was thought to be adaptive because children experience situations that typically involve less control than situations adults encounter.

## Goodness of Fit

Situations vary in the degree to which opportunities are provided for control, and effective adaptation requires appraisals and methods of coping that are appropriate to the situation (Kliewer & Sandler, 1992). If a situation is controllable, then appraising that situation as a challenge rather than as a stress and use of problem-focused coping efforts are likely to be adaptive. If a situation is uncontrollable, then coping methods that reduce distress—that is, emotion-focused, palliative methods—are likely to be more effective. That congruence between the situational demands, the person's appraisals of threat or challenge, and the subsequent coping methods employed is necessary for adaptation to stress has become known as the goodness-of-fit hypothesis, which has been discussed previously. Support for this hypothesis has been demonstrated with children and adolescents (Compas, Malcarne, & Fondacaro, 1988) and with adults. Parkes (1984), in a study of female nursing students ($N = 17$), found that those with internal locus of control beliefs were more likely to use problem- or emotion-focused strategies that match the controllability of the situation.

These findings also have implications for the goodness-of-fit of intervention efforts. Intervention efforts need to be designed with an "understanding of the process by which children who differ in their locus of control and self-esteem respond to stress" (Kliewer & Sandler, 1992, p. 109). For example, control-enhancing strategies are likely to be more effective for children with internal locus of control beliefs.

## Effects of Experience With Chronic Illness on Children's Perceptions of Control

Experience with uncontrollable events can lead to expectations of no control. Numerous studies have shown that adults with chronic illness have lower internal locus of control beliefs and higher beliefs in control by chance and powerful others than do healthy adults (Wallston & Wallston, 1981 as referenced in E. C. Perrin and Shapiro, 1985). Recognizing that different illnesses vary in amenability to control, a study assessed the health locus of control beliefs of mothers and their children with and without chronic illness (asthma, diabetes, seizure disorders, and orthopedic conditions; $N = 278$) between 5 and 16 years of age. It is thought that children who have chronic illness and are confronted with frequent hospitalizations are likely to have lower perceptions of internal control. However, there have been few studies that have addressed the impact of chronic illness on perceptions of control. The findings indicated that mothers of children with chronic illness had lower internal health locus of control scores than mothers of healthy children. However, mothers' health locus of control beliefs did not vary by age or specific illness of their children. Five- and

6-year-old children had lower internal health locus of control scores than those who were 9 to 16. On the chance and powerful other dimensions, 5- to 8-year-olds obtained the highest scores with no significant differences from those who were 9 years of age or older. Internal locus of control, as reflected in the total score, was lowest for the 5- to 6-year-olds, with significant increases at 7, 9, and 13 years of age. As a group, children with chronic illness reported lower beliefs in internal control of their health and lower beliefs in control by chance and powerful others than did children who were healthy. Locus of control beliefs of children with asthma or diabetes did not differ from those of healthy children. Healthy children had higher locus of control scores and lower chance and powerful other locus of control beliefs than children with seizure disorders and orthopedic problems.

There was a significant interaction with age. There were no significant differences between the youngest and oldest age groups. From 9 through 14 years of age, healthy children stated higher internal locus of control beliefs than did children with a seizure or orthopedic condition who seemed to hang on to beliefs in the external control of their health.

It is believed that children from approximately 6 months to 4 years of age are most vulnerable to transitory and long-term effects of hospitalization (see Bolig, Brown, & Kuo, 1992). However, there have been few developmental studies. In a study of 115 adolescents (13 to 19 years of age), adolescents hospitalized at various ages and those never hospitalized were not found to differ significantly in self-esteem or locus of control beliefs (Bolig, Brown, & Kuo, 1992).

What can be said is that children with different chronic illnesses at different ages may maintain different perceptions of control. Further research is necessary to delineate how interactions among illness, experiences, and developmental level influence children's perceptions of control.

## CAUSAL ATTRIBUTIONS

Emotional reactions and behavioral responses to an event are influenced by appraisals of stressfulness and perceptions of control and also by the cognitive interpretations or meaning the person ascribes to the event. In particular, explanations regarding the cause of stressful events have been related to psychological distress. C. Peterson and Seligman (1984) postulated that there are three dimensions of causal attributions: (a) the cause may be internal or external to the person, (b) it may be persistent (stable) or transient (unstable) over time, and (c) it may be limited to the specific event or it may be global and cause a variety of outcomes. In particular, internal causal attributions result in loss of self-esteem following negative events (C. Peterson & Seligman, 1984).

The particular explanatory style of habitually attributing positive events to causes that are external, unstable, and specific and negative events to causes that are internal, stable, and global has been termed maladaptive. This style has been associated with cognitive, motivational, and emotional deficits that have been termed *learned helplessness* (C. Peterson & Seligman, 1984). The *cognitive deficits* include inability to perceive existing opportunities to control outcomes. *Motivational deficits* include lowered response initiation and lowered persistence, or passivity. *Emotional deficits* include sadness and lowered self-esteem.

According to the reformulated theory of learned helplessness (Abramson, Seligman, & Teasdale, 1978), individuals who have a maladaptive explanatory style are predisposed to helplessness in the face of negative events (Nolen-Hoeksema, Girgus, and Seligman, 1986). This diathesis–stress model has spawned a substantial amount of research with adults that in general supports the role of causal attributions as a risk factor for distress in the face of stressful events (C. Peterson & Seligman, 1984).

## Maladaptive Explanatory Style and Children's Adjustment

The reformulated learned helplessness model has been applied to children also. In a study ($N = 96$) of eight 13-year-old children (Seligman et al., 1984), those who demonstrated the maladaptive explanatory style had higher levels of depressive symptoms than those who did not. Furthermore, the maladaptive attributional style predicted depressive symptoms 6 months later. In addition, children's attributional style for negative events correlated with their mothers' attributional style for negative events ($r = .39$, $p < .001$) but not with that of their fathers'. This suggests that children's explanatory style may be learned in part by imitating the primary caregiver (C. Peterson & Seligman, 1984). In a subsequent study ($N = 168$), researchers assessed the explanatory style of children 8 to 11 years of age five times during the course of a year (Nolen-Hoeksema et al., 1986). Explanatory style was found to be stable over the year and correlated with concurrent levels of depression and school achievement. It also predicted later changes in depression during the year.

In a study of undergraduates ($N = 65$) with a mean age of 19.6 years, researchers assessed the consistency and variability of causal attributions over time and across two stressors: academic and interpersonal (Compas, Forsythe, & Wagner, 1988). The findings indicated moderate to high levels of consistency in attributions for the same stressor over time and low consistency in attributions for the two different stressors.

Another study examined the relationships among learned helpless attributional style, depression, regimen adherence, and metabolic control in children ($N = 50$) 10 to 16 years old with diabetes (Kuttner, Delamater, & Santiago, 1990). The findings indicated that learned helplessness was associated significantly with depression but not with regimen adherence. Learned helplessness was not associated significantly with current metabolic control but accounted for 10% of the variance in mean level of metabolic control over a 1-year period. Regimen adherence accounted for 24% of the variance in current metabolic control. The findings did not support the hypothesis that learned helplessness is associated with poor metabolic control via poor regimen adherence. Researchers postulated that learned helplessness may be associated with increased stress, which in turn can directly impact metabolic control.

This association of maladaptive attributional style with adjustment difficulties is not limited to children with diabetes. A study of 96 youth 7 to 16 years old (M = 11.5 years) with insulin-dependent diabetes, acute lymphocytic leukemia, or sickle-cell syndromes assessed the relationship between attributional style and psychological symptomatology (Schoenherr, Brown, Baldwin, & Kaslow, 1992). The findings indicated that attributional styles were not associated with the illness-related parameters of disease onset, duration of illness, or specific diagnosis or with the demographic variables of socioeconomic status, gender, or race. However, attributional style was an efficient predictor of self-reported depressive symptoms when controlling for demographic and disease-related variables.

## Implications

Further explorations of the role of explanatory style in the adjustment of children with chronic illness is warranted because of the intervention implications. The reformulated learned helplessness theory asserts that explanatory style is an important target for therapy. For example, Dweck (1975) has shown that children who are given attribution retraining show decreases in helplessness deficits in cognitive tasks (Nolen-Hoeksema et al., 1986). It is particularly important to identify and rectify maladaptive attributional styles in children with chronic illness to avoid a learned-helplessness constellation of behaviors. Children with chronic illness need the cognitive flexibility to perceive opportunities to exercise control and the motivation to initiate and persist in coping efforts. Internal attributions for negative events are particularly deleterious in terms of loss of self-esteem.

## SELF-CONCEPT

Theoretical and empirical approaches to self-concept have differed in whether self-concept is seen as a generalized view across a number of domains or is domain-specific. The work of Harter (1986) has provided support for domain-specific judgments as well as a global sense of self-worth.

In Harter's work, children age 8 and older assessed themselves in five separate domains: (a) scholastic competence, (b) athletic competence, (c)
social competence, (d) physical appearance, and (e) behavior or conduct.
In addition, children also assessed themselves in terms of a general sense
of self-worth that reflected the degree to which they liked themselves and
the way they led their lives.

## Developmental Changes in Self-Concept

Changes in the content and structure of the self-concept occur with
development. The findings across a number of investigators reveal that
"with development, children shift their focus from behavioral characteristics of the self in the early years, to trait-like constructs during middle
childhood, and then to more abstract, psychological constructs during adolescence" (Harter, 1986, p. 143). The concept of *personness* as a generalization about the self and the corresponding sense of global self-worth
does not emerge until the approximate mental age of 8. It is during the
middle elementary grades that children begin to use social comparison to
make self-evaluative judgments. Self-concept then can vary, depending on
the reference group against which the comparisons are made.

Another way in which the self-concept changes developmentally is
in terms of intrapsychic conflict. Whereas 7th-grade students can identify
opposing characteristics within themselves, they do not typically report
them as conflicting. However, by 9th grade, they report opposites within
the self as in conflict. The sense of intrapsychic conflict declines somewhat
by the 11th grade.

Harter (1986) and her colleagues also have sought to delineate processes that underlie the development and maintenance of self-concept and
self-worth, providing support for two independent components to self-
worth. One component is based on James's (1892) notion that self-worth
reflects the degree to which one is successful in those domains that one
deems important. Another component is based on Cooley's (1902) view
of the self as social construction derived from the reflected appraisals of
others, particularly of parents and peers. In a series of studies, Harter (1986)
has demonstrated that children maintain a positive sense of self-worth by
discounting the importance of domains in which they are not performing
competently and by endorsing the importance of domains in which they
are competent. The importance of domains of scholastic competence, conduct, and appearance were more difficult to discount than the importance
of their athletic competence and social acceptance. Furthermore, children
with high self-worth tend to slightly exaggerate their competence.

Children's senses of control over their successes and failures also contribute to their sense of self-worth. Higher self-worth is associated with
taking more responsibility for success than for failure. This self-enhance-

ment strategy is acquired over the course of development in terms of scholastic competence. During the early grades, children take almost as much internal responsibility for their scholastic successes as their failures, but with development take less responsibility for their failures and maintain perceived internal control over their successes.

## Implications

We learned in chapter 3 that children's perceptions of self-worth correlate with the adjustment of children with chronic illness. The findings regarding the development of self-concept have implications for efforts to enhance self-worth: General strategies designed to convince someone that he or she is a worthwhile person are not likely to be very successful. . . . Rather, one must make adjustments at the domain level, which, in turn, will influence self-worth" (Harter, 1986, p. 165). It is necessary to (a) enhance the congruence between the importance and competence hierarchies by increasing skills in specific domains or by discounting importance, and (b) enhance perceptions of internal control over one's successes and decrease perceptions of responsibility for one's failures.

## CONCLUSION

It is clear that much of what is known from the literature about adult stress and the cognitive processes that serve to mediate and moderate the stress–adjustment relationship can be applied to children and adolescents. However, the application is modified by developmental changes that can be understood in terms of Piagetian stages of cognitive development.

The applicability of findings from the literature on adult stress to children and adolescents is conveyed by the evidence regarding major questions that have served to guide studies. First, there is a strong association between children's cognitive appraisal of the stressfulness of daily and major events and adjustment. Second, social support and perceptions of control moderate the relationship between stress and adjustment. Third, developmental transitions may be a time of particular vulnerability to stress. Fourth, there is evidence to support the goodness-of-fit relationship between characteristics of the event, appraisals of threat, coping methods, and adjustment.

Two other cognitive processes are also relevant to adjustment: causal attributions and self-concept. The maladaptive pattern of explanatory style found with adults also is evident with children and adolescents. Preventing the development of maladaptive explanatory styles in children with chronic illness is particularly important to avoid the constellation of behavior characterized by inability to perceive opportunities for control, passivity, sadness, and low self-esteem that have been termed *learned helplessness*. A better understanding is needed of how causal attributions and perceptions of control work together in developing self-concept.

Understanding the development of children's cognitive processes and their roles in moderating and mediating the stress–adjustment relationship has implications for efforts to enhance adjustment. The cognitive process of appraisal of stress, perceptions of control, causal attributions, and self-worth become salient intervention targets. We will review the finding regarding intervention efforts in subsequent chapters. However, it is first necessary to examine in more detail the parallel construct to stress—that is, the process of coping and its development.

# 9

# DEVELOPMENTAL CHANGES IN COPING

In this chapter, we will review the general findings regarding coping methods used by adults and the relationship of coping methods to adjustment. Next, we will discuss what is known about coping methods used by children in general and as a function of age and cognitive level. We will review findings of studies regarding the effectiveness of different types of coping strategies employed by children and discuss the implications of these findings regarding the development of children's coping methods.

## COPING METHODS AND ADJUSTMENT IN ADULTS

The literature on adult coping has yielded three consistent findings. First, the ways in which adults cope with stressful situations can be classified reliably in several ways. In terms of mode, coping can involve behavioral actions or intrapsychic cognitions. Coping strategies also can be classified as *active-* or *approach-oriented* (toward threat) or as *passive* or *avoidance-oriented* (away from threat) (Roth & Cohen, 1986). In terms of focus, *problem-focused coping* refers to efforts to modify the source of the problems; *emotion-focused coping* refers to efforts to reduce emotional distress (Folkman & Lazarus, 1980; Lazarus & Folkman, 1984). Second, coping methods vary as a function of situational differences. In particular, stressful situations

*215*

perceived as controllable elicit problem-focused coping; whereas stressful situations perceived as uncontrollable evoke emotion-focused coping in terms of optimizing one's goodness of fit with existing conditions (Band & Weisz, 1988; Lazarus & Folkman, 1984). Third, use of emotion-focused methods of coping with stress are associated with poor adjustment (Compas, Malcarne, & Fondacara, 1988).

The adult literature has served to guide the study of children's coping, but four specific questions remain: (a) Do children demonstrate the behavioral and cognitive, approach and avoidance, and problem- and emotion-focused coping methods used by adults? (b) Are there age-related changes in children's coping strategies? (c) Do children's coping strategies vary as a function of situational differences? and (d) How does emotional regulation affect children's coping strategies?

## COPING METHODS USED BY CHILDREN

The development of coping behaviors prior to preschool age has not been delineated, but it is clear that children as young as 6 years of age "are sufficiently aware of stress and coping in their own lives to report conditions and events that they find stressful and describe their own efforts to cope," (Band & Weisz, 1988, p. 251).

A review of 16 studies regarding children's coping that were published from 1981 to 1989 identified 145 coping strategies and categories (Ryan-Wenger, 1992). The following 15 groupings of coping strategies were derived inductively:

- aggressive activities
- behavioral avoidance
- behavioral distraction
- cognitive avoidance
- cognitive distraction
- cognitive problem-solving
- cognitive restructuring
- emotional expression
- endurance
- information seeking
- isolating activities
- self-controlling activities
- social support
- spiritual support
- stressor modification

Although the researchers did not attempt to group these hierarchically, the broad categories of behavioral and cognitive, problem- and emotion-focused, and approach and avoidant strategies identified in the adult literature were discernible. It is clear that the development of children's cognitive skills, social reasoning, and ability to regulate emotions could influence the development and use of specific coping methods. Consequently, a number of studies have tried to discover the coping strategies that children of various ages report using, or can identify, in relation to stressful events.

## COPING METHODS AS A FUNCTION OF AGE AND COGNITIVE LEVEL

The coping responses of children ($N = 73$) in three age groups (6, 9, and 12 years of age) were elicited by interviewers in relation to six domains of experience that were potential sources of everyday stress, one of which included going to the "doctor's office to get a shot" (Band & Weisz, 1988). Children were asked to report what they remembered doing and thinking, and their responses were classified in the broad categories of coping based on the primary–secondary control model (Rothbaum, Weisz, & Snyder, 1982; Weisz, Rothbaum, & Blackburn, 1984a, 1984b). *Primary control* is similar to problem-focused coping; it aims at influencing the event. *Secondary control* is similar to emotion-focused coping; it aims at maximizing one's goodness of fit with conditions as they are. The findings indicated that 6-year-old children used secondary-control strategies significantly less than did 9- and 12-year-old children. In terms of specific subtypes of coping, there was a significant decline with age in the proportion of avoidance responses to the medical situation and an increase in direct problem-solving. As has been found in the adult literature, the situations that evoked the greatest percentages of primary coping were those that were perceived as more controllable. However, the medical situation evoked secondary control approaches most frequently, and the use of these approaches tended to increase with age. Band and Weisz (1988) suggested that secondary-control coping strategies may develop more slowly than primary-control strategies, in part because of the need for cognitive maturity in secondary-control strategies and because cognitions are "hidden" and thus difficult for the child to learn through observation.

Altshuler and Ruble (1989) further addressed the difficulty young children may have in using avoidance strategies in a study ($N = 72$) of children 5 to 12 years of age. They hypothesized that young children may have more difficulty than older children in using cognitive, as opposed to behavioral, forms of distraction. The researchers presented scenarios to children about an uncontrollable positive or negative event (for example, a medical shot), and they asked children how the child character in the scenario would feel in that situation. They then classified children's responses into broad categories, including approach and avoidance. The avoidance category was subdivided into behavioral or cognitive forms of distraction. The findings indicated that avoidance strategies were the overwhelming coping choice of children at each of the three age groups for both the positive and the negative events. However, type of avoidance strategies suggested for the negative medical event varied with age. There was an increase in cognitive distraction and a decrease in escape with age. The 5- to 6-year-old children mentioned escape as frequently as behavioral distraction and mentioned cognitive distraction very infrequently. In contrast, the 10- to 11-year-old children mentioned escape strategies very infrequently, and mentioned similar proportions of behavioral and cognitive distraction.

These findings indicate that 5- to 12-year-old children demonstrate knowledge of approach and avoidance coping strategies, predominantly choose avoidance strategies, and suggest approach strategies, particularly information seeking, very infrequently. For 5- and 6-year-old children, avoidance strategies are primarily behavioral. It is not until children are 10 to 11 years of age do avoidance strategies involve similar proportions of behavioral and cognitive distractions. Furthermore, emotional distress may make it difficult for young children to think of strategies, resulting in a need to resort to escape strategies instead. Thus, young children may need guidance in using strategies of behavioral distraction (playing, reading, watching television) when faced with stressful medical events. Another implication of these findings is that more use of approach strategies and less use of avoidance coping methods may need to await the increased affective regulation that comes with increasing age.

The use of specific cognitive coping strategies as a function of age also has been addressed. The adult literature has identified a number of intrapsychic or cognitive coping strategies to be effective in attenuating pain and stress (J. M. Brown, O'Keefe, Sanders, & Baker, 1986). A study investigated the types of cognitions ($N = 487$) 8- to 9-, 10- to 11-, 12- to 13-, 14- to 15-, and 16- to 18-year-olds report in response to imagined stressors, including a dental shot (J. M. Brown et al., 1986). The researchers coded responses to a questionnaire into two categories. Coping categories were defined as imagining events that are inconsistent with the experience of pain and stress, such as relaxation or deep breathing, and attention diversion through thinking about objects in the environment, positive self-talk, thought-stopping, and thinking about the stressor in a problem-solving way. Catastrophizing categories involved a focus on or exaggerating of perceived negative aspects of the situation, denigrating self-statements, or thoughts of escape or avoidance. The findings indicated that coping increased significantly with age. Positive self-talk was the most commonly reported coping strategy employed in all age groups. Attention diversion was the second most common response. However, the researchers identified

64% of the subjects as predominantly catastrophizers, with a range of 79% for the 8- to 9-year-olds to 54% of the 16- to 18-year-olds. Focusing on negative affect and pain was most frequent, and thoughts of escape and avoidance were second in frequency across all age groups. There were no gender differences in rates of coping or catastrophizing. The high rate of catastrophizing and the persistence of predominance of catastrophizing cognitions into the late adolescent years is of concern because catastrophizing is associated with higher amounts of stress and anxiety (Chaves & Brown, 1987).

A study ($N = 130$) of children in the sixth, seventh, and eighth grades (10 to 14 years of age) investigated the extent to which children in the middle childhood years use the problem- and emotion-focused coping strategies evident in adult coping (Compas et al., 1988). These youngsters generated alternative solutions and reported using coping strategies to deal with interpersonal and academic stressors that could be described in terms of the problem-focused and emotion-focused coping framework developed by Lazarus and Folkman (1984). Whereas the generation and use of problem-focused coping was relatively consistent across the age and grade groups, emotion-focused solutions and strategies increased with the sixth- to eighth-graders. In general, there were few gender differences, although girls used more emotion-focused strategies than did boys in response to academic stressors.

The study provided some support for the hypothesis that children will match coping strategies to perceived controllability of the stressors. Both boys and girls reported more control over the cause of academic events than social events and correspondingly generated more problem-focused alternatives for academic stressors than interpersonal stressors. There were no differences in emotion-focused strategies as a function of perceived control.

Studies also have examined coping strategies of older adolescents. In a study ($N = 60$) that included an age range from adolescence (14 to 16 years old) through young adults (20 to 25 years old) to mature adults (30 to 46 years old), researchers assessed coping in relation to age and social cognitive maturity (Blanchard-Fields & Irion, 1987). Those studied endorsed more problem-focused coping strategies in controllable situations, whereas they endorsed more emotion-focused strategies in noncontrollable situations. In noncontrollable situations, both the adolescents and young adults endorsed more emotion-focused as opposed to problem-focused coping. In controllable situations, only the adolescents endorsed more emotion-focused than problem-focused coping. That is, adolescents endorsed more emotion-focused than problem-focused coping whether the stressful event was appraised as controllable or not. Social reasoning level rather than age or education level was the best overall predictor of emotion-focused coping. This suggests that "with increasing maturity, affective contexts may cause less disruption to coping strategies" (p. 148).

In general, differences in coping strategies as a function of gender have not been reported in children. However, gender-related differences in coping may emerge in adolescence. In a study ($N = 904$) of adolescents 14 to 17 years of age, the use of various coping strategies did not differ significantly by age. However, girls reported using social support and emotional regulation more often than boys, and boys reported using wishful thinking more often than girls (Stark, Spirito, Williams, & Guevremont, 1989).

## EFFECTIVENESS OF COPING STRATEGIES

The adult literature is consistent in showing a relationship between use of emotion-focused avoidant coping strategies and poor adjustment (Lazarus & Folkman, 1984). A review of studies found consistent support for the hypothesis that children who use *approach-coping strategies* characterized by seeking information (sensitizer style) had less distress in relation to stressful medical procedures and conditions than those who used avoidant strategies (Blount, Davis, Powers, & Roberts, 1991). In a similar way, using avoidance as opposed to approach strategies in adolescence also appears to be associated with adjustment difficulties.

In a study of youngsters 10 to 14 years of age, the number of problem-focused alternatives generated and strategies used in relation to interpersonal stressors were related negatively, whereas emotion-focused strategies were related positively to self-reported and mother-reported internalizing and externalizing behavior problems (Compas et al., 1988). The study provided limited support for the goodness-of-fit hypothesis that emotional and behavioral problems would be related to the degree of fit between appraisal of control and relative amount of problem- and emotion-focused coping used (Compas, 1987). Self-reported emotional and behavioral problems were associated with a mismatch between perceived control of social stressors and coping strategies (i.e., more problem-focused alternatives in response to stressors perceived as uncontrollable and more emotion-focused alternatives in response to stressors perceived as controllable).

Researchers examined adolescents who were depressed, exhibited conduct disorder, who were healthy, and who had rheumatic disease in a study ($N = 190$) of the coping methods employed by adolescents between the ages of 12 and 18 (Ebata & Moos, 1991). They found no significant group differences in approach coping. However, adolescents who were depressed and those who exhibited conduct disorder used more avoidance coping than the healthy adolescents and those with rheumatic disease. Approach coping was associated with higher levels of well-being, whereas avoidance coping was associated with higher distress. The results suggest that "efforts to change, manage, or positively reappraise a problematic situation actively, are important for good long-term adjustment" (p. 33).

The effectiveness of coping strategies also has been shown to vary as a function of children's cognitive development. In a study ($N = 64$) of children with diabetes (Band & Weisz, 1990), researchers formed subgroups on the basis of level of cognitive maturity: preformal operational ($n = 32$; $M = 8.8$ years) and formal operational ($n = 32$; $M = 14.6$ years). The two groups differed significantly in factual knowledge about their illness, coping approaches, and medical adjustment as rated by medical staff. Compared to the preformal group, children at the formal operational level had more advanced levels of knowledge about diabetes and used more secondary-control coping approaches, but had poorer medical adjustment ratings. Furthermore, there were differences between groups in how coping style, perceived control, perceived coping efficacy, and knowledge of diabetes contributed to medical and sociobehavioral adjustment. For the preformal operational level children, perceived control was the only variable related to adjustment—specifically, perceived control was related negatively to psychosomatic problems. For children at the formal operational level, greater knowledge was related to better ratings of medical adjustment. More primary versus secondary styles of coping were associated with more favorable medical and sociobehavioral adjustment, and perceived coping efficacy was related negatively to conduct problems. These findings attest to the need to recognize and understand that effective coping processes may differ from one developmental period to another.

The impact of illness and its treatment on children's sense of control has been an area of particular concern. We considered the cognitive process of perceptions of control earlier—how it changed developmentally—and the relation of perceived control to coping methods and adjustment. Control also has been a type of coping strategy that can facilitate adjustment. Researchers sought to identify the different types of control strategies used by children and adolescents ($N = 52$) with cancer, age 6 to 12 and 13 to 17, and the relationship between type of control strategies and adaptation (Worchel, Copeland, & Barker, 1987). Through factor analysis of responses to a questionnaire, they identified six types of control strategies: behavioral control, which included a variety of behaviors such as holding parents' hands or using deep breathing; cognitive control, which included thinking or talking about the illness or treatment; informational control, which included asking questions about the illness and treatment; and three types of dimensional control involving perceived control over treatments, other activities, and needs.

The findings indicated several age effects. Adolescents had higher levels than children of decisional control regarding meals and other activities and used more cognitive control strategies. Behavioral control strategies were most strongly related to nurses ratings of overall adjustment, to self-reported depressive symptoms, and to somatic complaints. Thus, poorer adjustment was associated with more use of behavioral control strategies, which was interpreted as indicating unsuccessful searching to find an effective solution. Cognitive control was related to nurses' ratings of passive noncompliance. Lack of decision making regarding meals and other activities was associated with parent-reported externalizing behavior problems, and decisional control over other activities was associated with poor overall adjustment as reflected in nurses' ratings. Lack of decisional control over treatments was associated with both internalizing and externalizing behavior problems.

In children, the link between perceptions of control and effectiveness of coping methods also has been addressed. Building on the findings of Compas and colleagues (Compas et al., 1988) that youngsters who reported the most behavioral and emotional problems were those who used coping methods that were incongruent with the controllability of the stressor, Weisz, McCabe, and Dennig (1994) investigated the effectiveness of coping methods in children ($N = 33$) ages 5 to 12 years ($M = 8.1$ years) with leukemia. They hypothesized that leukemia represents a stressor that is relatively low in controllability and that optimal adjustment would require adjusting to the stressor rather than trying to alter it. They elicited children's coping efforts with the disease and its treatments through an interview and classified them as primary-control coping (attempts to alter objective conditions), secondary-control coping (attempts to adjust to objective conditions), or relinquished-control coping (no attempt to cope). The findings indicated that use of secondary-control coping methods was associated positively with mother-reported general behavioral and emotional adjustment and illness-specific adjustment reflected in children's self-reported distress ratings and by behavioral observations during painful procedures.

The findings of this study of children with leukemia (Weisz et al., 1994) contrast with those of the previously reported study of children with diabetes (Band & Weisz, 1990). Secondary-control coping methods were associated with better adjustment among children with leukemia but poor adjustment among adolescents with diabetes. These diseases differ in relative controllability, and these two studies provide additional support for the hypothesis that effectiveness of coping methods is in part a function of the perceived and actual controllability of the stressor. Furthermore, Weisz et al. (1994) pointed out that medical conditions differ within and across illnesses in controllability, and over time different forms of coping are likely to be adaptive. That is, overgeneralizations regarding effectiveness of coping strategies must be avoided in favor of delineating effectiveness as a function of phases of specific illnesses.

The adult literature also suggests that coping effectiveness can vary as a function of the phase of the event. Researchers undertook a series of meta-analyses using 43 studies to compare the relative effectiveness of avoidant and attentional—that is, approach-oriented—strategies in reducing pain, stress, and anxiety (Suls & Fletcher, 1985). On the whole, they found little evidence that one strategy is superior to another. However, when temporal factors were considered, they did find differences. In the short run, avoidant strategies were generally more efficacious in reducing stress reactions when compared to attentional strategies, except those that emphasized the sensory, nonemotional aspects of the situation. In the long run, avoidance strategies resulted in better outcomes initially, but by the second week of exposure, attentional strategies were associated with more positive outcome (Suls & Fletcher, 1985). These findings indicate the importance of differentiating immediate and long-term effects, which is likely to be particularly germane to children with chronic conditions and of the way in which the threat is viewed. Schematizing the threatening stimulus in terms of its discrete sensory elements rather than its emotional value appears to enhance the efficacy of attentional strategies. There was a clear advantage when sensory monitoring was compared to avoidance strategies (Suls & Fletcher, 1985). It would appear that children's coping effectiveness can be enhanced by encouraging them to attend to sensory phenomena as a form of cognitive distraction rather than engaging in escape behaviors.

Siegal and Peterson (1980) examined the effectiveness in stress reduction of teaching specific self-control coping skills, such as relaxation, deep breathing, imagery, and calming self-talk, and of providing sensory information, including typical physical sensations, sights, and sounds, regarding the dental procedures preschool-aged (42 to 71 months) children ($N = 42$) would experience. Both treatments were significantly more effective than the contact control condition in reducing disruptive behaviors, ratings of anxiety and discomfort, and physiological arousal, but they did not differ significantly from each other. Thus, increasing attention and relabeling of the stressful aversive stimuli and distracting oneself from and blocking attention to aversive feelings were equally effective. Furthermore, both strategies were not too complex for preschool children (Siegel & Peterson, 1980).

## CONCLUSION

The major implications of these findings is that avoidant strategies are most prominent in children's and adolescent's coping strategies, but also most strongly associated with risk for adjustment difficulties. However, effectiveness of coping efforts has been found to vary as a function of cognitive–developmental level and situational characteristics, such as the temporal phase of the event. Furthermore, children's use of sophisticated cognitive distraction methods to cope with stressful health events lags behind their use of behavioral distraction coping methods. This lag appears to be related to the impact of affective arousal and the developmental maturity needed for effective emotional regulation. The literature is not yet clear about whether efforts to enhance adjustment should try to encourage coping strategies consistent with children's coping styles or, as the research with adults would suggest, to broaden their range to include both approach and avoidant styles (Blount et al., 1991). Perhaps the most important implication is that we should not expect children and adolescents to be able to employ sophisticated adult coping patterns. Furthermore, effective coping processes may differ from one developmental period to another. To alleviate distress and foster adjustment, those working with children who are confronting the affectively arousing stresses associated with chronic illness must base their interactions on the child's developmental level of coping skills.

# III

# ENHANCING ADAPTATION

# INTRODUCTION

# ENHANCING ADAPTATION

In Section III, we apply the knowledge base realized through the biopsychosocial framework to delineating salient intervention targets and effective intervention programs to foster the adaptation of children with chronic illness and their families. In chapter 10, we provide a conceptualization of intervention goals and processes. The primary goals in caring for children with chronic illness are to extend the duration and the quality of life. In meeting the objectives of diminishing the impact of the condition and preventing dysfunction, the focus is on the continuous process of adaptation by the children and their families to the stresses associated with chronic illness. A major mechanism of impact of chronic illness is through the disruption of normal processes of child development and family functioning. We review evidence that supports the suggestions of cognitive–behavioral and family system models that this impact can be lessened and adaptation promoted through reducing stress; enhancing support-eliciting, social problem-solving skills; and promoting effective parenting. We review the efficacy of specific intervention programs that target these adaptive processes.

In addition to the issues of goals, intervention targets, and intervention programs, in this section we also address two areas of specific relevance to children with chronic illness. We delineate in chapter 11 the changes in views regarding adherence to medical regimens that have occurred in conjunction with a change to a more family-centered, parent–professional, collaborative model of health care. Noncompliance with medical regimens is recognized as a common occurrence in pediatric patients. Efforts to identify the biomedical, psychological, and social–ecological parameters and processes associated with adherence continue, and multivariate models are beginning to emerge that offer the potential to facilitate adherence through the tailoring of consensual, mutually negotiated care plans.

We conclude the section in chapter 12 by considering pain management. Pharmacological approaches are beyond the scope of this book. Instead, we focus on psychologically based approaches to helping children cope with the pain associated with invasive medical procedures and illness-related pain. Consistent with our transactional, biopsychosocial, framework, we examine the methods of enhancing children's pain-coping skills and training parents to support their children's active coping efforts. Consistent with the overall approach of fostering adaptation by minimizing impact on normative life experience, the goals include helping children maintain the pleasures and joys afforded by their normal daily lives.

# 10

## INTERVENTION GOALS AND PROCESSES

In this chapter, we will provide a conceptualization of intervention goals and processes in terms of the continuous process of adaptation. Then, we will review the development of intervention models from those that are child-centered to those that are family-centered. In the remainder of the chapter, we will review findings from intervention studies that endeavor to prevent disruption of normal child development processes, reflected in school performance and peer relations, and parenting. We will address school reentry programs in general and the role of perceived social support and social cognitive problem-solving skills in particular and review findings from studies of a multicomponent intervention program to assist children with cancer with school and social reintegration.

Researchers within the biopsychosocial framework identified parenting as another salient intervention target to reduce parental stress and distress and enhance parenting skills conducive to child cognitive and social development. We will conclude this chapter with a review of studies that target parenting to foster children's behavioral adjustment and cognitive and social development. A multifamily group intervention program for children with diabetes exemplifies the application of this approach to the situation of chronic illness.

# CONCEPTUALIZATION

The biopsychosocial framework that we have applied to the process of adaptation to chronic childhood illness has implications for the conceptualization of intervention goals and processes. First, the focus is on positive adaptation by the children and their families to the stresses associated with a chronic illness. Comprehensive programs of care need to attend to the impact of the illness on the family and the child's academic and social adjustment, as well as on the child's physical health. Thus, the focus of intervention must be conceived broadly as fostering the adaptation of all children with chronic illness and their families, not just those who experience psychological crises (Drotar, 1981).

Second, adaptation is a continuous process. One of the cardinal characteristics of chronic illness is that cure is not likely. This impacts both the goals and processes of care. "Physicians and family are locked into an ambivalent partnership in which 'treatment' does not mean 'cure' and from which neither can exit" (Drotar, 1981, p. 216). The goal of care is to "diminish the impact of the illness and to prevent dysfunction where possible" (J. M. Perrin & MacLean, 1988b, p. 1325). In more specific terms, the goals of care are to

> Confine the consequences of the biologic disorder to its minimum manifestation, to encourage normal growth and development, to assist the child in maximizing potential in all possible areas, and to prevent or diminish the behavioral and social consequences. (Stein & Jessop, 1984, pp. 193–194)

Care goals are multidimensional, and they include both treatment and prevention. *Primary prevention* refers to preventing the occurrence of the illness. *Secondary prevention* refers to limiting the expression of the illness once it has occurred. *Tertiary prevention*, which is most relevant to chronic childhood illness, refers to limiting the effects of the illness by diminishing the disability and handicap the illness engenders (J. M. Perrin & MacLean, 1988b). *Disabilities* refer to functional limitations, whereas *handicaps* are barriers to participation resulting from an interaction between one's disability and one's physical and social environment (J. M. Perrin & MacLean, 1988b). "The prevention of a handicap may require different interventions from those needed to prevent disability" (p. 1325). Thus, comprehensive care requires treating both biomedical and psychosocial dysfunction and preventing disability and handicap.

Third, disease categories provide little information about the impact of illness on the children and their families. Throughout this book we have noted the considerable variability in impact among and within illnesses. There is a particular need to conceptualize and measure illness impact in terms of health outcomes that can capture the variability in biopsychosocial functioning of children and their families.

Kaplan (1990) has argued that behavior is the central outcome of health care and that there are only two health outcomes of importance: life expectancy (mortality) and the quality of life during the period that the person is alive (morbidity). *Quality of life* has been defined as functioning across the interrelated domains of mobility, physical activity, and social activity (Kaplan & Anderson, 1988). Some chronic childhood illnesses truncate life expectancy, and all may cause disabilities or interfere with the person's ability to perform age-appropriate daily activities. A comprehensive model of health care must include prognosis, or the probabilities of future changes in function or death, as well as mortality and morbidity (Kaplan, 1990). Viewed in this way, health care services for children with chronic illness, both treatment and prevention programs, are directed at these two behavioral health outcomes: extending the duration of life and improving the quality of life (Kaplan & Anderson, 1988).

Fourth, biological and psychosocial processes are mediators of the health outcomes of life expectancy and quality of life. In this regard, specific diagnoses are important because they lead to specific treatments. Biological mediators of health outcomes can be modified directly through medical or surgical treatments, such as insulin injections for children with diabetes or surgical excision of a brain tumor. Another way to improve health outcomes is to modify health behavior directly to enhance functioning—that is, quality of life—independent of improvements in the disease state. Examples include children with cystic fibrosis undertaking chest physical therapy to maintain pulmonary functioning or children with sickle-cell disease using pain management to increase participation in school and social activities. One implication of this perspective is that, although there may be numerous correlates of adaptation to chronic childhood illness, the focus of intervention efforts should be targeted on those biological and psychosocial processes that are linked to health outcome behaviors.

Fifth, it is hypothesized that a major mechanism of effect for chronic childhood illness on children and their families is through disrupting normal processes of child development and family functioning (J. M. Perrin & MacLean, 1988b). This impact is viewed through a stress and coping framework that calls attention to the treatment and prevention functions of stress reduction through techniques to manage stress and enhance coping through skill acquisition and social support.

Corresponding to the advances of health care that have prolonged the lives of children with chronic illness and to the changes in conceptualization of care goals, there also have been changes in the processes of providing health care. Because comprehensive care has biomedical and psychosocial components, care frequently must involve a multidisciplinary team of service providers. Communication, coordination, and integration are vital among members of the team and also among the team, the family, and the educational and social services systems of which the child and family are a part. Multidisciplinary services usually are provided through specialty clinics at tertiary care medical centers, which makes integration with the child's local primary care providers a necessity.

In addition to the team approaches, parents are increasingly responsible for implementing their child's treatment and prevention services and procedures; parents have acquired case manager and nursing roles along with their parenting roles. In a similar fashion, the home increasingly has become a treatment site in which complicated schedules of medication administration, injections, and physical therapies need to be integrated with routine family activities. The home also has become an educational setting, and parents have assumed the role of teacher both in terms of promoting cognitive and social development and also in terms of assisting with homebound education.

## MODELS OF INTERVENTION

Public policy over the past 30 years, which we will consider in chapter 13, as well as the needs of families, have brought about changes in attitudes and beliefs regarding the participation of parents in home care programs and early intervention efforts (Bazyk, 1989). Prior to the mid-1970s, most intervention efforts emanated from the health care system in medical settings. The prevailing medical model was child-centered. The health professional was viewed as the expert who brought about the necessary changes in the child, and parents were viewed as passive recipients of the intervention programs.

During the latter part of the 1970s, the prevailing model of intervention began to change to include much more extensive participation by parents. This change was reflected in, and stimulated by, public policy initiatives. For example, enactment in 1975 of Public Law 94-142, the Education for All Handicapped Children Act, provided a legal mandate for parents to be included in their child's educational program. "It created new expectations for parents to be part of the decision-making process; to be planners, coordinators, and advocates for their child's education; and to assume the role of teacher at home (Roger, 1986)" (Bazyk, 1989, p. 724). Treatment programs were extended to the home, and parents became therapists expected to carry out the prescribed regimens. When parents did not carry out the prescribed regimen, they were identified as noncompliant. Whereas the prevailing child-centered model was modified to include active parent participation, health professionals still functioned as experts who knew best and who made most of the treatment decision based on their judgment regarding the child's needs.

The importance of families in facilitating the development of young children with special needs was further emphasized through the passage in 1986 of Public Law 99-457, Handicapped Infant and Toddler Program. "This law represents a philosophical shift from child-centered to family-centered intervention" (Bazyk, 1989, p. 724). The critical difference is the recognition that families incorporate the needs of the child within the context of the needs and priorities of the family (Shelton & Stepanek, 1994). Families are recognized as the constant in the child's life, and families are the consumer of services as well as the decision makers. Professionals are agents of the family and promote family decision making and competencies. Intervention goals are based on the needs of the entire family. This change in goals also requires a change in the role of health care providers from experts to those seeking to establish a parent–professional collaborative relationship that supports parents in meeting their goals. In this model, health care providers "serve as consultants to the parents to help them acquire the knowledge and skills that they need to care for their children with special needs" (Bazyk, 1989, p. 725). Furthermore, it is recognized explicitly that "parents are the specialists in knowing their child and their family" (Bazyk, 1989, p. 726). In a collaborative model, activities are not prescribed for parents, and lack of follow-up with home activities is not viewed as "noncompliance." The home activities need to fit the degree to which individual parents want to be, and realistically can be, involved given their other obligations.

This movement from a child-centered to a family-centered model requires a change in beliefs, attitudes, and behaviors of health care providers in order to promote greater participatory involvement by the family. The traditional model of providing health care promotes child and parental dependency on health care providers (Dunst, Trivette, Davis, & Cornwell, 1988). In contrast, family-centered health care is based on principles that are designed to foster empowerment of families. Dunst et al. (1988) have outlined basic principles of health provision that underlie empowerment and effective helping. First, they argued that a positive, proactive stance is necessary in which people are viewed as competent or as having the capacity to become competent. Second, failure to display competence "is not due to inherent personal deficits but rather to the failure of the social systems to create opportunities for competencies to be displayed" (Dunst et al., 1988, p. 72). *Enabling* involves creating opportunities for competence to be displayed. Third, individuals need the necessary information to make informed decisions, to develop necessary competencies, and to attribute behavior change to their own actions.

These principles result in expanding the role of health care providers to include "the empowerment of families to become more actively involved and in control of identifying and meeting the needs of their health impaired children" (Dunst et al., 1988, p. 79). Taken from the social-systems perspective, empowerment can be defined operationally as enabling—that is, proactively creating opportunities for individuals and families

> To become better able to solve problems, meet needs, or achieve aspirations by promoting acquisition of competencies that support and strengthen functioning in a way that permits a greater sense of individual or group control over its developmental course. (Dunst et al., 1988, p. 72)

In the remainder of this chapter, we will consider intervention in terms of efforts to address the hypothesized mechanisms of effect. That is, we will focus on efforts to prevent disruptions of normal child development processes, reflected in school performance and peer relations, and parenting. In subsequent chapters in this section, we will address two aspects of medical management of importance to the health outcomes of extended life and quality of life: adhering to medical regimens and managing pain.


## SCHOOL PERFORMANCE AND PEER RELATIONS

As we have emphasized previously, one of the objectives in lessening the impact of chronic childhood illness is to avoid disrupting normal processes of child development. It has been noted that "the normalization of the child largely depends on the social and academic progression that occurs in the school setting" (Sexson & Madan-Swain, 1993, p. 124).

However, it has been estimated that almost 40% of children and adolescents with chronic illness experience school-related problems (Bloch, 1986). As discussed in chapter 4, primary among these problems are difficulties with social and peer interaction and school performance. Preventing these school-related problems is integral to optimal overall adaptation to an illness.

School performance difficulties come about in two ways. First, some children with chronic illness experience cognitive impairment as a direct consequence of their illness, such as patients with sickle-cell disease who have strokes, or as a consequence of treatment, such as radiation for a brain tumor. Sometimes the cognitive impairment produces major performance difficulties such as that found with traumatic brain-injured children. More frequently, the cognitive impairment produces performance problems similar to those found in children with learning difficulties. For example, in the classic Isle of Wight Survey, children with chronic illness had an increased incidence of severe learning problems (14%) compared to healthy control children (4.5%; Sexson & Madan-Swain, 1993). Second, some children with chronic illness do not have cognitive impairment but fail to achieve their potential compared to their physically healthy peers (Sexson & Madan-Swain, 1993). This suggests that mediating processes such as absenteeism; child emotional difficulties reflected in anxiety or depression; illness or treatment effects such as attentional problems, fatigue, lethargy, and functional limitations on activity; and attitudes of parents and school personnel may account for these learning problems.

Homebound instruction may help the student deal with the academic problems associated with absenteeism. However, many children with chronic illness have frequent periods of short absences that may be insufficient at any one time to warrant homebound services. Furthermore, homebound instruction cannot replace the role of the school setting in fostering social and emotional development (Sexson & Madan-Swain, 1993). Homebound instruction can be a useful adjunct, but it is not a primary solution.

The overall educational situations for children with chronic illness have been well summarized by Sexson and Madan-Swain (1993).

> At some time during their school careers many children with chronic illness will require some type of special consideration by the school. Although most children with chronic illness do not need specific special education placement, they require coordinated school interventions to maximize school attendance and facilitate educational and social growth. (p. 115)

Meeting the educational needs of children with chronic illness requires cooperative efforts among health care providers, the child and family, and the school system. These services frequently are conceptualized as *school reentry*—that is, the process of reintegrating the child into the school setting after a diagnosis of a chronic illness or a prolonged absence because of the illness. Successful school reintegration programs focus on meeting the child's special needs by enhancing the child's academic and social skills, by appropriately modifying the school environment, and by helping parents be effective advocates for the needs of their children.

### School Reintegration Programs

To address the school reentry process of children with chronic illness, many medical specialty teams incorporate school liaison as a component of services provided to children. These services vary in structure, from relatively unsystematic efforts to formal programs with multiple components. One such multiple component program is the school reintegration project developed by Katz and colleagues for children with cancer (Katz, Rubenstein, Hubert, & Blew, 1988; Katz, Varni, Rubenstein, Blew, & Hubert, 1992). The primary goal of the program is to reintegrate children with cancer into school as soon after the diagnosis as possible to prevent adjustment problems associated with disruption of school participation and social support.

This school reintegration program has four specific components. *Preliminary intervention* activities are initiated as soon after the diagnosis as feasible and include assessing the child's school behavior and parents' involvement with the school prior to the illness and arranging interim educational programs prior to school return. *Conferences* with school personnel focus on helping school personnel understand basic issues about the child's illness and treatment, including scheduling medical treatments and their side effects, planning for absences, anticipatory psychosocial adjustment issues such as the reaction of school personnel and other children to the child, and the formulation of an individualized educational plan. *Classroom presentations* occur with the child present and provide the child's peers with age-appropriate information about the child's illness, medical procedures and treatments, and common side effects such as vomiting, hair loss, and weight gain, and the importance of social support and the negative consequences of teasing. *Follow-up contact* with school personnel and parents occurs after the child returns to school and continues as needed.

The effectiveness of this school integration program was evaluated in a study of 49 children with newly diagnosed cancer. A comparison group consisted of 36 children who had been diagnosed with cancer within 36 months before the project was initiated (Katz et al., 1988). The study design included pre- and post-evaluations for the intervention group on parent, teacher, and child reports of adjustment; grades and absenteeism; and comparisons of the intervention group post measures with the data obtained from the comparison group. The findings indicated that, compared to pre-test measures, the children in the intervention group exhibited fewer parent-reported internalizing and overall behavior problems and more social competence; less self-reported depressive symptoms and greater perceived social competence and physical competence; and better teacher-reported school adjustment. There were no significance differences in school attendance or grades between the intervention group and the comparison group. However, the intervention group had significantly higher parent-reported social competence scores, higher social and general perceived competence, and better teacher-reported school adjustment than the comparison group. Teachers, parents, and children all expressed high evaluative ratings of the utility and value of the school reintegration program (Katz et al., 1992).

### Social Support and Social Skills

The transactional stress and coping model of adaptation to chronic childhood illness calls attention to the mediating role of perceived social support in ameliorating stress. *Perceived social support* "refers to the cognitive appraisal by individuals that they are cared for and valued, that significant others are available to them if needed, and that they are satisfied by their interpersonal relationships" (Varni, Katz, Colegrove, & Dolgin, 1994, p. 21). Children with chronic illness are at risk for peer difficulties because of negative reactions to their physical changes and from disruption of social contact brought about by illness. Recognizing that the social environment of the school setting may be particularly problematic for children with newly diagnosed chronic illness, studies have attempted to delineate whether perceived social support serves as a protective factor in adaptation to chronic illness.

The unique and combined relationship of family support and peer support was investigated in a study of 153 children, 4 to 16 years of age (M = 10.4 years) with an array of chronic illness, including juvenile diabetes, spina bifida, juvenile rheumatoid arthritis, cerebral palsy, and chronic obesity (Wallander & Varni, 1989). The findings indicated that children with high social support from both family and peers had significantly lower mother-reported internalizing and externalizing behavior problems than children with high social support from only one of these sources. Both family support and peer support contributed independently to reported externalizing behavior problems, but only peer support contributed to internalizing behavior problems. The findings suggested that children with chronic illness can potentially benefit from efforts to improve social support, such as through family counseling or social skills training.

A study with 30 children, 8 to 13 years of age (M = 10.7 years) with newly diagnosed cancer assessed the role of perceived social support from parents, teachers, classmates, and close friends in self-reported depression, anxiety, self-esteem, and parent-reported internalizing and externalizing behavior problems (Varni et al., 1994). The findings indicated that perceived teacher support and parent support showed the predicted association with measures of adjustment. However, it was perceived social support from classmates that was the most consistent predictor of adjustment. Higher perceived social support from classmates predicted lower depressive symptoms, state anxiety, trait anxiety, social anxiety, internalizing behavior problems, and externalizing behavior problems. The general lack of association of social support from friends with adjustment suggests that best-friend relationships are not as influential for adjustment as supportiveness of classmates in general.

The particular importance of social support from classmates is reflected in other findings as well. For example, perceived social support from classmates also has been found to be a significant predictor of depressive symptomatology and self-esteem in children with physical handicaps (Varni, Rubenfeld, Talbot, & Setoguchi, 1989a, 1989b). In addition, perceived social support from classmates was found to be related to overall adjustment in elementary school children without illness problems (La

Greca & Santogrossi, 1980). Furthermore, the association of peer rejection with poor psychological adjustment is well established in the literature (see Coie, 1985).

It has been hypothesized that children's social skills are important to eliciting and maintaining social support from peers. A distinction has been made between social skills and social competence. *Social skills* have been defined as observable behaviors that a child engages in when faced with an interpersonal situation (Walco & Varni, 1991). *Social competence* "represents an evaluative judgement that the child performs age-appropriate adaptive behavior in those areas that are considered socially important by significant others" (p. 229).

Because of their importance to children's adjustment, efforts have been directed toward developing methods to improve children's social skills and peer relationships. Representative of those efforts is the work of La Greca and Santogrossi (1980) in using a behavioral group approach for social skills training with elementary school children (third to fifth grade) who showed difficulty relating to peers. The training procedure consisted of weekly, 90-minute sessions for 4 weeks. Based on the literature regarding correlates of peer acceptance in elementary schoolchildren, eight skill areas were selected for training: (a) smiling/laughing, (b) greeting others, (c) joining ongoing activities, (d) extending invitations, (e) conversational skills, (f) sharing and cooperation, (g) verbal complimenting, and (h) physical appearance/grooming (La Greca & Mesibov, 1979). The main treatment procedures were modeling, coaching, behavioral rehearsal with videotaped feedback, and homework assignments. In contrast to an attention–placebo group and a waiting-list control group, children in the social skills training group demonstrated increased skills in role playing, greater knowledge of how to interact with peers, and more initiation of peer interactions in school.

Research in the area of improving children's social skills has moved to identifying situation-specific social skills deficits as a prerequisite for treatment planning. Representative of this line of research is the work of Dodge and colleagues on generating a taxonomy of situations most likely to lead deviant elementary schoolchildren (Grades 2 to 4) to experience social difficulties (Dodge, McClaskey, & Feldman, 1985). In constructing a taxonomy of problematic situations, 50 elementary schoolteachers and 6 child clinical psychologists identified frequently occurring social situations likely to result in problems among schoolchildren. Factor analysis yielded six situations conceptualized as social tasks: (a) peer group entry, (b) response to peer provocations, (c) response to failure, (d) response to success, (e) social expectations, and (f) teacher expectations. Based on sociometric interviews, peer nominations and ratings of how much they liked each other were elicited, and children were classified as socially rejected or socially adaptive. Based on teacher responses on the Child Behavior Checklist (Edelbrock & Achenbach, 1984), children were classified also as aggressive or nonaggressive. Children's behavioral responses during role playing to these social tasks were obtained for subgroups of aggressive/rejected and nonaggressive/adaptive children. Overall, the adaptive group performed more competently than the aggressive group, particularly in response to peer provocation. Dodge et al. (1985) advocated a profile approach to identifying skills and deficits with specific children. The *profile* would be made up of a two-dimensional matrix of situation contexts and component-skill deficits that would serve as a basis for social skills training for the individual child.

## Social–Cognitive Problem-Solving Strategies

In addition to social skills for specific situations, children need to know how to apply those skills—that is, they need social–cognitive problem-solving strategies. Higher levels of social–cognitive problem-solving skills have been found to be related to psychosocial adjustment (Walco & Varni, 1991). One important social problem-solving skill is the ability to generate effective methods for resolving interpersonal conflicts.

The Interpersonal Cognitive Problem-Solving Model, formulated by Spivack, Platt, and Shure (1976), has spawned a considerable amount of research. This model includes training in five component skills: (a) problems recognition, (b) alternative thinking, (c) means–end thinking, (d) consequential thinking, and (e) evaluative thinking (Walco & Varni, 1991). Another model is that formulated by D'Zurilla and Goldfried (1971), which also includes five components: (a) problem orientation, (b) problem definition and formulation, (c) generation of alternative solutions, (d) decision making, and (e) solution implementation and verification.

Intervention efforts to enhance children's social support typically incorporate social skills training and social–cognitive problem-solving training in various packages. The literature indicates that children can learn these skills and problem-solving strategies and improve psychosocial adjustment. As a consequence, training programs for social skills and problem-solving strategies are being formulated for the specific problematic social tasks confronted by children with chronic illness.

## Social Skills and Cognitive Problem-Solving Training for Children With Cancer

Varni, Katz, and their colleagues have developed and evaluated empirically the efficacy of an intervention program to assist in the school and social reintegration of children with cancer. The rationale for the intervention program is based on several lines of research. Previous research has indicated that perceived social support may attenuate the impact of stressful life events and chronic strain on the psychological adjustment of children with chronic illness. More specifically, the importance of perceived social support from parents, teachers, and classmates as predictors of adjustment in children with chronic illness has been demonstrated empirically (Varni & Setoguchi, 1991; 1993, Varni, Setoguchi, Rapport, & Talbot, 1991; 1992). As we discussed previously, these studies indicated that perceived classmate support was the most significant predictor of depressive symptoms, trait anxiety, and general self-esteem (Varni, Katz, & Waldron, 1993).

Another line of research is based on the observation that children with cancer often experience a disruption of their social relations and typically have not developed the social competence necessary to cope with the stress associated with their disease. For example, teachers rated children with cancer as less sociable, less prone to leadership, and more socially isolated and withdrawn (Noll, Bukowski, Rogosch, LeRoy, & Kulkarni, 1990). Children with newly diagnosed cancer have been found to have difficulty confronting social situations involving teasing and name calling, assertiveness, and problem-solving (Katz & Varni, 1993).

Based on these findings, Varni and Katz hypothesized that social-skills training should enhance social competence of children with cancer and other chronic illness, facilitate social interactions, and result in greater perceived social support and fewer subsequent adjustment problems (see Varni, Katz, & Waldron, 1993).

To address these hypotheses, researchers assessed the benefits of an explicit social-skills training component in facilitating school reintegration (Varni, Katz, Colegrove, & Dolgin, 1993). Sixty-four children with newly diagnosed cancer, 5 to 13 years of age, were assigned randomly to either a group that received social skills training in addition to routine school reintegration services or to a school reintegration group only.

The social skills training was made up of three curriculum modules, each of which was 60 minutes long and provided individually. The *social–cognitive program-solving module* taught children to identify the problems, consider the antecedents, explore the possible resolutions, and evaluate outcome to guide future responses in relation to interpersonal difficulties with peers, parents, teachers, and siblings. The *assertiveness training module* taught children how to express their thoughts, wishes, and concerns to others, with an emphasis on home activities and medical care at school. The *handling-teasing-and-name-calling module* taught children how to cope with verbal and physical teasing associated with changes in their physical appearance. The children were given specific homework assignments at the end of each session, and they used demonstration videotapes and a treatment manual in the sessions. The primary care-providing parent participated in one session at the beginning of the intervention and was encouraged to support his or her child's social–cognitive problem-solving efforts. Children were seen for two follow-up social skills booster sessions at 3 weeks and 6 weeks, following their return to school.

The findings indicated that at the 9-month follow-up, children receiving the social problems-solving skills training evidenced significantly less parent-reported internalizing and externalizing behavior problems and significantly greater classmate and teacher social support and school competence than the children in the comparison condition who received only the routine school reintegration services.

In a subsequent analysis of the 9-month findings (Varni, Katz, Colegrove, & Dolgin, 1993), higher perceived classmate social support was related to lower depressive symptoms, state, trait, and social anxiety, and lower internalizing and externalizing parent-reported behavior problems. Higher perceived teacher social support was related to lower externalizing behavior problems. Perceived classmate social support was the most consistent predictor of adaptation.


# PARENTING

The transactional stress and coping approach to adaptation to chronic childhood illness emphasizes three processes that influence child development and functioning directly through parenting: (a) parental beliefs regarding development and health and illness, (b) parental stress related to both illness tasks and daily hassles, and (c) parental distress. These parental processes also serve as salient intervention targets.

Adaptation to chronic childhood illness can be fostered by intervention programs designed to reduce parental stress and distress and to enhance parenting skills conducive to child cognitive and social development. To date, there are few empirical studies of the effectiveness of intervention programs that target improving parenting as a method of fostering adaptation to chronic childhood illness. Before reviewing an example of this type of approach, it is useful to recognize that the mental health and child development literature contains examples of parenting intervention programs with well documented effectiveness in improving children's behavior problems and cognitive and social functioning. A brief review of illustrative examples is useful in identifying what eventually could be realized with systematic efforts to develop parenting intervention programs for children with chronic illness.

## Behavioral Adjustment

The parenting training program developed by Rex Forehand and his colleagues over a 20-year period is exemplary (Forehand, 1993). Because this program focuses on children who are noncompliant in multiple situations, it may have particular application to situations in which adherence to medical regimens is a problem. The program rationale is based on teaching parents effective procedures for interacting with their children. The parenting program is designed to teach parents two sets of skills. The first set of skills are those designed to improve the parent–child relationship, as well as to increase the child's desirable behaviors. There are three component skills: (a) attending to a child's activities, (b) praising or rewarding the child's positive behavior, and (c) ignoring minor unacceptable behavior. The second set of skills are those that assist parents in dealing with problematic child behaviors and noncompliance. There are two component disciplinary skills: (a) giving instructions and (b) using the time-out procedure.

These two sets of parenting skills are taught in a systematic manner in eight to ten sessions. The skill and rationale are described for the parents, and then the therapist models the skill; parents practice the skill with the therapist; parents practice the skill with the child in the therapy room and receive feedback from the therapist; and parents and therapists discuss ways to use the skill in various situations at home. Numerous evaluations of this parenting program have been conducted, and the findings indicated that the program is effective with parents of various educational and intellectual levels (Forehand, 1993).

### Cognitive and Social Development

There have been a number of intervention programs that have been designed to help parents interact with their infants and young children in ways that foster cognitive and social development. Bronfenbrenner (1975) concluded that a focus on parental involvement, the mother–child interaction system, and the parents as the primary agents of intervention are critical to effective programs. These programs have focused on economically disadvantaged children, and some have included a day-care component. Over time, programs with demonstrated effectiveness have been applied to groups of children who are at risk for developmental problems. Our own work with adolescent mothers is an example (Thompson, Cappleman, Conrad, & Jordan, 1982). The infants of adolescent mothers are at risk for medical, developmental, behavioral, and learning problems. However, high-quality antenatal care can reduce the risks of medical problems. The goal of our study was to foster the development of infants of adolescent mothers by teaching mothers to interact in developmentally conducive ways with their infants through incorporating the Partners for Learning Curriculum (Sparling & Lewis, 1984) into a home-based intervention program.

The Partners for Learning Curriculum (Sparling & Lewis, 1984) is a series of learning activities for mothers and children from birth to 24 months of age. These activities are designed to foster physical, motor, perceptual, cognitive, language, and social development. This curriculum was incorporated into monthly home visits made by a nurse clinician for 2 years after the birth of the child. A comparison group did not receive the intervention program, but participants in both groups received developmental follow-up assessments at 9, 12, and 30 months. Mothers were invited to participate in either the control group or the intervention group on the basis of a randomly determined sequence. All mothers were 18 years old or younger when they delivered their babies, all were African Americans, and all were of low socioeconomic status. Nineteen mothers and infants in the control group and 18 in the intervention group completed the study.

The findings indicated that all infants in both groups had normal scores on the Denver Developmental Screening Test at 9 months of age. At 12 months of age, the intervention group had a mean Bayley Mental Developmental Index of 116.32 ($SD$ = 11.07; range 98–137) compared to the mean for the control group of 110.16 ($SD$ = 13.50; range 89–131) ($p$ > .10). At 30 months of age, the intervention group had a mean Stanford-Binet intelligence quotient of 97.95 ($SD$ = 12.71; range 77–121) compared to the mean of 89.50 ($SD$ = 16.17; range 65–116) for the control group ($p$ < .08). Furthermore, 50% of the children in the control group had cognitive functioning that fell within the at-risk level (i.e., IQ ≤ 84) ($p$ ≤ .05), compared to only 11% of those in the intervention group. Analysis of mother–child interaction during a 20-minute videotaped play session at 30 months of age revealed that mothers in the intervention group gave more praise and positive feedback to their children, who in turn were more cooperative than the children in the control group. Thus, the results provided support for the effectiveness of intervention in promoting developmentally conducive interactions of adolescent mothers with their infants. The effect was relatively small, but the intervention program was also modest, consisting of only monthly home visits with no day-care setting components.

This curriculum was a component of a much larger intervention program for low birth weight (≤ 2500 grams) premature (gestation ≤ 37 weeks) infants. The Infant Health and Development Program is an eight-site, randomized clinical trial of the efficacy of combining early child development and family support services with pediatric follow-up in reducing developmental, behavioral, and health problems among these at risk infants (Gross, 1990). A large group of infants ($N$ = 985) were assigned randomly to the intervention ($n$ = 377) or control ($n$ = 608) groups, and received developmental follow-up assessments at eight clinic visits through 36 months of age (corrected for prematurity).

The intervention program had three components. The home visit component consisted of weekly visits for the first year and biweekly visits thereafter, during which health and developmental information and family support were provided and two curricula were implemented. The Partners for Learning Curriculum (Sparling & Lewis, 1984) emphasized cognitive, linguistic, and social development through a program of games and activities for parents to use with their children. The second curriculum focused on helping parents to manage self-identified problems (Wasik, 1984). The second component was participation for 5 days a week in a child developmental center program from 12 through 36 months of age, which continued to implement the learning activities used by the home visitors. The third component was bimonthly parent group meetings, beginning at 12 months, to provide information on child rearing, health, safety, and other parental concerns.

The primary findings were that children who received the intervention program had significantly higher IQ scores and significantly fewer mother-reported behavior problems at 36 months (corrected age) than the children in the control group. The effect in terms of cognitive development for the subgroups ($\geq$ 2001 grams) was 13.2 IQ points and for the lighter subgroups ($<$ 2001 grams) was 6.6 IQ points. There also was a small, but significantly higher, level of mother-reported minor illness in the intervention group. The program was effective in decreasing the number of low birth weight premature infants at risk for developmental disability, but the program was not effective for the subgroup with birth weight less than 1500 grams and with IQ scores less than 70. This indicates the continuing need to develop intervention programs that are effective for children who are at high biological risk for developmental disabilities.

## Multifamily Group Intervention for Children With Diabetes

The concepts and procedures associated with parenting intervention programs designed to foster developmentally conducive parent–child interaction are beginning to be applied to the specific situation of children with chronic illness. An example is the intervention program developed by Satin, La Greca, Zigo, and Skyler (1989) for adolescents with diabetes. This program is illustrative because it contains several components that are designed to increase family support and positive family interventions around diabetes management to improve metabolic status and overall psychosocial functioning.

Families of 32 adolescents (M = 14.6 years) with insulin-dependent diabetes were assigned randomly to one of three groups: multifamily, multifamily plus parent simulation of diabetes, and control. The family component was the same for both intervention groups. There were three to five families per group, and the groups met together for six weekly sessions of 90 minutes each. Discussion facilitators—a psychiatric social worker and a nurse clinician—endeavored to promote independent problem-solving skills regarding managing diabetes. Family members were encouraged to discuss feelings and to communicate with each other in an assertive and positive manner. The parents in the family intervention plus simulation group simulated diabetes management for one week. The *simulation* consisted of administering twice-daily measured injections of normal saline; measuring four times daily urinary glucose and ketones using simulated urine, and recording the results in a diabetes-monitoring diary; following a meal plan and exercise plan; and submitting to blood tests for glycosylated hemoglobin. The adolescent patients served as "coaches" to their parents during these simulation exercises.

The findings indicated that participants in the small multifamily groups, with and without the simulated experience component, exhibited improvements in metabolic functioning relative to controls at both the 3- and 6-month assessment periods. Adolescents in both intervention groups reported more positive perceptions of a "teenager with diabetes" at post-treatment than did the control group, but there were no significant changes post intervention in either adolescents' or parents' perceptions of family functioning.

## CONCLUSION

The conceptualization of intervention goals in terms of increasing longevity and enhancing the quality of life leads to the specific objective of limiting the impact of the biological disorder and fostering adaptation of children and their families to the stresses associated with chronic illness. One method of accomplishing these goals and objectives is preventing or minimizing disruptions of normal child development processes reflected in school performance and peer relations and parenting.

The importance of social and academic progression in school to the goals of normalization of children with chronic illness has been established clearly. Preventing the school-related problems of poor school performance and difficulties with social and peer interactions is an integral part of adaptation. School reintegration programs involve cooperative efforts among health care providers, the child and family, and the school system, and they identify eliciting and maintaining peer support as key objectives. In addition, specific methods have been developed to improve children's social skills and social cognitive problem-solving skills. The effectiveness of these skill training programs is well established, and they now are being modified to be specific to the challenges confronted by children with chronic illness. Although continued efforts are needed to refine these intervention components, the evidence regarding efficacy is sufficiently strong to warrant integration of school reintegration and social problem-solving skill training into comprehensive care programs for children with chronic illness.

As parents increasingly become involved in, and responsible for, sophisticated health care regimens for their chronically ill children, they are going to need assistance in developing the requisite stress-coping and problem-solving skills necessary for managing these regimens. Parents also are going to need assistance in developing and maintaining parent–child interaction patterns that foster cognitive and psychosocial development of their children and their children's coping skills. As we will discuss further in the next chapters on adherence, pain management, and public policy, parents need to be viewed as active participants in shaping as well as implementing the health care plan for their children. This requires adoption of a parent–professional partnership model of care in which professionals serve as educators and consultants to parents. Parents need to become advocates for their children, particularly in terms of educational services, and as a consequence need to learn advocacy skills. There is a compelling need to develop and evaluate systematically intervention programs designed to meet these parental needs for knowledge and skills that arise out of their expanding role in caring for their children.

Parent–professional collaboration is essential, but it also needs to be recognized that the needs of all parents are not met through professionally guided services. Parents frequently use and benefit from naturally occurring support services—friends and social and religious affiliations. Furthermore, parents often find self-help groups and programs to be emotionally supportive and effective sources of information and practical problem-solving skills. For example, the Candlelighters Childhood Cancer Foundation is an international network of parent support groups. The name *Candlelighters* derives from the belief that "it is better to light one candle than to curse the darkness." The goals of Candlelighters groups include providing an emotional support system and guidance in coping with the impact of cancer on the family and identifying family needs to facilitate the response of medical and social service systems. Some groups conduct separate meetings for teenage patients and their siblings. In recognition of the logistical difficulty some parents have in participating in parent support groups, other parent-to-parent programs train parents of children with a handicap or illness to provide support and coping suggestions, on an individual basis, to parents of newly diagnosed patients (see Anderson, 1985; Chesler, Barbarin, & Lebo-Stein, 1984; Iscoe & Bordelon, 1985).

As with training in school reentry and social problem-solving skills, a number of programs to enhance parenting skills and to provide advocacy training and social support have been developed, and their effectiveness has been demonstrated. The next step involves integrating the school, child, and parenting programs into the array of comprehensive health services offered to children with chronic illness and their families. From among this array of services, individualized care plans can be formulated to match specific child and family needs. To improve the quality of life, this level of psychosocial intervention is a necessary companion to the biomedical health care components that so successfully have extended the lives of many children.

# 11

## ADHERENCE

Complying with instructions, requests, and expectations is important in the everyday life of all children, not just those with developmental and medical problems. Noncompliance has been viewed as the root cause of most behavioral problems that parents bring to the attention of their pediatricians, such as discipline, eating, and dressing problems (see Christopherson, 1994 for a review). Compliance involves learning and developing self-regulatory capabilities. Failing to develop these basic skills can be a major reason for difficulties in complying with medical regimens.

In this chapter, we will consider adherence or compliance with medical regimens, beginning with a general discussion of the scope of the issue and evolving perspectives in terms of conceptualizations and measures. More specifically, we will review the evolution of the view of adaptive noncompliance and corresponding changes in pediatric compliance research. Then, we will apply the biopsychosocial framework to integrate findings of studies of factors affecting adherence in terms of biomedical, child, and social–ecological parameters. As with adaptation in general, this biopsychosocial framework has led to the formulation of models of adherence, three of which we will present and review. We will follow with a consideration of studies that address the interaction among these parameters with regard to three specific situations: pediatric appointment keeping, regimen complexity, and decision making. We will conclude this chapter with a review of the effectiveness of educational and behavioral strategies to improve compliance and of the advent of the process of tailoring a mutually negotiated regimen or management plan.

## SCOPE AND PERSPECTIVES

Adhering to treatment or complying with medical regimens is necessary to maximize treatment effectiveness. However, it is recognized that noncompliance with medical regimens is a relatively common occurrence. Reports in the literature indicate that there is considerable variability in adherence to prescribed medical regimens for both acute and chronic illnesses (see L. H. Epstein & Cluss, 1982; Haynes, Taylor, & Sackett, 1979; La Greca, 1988). Because of its importance to treatment outcome and to quality of life, delineating the processes associated with adherence has been an area of increasing research interest.

The terms *adherence* and *compliance* are used interchangeably in the literature, frequently within the same article. There have been many definitions, but the definition formulated by Haynes (1979) is cited frequently. *Compliance* is "the extent to which a person's behavior (in terms of taking medications, following diets, or executing lifestyles change) coincides with medical or health advice" (pp. 2–3). *Adherence* has been conceptualized in three general ways (La Greca, 1988). One approach views adherence in a categorical manner, with anything less than the minimum level needed for treatment to be effective considered unsatisfactory. Specific criteria or cutoff scores are established to identify adherent and nonadherent patients. One major difficulty with this approach is the lack of knowledge regarding what constitutes an adequate level of compliance for specific health problems. A second approach is to combine multiple indicators of compliance across a number of components of the treatment regimen. A third approach views adherence as a continuum. Level of adherence in any given situation is reflected by the number of adherence behaviors completed divided by the number that are prescribed.

There also has been considerable variability in the methods used to assess adherence. L. H. Epstein and Cluss (1982) categorized methods as indirect and direct. *Indirect methods* include patient or parent reports, physician estimates, pill and bottle counts, and mechanical devices that record behaviors such as the number and time of pill removal from prescription bottles. *Direct methods* include blood/serum assays to assess concentration of the prescribed drug in the blood, and urine assays for detection of excreted medication or drug metabolite. These direct and indirect methods vary in validity, practicability, and expense.

L. H. Epstein and Cluss (1982) pointed out that therapeutic outcome, although frequently employed, can be a misleading indicator of compliance.

The reason is the lack of one-to-one correspondence between adherence and outcome. La Greca (1988) commented: "Adherence to a prescribed regimen does not guarantee symptom remission or disease recovery. The state of the art in medicine is such that treatment is not always effective" (p. 302).

Given the variability in conceptualizations, definitions, and measurement, it is not surprising that there is considerable variability in reported rates of adherence for both adult and child patients. L. H. Epstein and Cluss (1982) noted that compliance rates in the literature range from 18% to 90%. Deaton (1985) maintained that about one third to one half of all medical recommendations are not adhered to. In a similar way, Litt and Cuskey (1980) estimated the average noncompliance rate to be 50% for pediatric populations, with a range of 20% to 80%. In their review of pediatric studies over a 20-year period, from 1970 to 1989, Dunbar-Jacob, Dunning, and Dwyer (1993) reported that the median adherence rate has remained consistent at 50%.

Part of the variability in compliance rates is a function of the recommendations made. Sackett and Snow (1979) reviewed approximately 40 studies and organized the findings into clinically meaningful categories in terms of type of recommendation (appointment-keeping, short- or long-term medications, diets) and intent of the recommendation (prevention or management/cure). The findings across studies suggested compliance of appointment keeping of only about 50% if the appointment was initiated by a health professional; the rates were somewhat higher if the patient was a child. However, when the appointment was scheduled by the patient, compliance rates were approximately 75%. Compliance with appointment keeping for prevention ranged from 10% to 65%. Compliance for management or cure ranged from 55% to 84%. Only two studies addressed compliance with short-term medication for prevention, and both reported 60% to 64% compliance rates. In a similar way, two studies that addressed compliance with short-term medications for treatment or cure reported 77% and 78% compliance rates. The compliance rate for long-term medications for prevention ranged from 33% to 94%, with a mean of 57%. For long-term medications for treatment or cure, the compliance rate ranged from 41% to 69%, with a mean of 54%. The compliance rates for diets ranged from 8% to 70%.

In reviewing these findings, Sackett and Snow (1979) made the important point that while average compliance rates can be reported for a study, what is really crucial is the distribution. It makes a difference clinically if the distribution of compliance across a patient population follows a normal curve, with most cases clustered around the mean, or if compliance follows a U-shaped curve, with one third of the patients taking almost none of the medicines, one third taking almost all of the prescribed medicines, and the remaining one third scattered in between.

## Adaptive Noncompliance

The literature reflects that a gradual change is taking place in assumptions regarding adherence, which is affecting how adherence is being studied (Deaton, 1985). Traditionally, the physician has been viewed as the expert and patients are expected to do what they are told or prescribed to do. Lack of treatment effectiveness was viewed in large part as a result of lack of adherence to the treatment regimen. Noncompliance was problematic and maladaptive. Clinical and research attention was directed toward identifying noncompliers and persuading them to comply.

> Implicit in this perspective, however, is the assumption that the doctor knows best and that the most functional and adaptive patient behavior is to comply fully with medical recommendations, regardless of their effectiveness, or of the cost, inconvenience, and discomfort to the patient or family. (La Greca, 1988, pp. 299–300)

Noncompliance was viewed as indicating irresponsibility, carelessness, or forgetfulness. Haynes (1979) challenged this traditional view, noting that in all but a few legally defined situations, "the individual in our society has a right to refuse to follow health advice" (p. 3). However, of all those who do not comply, only a subset actively refuse assistance to improve compliance:

> Thus, we see the study of compliance problems, aside from its phenomenological aspects, as a means to an end of assisting those who are seeking health and the benefits of modern medicine but who, for whatever reason, have difficulty sticking with the often inconvenient, stigmatizing, or expensive treatments currently in use. We now know that many of these people will volunteer for and respond to compliance-improving strategies, and we believe that we and other health professionals owe them the same efforts in this regard as we do for the other elements of diagnosis, therapy, and compassionate care. (p. 3)

The view of the patient "as a decision-making individual who evaluates medical treatment in terms of its efficacy and also with regard to the physician's past performance, the patient's own health and illness experience, and the experience of others" (Deaton, 1985, p. 3) further contrasts with the view of noncompliance as a character flaw. A patient's decision not to adhere may be a well reasoned, adaptive choice. Corresponding to this view of patients and parents as decision makers in consultation with educator–physicians, clinical and research efforts are beginning to investigate the nature of patient's and parent's decision-making processes and how these relate to outcome.

### Evolution of Pediatric Compliance Research

Dunbar-Jacob, Dunning, and Dwyer (1993) reviewed the literature to identify studies related to adherence in pediatric populations that were published from 1970 to 1989. Articles related to substance abuse were excluded. They identified 91 research articles and summarized them by 5-year intervals. The findings provided a useful synopsis of the status of pediatric adherence research.

The number of papers increased progressively over 5-year intervals from 1970 through 1980 to 1984, in which there were 37 papers from 35 studies. Since then there has been a leveling off in numbers, with 29 papers from 27 studies published from 1985 through 1988. Over time the ages of the patients addressed in these studies have become increasingly older, with 50% focusing on adolescents and only 20% focusing on infants and preschool children.

Research has shifted from acute illness to chronic disease, with nearly 70% of the studies in the latter half of the 1980s addressing adherence in chronic illness. The proportion of studies directed at prevention are relatively low. It is surprising to note that the range of illnesses included in these studies has been small. Among the acute illnesses, the most frequent illness studied has been otitis media, which makes up 64% of the studies. Among the chronic illnesses, diabetes has received the most attention, making up about one third of the studies, followed by asthma (20%), epilepsy (11%), and juvenile arthritis (9%). "Most of what we know about compliance with pediatric regimens has come from studies of compliance to antibiotic regimen for otitis media and from the studies of compliance to diabetic and asthma regimens, principally focused on medication and urine/blood testing" (Dunbar-Jacob et al., 1993, p. 38). Furthermore the otitis media studies have been done with infants and toddlers, whereas the chronic illness studies have been done with school-age children and adolescents.

Medication taking in both acute and chronic illnesses has been the most frequently examined aspect of compliance (46% of studies) followed by studies of compliance to multicomponent regimens (23% of studies) primarily involving diabetes. Appointment keeping and dietary studies have been studied at a relatively low rate. "Thus, our knowledge of compliance behaviors has been formed by the examination of a few behaviors in a very few illnesses at relatively discrete stages of development" (Dunbar-Jacob et al., 1993, p. 39).

The majority (79%) of this research on pediatric adherence has been atheoretical. When studies have been theoretically driven, the Health Belief Model (which we will describe subsequently) has been predominant, with a majority of studies focusing on the health beliefs of the mothers.

No comparative studies of efficacy of different models in predicting or in improving compliance were identified. Furthermore, these studies also have lacked a developmental perspective. No studies identified addressed the nature of changes in compliance to either acute or chronic illness as the child matures. Self-reporting has become the major assessment strategy, accounting for one third of studies during the past 5 years and most frequently is used in combination with biological assays.

The majority of the 91 studies were interventional, but few (16%) used a randomized, control group design, and most were descriptive (16%) or correlational (35%) in nature. The majority of studies reported improvement in adherence of about 33% on average. Fear arousal techniques have declined, whereas educational, behavioral, and multicomponent educational and behavioral strategies have increased.

This review makes clear that our knowledge base regarding pediatric compliance is limited. The field needs to move to more theoretically driven studies that employ experimental designs in evaluating models that seek to predict or improve compliance and that incorporate a developmental approach with a wide range of illnesses.

## FACTORS AFFECTING ADHERENCE

The biopsychosocial framework that we have developed with which to view adaptation to chronic childhood illness unites three parameters (biomedical, individual, and socioecological) to provide an integrating focus. This same three-dimensional framework can be applied when considering factors affecting adherence.

### Biomedical Parameters

As we discussed in chapter 1, there is considerable variability in illness characteristics in terms of type, severity, age of onset, manifestations, course, and outcome and in the management demands placed on individuals and their families by the treatment regimen for specific illnesses. In turn, the extent and nature of general and disease-specific illness and treatment regimen characteristics affect adherence. Five dimensions of biomedical parameters have been investigated: (a) illness type, (b) illness severity, (c) illness chronicity, (d) treatment regimen complexity, and (e) treatment consequences.

In their classic work on compliance in health care, Haynes, Taylor, and Sackett (1979) reviewed 537 articles regarding the magnitude of the problems and determinants of compliance. With the exception of psychiatric conditions, compliance was not found to be related to illness type

(Haynes, 1979). Studies of disease severity also have not consistently found a relationship with compliance (Haynes, 1979). Furthermore, increasing severity of symptoms is associated with decreasing, rather than increasing, levels of compliance (Haynes, 1979). However, the degree of disability produced by the illness is positively associated with compliance (Haynes, 1979).

Although the literature frequently characterizes illnesses into acute and chronic conditions, the duration of health problems varies along a continuum. Across illnesses, chronicity has been associated with poorer treatment adherence (La Greca, 1988). Based on an extensive review of the literature, Haynes (1979) maintained that "the duration of treatment has an unequivocal effect on compliance: adherence to treatment decreases with time" (p. 59). Often adherence appears to be linked to symptoms—once symptoms abate, patients cease taking medications (La Greca, 1988). Although this affects short-term illnesses, such as the frequently cited lack of adherence to the prescribed 10-day period of antibiotics for infection, many chronic illnesses are characterized by recurring symptom patterns or by the need for prophylactic medication, such as penicillin during early childhood to prevent infections in children with sickle-cell disease and anticonvulsants to prevent seizures in patients with epilepsy.

Complexity of the treatment regimen also varies across illnesses and during phases within illness groups. Two broad components of treatment regimens are the taking of medications and lifestyle changes such as modifying diets or activity levels. As the complexity of the treatment regimen increases, within a specific modality such as number, dosage, and timing of medications, and in terms of multiple modalities such as diet, exercise regimens, and medications, adherence decreases. Haynes (1979) summarized the findings: "The more treatments prescribed, the lower the compliance rate" (p. 59). Also, it is recognized that lifestyle changes are more difficult to comply with than the taking of medications (Hulka, 1977). For some patients, cost of treatment is also a barrier to compliance (Haynes, 1979).

Adherence is also a function of positive and negative consequences. La Greca (1988) summarized the evidence from studies across a number of illnesses. Her findings indicated that: (a) adherence is better when adherence behaviors bring immediate, positive results, such as pain relief or symptom reductions or immediate negative results; (b) adherence is more difficult with regimens that interfere with normal development or daily activities; (c) adherence is more difficult with regimens that produce negative physical and cosmetic side effects; and (d) adherence to future-oriented regimens designed to prevent or forestall illness complications requires a particularly high level of motivation.

## Child Parameters

Individual differences in development, behavioral style, and responsiveness to treatment are child parameters that affect adherence. As discussed in chapter 7, children's conceptualizations of health, illness, pain, and death follow a developmental perspective that generally lags somewhat behind their level of cognitive development, particularly in terms of understanding of cause and effect relationships, immediate versus future benefit, and the necessity and benefits of painful procedures. In the same way, the child's level of social and emotional development affects adherence in terms of capacity for self-regulation of emotions and behaviors and response to social and peer demands. For example, La Greca (1988) pointed out that adolescents have difficulty adhering to treatment regimens that produce undesirable side effects and may deny or neglect their medical care to avoid appearing different from their peers.

Individuals also vary in their responsiveness to treatment regimens. There are individual differences in absorption rates for drugs and in metabolism that can affect treatment effectiveness and side effects. This variability in response to treatment can impact motivation to adhere to the treatment regimen (La Greca, 1988). However, treatment regimens are based largely on the average patient's typical response to a regimen. Individual variability in responsiveness needs to be considered to enhance both treatment efficacy and adherence. In particular, research is needed to delineate coping skills and behavioral styles conductive to adherence (La Greca, 1988).

The research program of Jacobson and Hauser and their colleagues has addressed the role of patient coping abilities and psychological adjustment on adherence of children and adolescents ($N = 61$), ages 9 to 16 years, to a diabetes regimen over a 4-year period (Jacobson et al., 1990). They addressed adherence in terms of ratings by a pediatrician or diabetes nurse specialist of diet, metabolic monitoring, and insulin use. They measured psychological adjustment using an index derived from six interrelated measures of the child's adjustment: (a) self-esteem, (b) parent-reported behavioral problems, (c) child-reported behavioral problems, (d) self-perceived competence, (e) parent-reported competence, and (f) self-reported adaptation to diabetes. Patient coping was assessed in terms of locus of control and ratings of ego defense mechanisms and adaptive strengths.

The findings indicated that the rate of adherence decreased significantly over the 4-year period, but the relative adherence of individuals remained stable. That is, patients did not tend to change their position within the group in terms of adherence. Age at study inception was associated significantly with adherence. Younger children were more adherent than older children. Higher psychological adjustment ratings at study inception also were associated with better adherence. Patients who used more mature defenses and who demonstrated greater adaptive strengths were more likely to remain adherent over the 4-year period. Hierarchical regression analyses revealed that age at study inception, psychological adjustment, and ego defense levels were associated significantly with the composite measure of adherence and accounted for 47% of the variance. With the effects of age controlled, both adjustment and maturity level of ego defenses remained significant. Similar findings occurred with each component of adherence—that is, diet, metabolic monitoring, and insulin use. One implication of these findings is that a patient's pattern of adherence established initially persists over time, as do the initial associations between adherence and psychosocial functioning in terms of adjustment and coping.

## Social–Ecological Parameters

The major sources of ecological influence on adherence are the family and the relationship the doctor has with the patient and the family. As discussed previously, the family is affected by chronic childhood illness in terms of time demands and disrupted and changed routines and lifestyle. In turn, the family influences adaptation of the patient, particularly through the degree of emotional and instrumental support it provides. All family members are impacted by the child's chronic illness, but most often mothers assume the major responsibility for implementing the treatment regimen. Thus, maternal functioning, particularly in terms of stress, coping, and distress, is likely to affect adherence. Furthermore, the maternal processes associated with parenting, such as knowledge and beliefs regarding cognitive and social development and child management skills, along with health beliefs and specific disease-related knowledge and skills, are also likely to affect adherence.

Evidence regarding the contribution of parental processes to adherence is beginning to emerge. Researchers investigated the role of parenting style in adherence with a cancer treatment regimen in a study of 77 children, 3 to 10 years of age ($M = 69.4$ months) with various types of cancers (Manne, Jacobsen, Gorfinkle, Gerstein, & Redd, 1993). The researchers administered the Parenting Dimensions Inventory (Power, 1989) to the primary caregivers (63 mothers, 13 fathers, and 1 grandmother). This inventory assesses (a) parental support, in terms of nurturance, sensitivity to the child's input, and a nonrestrictive parenting attitude; (b) control in terms of type and amount, and (c) structure, in terms of involvement, consistency, and organization. The pediatric nurse practitioner completed the adherence rating scale, which had two dimensions. *Procedure-related adherence* included cooperation with conduction of mouth care, central access line care, other hygiene care, and physical examinations. *Appoint-*

*ment and symptom-reporting adherence* included arrival for appointments, cancellation or delay of appointments, and timeliness of reporting reactions to treatment.

The findings indicated that two child parameters were related to adherence. Younger children were more likely to exhibit procedural adherence difficulties, and children who were more functional and physically active had more procedural and appointment and symptom-reporting adherence difficulties. The parenting parameters also were related to adherence. Caregivers who were more supportive—that is, who were more sensitive to their children's input, had a less restrictive attitude toward child rearing, and were more nurturant—had fewer appointment and symptom-reporting adherence problems. The other parenting dimensions of control and consistency were not significantly related to either procedure-related or appointment and symptom-reporting adherence. Lower socioeconomic status also was associated with appointment and symptom-reporting difficulties. Furthermore, there was an interaction of child functional status and parenting style such that the highest level of appointment and symptom-reporting adherence problems were reported in the most functional, physically active children with low levels of supportive parenting style.

In addition to child-rearing attitudes and practices, the relationship of other aspects of parenting, such as problem-solving skills, to adherence are beginning to be addressed. For example, in a study of 30 children with phenylketonuria, researchers addressed the relationship of parental problem-solving skills and stress to dietary compliance. Based on the children's mean blood phenylalanine levels for the previous 6 months, parents were included in a good ($n = 19$) or poor ($n = 11$) control group. Parents (27 mothers and 3 fathers) provided problem-solving responses to audiotaped descriptions of 12 situations involving dietary decisions typical of those encountered by children with phenylketonuria. Half of the situations portrayed high stress in terms of increased time pressure and competing activities. The researchers rated the overall quality of the parents' problem-solving responses and the number of different alternatives generated. They assessed family functioning in terms of the Family Environment Scale (Moos & Moos, 1981).

The findings indicated that parents whose children were in good dietary control produced higher quality responses, a higher number of responses, and integrated more behaviors into their solutions than parents of children in poor metabolic control. Stress reduced the quality of problem-solving in both groups. The level of support and perceived cohesion within the family and the degree of conflict between family members was not associated with adherence, but parents of children in good control had higher scores on the control scale than parents of children in poor control.

In a study of 25 children and adolescents, 7 to 17 years of age ($M = 12.5$ years), Chaney and Peterson (1989) addressed the role of family factors in managing juvenile rheumatoid arthritis. They assessed family functioning in terms of the cohesion and adaptability dimensions of the Family Adaptability and Cohesion Evaluation Scales III (Olson, Portner, & Lavee, 1985), which was completed by the parent and patient. The researchers assessed number of coping behaviors, life stresses, and level of family satisfaction for each parent. They used a self-monitoring, weekly medication diary, completed by the parents, to assess adherence. The findings indicated that more extreme levels of family functioning (that is, those further from the center of the circumplex model) were associated with lower levels of medication compliance. Families that identified a greater number of life stresses had lower levels of medication compliance. Higher levels of medication adherence were associated with mothers who endorsed a greater number of coping behaviors and fathers who reported higher levels of family satisfaction.

The previously described study of children and adolescents with insulin dependent diabetes over a 4-year period (Jacobsen, Hauser et al., 1990) assessed the contribution of the family environment to patient adherence (Hauser et al., 1990). Family functioning was assessed in terms of parent and patient scores on five subscales of the Family Environment Scale (Moos & Moos, 1981): (a) conflict, (b) cohesion, (c) expressiveness, (d) organizational control, and (e) independence. The findings indicated that parent's perceptions of family support in terms of cohesion—that is, commitment and help that family members provide for one another—were associated with patient adherence during the first year of illness, and both parents' and youngsters' initial perceptions of family cohesion were associated with improved adherence over time. Both parents' and youngsters' perceptions of family conflict were associated with lower levels of adherence during the first year of the illness, and youngsters'—but not parents'—perceptions of family conflict were associated with follow-up levels of adherence. Parents', but not youngsters', initial perceptions of degree of family organization were linked with initial and follow-up adherence levels. No significant relationships were found between youngsters' or parents' perceptions of family valuing of independence and adherence. Parents' perceptions of higher levels of expressiveness were initially associated with better follow-up levels of adherence—the only significant relationship in terms of family expressiveness. This type of research focus on identifying patterns of family functioning associated with adherence will likely lead to identifying high-risk subgroups and specific intervention efforts.

A number of aspects of the health care setting and the doctor–patient relationship have been identified as influencing adherence. For example, a consistent finding has been the negative association of compliance with waiting time (Litt & Cuskey, 1980). The longer the waiting time, the lower the compliance. La Greca (1988) summarized the main findings about doctor–family relationships. Adherence is enhanced when (a) parents are satisfied with the medical care provided for their child; (b) the medical provider is perceived as friendly, warm, and emphatic; (c) there is consistency in who is providing the care; and (d) there is effective communication—for example, as reflected by an emphasis on treatment instructions.

Parents have to balance their child's health needs with the other aspects of their child's and family's daily lives and goals. Preserving as much "normality" in the child's life as possible is an often expressed goal against which treatment requirements are balanced. As parents increasingly are being asked to be primarily responsible for implementing complex medical regimens, opportunities need to be provided for parents to acquire the requisite knowledge and problem-solving skills.

## MODELS OF MEDICAL ADHERENCE

Several efforts have been made to formulate multivariate conceptual models of adherence to medical regimens. All these models incorporate combinations of biomedical, child, and social–ecological parameters, but specific variables and underlying theoretical perspectives vary.

### Health Belief Model

One model that has influenced thinking about adherence and its determinants is the Health Belief Model (see Becker, Maiman, Kirscht, Haefner, Drachman, & Taylor, 1979). This theory is based on the decision-making concepts of *valence*—that is, the attractiveness of a goal—and *subjective probability*—that is, a personal estimate of the likelihood of goal attainment (Becker et al., 1979). Those following the Health Belief Model postulate that the individual's decision to undertake a recommended health action depends on the individual's perceptions of susceptibility to the specific illness; severity of the condition; efficacy or benefits of the prescribed actions in preventing or reducing susceptibility or severity; and the physical, psychological, financial, and other barriers associated with initiating or continuing the recommended actions. Becker et al. (1979) reported that the relationship between health beliefs and compliance is stronger when assessed concurrently as opposed to predictively. "This may suggest that the relationship between health beliefs and compliance is at least partly bidirectional" (p. 81).

Although this conceptual framework is interesting, with its focus on the role of perceived benefits versus perceived costs in decisions to adhere to health care recommendations, few studies employing the model have been accomplished with children with chronic illness. Furthermore, the applicability of the Health Belief Model for developing adherence intervention programs is not clear (La Greca, 1988). However, this model has been important because it has stimulated thinking about compliance in a multivariate manner.

Iannotti and Bush (1993) have modified the Health Belief Model to incorporate cognitive–developmental processes that are essential to adherence to a medical regime. Their Children's Health Belief Model emphasizes the role of memory, causal thinking, and personal control as the source of motivation to be compliant. Personal control subsumes the concepts of self-regulation, autonomy, locus of control, and self-efficacy. In addition to these cognitive–developmental processes, the Children's Health Belief Model also identifies social, cultural, and socioeconomic factors reflected in the family, peers, and neighborhood environment as influencing adherence. Iannotti and Bush (1993) reported the findings of a study of elementary schoolchildren ($N = 240$) in Grades 3 through 7 that provided support for the Children's Health Belief Model. The primary caregivers' attitudes influenced their children's readiness and expectations to take medicines, and there was significant correlation between the primary caregivers' readiness, cognitive–affective, and enabling variables and the corresponding variables for their children. Furthermore, the children's own cognitions and attitudes had a stronger influence on children's readiness and expectations to take medicines.

## Self-Regulation Model

Leventhal (1993) has reviewed existing models of compliance and adherence as a basis for formulating a self-regulation model that offers a lifespan perspective in which *necessities*—acts that one must do—are converted into *preferences*—acts that one wishes to do. Leventhal (1993) maintained that there is a conceptual difference between compliance and adherence and that the shift in the literature from compliance to adherence represents a moving away from models emphasizing obedience to models emphasizing the autonomy and self-regulatory activity of the patient.

Leventhal (1993) traced the development of models of adherence. Early efforts framed the issue as a personal problem and led to identifying personality characteristics associated with failure to comply. Reframing compliance as a situational problem led to identifying situational characteristics—such as how and where appointments were scheduled—as associated with adherence. This focus on situational characteristics set the stage for operant behavioral models that focused on the role of environmental cues and rewards and cognitive behavioral models that emphasized the role of communication, social learning, and decision making as reflected in the Health Belief Model.

Findings across models indicated that adherence is a multivariate problem in terms of different behaviors—such as appointment keeping and medication taking—that are influenced by multiple personal processes and situational factors. Behavioral approaches are highly successful in producing initial change, but change rarely persists over time. These findings called attention to the need to develop effective strategies to maintain behavioral change.

Leventhal (1993) identified four sets of factors that need to be incorporated into models of adherence to address the issue of maintenance: (a) motivational variables, (b) skill factors, (c) appraisal of outcome, and (d) ability to regulate the internal and external environment. *Motivational variables* reflect processes that are responsible for the desire to adopt or stop specific behaviors. *Skill factors* involve both the selection and execution of specific behaviors. *Appraisal* involves knowledge about appropriate outcomes and attribution of failure to external factors and successful management to personal skill and competence. *Environmental regulation* includes the ability to manage feelings of anxiety and distress evoked by stressful life events or self-appraisals. In Leventhal's view, too much emphasis for maintenance failures has been placed on self-efficacy and behavioral skills and too little on motivation for change. More specifically, what people know and feel about themselves and specific health threats "generates the motives that drive the skills needed to minimize risk" (Leventhal, 1993, p. 101). This view is reflected in a self-regulation framework that Leventhal (1993) has formulated regarding adherence. In this framework, the individual is seen as actively constructing a representation of illness threats and short-term and remote goals that in turn guide coping efforts and criteria for success. The representation, coping, and appraisal processes are influenced by a contextual framework that includes the self-system and cultural and health care institutional factors. Actively constructing a representation leads to focusing on how health threats are framed as an important influence on motivation.

### Systems-Theory Model

The research program of Hanson (1990) is illustrative of a systems-theory approach to adaptation to a specific illness, insulin-dependent diabetes, in which adherence plays a central role. Because research indicates that poor glycemic control is associated with both short-term and long-term complications, the primary health care goal is to attain good metabolic control. Treatment has focused on promoting adherence to the treatment regimen for diabetes, which is complex. As with other illnesses, the direct association between adherence and metabolic control is not one-to-one. The inconsistent findings can be attributed to several factors, including individual variability in response to components of the treatment regimen—such as diet and exercise—and hormonal changes and because some components of adherence—such as the frequency of blood glucose testing—are not expected to relate directly to blood glucose levels (Hanson, 1992).

Hanson and her colleagues have assessed whether five key psychosocial constructs are linked directly with metabolic control or indirectly through their association with adherence: (a) family relations, (b) family knowledge about diabetes, (c) adolescent social competence, (d) life stress, and (e) adolescent age.

The findings across several studies have indicated that some of these variables affect metabolic control directly but others operate through the relationship between adherence and metabolic control. Positive family functioning was associated with improved adherence, which in turn was associated with good metabolic control. In contrast, life stress was directly related to metabolic control. Adolescent age had both direct and indirect effects on adherence. Older adolescents had less positive family relations, more negative coping behaviors, and less parental support of treatment, all of which were associated with poor treatment adherence (Hanson, 1992). Knowledge about diabetes was not linked directly or indirectly to metabolic control. Social competence was not related to metabolic control but buffered the relationship between high life stress and poor metabolic control.

## INTERACTIONAL PERSPECTIVES

Recent efforts to delineate the determinants of compliance have begun to focus on the interactions among biomedical, individual, and social–ecological parameters. Furthermore, these more recent approaches emphasize processes as opposed to static factors. We will review three studies that illustrate this interactional, process-oriented approach.

### Pediatric Appointment Keeping

In pediatric health care settings, 20% to 50% of patients do not keep scheduled appointments (Meichenbaum & Turk, 1987). In particular, there is an increased risk for missed appointments for nonurgent or screening visits compared with acute care or chronic illness visits (see Catlett, Thompson, Johndrow, & Boshkoff, 1993). Previous research has focused on the contributions of demographic parameters to lack of appointment keeping and to the role of financial inducements in improving appointment keeping. However, there has been little focus on delineating the role of processes of daily living such as stress, coping, and social and instrumental support in appointment keeping (Catlett et al., 1993). These processes were assessed within the context of a longitudinal, developmental follow-up project for very low birth weight infants.

The findings indicated that the stress of daily living reported by mothers was a significant predictor for failing to return for the developmental follow-up assessment when the infant was 6 months old (corrected age). The significant predictors for return at 24 months (corrected age) included both biomedical and psychosocial parameters. Of the 124 study participants eligible for the 24-month developmental follow-up examination, 87 returned, 3 had their examinations completed in the hospital or at home, and 34 failed to complete the evaluation. The subgroup that did not complete the evaluation had a lower percentage of parents who were married, a higher percentage who were non-White, infants with higher gestational age, lower maternal intelligence, and lower maternal efficacy ratings than the subgroup who did complete the evaluation. However, there were no significant differences in socioeconomic status, birth weight, or the infants' neurobiological risk score nor maternal ratings of stress regarding daily hassles or tasks associated with caring for very low birth weight infants, coping methods, or psychological distress. Thus, maternal perceptions of daily stress were predictive of difficulties in returning for the 6-month follow-up visit, but maternal marital status, intellectual level, and self-efficacy beliefs were predictive of returning for the 24-month follow-up. This study also demonstrated that providing transportation was a successful intervention strategy to maintain developmental follow-up for a subgroup at high risk for dropping out because of a constellation of biomedical, demographic, and psychosocial factors.

### Regimen Complexity and Patient Skill Level

La Greca (1988) proposed that active knowledge of the illness and skill level needed in using therapeutic apparatus and performing techniques may mediate treatment adherence for complete regimens. A study of cognitive and behavioral knowledge contributions to managing insulin-dependent diabetes relates directly to this hypothesis (S. B. Johnson et al., 1982). With 151 children and adolescents, age 6 to 18 years of age with insulin-dependent diabetes and 179 parents, this study addressed knowledge about diabetes across three domains: (a) general information, (b) problem-solving, and (c) skill at urine testing and self-injection of insulin. All patients and parents received some form of diabetes education, albeit through different educational programs used at different outpatient clinics.

Both parents and children demonstrated poorer problem-solving skills than knowledge of general information. Girls were more accurate than boys, older children were more knowledgeable than younger children, and mothers were more knowledgeable than fathers and children. Children's and parent's knowledge of diabetes often was found to be "simplistic, lacking sufficient understanding of the relationships between insulin, illness, exercise, and stress to make accurate daily management decisions" (S. B. Johnson et al., 1982, p. 713).

More than 80% of the children made significant errors on urine testing, and approximately 40% made serious errors in self-injection of insulin. The most frequent error made was injecting insulin with bubbles. Girls were more accurate with these skills than boys and older children were more accurate than younger children. Furthermore, skills at self-injection and urine testing were not highly related to the other dimensions of knowledge, general information, and problem solving. The duration of diabetes was not significantly related to knowledge or skill. These findings indicated the continuing need for educational approaches that are developmentally targeted and strive to achieve functional knowledge in terms of problem-solving and technical skills.

## Adherence Decision Making

Deaton (1985) addressed the issue of adaptive noncompliance in a study of children ($N = 30$) 6 to 14 years of age with asthma. Asthma is the most commonly occurring chronic childhood illness, and the treatment regimen is complex, difficult to implement, and only partially efficacious (Deaton, 1985). Thus, noncompliance or partial compliance may be seen by some parents as a viable alternative to complete adherence to the treatment regimens. The study focused on identifying adaptive and maladaptive decision makers and to evaluate the relationship between adaptiveness and outcome in terms of illness control and quality of life.

The researchers conducted a structured interview in which parents gave a description of the child's asthma, its impact on the family, the treatment regimen and side effects, and the extent and reasons for non-compliance. As an indication of accuracy of their knowledge regarding their child, parents also predicted their child's performance on four tasks in comparison to normative scores for same-age peers. Based on the interview, an Adaptiveness Rating Scale was completed to rate the patient's decisions about compliance, regardless of the extent of compliance. The scale included eight dimensions: two each relating to activeness and clarity of the compliance choice, knowledge of the child and whether this had a role in making compliance decisions, knowledge of the regimen, and how compliance decisions are evaluated. Parent-reported level of compliance with medications and behavioral recommendations were rated, as was the child's quality of life based on extent of restrictions on normal activities and family attitudes.

The findings indicated that (a) parents tended to underutilize medications increasingly over time; (b) compliance with medications, but not behavioral recommendations, was related particularly to physician ratings of asthma severity; (c) compliance with medications and behavioral recommendations was not significantly related to medical outcome, quality of life, or school absences; (d) medication compliance, but not behavioral compliance, was correlated with parent's rated adaptiveness; (e) rated adaptiveness was correlated positively with quality of life; and (f) the more accurate parents were in their predictions of their child's task performance, the more adaptive their decisions regarding compliance tended to be.

In commenting on these findings, Deaton (1985) noted that "many parents obviously viewed modification of the treatment regimen as an option" (p. 12). This was an active decision, not one representing forgetfulness, irresponsibility, or carelessness. Furthermore, "the adaptiveness of the decision was a better predictor of outcome than was the actual degree of compliance" (p. 12). The findings also have clinical implications in terms of supporting the growing emphasis on patient education and patient–physician partnership in which both have their own areas of expertise. This approach is likely to facilitate more adaptive decision making by enhancing level of communication and mutual respect between patients and physicians.

## INTERVENTION

The importance of adherence to the goal of improving quality of life is well recognized. "If health compliance behaviors can be promoted and maintained, the likelihood of a child living a more normal life, in spite of chronic illness, is greatly increased" (Krasnegor, 1993, p. 357). Numerous studies have attempted to improve adherence to medical regimens, and several excellent reviews are available (e.g., L. H. Epstein & Cluss, 1982; Haynes et al., 1979; Sackett & Haynes, 1976).

Haynes (1976) classified strategies for improving compliance used in studies of therapeutic regimens into three broad categories: educational, behavioral, and combined educational and behavioral. *Educational strategies* attempt to improve compliance by transmitting information about the illness and its treatment to patients. The intermediate objective is patient knowledge and attitudes, and the information may or may not incorporate a motivational fear or positive appeal format (Haynes, 1976). *Behavioral strategies* focus on changing the behavior involved in compliance and include attempts to reduce barriers, cue or stimulate compliance, and reinforce or reward compliance.

Based on an appraisal of effects across studies, Haynes (1976) reported that the success rates for improving compliance were 64% for educational strategies, 85% for behavioral strategies, and 88% for combined educational and behavioral strategies. The success rates for the associated therapeutic outcomes were 50% for educational strategies, 82% for behavioral strategies, and 75% for combined strategies.

Several studies addressed the determinants of compliance. The lack of a significant relationship between patient's knowledge about their illness and compliance and between intelligence quotient and compliance has been noted (see Haynes, 1976). Although knowledge of the therapeutic regimen is necessary, it is not sufficient: "It is becoming equally clear that the proportion of patients who fail to comply because they lack knowledge or intelligence is small indeed" (Haynes, 1976, p. 81).

In contrast to the findings regarding educational strategies for enhancing compliance, the evidence for the effectiveness of behavioral strategies in general is strong. L. H. Epstein & Cluss (1982) reviewed and organized the findings regarding behavioral approaches to increasing adherence in terms of stimulus control, self-control, and reinforcement approaches. *Stimulus-control techniques* include increasing the saliency of pills (e.g., through flavoring pills) and tailoring the drug regimen to habitual events in the patient's lives. *Self-control techniques* include self-regulation of dosage, self-monitoring of symptoms, and self-monitoring of medications. *Reinforcement methods* include reinforcing symptom reduction, medication use, health contracts, and feedback of drug levels.

Based on their review, L. H. Epstein and Cluss (1982) maintained that self-monitoring approaches are less effective than reinforcement or feedback approaches. There have not been enough comparative studies of stimulus-control techniques to determine their relative effectiveness. Reinforcement approaches typically have involved return of security deposits or incentives for children for adherence. Feedback of whether drug levels are in the therapeutic range is relatively simple and cost-effective. Self-reinforcement and drug-feedback approaches are also consistent with the increasing focus on patients and parents as decision makers and physicians and health care providers as educator–consultants in enhancing adherence.

Also consistent with the focus on the patient as decision maker is the process of tailoring a consensual regimen. Fink (1976) described the assumptions underlying the process of tailoring the *consensual regimen*, which is a mutually negotiated regimen or management plan. First, "there is no such thing as a standard regimen for a standard patient" (Fink, 1976, p. 110). That is, all patients interacting with their health care provider present a unique combination of circumstances to which the regimen must be adopted. Second, health decisions and behaviors are carried out in the context of the person's total life. As a consequence, current life priorities, family and social stress, and sociocultural aspects of health and illness directly affect adherence. Third, the individual's health problems are always changing in terms of components with which the patient is self-sufficient and those with which assistance is needed. Fourth, the provider–patient relationship is most appropriate and effective when it is characterized by "mutual participation." Fifth, the goal of compliant behavior is to achieve client-focused as well as provider-focused objectives.

In their review of behavior strategies to enhance compliance, L. H. Epstein and Cluss (1982) reported on two studies in which principles of tailoring were used and appeared to be effective singly and as one component of a multicomponent package. However, Fink (1976) commented that tailoring "is as much a process or relationship of provider and patient interaction as it is a set of tasks" (p. 110). This suggests that future targets for research on factors affecting compliance, and efforts to enhance compliance, could focus on the extent to which the provider–patient relationship is one of "mutual participation."

## CONCLUSION

Adherence is a multifaceted process characterized by variability in conceptualizations and measures and variability in reported rates that hovers at about 50%. There has been a movement away from viewing noncompliance as indicative of patient character flaws, disobedience, or forgetfulness to that of an adaptive choice of a decision-making individual.

It is somewhat surprising that our knowledge about adherence is based on the examination of a few behaviors in a very few illnesses in studies lacking theoretical and developmental perspectives. Nevertheless, applying the biopsychosocial framework to consider factors affecting adherence delineates aspects of the regimen and psychological and social–ecological parameters of importance. Regimens that are complex, interfere with normal activities, produce negative side effects, and are future-oriented are most challenging. Adherence is also a function of the child's social, emotional, and cognitive development and coping skills. Among social–ecological processes, maternal functioning, family functioning, parenting (child-rearing attitudes and problem-solving skills), and doctor–family relationships are all contributing processes.

Research has moved to the model-building stage, in which combinations of biomedical, child, and social–ecological parameters are hypothesized to act together to influence adherence. As with psychosocial adjustment, key processes across models include cognitive processes, problem-solving skills, and family relationships. Intervention studies to foster adherence have provided considerable support for the effectiveness of behavioral approaches to enhance self-regulation and self-reinforcement skills. This skill-based approach, combined with tailoring a mutually negotiated management plan, is consistent with the view of patients and parents as decision makers in consultation with educator–physicians. The next step in the research process is to elucidate the decision-making process, particularly with regard to the overall intervention strategies to enhance adaptation by preventing or minimizing disruptions of normal child development processes reflected in school performance and peer relations and parenting.

# 12

# PAIN MANAGEMENT

This chapter will consider briefly the nature and types of pain and approaches to pain management. We will focus on coping with two types of pain of particular relevance to adaptation to chronic childhood illness: (a) pain associated with invasive medical procedures and (b) chronic and recurrent pain.

We will review findings from studies that endeavor to help children cope with invasive medical procedures by providing information and training skills in coping. We will follow by considering the role of parents (presence, anxiety and parenting style, explanations and distraction techniques, and coaching) in fostering their children's ability to cope with procedures. We will review the effectiveness of a multicomponent, cognitive–behavioral intervention in reducing children's distress during bone marrow aspirations.

In terms of coping with chronic and recurrent pain, we will follow a similar pattern. We will review the findings regarding two types of cognitive–behavioral treatment approaches: (a) pain perception regulation techniques and (b) pain behavior-modification techniques. We will conclude the chapter by formulating guidelines to help children cope with pain.

# PAIN: A MULTIDIMENSIONAL EXPERIENCE

In chapter 7, we discussed the unavoidability of pain in children's daily lives and its association with illness and treatments. Pain was defined as a complex, multidimensional experience involving two components. The sensory component, nociception, is related directly to activity in neural pathway response to tissue damage (P. J. McGrath et al., 1990). The response component includes psychologic, physiological, emotional, and behavioral responses to the nociception. This response dimension is affected by intrinsic factors, such as the child's anxiety, depression, and fear, previous experience with inadequately managed pain, and lack of control. The response dimension also is affected by extrinsic factors, such as the anxiety and fear of parents, parental reinforcement of under- or overreaction to pain, and the invasiveness of the treatment regimen (P. J. McGrath et al., 1990).

It is customary to distinguish three types of pain: acute, chronic, and recurrent. With regard to pain experienced by children, four categories have been delineated based on etiology: pain associated with (a) physical injury or trauma, (b) disease states, (c) medical/dental procedures, and (d) idiopathic (unknown) (Varni, Katz, & Dash, 1982).

Approaches to pain management can involve analgesics, behavioral intervention, or a combination. "The goal of analgesia is to provide maximum pain relief with minimal side effects" (P. J. McGrath et al., 1990, p. 816). A consideration of pharmacological approaches is beyond the scope of this book. The interested reader is directed to the report of the Consensus Conference on the Management of Pain in Childhood Cancer (Schechter, Altman, & Weisman, 1990) for an overview of principles and procedures. We will address the process of coping with the pain of invasive medical procedures and chronic and recurrent pain in this chapter. Efforts to enhance coping with pain typically employ cognitive–behavioral therapy (CBT) approaches. The rationale for this approach is that cognitions and socioenvironmental processes influence the perception, interpretation and behavioral responses to pain. Thus, CBT approaches are directed at regulating pain perception and modifying social and environmental processes, such as parent response, that affect the behavioral expression of, and response to, pain.

# COPING WITH INVASIVE MEDICAL PROCEDURES

It is estimated that each year 5 million American children undergo medical procedures for diagnosis or treatment (Bush, Melamed, Sheras, Greenbaum, 1986). Children with chronic illness are confronted with the challenges of coping with frequent and repetitive painful medical procedures. For example, children with cancer such as acute lymphoblastic leukemia typically undergo three or more years of treatments that involve frequent invasive procedures, including intramuscular and intravenous injections, lumbar punctures, and bone marrow aspirations. The frequency of procedures is conveyed in a study of 70 children, 3 to 10 years of age, with a diagnosis of cancer (Jacobsen et al., 1990). On average, the children had been diagnosed 32 months previously and had undergone 93 venipunctures, with a range of 2 to 300.

The findings are contradictory about whether children *habituate*—that is, become less distressed—to repeated invasive cancer treatment procedures (Jacobsen et al., 1990). A modest effect of less distress over time was found, which became nonsignificant after the effects of child age and quality of venus access were controlled statistically (Jacobsen et al., 1990).

Many clinics use psychological methods to help children through these painful medical procedures, but for the most part these methods have been based on clinical experience. Only recently has a behavioral science basis emerged for efforts to enhance coping with invasive medical procedures. Several reviews of conceptualizations, approaches, and findings regarding coping with invasive medical procedures are now available (see Dahlquist, 1992 and Jay, 1988 for reviews).

In general, there are two main psychological approaches to helping children cope with stressful medical procedures: providing information and training in coping skills.

## Information Strategies

*Information strategies* seek to reduce distress by making the procedure more predictable through verbal explanation, demonstration, or modeling of what will happen (Dahlquist, 1992). In terms of *verbal explanation*, "it is probably most accurate to conclude that sensory plus procedural information is more effective than procedural information alone in decreasing distress associated with a medical procedure" (Dahlquist, 1992, p. 347). *Demonstration* typically involves the "tell–show–do" method. The child is told what will happen in developmentally appropriate language and shown how the procedure works on a doll prior to performing the procedure with the child. Although this procedure is used widely, there have been few studies of effectiveness and of the mechanisms accounting for the effect (Dahlquist, 1992). The effectiveness of pain *modeling* in conveying information and reducing children's distress and disruptive behavior has been well documented by Melamed and her colleagues (see Melamed & Siegel, 1975). Effectiveness of modeling techniques have been related to timing and to the extent of the child's previous experience with medical procedures. For example, when only limited time is available for preparation, modeling may not be helpful and distraction may be the treatment choice

(Dahlquist, 1992). Modeling also appears to have a more beneficial effect with children lacking in experience with the medical procedures and may have a detrimental effect on experienced children. "Modeling and information appear to be most useful for naive, inexperienced patients, where anxiety appears to be based on their unfamiliarity with the medical procedure" (Dahlquist, 1989, p. 362). Experienced children may become sensitized when exposed to modeling or information and may benefit more from specific training in ways to cope with the procedure (Dahlquist, 1989).

## Coping Strategies

Efforts to enhance children's skills in managing the stress and pain associated with invasive medical procedures has been based primarily on cognitive–behavioral coping skills training with children and their parents. The rationale for using cognitive–behavioral strategies is that patient's cognitions influence their stress reactions (Jay, 1988). Training programs to develop cognitive–behavioral coping skills typically involve teaching children a package of coping skills, including deep breathing; attention distraction; muscle relaxation; relaxing imagery, emotive imagery, such as children imagining themselves as superheroes undergoing a test of their powers; and behavioral rehearsal (Dahlquist, 1992). Typically, children choose which specific coping skills they prefer to use. The therapist is customarily present as a "coach" during the medical procedure and prompts the child to use the strategies and praises the child for coping efforts. The training typically is accomplished in a single session of approximately 45 minutes. The effectiveness of cognitive–behavioral coping skills training is well documented, with distress reduction typically reported at 50% or more (Dahlquist, 1992). Whereas these single-session training programs have immediate effects, maintenance across subsequent invasive procedures has been disappointing, suggesting the need for more extensive training and the ongoing participation of a coach (Dahlquist, 1992).

The treatment program developed by Dahlquist (1992) for children with cancer at the Texas Children's Hospital teaches children deep breathing, progressive muscle relaxation involving eight muscle groups, relaxing imagery, and use of positive self-statements. The therapist serves as coach during the actual medical procedure. Initial findings suggested that six sessions may be effective in maintaining decreases in behavioral distress. However, given the individual differences in children's abilities to remain calm independently, the continued presence of a coach during aversive medical procedures may be necessary. This need for ongoing coaching raises concerns in terms of available personnel and costs and focuses attention on the role of parents during stressful procedures.

## The Role of Parents

In recognizing the contribution of social and environmental factors in eliciting and maintaining children's responses to pain, attention has been focused on the role of parents in enhancing children's coping with painful medical procedures. Investigations have addressed four aspects of parental impact: (a) presence, (b) parental anxiety and parenting style, (c) use of explanations and distractions, and (d) coaching.

### Presence of Parents

Four studies have used randomized designs to examine the effects of parental presence or absence during invasive medical procedures (Jacobsen et al., 1990). One research group found that children accompanied by their mothers were less distressed during anesthesia induction prior to tonsillectomy, but that presence of a parent during hospital admission procedures for elective surgery had no effect on child distress (Vernon, Foley, & Schulman, 1967). However, mother presence was associated with more distress in children aged 4 to 10 years prior to, but not during, a venipuncture blood sample draw (Gross, Stern, Levin, Dale, & Wojnilower, 1983). In a similar way, 18-month-old and 5-year-old children (Shaw & Routh, 1982) demonstrated more distress while receiving routine immunization injections if their mothers were present compared to children whose mothers were absent. Shaw and Routh (1982) interpreted these findings in terms of operant conditioning. Mother presence served as a stimulus for expressions of distress, which is reinforced with attention and comforting. Despite distress, children inhibited their expression of distress in the absence of the comforting stimulus represented by mother. Shaw and Routh (1982) also cautioned that these studies provide an explanation of a possible mechanism of effect for the distress children display and should not be interpreted to mean that children should be separated from their mothers during painful procedures. Jay (1988) commented: "Even though children may display greater *behavioral* distress in the presence of parents, their cognitive, affective, and physiological distress may be lessened by the presence of a supportive figure" (p. 417). In this regard, the children almost uniformly reported that the "thing that helped most" during painful experiences was having their parents present (Ross & Ross, 1984). These studies indicate the necessity for evaluating distress multidimensionally.

A subsequent study (Gonzalez et al., 1989) examined the effect of parental presence multidimensionally and also addressed an alternative explanation to operant conditioning: Children are more emotionally aroused by mother absences but may express their arousal behaviorally only if disinhibited by mother's presence. Children 13 months to 7 years 9 months of age receiving injections for immunizations or antibiotics and their mothers were assigned randomly to parent-present ($n$ = 23) or parent-absent ($n$ = 24) conditions. Older children (M = 5 years, 6 months), but not younger children (M = 3 years), demonstrated significantly more behavioral distress—specifically, crying—when the parent was present. In terms of psychological responses, children in the parent-present and parent-absent conditions had comparable heart rates. In terms of self-report obtained from the older group, children overwhelmingly (86%) stated a preference for the parent-present condition for any future injections. The findings did not support the hypothesis of increased physiological arousal with parent absence during injections, but disinhibition of behavioral reactions during a painful experience does occur, and children feel more distress in the parent-absent condition than they do in the parent-present condition. Gonzalez et al. conclude that while a child may behave a bit worse, the importance of parental pressure must not be underestimated. Research needs to focus now on identifying how to render parental presence conducive to reducing child distress during painful procedures.

### Parental Anxiety and Parenting Style

It has been hypothesized that mothers who display more anxious behavior prior to an impending stressful event would have children who also would show more anxiety-related behavior (Bush et al., 1986). Support for this hypothesis was provided in a study of 50 mother–child dyads of 4- to 10-year-old children seen at pediatric outpatient clinics. Maternal self-reported trait and state anxiety was correlated significantly with their report of their children's level of anxiety (Bush et al., 1986). In a similar way, a positive relationship between parental anxiety and children's distress during bone marrow aspirations also has been reported (Jay, Ozolens, Elliott, & Caldwell, 1983).

Parental anxiety also has been related to parenting style and to behavior during stressful medical procedures. The interactions of 66 children with cancer and their parents were evaluated during a routine bone marrow aspiration or lumbar puncture (see Dahlquist, 1992). Anxious parents of children 2 to 7 years of age were more agitated and less reassuring during the procedures and reported using discipline methods that were less consistent, organized, nurturant, and reliant on rule-setting and more punitive than did less anxious parents. These anxious parents also perceived their children as more anxious prior to the procedures. Young children of parents who reported the parenting behavior pattern just described demonstrated higher levels of behavioral distress during the anticipatory phase of the medical procedure. Dahlquist (1992) commented: "It appears that non-nurturing, punitive, inconsistent, insensitive, disorganized, or overly permissive discipline styles are likely to be associated with greater distress in young children undergoing stressful medical procedures" (pp. 368–369).

In the study of the 50 mother–child dyads seen in pediatric outpatient clinics (Bush et al., 1986), parenting patterns also were related to child distress. Mothers whose parenting had an emotive emphasis characterized by agitation, ignoring, and reassurances were likely to have children who demonstrated more distress (Bush et al., 1986). Children whose mother's parenting was characterized by supporting the child's coping efforts through providing information and low rates of reassurance exhibited low rates of distress. Low rates of child distress also were associated with maternal use of distraction and low rates of ignoring.

### Parental Explanations and Distractions

In a study ($N = 70$) of children 3 to 10 years of age seen in an outpatient oncology clinic during which venipuncture was performed, the researchers reported that the most frequent child distress behavior was verbal expressiveness of pain and fear (77%), muscular rigidity (63%), and crying or screaming (63%) (Jacobsen et al., 1990). The most frequent parent behavior was emotional support (63%), followed by distraction (56%) and explanation (46%). Child distress during needle insertion was not influenced by whether parents engaged in distraction. Parental explanations were found to have either a soothing or an inflammatory effect on child distress, depending on the child's existing level of distress and the phase of the procedure. Explanations were beneficial if provided at the onset to an already distressed child. Explanations had an inflammatory effect if provided to a distressed child during the procedure and if provided to a nondistressed child at the beginning of the procedure.

In a subsequent study (Manne et al., 1992), sequential analyses were used to assess the relationship among adult and child behaviors during invasive medical procedures. Children ($N = 43$) between the ages of 3 and 10 years undergoing a venipuncture procedure in the course of cancer treatment participated in the study. The findings indicated that adult use of distraction resulted in both an increase in child coping behavior and a reduction in momentary child distress behaviors and crying. Adult explanations, commands to engage in coping behaviors, giving control to the child, praise, criticism, threats, and bargaining all resulted in decreased likelihood that the child would engage in coping behavior. Giving the child control over some aspect of the procedure—in other words, procedural control rather than behavioral control as discussed in the study by Blount et al. (1989)—resulted in reductions in distress. Directives to cope were associated with less distress subsequently only for children who were upset at the onset. The researchers concluded that, to help their children cope with invasive medical procedures, parents should be encouraged to use distraction, contingent praise, and active directives to cope, and they ought to avoid explanations.

Parental explanations have been found to be ineffective in decreasing child distress, and parental reassurance also has been demonstrated to be ineffective. In a study of 3- to 7-year-old children undergoing a routine intramuscular immunization injection, 42 child–mother dyads were assigned randomly to a parental reassurance, parental nonprocedural talk (distraction), or control group (Gonzalez, Routh, & Armstrong, 1993). Children in the maternal distraction group demonstrated significantly less distress—more specifically, less crying—than the children in the reassurance and control groups who did not differ significantly from each other. Thus, maternal distraction, not reassurance, was found to ameliorate child distress.

### Parental Coaching

In a study of 23 children 5 to 13 years of age with acute lymphocytic leukemia who were undergoing bone marrow aspirations and lumbar puncture, Blount et al. (1989) examined parental behaviors that were followed by or preceded by child distress or coping. The children had not participated in training for coping skills. Child coping behaviors of nonprocedural talk and distractions typically were preceded and followed by nonprocedural talk to the child. Deep breathing was associated with parental commands to "take a deep breath." Reassuring comments, apologies, criticism, and giving behavioral control to the child (e.g., "Tell me when you are ready") were associated with parental distress.

This study was followed up by a study to evaluate the effectiveness of an intervention targeting parent-training of behaviors associated with less child distress (Powers, Blount, Bachanas, Cotter, & Swan, 1993). Four children 3 to 5 years of age receiving intravenous and intramuscular injections in an outpatient clinic were taught to engage in distraction activities such as play or conversation prior to the procedures and in active breathing or counting strategies during the procedures. Parents were taught to engage their children in distraction activities prior to the procedure and to coach the children's use of breathing and counting strategies during the procedure. Intensive training, consisting of modeling, role playing, and rehearsal of child coping and parent coping skills was conducted for two to four sessions lasting 45 minutes. This was followed by maintenance-promoting training involving brief rehearsal of previously learned skills for two to four sessions lasting 15 minutes. The trainer was not present to coach the parents or children during the actual procedure. The findings indicated that both parents and children learned and employed the coping strategies that were taught and distress decreased. Despite improvements, variability also was demonstrated over repeated procedures. Children used coping behaviors but also exhibited some distress. Not all children or their parents maintained behavioral change at all times after training. This suggests that some parents and children may need more intensive follow-up training and maintenance-promotion efforts.

## Multicomponent Cognitive–Behavioral Intervention

The efficacy of a cognitive–behavioral intervention package in reducing children's distress during bone marrow aspirations was compared with that of pharmacologic intervention (oral Valium) and a minimal treatment–attention control condition (Jay, Elliott, Katz, & Siegel, 1987). The subjects were 56 children, 3 and a half to 13 years of age, with leukemia. The researchers provided three intervention conditions in a randomized sequence within a repeated-measures counterbalanced design. In the control condition, children watched cartoons for 30 minutes prior to the bone marrow aspiration, which did not preclude the routine support and reassurance provided by parents and nurses. The pharmacologic intervention consisted of the administration of oral Valium (0.3 mg/kg) 30 minutes before the procedure. The cognitive–behavior therapy intervention included a package of five components: (a) filmed modeling (11 min) of positive coping behaviors, such as breathing exercises and imagery and positive coping self-statements; (b) breathing exercises; (c) imagery and distraction; (d) positive incentive (a trophy presented noncontingently); and (e) behavioral rehearsal (e.g., play doctor and give a bone marrow aspiration).

The findings indicated that children exhibited significantly less behavioral distress, reported significantly lower levels of pain, and had significantly lower pulse rates when in the cognitive–behavior therapy condition than when in the Valium or control conditions. The cognitive–behavioral treatment produced behavioral distress scores that were 18% less and self-reported pain scores that were 25% less than those reported in the control condition.

Because of its demonstrated efficacy, cognitive–behavioral therapy for children with cancer has become almost a routine component of bone marrow aspirations and lumbar puncture procedures. However, Jay & Elliott (1990) noted that parents still experience these procedures as highly traumatic, which has led to developing an adult-focused intervention to reduce parental distress.

The efficacy of a stress-inoculation program designed to ameliorate parents' stress associated with their child's painful procedures was compared to providing a child-focused cognitive–behavioral therapy intervention only. The stress-inoculation program was designed to teach parents coping strategies for their own anxiety; it was not designed to teach parents to intervene directly with their children. The program included three components: (a) filmed modeling and education, (b) brief self-statement training, and (c) relaxation training combined with coping imagery (Jay & Elliott, 1990). Parents viewed a 15-minute video that provided information about bone marrow aspirations, lumbar punctures, and pediatric cancer treatments and a model of a parent using positive coping behaviors and cognitions during the procedures. Self-statement training was conducted for 15 minutes and addressed cognitive–behavioral principles, the parent's own cognitions and feelings during the child's procedures, and the development of individualized self-statements such as "I don't like this, but I can handle it." The relaxation training session was 15 minutes, during which instructions were provided for muscle relaxation and guided imagery.

Parents assigned to the child-focused intervention received no direct intervention themselves but accompanied their children in the cognitive–behavioral therapy condition or the cognitive–behavioral therapy plus Valium condition. The subjects included 72 parents (79% mothers) of children aged 3 to 12 years with leukemia who were undergoing bone marrow aspirations ($n = 28$) or lumbar punctures ($n = 44$).

The findings indicated that parents in the stress-inoculation condition reported lower state and trait anxiety scores and higher positive self-statement scores than did parents in the child-focused condition. Over time, parents in both conditions demonstrated improvement on state and trait anxiety, but the stress-inoculation group demonstrated significantly larger decreases than the child-focused intervention group.

Another approach to reducing stress associated with painful treatment procedures involved components directed at both parents and their children (Manne et al., 1990). The subjects were 23 children 3 to 9 years of age with cancer who required physical restraint to complete venipuncture. Patients and their parents were assigned to either a behavioral intervention group or to an attentional control group. The behavioral-intervention group included attentional distraction by substitution of an incompatible positive response (blowing into a party blower) for undesirable behavior (crying), paced breathing, and positive reinforcement contingent on cooperation. Parents were trained in behavioral coaching of the child's breathing and use of the party blower.

The findings indicated that observed child distress, parent-rated child distress, and parental ratings of their own distress were reduced significantly in the intervention group but not in the attentional-control group. The reductions were maintained across the course of three intervention trials. However, child self-reported pain and nurses ratings of child distress were not affected significantly.

The findings of these studies that have employed multiple cognitive–behavioral therapy components to reduce child stress or parent stress during painful procedures do not enable assessment of the effectiveness of the individual components. It is likely that different components are effective as a function of individual and family characteristics. Furthermore, these multicomponent cognitive–behavioral therapy packages all were designed to be brief and cost effective. It may continue to be cost effective to provide package programs that are likely to have broad effectiveness rather than attempting to delineate a "cafeteria-style" approach in which only specific components are selected to maximize the fit with individual and family characteristics. This is an area for future research.

## COPING WITH CHRONIC AND RECURRENT PAIN

In addition to the pain associated with invasive medical procedures, chronic and recurrent pain is a frequent concomitant of a number of illnesses and conditions. In particular, pain of this type occurs with specific conditions such as sickle-cell disease, hemophilia, and juvenile rheumatoid arthritis and may be the defining problem, as with recurrent abdominal pain. Affecting an estimated 10% to 15% of school-age children (Apley, 1975), recurrent abdominal pain is characterized by repeated episodes of pain that interfere with the child's daily functioning. Organic causes for the abdominal pain include dysfunctional bowel disorders, pancreatitis, and peptic disease. However, organic causes can only be identified in about 10% of these cases. Many children continue to experience abdominal pain for years, attesting to the need for effective management strategies for recurrent abdominal pain as well as for recurrent and chronic pain associated with other pediatric conditions.

Cognitive–behavioral treatment approaches to managing chronic and recurrent pediatric pain have been characterized by two types of techniques (Varni, Walco, & Wilcox, 1990). Techniques to regulate pain perception include self-regulatory techniques, such as progressive muscle relaxation, meditation, and guided imagery. Techniques to modify pain behavior identify and modify socioenvironmental factors that influence pain expression and rehabilitation.

### Regulating Pain Perception

Varni and his colleagues have reported on a series of studies that have demonstrated the efficacy of cognitive–behavioral therapy techniques for treating chronic arthritic pain in both children and adults with hemophilia (Varni, Walco, & Katz, 1989). Instruction in self-regulation consists of three phases. In the first phase, children are taught a 25-step progressive muscle relaxation sequence. This involves having children alternately tense and relax the major muscle groups. In the second phase, children are taught meditative breathing exercises. Children are instructed to inhale medium deep breaths through the nose and slowly exhale through the mouth. While exhaling, children are instructed to say the word *relax* and to visualize it in warm colors written on a chalkboard. In the third phase, children are instructed in the use of guided imagery techniques. Children are instructed to imagine themselves actively participating in pleasant, distracting scenes that they select themselves.

The program at Duke University developed by Gil and colleagues has examined the relationship of strategies of coping with pain in children with sickle-cell disease. In a study of children with sickle-cell disease (N = 72) who were 7 to 17 years of age (M = 11.1 years), researchers assessed adjustment multidimensionally in terms of parent- and child-reported psychological distress; parent-reported child activity during painful episodes; and health care use (Gil, Williams, Thompson, & Kinney, 1991). The findings indicated that children's pain-coping strategies characterized by passive adherence and negative thinking—that is, thinking patterns such as catastrophizing and self-statements of fear and anger—were associated with psychosocial and functional impairment. More specifically, use of passive adherence strategies was associated with more frequent visits to the emergency room and less activity during painful episodes according to parental report. Negative thinking also was associated with less activity during painful episodes and higher levels of self-reported psychological distress. Active coping attempts, reflected in multiple cognitive and behavioral coping strategies including diverting attention, calming self-statements, and reinterpreting pain sensations, were associated with fewer visits to the emergency room and more activity during painful episodes.

A follow-up study revealed relative stability over a 9-month period in pain-coping strategies for children but less stability for adolescents (Gil et al., 1993). Baseline pain-coping strategies were predictive of adjustment at follow-up: Passive adherence was associated with more frequent health care contacts and coping attempts were associated with higher levels of school, household, and social activity during painful episodes. Furthermore, increases in negative thinking over time were associated with further increases in health care contacts. These findings suggest that training to develop pain-coping for children would be potentially useful in fostering adjustment.

## Pain Behavior Modification

The research program of L. S. Walker and colleagues at Vanderbilt University Medical Center on pediatric abdominal pain has been guided by a conceptual framework that incorporates stress and coping, family systems, and social learning theories (see L. S. Walker et al., 1993 for a review). Consistent with other model-driven research portrayed in this book, the goal is to identify potential targets for the prevention and treatment of recurrent abdominal pain. In a series of studies on pediatric patients referred to a tertiary care setting, patients with recurrent abdominal pain were found to have higher levels of internalizing emotional problems than well patients but not significantly higher than patients with organic etiologies for their pain. Both children with recurrent abdominal pain and with organic etiologies for abdominal pain had lower levels of emotional distress and internalizing problems than psychiatric patients with mood and anxiety disorders. Patients with recurrent abdominal pain had levels of mother- and teacher-reported competence that were comparable to well children and significantly higher than that reported for psychiatric patients.

L. S. Walker, Garber, Van Slyke, and Greene (1995) addressed questions regarding long-term outcome of physical and emotional symptoms, functional disability, and use of health services with 31 patients (M = 17.56 years) with recurrent abdominal pain 5 to 6 years after initial evaluation. Compared to 41 former well patients, the former patients with recurrent abdominal pain had significantly more pain in the past two weeks and in the previous year, had experienced more somatic complaints and had more difficulty with daily activities as a result of health problems in the past two weeks, and higher levels of mother-reported internalizing symptoms such as anxiety and depression. Patients with recurrent abdominal pain also reported twice as many absences from school or work, made more mental health visits, and demonstrated a trend for more medical clinic visits. Furthermore, only 1 of the 31 patients (3%) initially considered to have recurrent abdominal pain subsequently was found to have evidence of organic disease. "Thus, it appears that as they reach adolescence and young adulthood, many former RAP patients may continue to be characterized by somatic and emotional distress that interferes with their daily activities" (L. S. Walker et al., 1995, p. 243).

Additional studies in this series indicated that psychosocial variables were indicators of concurrent disorder and continued somatic complaints at follow-up. More specifically, high levels of stress associated with negative life events within the family appeared to constitute a risk factor for emotional disorder and symptom maintenance, particularly among those children who lacked competence. Thus, efforts to enhance functioning may focus on modifying a stressor, such as by reducing family conflict, and on increasing the child's ability to deal with stressors, such as through teaching stress-management and pain-management techniques. Furthermore, the findings of high incidence of illness in the families and the solicitous nature of parents' responses to their children's pain provide support for the role of parent modeling and social reinforcement in the child's symptom complaints and functional disability. Parent behavior can be a target for intervention efforts to promote a change in the child's functioning. More specifically, parents can be encouraged to change their response to the child from one characterized by giving them increased attention and relieving them of responsibilities contingent on reports of abdominal pain to encouraging them to cope with symptoms that may persist for some time. L. S. Walker commented: "It may be useful to reframe the parent's role from that of protector to that of coach" (L. S. Walker et al., 1993, p. 210).

This focus on parental involvement to enhance coping with chronic and recurrent pain as well as with painful procedures is based on the recognition that children's ability to implement adaptive coping skills is influenced by their family environment (Sanders, Shepherd, Cleghorn, & Woolford, 1994). The social-learning perspective calls attention to the role of caregivers in providing discriminative cues and selective reinforcement of behavioral expression of pain. Parental attention, reinforcement, and modeling may affect the child's pain.

> Consequently, training parents to alter attending behaviors that reinforce pain behaviors and to support their children's well behavior or active coping (e.g., positive self-talk, persistence with tasks, relaxation, or distraction) may be useful. Parents can be trained to prompt self-management skills and to withhold reinforcement for pain behavior (extinction). Such parent–child collaboration may improve children's implementation of self-management skills, decrease relapse, and at the same time decrease parent's anxiety and uncertainty about how to help their child. (Sanders et al., 1994, p. 307)

The efficacy of a cognitive–behavioral family intervention, with its dual emphases on teaching children pain-coping skills and training parents, has been assessed in two studies of children with recurrent abdominal pain. In the first study, Sanders et al. (1989) randomly assigned 16 children to a treatment or wait-list control condition. Children and their mothers ($n = 8$) in the treatment condition participated in an eight-session program with two components. The behavioral component included self-monitoring of pain, a differential reinforcement of other behavior schedule for increasing pain-free periods and prompting distraction, and competing activities. The cognitive self-control component included self-monitoring, self-instruction, self-efficacy statements, self-administration of rewards, self-induced relaxation, and an imaginal strategy to reduce pain. Researchers also incorporated generalization and relapse-prevention training into the treatment program (Sanders et al., 1989). The findings indicated that both the treatment and wait-list control groups improved in child and parent measures of pain over the course of the treatment and 3-month follow-up phases. However, those in the treatment condition improved more quickly and had a larger proportion of complete elimination of pain (87.5% versus 37.5%). Furthermore, the effects generalized to the school setting in which teachers observed an improvement in the treatment group at follow-up and a slight deterioration in the control group (Sanders et al., 1989).

The second study compared cognitive–behavioral family intervention to standard pediatric care with 44 children 7 to 14 years of age with recurrent abdominal pain (Sanders et al., 1994). Children and their mothers were assigned randomly to treatment conditions. The cognitive–behavioral family intervention was similar to that described previously. There were six sessions, 50 minutes in length, consisting of three components: (a) explanation and rationale, (b) contingency management training for parents, and (c) self-management training for children. The standard pediatric care involved providing reassurance from a gastroenterologist within the context of a caring, supportive, noncritical, therapeutic relationship. The findings indicated that both treatment conditions resulted in significant improvements in pain intensity and pain behavior. However, the children receiving the cognitive–behavioral family intervention had a higher rate of complete elimination of pain at the 6-month follow-up (67% vs. 28%) but not at the 12-month follow-up (59% vs. 37%); lower levels of relapse in terms of fewer episodes of pain at the 6- and 12-month follow-up by parent report and the 12-month follow-up by child report; and less interference of pain with the child's activities at the 6- and 12-month follow-up by child and parent report. Furthermore, pain reduction was associated with reductions in both internalizing and externalizing mother-reported behavior problems.

In sickle-cell disease, vaso-occlusion leads to bone or joint pain that can last for hours to several days. These "painful crises" can be debilitating and are a cause for hospitalization. There is wide variability in patients' ability to tolerate pain, and most health care programs for patients with sickle-cell disease have a small group of patients who have frequent painful crises and hospital admissions. For example, Walco and Dampier (1987) reported on the 260 pediatric and adolescent patients (birth to 25 years of age) followed by their program. Over a 12-month period, 194 (74.6%) had no admissions to the hospital for pain. Of the 66 (25.4%) requiring admission, 54 were hospitalized only once, with an average stay of 7 days. However, 12 patients were admitted 3 to 15 times and had lengths of stay of 10 to 12 days. This group of patients accounted for one half of the total hospital days.

Based on their clinical experience, Walco & Dampier (1987) have formulated a treatment strategy for the overutilizing patients that includes a fixed schedule of tapering analgesic dosages and a structured program to promote a more adaptive lifestyle. Patients are taught to avoid the organic or psychogenic dichotomized way of thinking about pain. Intermittent sickle-cell pain is presented as a lifelong problem, and cognitive and affective factors are identified as mediating the ways in which patients tolerate the discomfort and function in their environments. Coping is emphasized, and the notion of curing the pain is deemphasized. Patients are taught techniques to regulate pain-perception modalities and to modify pain behavior. Walco and Dampier (1987) reported positive clinical results with this program, but the treatment program has not been subjected to rigorous controlled intervention.

## CONCLUSION

This brief review of children's coping with painful medical procedures and with chronic and recurrent pain provides considerable support for the view that parent and child behaviors interact to effect coping with pain. As discussed in chapter 7, cognitive development underlies increasing understanding of pain. Tolerance and expression of pain also change with development. The vast majority of children function well socially and academically while dealing with pain associated with their chronic illness and its treatment. However, there is a small subset of children who "miss school, withdraw from social activities, become preoccupied with their pain, and begin early their careers as pain patients" (P. J. McGrath et al., 1986, p. 229).

The behavioral science knowledge base now exists to help children cope with invasive medical procedures. Brief cognitive–behavioral intervention packages can be employed effectively to teach children to control their pain perceptions, primarily through distraction techniques. Cognitive–behavioral intervention also can be employed to teach parents how to support their child's active coping efforts by coaching the use of distraction techniques and avoiding the use of explanation and reassurance. Commenting on her clinical experiences, Jay (1988) stated:

> With few exceptions, the children who cope most effectively with traumatic medical procedures are those whose parents do not reinforce pain behavior with overwhelming amounts of sympathy, nurturance, or attention. In other words, coping behaviors rather than distress behaviors are reinforced, nor do these parents openly display their own personal anxiety and distress. (p. 416)

In a similar way, considerable support also has been provided for the efficacy of cognitive–behavioral intervention packages in lowering the distress and functional impairment associated with chronic-illness related pain. These interventions teach children strategies to manage pain and teach their parents to coach their children to use distraction and to support their children's active coping efforts.

This body of behavioral–science knowledge provides a basis for formulating guidelines to help children and their families cope with pain. First, the organic and psychogenic dichotomy viewpoint should be avoided. "Psychogenic and organic causes of pain can co-exist. . . ." (P. J. McGrath et al., 1986, p. 230). Furthermore, psychological and physiological processes interact in the phenomenological experience of pain, and the response of the social–ecological environment can elicit, maintain, or decrease the expression of pain and coping behaviors. One effective method we have used at Duke University Medical Center is the analogy of a radio to reflect this interaction. We have children and their parents think about a radio playing in the background that they are unaware of until a particular song is played. The radio signal was there all the time but they did not hear it until their attention was elicited and focused. In this way the mind, through the attention and the association of thoughts and feelings, serves as an amplifier of the existing signal. In the same way, thoughts and feelings serve as the volume knob for the pain signals and can be used for self-regulation.

This focus on thoughts and feelings is related to another guideline: establishing the context and the meaning of pain. The clinician should attempt to establish the relationship between the pain the child is experiencing and life situations (P. J. McGrath et al., 1986). Parents and children attach meaning to pain, such as punishment for faults or transgressions, that influence how they respond to pain. Some patients and families will need help in changing their thinking patterns to enable them to cope effectively with pain.

Another guideline is emphasizing coping with pain rather than curing it, with the corollary emphasis on teaching coping skills and encouraging maintaining daily activities. A focus on coping skills and social problem solving avoids blame and self-pity and helps children continue to enjoy the pleasures afforded by their normal daily activities. In this way, strategies to manage pain are consistent with the overall approach of fostering adaptation to chronic childhood illness by minimizing the impact on normative life experiences.

# IV

## GOALS FOR PUBLIC POLICY AND RESEARCH

# INTRODUCTION

# GOALS FOR PUBLIC POLICY
# AND RESEARCH

Section IV addresses the implications of the biopsychosocial framework for social policies regarding children with chronic illness and their families and the future research agenda. Chapter 13 makes the bridge between our framework and public policy. The biopsychosocial framework suggests that our objectives include meeting the special needs of families with children with chronic illness in ways that maintain a normative developmental course and facilitate effective parenting. We will review the impact of federal legislation for children with developmental disabilities and handicaps as illustrative of what can be accomplished through the advocacy of parents and the scientific health care community to improve the well-being of children and their families. There is a specific need to support parents in their efforts to promote optimal development and adaptation of their children with chronic illness.

Chapter 14 guides the formulation of the continuing research agenda. We summarize the findings provided by the biopsychosocial conceptual framework in terms of answers to the four questions that constitute the major objectives of this book: (a) What are the frequencies and types of adjustment problems? (b) What are the biopsychosocial correlates of adjustment? (c) What are the salient intervention targets? (d) What are the effective intervention programs?

This review leads to the delineation of two research goals. First, studies need to continue at the analytic level of research. However, studies need to be developmental, not cross-sectional. There is a compelling need to determine how psychosocial adjustment, mediating and moderating adaptational processes, and their interrelationship change over time in relation to individual and family developmental phases and illness course. Second, although the knowledge base is incomplete, it is sufficient to move to the next level of research—that is, the experimental level. Intervention studies are needed to confirm what is known about adaptational processes and to refine further the biopsychosocial models that will guide subsequent research efforts to enhance the quality of life of children with chronic illness and their families.

# 13

## POLICY IMPLICATIONS

This chapter introduces what is meant by public policy and then considers how our biopsychosocial framework can inform policy considerations for children with chronic illness and their families. We will follow with a discussion of the organization and financing of needed services. The biopsychosocial perspective has identified the role of the family in general, and parenting in particular, as important in adapting to chronic childhood illness. We therefore will consider the role of public policy in supporting parenting and family functioning. We will follow with a review of federal legislation in two areas that can serve as models of social policy formation: developmental disabilities and education of children with handicaps. We will end the chapter by considering the implications of the public policy process for efforts to enhance adaptation to chronic childhood illness.

### PUBLIC POLICY

Public policy is one method by which we, as a society, make explicit statements regarding what we are trying to achieve and how we are going to go about the process of achieving it. "A public policy statement represents the consensus of the general population on significant issues: it also represents the allocation of scarce public resources to such issues" (Gallagher, 1989, p. 387).

Public policy usually is expressed through federal or state laws and regulations and the corresponding allocation of resources. Adopting public policies is made easier when the need for allocating resources to particular groups is clear and compelling, such as with people who are poor and people with disabilities (Gallagher, 1989). Thus, public policy typically is formulated through the interactive processes of demonstrating a need and advocating that the need be met. Children cannot advocate for themselves, and therefore they must rely on others to make known their needs in a clear and compelling manner.

> The shape and scope of policies for children are very much products of our political system, which is premised on negotiation and compromise. Thus, the values held by individual policymakers, fiscal considerations, and partisan politics all affect the policy agenda and dictate a political strategy that may affect comprehensive change or promote only incremental change. (Garwood, Phillips, Hartman, & Ziegler, 1989, p. 436)

Even though incomplete, the knowledge base regarding normal and at risk child development and the understanding of the process of adapting to chronic childhood illness has accumulated to the point that it can serve as a basis for advocating for children's needs. However, it is essential that those making social policies recognize what is known, what is not yet known, and what needs to be discovered (Horowitz & O'Brien, 1989).

## BIOPSYCHOSOCIAL PERSPECTIVE

The biopsychosocial framework through which we have been viewing adaptation to chronic childhood illness has implications for, and provides a perspective on, social policy for children with chronic conditions and their families. First, the framework provides a transactional, social–ecological perspective. Such a perspective necessitates integrating biological, psychological, and social domains in accordance with systems theory, and also requires attention to the match between environmental parameters and individual child parameters.

Second, the modified categorical approach discussed previously is an essential framework for delineating the specific and common impacts of illnesses and for the advocacy efforts necessary for forming social policy. The numbers of children and families affected by a specific illness are relatively small. However, across all the chronic conditions of childhood, there are more than 1 million children whose lives, along with the lives of their families, are affected. Advocating for the common needs of these children and families increases the likelihood of policy initiatives.

Third, the focus of the framework is to extend the duration of life and improve the quality of life, as discussed in chapter 9. This focus also applies to social policy initiatives.

Fourth, the framework identifies disruption of the processes of normal development and family functioning, particularly parenting, as the mechanism of dysfunction or morbidity (J. M. Perrin & MacLean, 1988b). Thus, the framework suggests that policy objectives should include meeting the special needs of children with chronic illness in a way that will maintain a normative developmental course and make parenting less difficult. More specifically, the framework suggests that policy initiatives could be directed toward reducing stress and increasing support as ways of maintaining normal development and fostering family functioning.

## ORGANIZATION AND FINANCING OF NEEDED SERVICES

For our purposes, delineating an exhaustive list of needs is not necessary. Instead, it is necessary to recognize the broad-based needs that fall within the purview of society in general, and the function of government in particular, to provide for the well-being of all citizens. Perhaps most obvious is the need for medical care. This includes special medical and surgical services, as well as primary health care services. What may not be as readily apparent are the associated needs for trained health care providers from a number of disciplines and for access that relates to the geographic distribution of health care facilities and services and to availability of adequate transportation.

In addition to medical services, an array of support services are needed also. These include counseling services, provisions for respite care, home care equipment and skills, and support groups. Educational and vocational services are needed also. Almost all children with chronic illness will at some time in the course of their illness need special education or related services, hospital schooling, or homebound education. There is a related need for school personnel to be trained about chronic illness, particularly emergency procedures. Training also is necessary regarding the impact of chronic illness and its treatment on daily functioning and school performance in terms of absences, fatigue and lethargy, physical and mental impairments, changes in physical appearance, and impact on self-esteem and peer relations.

"Diversity and fragmentation characterize the organization of services for chronically ill children" (J. M. Perrin & Ireys, 1984, p. 235). This often results in a high degree of frustration and stress and points to the particular need for integrating services—among health care specialties and also among health care, support, and educational services. This need for assistance with integration is reflected frequently in terms of case-management services.

Another major source of stress in caring for children with chronic illness is the economic impact. While it is difficult to generate exact cost figures, two facts are clear: The costs are high and the sources of support leave many gaps in coverage. Cost includes direct health care services, related support and educational services, and also indirect costs, such as those associated with transportation and lost wages. There are substantial gaps in the network of programs and resources available to support the costs of these needed services. Broadly defined, there are six primary sources of payment for health care for children with chronic illness: (a) private insurance companies, (b) disease-oriented voluntary associations, (c) Medicaid, (d) State Crippled Children Service Programs, (e) special state programs, (f) and out of pocket monies (J. M. Perrin & Ireys, 1984).

Private health insurance covers children as dependents of employed parents. However, there are major shortcomings in coverage (J. M. Perrin & Ireys, 1984). Health insurance is actually medical care insurance, which covers hospital and physician costs but not the array of other health care and support services needed by children with chronic illness and their families. Furthermore, insurance plans have various exclusions that serve to limit coverage—such as waiting periods for preexisting conditions—and it is often difficult for young adults to obtain their own health insurance once they are no longer covered by their parents' policy. The central problem of health care insurance is *shared-risk* (J. M. Perrin & Ireys, 1984). That is, the plan needs to spread out the cost of providing health care for individuals who are likely to incur high medical costs or else the premiums for the high-risk individual will be unattainably high. Several states have developed shared-risk arrangements among insurance providers.

Private health insurance has shortcomings with regard to covered services and costs, but many families of children with chronic illness do not have private health insurance and rely on public support or their own resources.

The Medicaid Program, Title XIX of the Social Security Act, is the largest public sector health care financing program for children (J. M. Perrin & Ireys, 1984). Medicaid is funded jointly by federal and state governments and requires certain services and allows payment for other services for low-income families. In many states, eligibility is tied to the welfare program, Aid to Families With Dependent Children. Similar to the shortcomings of private insurance, Medicaid does not pay for the array of services needed by children with chronic illness and their families. Furthermore, many low-income families, perhaps as high as 40%, are not eligible for Medicaid (see J. M. Perrin & Ireys, 1984).

The Crippled Children's Service Program was the only major public source of support for the care of children with chronic illness in low-income families prior to Medicaid (J. M. Perrin & Ireys, 1984). The program was started in 1935 and involved federal grants to states, which the states then matched, to provide services to children who were suffering from crippling conditions. Federal statutory requirements for state programs were removed in 1981 with the passage of the Maternal and Child Health Block Grant. Federal monies were reduced, but most state programs continued. Such a state program "sets and disseminates standards of care, provides for a fairly broad set of services, and covers children from a wide range of income levels . . . [and] represents an area in which both the organization and the financing of care merge" (J. M. Perrin & Ireys, 1984, p. 246). However, over time, many state Crippled Children's Service Programs have focused disproportionately on a small number of diseases, such as orthopedic diseases, or on a small set of services, such as hospital and physicians services. For example, the Crippled Children's Service Program in some states may not reimburse for psychological services.

In addition to private insurance and the major public support programs of Medicaid and the Crippled Children's Service Program, some support is provided through federal categorical grants to states and through disease-oriented associations. Examples of a categorical program are the Genetic Disease Program and the Hemophilia Treatment Center Project. In addition to serving an advocacy function, disease-oriented associations, such as the Cystic Fibrosis Foundation, endeavor to use their funds to fill in some of the gaps for support of services and needs that are not otherwise reimbursable. Disease-oriented associations typically allocate funds for medical, patient education, and community services, as well as research and training.

Out-of-pocket expenses for families of children with chronic illness are substantial. These include costs for direct services that are not reimbursable, such as deductibles and copayments for medical services, other direct costs, such as for transportation and parking, and indirect costs associated with lost wages as a result of time off from work to care for the child and take the child for needed inpatient and outpatient health care.

In-depth consideration of the organization and financing of services for children with chronic illness and their families is beyond the scope of this book, and we refer the interested reader to the thorough coverage of these topics found in Hobbs & Perrin (1985). At this time, the health care system in the United States is undergoing unprecedented changes propelled by a determination to reduce costs. There is also an expressed recognition of the need for "universal coverage," but this seems to run contrary to reducing health care expenditures. As the health care system is being redesigned, it will be necessary to advocate for the needs of children with chronic illness and their families. It would appear that there are opportunities to advocate for preventive services and for integrating services as ways of addressing the need to reduce health care costs for such an at risk population.

## PARENT SUPPORT POLICIES

The role of the family in general, and the process of parenting in particular, in promoting children's cognitive and psychosocial development and in mediating the stresses associated with chronic childhood illness is now well substantiated and recognized. Attention needs to be directed to the role of social policy in supporting parenting and family functioning. These policy initiatives must recognize social and economic changes that impact family structure and functioning of families in general, as well as those with children with chronic illness.

Data from a number of sources indicate that American families are experiencing increasing levels of stress and structural change. An increasing number of families are headed by one parent. One in three marriages end in divorce, and out-of-wedlock birth now constitutes about 20% of all births (Stipek & McCroskey, 1989). Forty to fifty percent of children can expect to spend at least 5 years in a single-parent home (Horowitz & O'Brien, 1989). More than ever, the only parent, or both parents, are working outside of the home. For example, more than 70% of mothers of school-aged children and more than 55% of mothers of children who are under 6 years of age work outside of the home (Stipek & McCroskey, 1989). However, increasing numbers of families are experiencing serious economic problems. More than 25% of all children and more than 50% of minority children are being raised in poverty (Horowitz & O'Brien, 1989).

The lack of adequate day-care programs, in terms of both quantity and quality, limits employment opportunities and has negative consequences for children. Current social policies that affect the quantity and quality of day care are inadequate (Stipek & McCroskey, 1989). Federal support for child care is provided through the dependent care tax credit, which benefits middle- and upper-income families, and direct assistance to poor families comes primarily through Title XX of the Social Services Block Grant, approximately 18% of which is spent on child care (Stipek & McCroskey, 1989).

Income-support programs have included in-kind benefits such as food stamps and Medicaid, income transfer benefits such as Supplemental Security Income for individuals with disabilities, and direct support through Aid to Families With Dependent Children. The adequacy of these income-support programs has been challenged consistently, and currently President

Bill Clinton and the 104th Congress are formulating policies intended to end welfare as we know it.

Related to the issue of child care are workplace policies regarding parental leave and work schedules that have particular relevance to stress experienced by parents of children with chronic illness. Currently, fewer than half of workers receive paid sick leave and fewer receive personal leave days to attend to sick children (Stipek & McCroskey, 1989). In 1993, Congress passed the Family and Medical Leave Act, which grants 12 weeks unpaid leave to employees under circumstances including the birth or adoption of a child; foster care placement; when employees are needed to care for a child, spouse, or parent who has a serious health condition; or when employees cannot perform their responsibilities because of a serious health condition. Eligibility requirements include having been with the employer for at least 12 months, during which time the employee must have worked at least 1,250 hours. Spouses employed by the same company receive a combined total of 12 weeks for the birth or adoption of a child or for care of a sick family member. However, small companies employing fewer than 50 employees are exempt.

In advocating for the needs of children with chronic illness and their families, the current social and economic impacts on family functioning in general must be recognized. Because of the increase in single-parent families and the frequent need for the primary caretaker to work outside of the home, income support, quality day-care services, and enlightened leave policies are needed just as much as a network of integrated and affordable health care and support services. Furthermore, meeting these needs is all the more necessary because of the increasing demands placed on parents to be responsible for home health care provisions for their children, as well as their role in fostering cognitive and social development of their children.

## MODEL FEDERAL LEGISLATION

The quality of children's lives increasingly became a matter of policy concern to the federal government during the first half of this century. The social climate of the 1960s served to expand greatly federal activity on behalf of children with such programs as HeadStart and Medicaid (Garwood, Phillips, Hartman, & Zigler, 1989).

Two interrelated areas of social policy that have particular relevance for children with chronic illness are developmental disabilities and education for children with handicaps. These areas illustrate the process of policy formulation over time through a continuous process of advocacy involving lay and professional groups. These areas also focus on improving quality of life by fostering normalization of developmental experiences and family functioning.

## Developmental Disabilities

The starting point for the evolution of the concept of developmental disabilities can be considered to be President John F. Kennedy's Panel on Mental Retardation, which was charged to develop a plan to address mental retardation (see Thompson & O'Quinn, 1979). The panel made a number of recommendations regarding the prevention and treatment of mental retardation based on several key concepts and findings. First, the panel emphasized prevention and the need for sustained and mutual stimulation of mother and child. Mentally retarded infants could be cared for at home if mothers were provided skilled advice and encouragement. Second, the panel emphasized the need for a continuum of care and interdisciplinary services (i.e., the blending of medical, educational, and social services required to minimize disability at every point in the lifespan).

In 1963, Congress enacted two programs specifically for citizens with mental retardation (Chiles, 1987). Public Law 88-156, entitled the Maternal and Child Health and Mental Retardation Planning Amendments of 1963, provided funds for comprehensive state planning to prevent mental retardation and to serve those affected (Chiles, 1987). Public Law 88-164, entitled the Mental Retardation Facilities Construction Act of 1963, enabled the construction of research and training facilities. This law also created university-affiliated facilities to offer model clinical services for mentally retarded individuals and to train personnel from a number of biomedical, psychosocial, and educational disciplines in interdisciplinary assessment and treatment services (see Thompson & O'Quinn, 1979). Through the legislative process of continuing the funding for these programs, the field of developmental disabilities emerged as it gradually was recognized that many individuals who were not mentally retarded had similar needs.

Public Law 91-517, passed by Congress in 1970, entitled the Developmental Disabilities Service and Facilities Construction Amendments of 1970, amended the 1963 law (88-164) by replacing the term *mental retardation* with *developmental disabilities*. This law also replaced the authority for federal construction of mental retardation facilities with a federal–state formula grant program. The objective of this program included assisting states in developing and implementing a comprehensive state plan to meet the needs of developmentally disabled persons, including constructing facilities, providing services, and training specialized personnel. The new law established a definition for developmental disabilities:

> A disability attributable to mental retardation, cerebral palsy, epilepsy, or another neurological condition of an individual found by the Secretary (Health, Education, and Welfare) to be closely related to mental retardation or to require treatment similar to that required for a men-

tally retarded individual, which disability originates before such individual attains age eighteen, which has continued or can be expected to continue indefinitely, and which constitutes a substantial handicap to such individual. (Developmental Disabilities, p. 1325)

In the early 1970s, congressional hearings were held to extend and to improve the programs initiated under Public Law 91-517. Representatives from a number of professional and lay organizations testified, including the National Society for Autistic Children, the National Association for Retarded Children, the Muscular Dystrophy Association of America, the United States Cerebral Palsy Association, the American Speech and Hearing Association, and the National Association of State Mental Health Program Directors. The point was made that the definition of developmental disabilities under Public Law 91-517 was too restrictive and that many persons who were in fact developmentally disabled and who could benefit from the services mandated by the act were omitted. The result was Public Law 94-103, entitled the Developmentally Disabled Assistance and Bill of Rights Act (1975), which broadened the definition of developmental disabilities to include autism and dyslexia resulting from mental retardation, cerebral palsy, epilepsy, or autism. This law also required an independent study with respect to which disabilities should be included or excluded in the definition of developmental disability.

A national task force subsequently clarified that the term *developmental disabilities* was not a general catch-all but referred to a group of people experiencing a chronic disability that substantially limits their functioning in a variety of broad areas of major life activity central to independent living: self-care, receptive and expressive language, learning, mobility, self-direction, capacity for independent living, or economic self-sufficiency. This definition was incorporated into Public Law 95-602, entitled Rehabilitation, Comprehensive Services, and Developmental Disabilities Amendments of 1978.

There are several aspects of this process of policy formation that are important. First, the scientific and professional community, in concert with advocacy groups representing individuals with special needs, provided the foundation for what was needed and what was possible. Second, while the processes started out addressing the needs of one particular group (those with mental retardation), the legislation became more generic to accommodate other individuals with different diagnostic labels but with common needs. Rather than viewing this as a step backward in terms of programs for mentally retarded citizens, then Senator Lawton Chiles (1987) maintained that "we may make more progress by forcing states and local communities to address the needs of all handicapped citizens in a collective and coordinated fashion" (p. 793). Third, the focus on functional limitations is a way of delineating a common denominator across a number of disparate conditions. The parallel with the noncategorical approach to chronic childhood illness and emphasis on quality of life–health outcome is readily apparent. Fourth, the changing role of the federal government is also apparent. Rather than construct facilities and maintain service programs, federal dollars are now directed to strengthening the capacity of states and local communities to meet human needs by supporting initial planning, program start-up, and research models and demonstration (Chiles, 1987).

## Education of Children With Handicaps

During the same time period that policies for children with developmental disabilities were being formulated, policies were being formulated for education of children with handicaps. We can begin our consideration of this process with the passage by Congress in 1968 of Public Law 90-538, entitled the Handicapped Children's Early Education Program. This was the first federal special education program targeted exclusively for the needs of young children with disabilities. It was a demonstration program rather than a service program (Hebbeler, Smith, & Black, 1991). The objective was to stimulate early childhood special education programs.

Public Law 91-230, passed by Congress in 1970, was entitled the Education of the Handicapped Act. Grants were authorized to assist states in initiating and improving programs for educating children with handicaps at the preschool, elementary-, and secondary-school levels (Hebbeler et al., 1991).

Public Law 93-380, entitled the Education Amendment of 1974, amended 91-230 and added new requirements for state plans, including due-process guarantees and least-restrictive environment provisions in return for federal grants for services at the preschool, elementary-, and secondary-school levels (Hebbeler et al., 1991).

In 1975, Congress passed Public Law 94-142, The Education for All Handicapped Children Act. This was truly a landmark piece of legislation and mandated a free, appropriate public education for all eligible persons 3 to 21 years of age. This legislation sought to implement several key concepts (Gallagher, 1989). First, no child would be denied special services—that is, services were to be available to all children with handicaps. Second, a nondiscriminatory evaluation was required. Third, each child was to have a written, individualized educational program with clear objectives and records of performance toward those objectives. Fourth, services were to be provided in the least restrictive environment, so that the child could be as close as possible to a normal classroom setting. Fifth, there were requirements for due process, so that parents could protest the plan. Sixth, parents were ensured a role in developing their child's program.

Public Law 94-142 encompasses a wide spectrum of children with handicaps, including those who are mentally retarded, hearing-impaired, deaf, speech-impaired, visually handicapped, seriously emotionally disturbed, orthopedically impaired, or other health-impaired children, or children with specific learning disabilities who require special education and related services (D. K. Walker & Jacobs, 1985). *Related services* refer to developmental, corrective, and other supportive services as required to assist children with handicaps to benefit from special education and include transportation, specific therapies, early identification, counseling services, medical evaluation and diagnostic services, school health services, social work services in schools, and training for parents (D. K. Walker & Jacobs, 1985).

Some children with chronic illness would qualify for special education services because of specific handicaps, such as those with cognitive impairment. However, most of the children with chronic illness do not have these types of handicaps but could potentially qualify for services under the categories of *orthopedically impaired* and *other health impaired*. *Orthopedically impaired* means a severe orthopedic impairment that affects a child's education performance and includes impairments caused by congenital anomaly, disease, or trauma. *Other health impaired* means "limited strength, vitality or alertness due to chronic or acute health problems such as a heart condition, tuberculosis, rheumatic fever, nephritis, asthma, sickle cell anemia, hemophilia, epilepsy, lead poisoning, leukemia, or diabetes, which adversely affects a child's educational performance" (Baird & Ashcroft, 1985, p. 657).

A difficulty arises in implementing this legislation because the majority of children with chronic illness are not going to require placement in special education classes (D. K. Walker, 1987). Whether or not children with chronic illness are eligible for services revolves around the related-services provision of the law (D. K. Walker, 1987). At one time or another, almost all children with chronic illness will need one or more of the school-related services provided under the law. However, since *related services* are defined as those required to benefit from special education, children with chronic illness who do not need or qualify for special education may not receive the services. The illness condition must affect adversely a child's educational performance to qualify for special education services. The main determinant of whether children with chronic illness require something other than normal classes is the extent to which their illnesses interfere with daily functioning and learning (D. K. Walker, 1984). Little guidance is given regarding the criteria for impact other than the handicap must be serious enough to impede successful progress in a regular education program (D. K. Walker & Jacobs, 1985). There is wide variability in how schools determine eligibility. Some children with chronic illnesses are designated as special education students and receive the needed related services, whereas some students are denied services.

Another way in which some schools provide services for children with chronic illness is through the school health program (D. K. Walker, 1987).

> At a minimum, school health services for these children should include assistance with medication, implementation and monitoring of medical treatment procedures, staff training and preparation for emergencies, and coordination with the child's medical providers outside of the school setting. (D. K. Walker, 1987, p. 118)

However, there is no federal statute that governs what services schools provide. Therefore, states develop their own guidelines. Wood, Walker, and Gardner (1986) conducted a survey of state policies and guidelines for administering medication and selected nursing procedures. The nursing procedures included catheterization, managing seizures, respiratory care, tube feeding (including nasal gastric and gastric tubes), positioning, colostomy/ileostomy care, and other procedures (including allergy shots). The survey found that 26% of the states had no written guidelines regarding any of the nursing procedures. Of the states with written guidelines, all had guidelines for medication administration, 12% had guidelines governing the selected school nursing procedures, and 6% had guidelines governing all procedures except respiratory care. Thirteen states (26%) had guidelines only for administering medication.

A decade after its enactment, Public Law 94-142 was amended through Public Law 99-457, entitled the Education for the Handicapped Act Amendments of 1986 (Part H), to include services for infants and toddlers who had, or who were at risk for developing, handicapping conditions. It also sought to facilitate coordination of multidisciplinary services across community agencies by requiring a designated lead agency, case manager, multidisciplinary assessment, and a state interagency coordinating council (Gallagher, 1989). The law sought to empower parents and make them a significant factor in planning for their child's life. The law required an Individualized Family Service Plan, which was to be reviewed with the family at 6-month intervals and required the participation of a parent or guardian.

This law also addressed the need to reform the classification system for exceptional children based on etiological categories. Eligibility for services was defined in terms of children, from birth to age 2, who need early intervention services because they are experiencing developmental delays in cognitive development, physical development, language and speech development, psychosocial development or self-help skills, or have a diagnosed physical or mental condition that has a high probability of resulting in developmental delay (Gallagher, 1989). Those at risk for, as well as those who have, a developmental delay were eligible for services under this law. Early intervention services included, but were not limited to, family training, counseling, and home visits; specific services such as special instruction, speech pathology, and audiology, occupational therapy, physical therapy, and psychological services; case management services; medical diagnostic and evaluation services; early identification, screening, and assessment services; and health services necessary to enable the infant to benefit from early intervention (Garwood, 1987).

Implementing and evaluating public policies over time results in an appreciation of needs that remain to be met. For children with chronic illness and their families, additional legislation may be necessary to provide the needed array of health, education, and social services. For example, with the current move to avoid unfunded mandates and to change from federally prescribed programs to block grants to states, legislation may need to be enacted at the state level to ensure that the education and social services needs of children with chronic developmental and medical problems can be met. Legislation also may be needed to ensure that managed care health plans not exclude or underserve children with chronic conditions. However, not all needs require legislation. More than ever, there is a need for flexibility within and among systems to use the resources available to develop individualized care plans that foster quality of life. In this regard, moving to block grants with an emphasis on local decision making regarding resource allocations and programming may facilitate such flexibility. It is necessary to think about people, programs, and agencies in noncategorical ways.

## CONCLUSION

There are several aspects of the public policy process that are important to recognize. First, the cumulative impact of the continuous process of advocating for the special needs of a group of individuals, those with developmental disabilities and handicaps, has resulted in the legal mandate of an appropriate education for all individuals with handicaps, including those with chronic illness.

Second, what has been accomplished has been done through this purposeful evolution of federal policy (Hebbeler et al., 1991). Knowledge has been generated and shared, training programs have been developed, and states are building the infrastructure for administering and funding programs. "Accomplishments at the local, state, and federal levels are being realized through the efforts of a political constituency of parents and professionals that federally funded programs helped to empower" (Hebbeler et al., 1991, p. 111).

Third, it is clear that there are limits to what federal policy can achieve. "Federal policy can point the way and certainly help with funding, but the commitment that will ultimately achieve the final goal must come at the state and local levels" (Hebbeler et al., 1991, p. 111).

Fourth, the services that children with special needs receive varies as a function of the particular school system they attend. Resources vary widely, as do skill, commitment, and attitudes. The law can require an individualized educational plan (IEP), but the *appropriateness* of that plan is another matter. Review of the literature indicates "that IEPs are not functioning as designed, including being inept at structuring specially designated instruction" (Smith, 1990, p. 7). The IEP can be considered a formalization of diagnostic prescriptive teaching. Evaluative studies of IEPs have failed to find the link between the IEP and actual classroom instruction that the law requires (Smith, 1990). In particular, the IEP often fails to link psychoeducational assessment and planned educational programming as reflected in goals and objectives based on assessment findings and against which performance is monitored (Smith, 1990). Furthermore, there are questions about the underlying assumption that assessment, as it is frequently undertaken, is useful for instructional planning (Smith, 1990).

Fifth, these federal policies specifically sought to involve parents in planning for their children and to empower them—for example, by requiring participation in the formulation of IEPs. However, obtaining needed specialized services for their children can be a formidable task. As a result, the federal government has funded a number of parent-training demonstration projects that focus on teaching parents a repertoire of advocacy skills necessary to understand and negotiate the educational maze. Whereas these programs were developed primarily for parents of children with developmental disabilities, other programs have been developed to provide parents of children with chronic health problems the communication and advocacy skills they need to deal effectively with the educational and medical systems (Hixson, Stoff, & White, 1992).

Sixth, there is a role for the scientific community, in concert with advocacy groups, in the legislative process. Legislation typically reflects prevailing views in the scientific community, in this case regarding child development. Gallagher (1989) has noted: "Each piece of legislation or regulation regarding the well-being of children represents a hypothesis or a set of assumptions about human behavior" (p. 387). For example, one hypothesis reflected in the legislation for children with developmental disabilities and handicaps is the value of early intervention for cognitive and social development. It is important to recognize that researchers have an obligation to be responsive to societal needs for information to guide policy information. Even though understanding is incomplete, the knowledge base is in many instances sufficient to guide social policy. "Children cannot wait to grow up until we know all that we need to know to take effective action in every case" (Horowitz & O'Brien, 1989, p. 444). Effectiveness of programs needs to be evaluated in terms of evidence regarding the basic hypotheses. In turn, these findings can enhance the knowledge base and serve to guide future policies.

Seventh, in this evaluative process, we cannot expect more of policy initiatives than they were intended to accomplish. For example, Horowitz & O'Brien (1989) cautioned that there is a need to put early intervention efforts in perspective: "Development is not a disease to be treated. It is a process that needs consistent nurturance. There is no reason to expect that an intensive program of early stimulation is an inoculation against all further developmental problems" (p. 444).

# 14

## CONCLUSION AND FUTURE RESEARCH GOALS

This chapter concludes the book by revisiting the goal and objectives as a basis for formulating the next steps in the research process. We will assess briefly the current state of knowledge in relation to four major questions and we will identify general research needs. We will make the case for moving to the experimental level of research.

### BIOPSYCHOSOCIAL PERSPECTIVE ON ADAPTATION

Adaptation is the process of accommodation that occurs between the developing child and his or her environment and is reflected in duration and quality of life. Chronic childhood illness can disrupt normal processes of child development, family functioning, and the transactions between the child and his or her environment and can be viewed as a potential stressor to which the child and family systems need to adapt.

The purpose of this book is to employ a biopsychosocial conceptual framework to enhance our understanding of the processes associated with adaptation to chronic childhood illness. This enhanced understanding will enable researchers to delineate salient intervention targets and develop effective prevention and treatment programs to enhance quality of life. The conceptual framework is derived from models that reflect the current analytic level of research in the field and can be viewed as a matrix formed by the transactions of the biomedical, social–ecological, and psychological dimensions of chronic childhood illness with the developmental phase of children and their families. This matrix delineates adaptive tasks that need to be addressed throughout the life course and processes and factors hypothesized to mediate or moderate the stresses of chronic childhood illness and quality of life.

It is premature to adopt a noncategorical—that is, a general as opposed to a disease-specific—approach. Rather, we suggest a modified categorical approach that enables considering adaptation as a function of tasks and processes that are illness-specific as well as those that are common across illnesses.

The use of this conceptual framework and matrix has increased our understanding of chronic childhood illness and also identified the next steps in the research process. The status of current knowledge and understanding can be summarized in terms of the objectives of the book to address four specific questions: (a) What is known about psychosocial adjustment? (b) What is known about the correlates of adjustment? (c) What are salient intervention targets? (d) What methods are effective in enhancing adaptation?

## PSYCHOSOCIAL ADJUSTMENT

Adaptation is frequently assessed in terms of psychosocial adjustment— that is, the degree to which behavior and functioning is age-appropriate, normative, and follows a trajectory toward positive adult functioning (Wallander & Thompson, 1995). Psychosocial adjustment is multidimensional and involves psychological adjustment manifested in terms of behavioral and emotional problems, low self-esteem, and psychiatric disorders; social adjustment, as reflected in peer relationships; and school performance.

It is now clear that comprehensive assessment of children's psychological adjustment requires use of multiple informants. Parents' level of stress and distress affect their view of their children's functioning. Furthermore, the phenomenological aspects of distress are subjective experiences that require self-report. These measurement issues not withstanding, children with chronic childhood illness are at increased risk for behavioral and emotional problems. These problems primarily reflect internalizing anxiety-based problems that are easy to overlook in the face of pressing health problems. Externalizing problems, while relatively infrequent, are likely to be manifested in oppositional behavior, which is of particular relevance to adherence with complex medical regimens.

It is also clear that children with chronic illness are at increased risk for school performance difficulties. Children with chronic illness also appear to be at increased risk for difficulties in social adjustment. However, our behavioral-science knowledge base is just beginning to be formed regarding this dimension of children's adjustment.

The level of research regarding the psychosocial adjustment of parents and siblings has lagged behind that of children with chronic illness. It is now known that parents and siblings have increased risk for adjustment difficulties, but good adjustment is also possible.

Our knowledge about the psychosocial adjustment of children with chronic illness and of their parents and siblings is based almost entirely on cross-sectional studies. The few developmental studies that have been accomplished suggest that there is considerable variability at the level of the individual in adjustment, particularly with child self-reported adjustment. It is imperative that longitudinal investigations be implemented that trace the change and stability over time in adjustment of children with chronic illness and their parents and siblings, as a function of illness course and developmental level and transitions. Efficient prevention and intervention efforts require specifying individuals and time periods of particular high risk.

## CORRELATES OF ADJUSTMENT

The search for correlates of psychosocial adjustment of children with chronic conditions has focused on biomedical, that is, illness or disease condition, parameters, family functioning, and child characteristics. The most consistent finding within biomedical parameters has been the increased risk for adjustment problems in children whose condition involves brain impairment. Family functioning characterized as low in cohesion and supportiveness and high levels of maternal distress consistently have been found to be associated with adjustment difficulties. Models also are beginning to address the role of individual child characteristics. The main focus has been on psychological processes. In particular, high levels of perceived stress and low levels of self-esteem have been identified as correlates of adjustment difficulties. In addition to psychological processes, there is a particular need to address how adjustment, adaptational processes, and their interrelationship vary as a function of gender and race, which are individual characteristics that also reflect the influences of biological and sociocultural processes.

In general, current models account for 30% to 50% of the variance in the adjustment of children with chronic illness. Thus, there is a substantial portion of variance that remains to be accounted for, attesting to the need to include additional dimensions and processes into models. In this regard, children's social skills and peer support appear to be promising processes for inclusion.

The search for correlates of parental and sibling adjustment also has lagged behind the search for correlates of adjustment in children with chronic illness. Most of our knowledge base regarding parental adjustment concerns maternal adjustment. There is clear support for the role of stress processing, in terms of cognitive appraisals and coping methods, in maternal adjustment. More specifically, maternal perceptions of stress related to daily hassles and to illness tasks and high levels of use of palliative coping in relation to adaptive coping methods are related to adjustment difficulties. In addition, the role of social support, particularly as reflected in family functioning in mitigating stress, is also apparent. While there is no one-to-one relationship between severity of the child's illness and maternal adjustment, the degree of the child's functional limitations does appear to impact on maternal adjustment.

Studies of the correlates of sibling adjustment have focused on non-dynamic factors such as birth order, gender, and age spacing, and no broad conclusions are evident yet. What is particularly lacking is an understanding of the contribution of healthy siblings to the adjustment of the chronically ill child.

Parent–child dyads and sibling dyads are interrelated subsystems within the family. The unique and combined contributions of each of these subsystems to psychosocial adjustment in the face of chronic childhood conditions needs to be addressed. There is a need for longitudinal studies that trace the relationship over time among condition parameters, child characteristics, family processes, and adjustment of all members of the family. In addition, there is a compelling need for studies that examine how different patterns of interrelationships among adaptational processes and adjustment occur for subgroups constituted on the basis of illness, race, and gender. For example, findings from our research program suggest that different patterns of relationships among correlates and adjustment occurred within subgroups formed on the basis of race, illness type, and gender.

## SALIENT INTERVENTION TARGETS

With chronic childhood illness viewed as a potential stressor to which children and their families must adapt, one of the primary mechanisms for promoting adaptation is preventing disruption of normal processes of child development and family functioning. The increasing knowledge base regarding the correlates of adjustment and risk and resiliency factors identifies three primary intervention targets to prevent disruption of these normal processes: (a) stress reduction, (b) enhancing support-eliciting and social problem-solving skills, (c) and effective parenting.

Stress processing involves the cognitive processes of appraisal, as well as specific coping methods. In particular, attention is focused on identifying a goodness of fit between specific coping strategies, characteristics of the stressor, and preferred behavioral styles. Both a combination of palliative and adaptive coping skills are necessary to deal with controllable and noncontrollable aspects of the adaptive tasks generated by chronic illnesses and their treatments.

Perceived social support, particularly perceived classmate support, appears to serve as a protective factor in adaptation to chronic childhood illness. Children's social skills are important to elicit and maintain peer social support. Research in the area has moved to identifying situation-specific deficits in social skills as a prerequisite for planning treatment. In addition, children need to know how to apply these skills—that is, they need social–cognitive problem-solving skills that have been found to be associated with better psychosocial adjustment.

The research in child development consistently points to the role of effective parenting in promoting children's cognitive and psychosocial development. Parents' beliefs and expectations guide their proactive and reactive responses in parent–child interactions. Parenting characterized as authoritative, involving the dimensions of warmth, control, and psychological autonomy, has been associated positively with psychosocial development and academic functioning. Furthermore, there is considerable evidence that mothers' levels of psychological distress influence perceptions of, and behavioral interactions with, their children, which in turn affects child competence.

These parental processes also could serve as salient intervention targets. That is, adapting to chronic childhood illness could be fostered by intervention programs designed to reduce parental stress and distress and to enhance parenting skills conducive to child cognitive and social development. Parents also have a role to play in supporting their children's active coping efforts to make the accommodations necessary to deal effectively with adaptive tasks and to maintain normative, age-appropriate, interactions and functioning. In particular, parents can learn to be effective coaches for their children's efforts to reduce stress, enhance social support and social problem-solving skills, and manage pain.

The focus on enhancing parenting skills is consistent with the movement toward a more collaborative relationship model of health care delivery. This model recognizes parents as active decision makers in the care of their children and health care providers as educators and consultants. In this regard, noncompliance need not be viewed as irresponsible but could reflect a well reasoned, adaptive choice. In particular, parent–professional partnership models enable an integration of illness tasks with family priorities as manifested in the process of tailoring a consensual treatment regimen.

## EFFECTIVE METHODS IN ENHANCING ADAPTATION

Interventions based on social-learning theory are proving to be effective in relation to the three primary intervention targets. Considerable support has been provided for the role of cognitive–behavioral interventions in improved stress management and in enhancing support eliciting social problem-solving skills. Furthermore, cognitive–behavioral intervention is effective in improving pain-management skills. Cognitive–behavioral intervention programs directly target children's skill development and also enable parents to participate in the process of fostering the skill development of their children. Well established methodologies are now being modified to be specific to tasks confronted by children with chronic illness. The programs developed by Varni (Varni, Katz, Colegrove, & Dolgin, 1993; Varni, Katz, & Waldron, 1993) and Katz (Katz et al., 1988; Katz et al., 1992) to assist children with cancer in school and social reintegration are exemplary models.

The methods associated with enhancing parenting by fostering developmentally conducive parent–child interactions are beginning to be modified to the specific situation of children with chronic illness. Well established parent training programs to address children's behavior problems and to foster children's cognitive and social development exist and can be modified to fit the specific situation of children with chronic illness.

## THE NEXT STEP

The current behavioral-science knowledge base is certainly incomplete, but it is sufficient to warrant moving to the next stage of research—the experimental level. This would involve systematic intervention-outcome studies using the social learning theory-, cognitive–behavioral-, and family-system based interventions outlined previously. The intervention approaches are necessarily multicomponent, and no one study will employ all components. However, intervention studies are necessary to confirm our knowledge about hypothesized adaptational processes. For example, if stress appraisal is hypothesized to be contributory to adjustment, modifying stress appraisal should reduce psychological distress. In this way, experimental-level research will enable further refinement of the biopsychosocial models that will guide subsequent research efforts to enhance adaptation and quality of life of children with chronic illness and their families.

# REFERENCES

Abramson, L. Y., Seligman, M. E. P., & Teasdale, J. D. (1978). Learned helplessness in humans: Critique and reformulation. *Journal of Abnormal Psychology, 87,* 49–74.

Achenbach, T. M., & Edelbrock, C. S. (1978). The classification of child psychopathology: A review and analysis of empirical effects. *Psychological Bulletin, 85,* 1275–1301.

Achenbach, T., & Edelbrock, C. (1983). *Manual for the Child Behavior Checklist and Revised Child Behavior Profile.* Burlington, VT: Queen City Printers.

Achenbach, T. M., McConaughy, S. H., & Howell, C. T. (1987). Child/adolescent behavioral and emotional problems: Implications of cross-informant correlations for situational specificity. *Psychological Bulletin, 101,* 213–232.

Altshuler, J. L., & Ruble, D. N. (1989). Developmental changes in children's awareness of strategies for coping with uncontrollable stress. *Child Development, 60,* 1337–1349.

American Psychiatric Association. (1980). *Diagnostic and statistical manual of mental disorders* (3rd ed.). Washington, DC: Author.

American Psychiatric Association. (1987). *Diagnostic and statistical manual of mental disorders* (3rd ed., rev.). Washington, DC: Author.

American Psychiatric Association. (1994). *Diagnostic and statistical manual of mental disorders* (4th ed.). Washington, DC: Author.

Anderson, B. (1985). Parents of children with disabilities as collaborators in health care. *Coalition Quarterly, 4,* 1–18.

Anderson, B., Miller, J., Auslander, W., & Santiago, J. (1981). Family characteristics of diabetic adolescents: Relationship to metabolic control. *Diabetes Care, 4,* 586–594.

Angold, A., Weissman, M. M., John, K., Merikangas, K. R., Prusoff, B. A., Wickramaratne, G., Gammon, D., & Warner, V. (1987). Parent and child reports of depressive symptoms in children at low and high risk of depression. *Journal of Child Psychology and Psychiatry, 28,* 901–915.

Apley, J. (1975). *The child with abdominal pain.* London: Blackwell.

Arslanian, S., Becker, D., & Drash, A. (1995). Diabetes mellitus in the child and adolescent. In M. S. Kappy, R. M. Blizzard, C. J. Migeon (Eds.), *The diagnosis and treatment of endocrine disorders in childhood and adolescence* (4th ed., pp. 961–1026). Springfield, IL: Charles C Thomas.

Austin, J. K., & Huberty, T. J. (1993). Development of the Child Attitude Toward Illness Scale. *Journal of Pediatric Psychology, 18,* 467–480.

Baird, S. M., & Ashcroft, S. C. (1985). Need-based educational policy for chronically ill children. In N. Hobbs & J. M. Perrin (Eds.), *Issues in the care of children with chronic illness* (pp. 656–671). San Francisco: Jossey-Bass.

Baldwin, A. L. (1967). *Theories of child development.* New York: Wiley.

Band, E. B., & Weisz, J. R. (1988). How to feel better when it feels bad: Children's perspectives on coping with everyday stress. *Developmental Psychology, 24,* 247–255.

Band, E. B., & Weisz, J. R. (1990). Developmental differences in primary and secondary control coping and adjustment to juvenile diabetes. *Journal of Clinical Child Psychology, 19,* 150–158.

Bandura, A. (1977). Self-efficacy: Toward a unifying theory of behavioral change. *Psychological Review, 84,* 191–215.

Banez, G. A., & Compas, B. E. (1990). Children's and parents' daily stressful events and psychological symptoms. *Journal of Abnormal Child Psychology, 18,* 591–605.

Barakat, L. P., & Linney, J. A. (1992). Children with physical handicaps and their mothers: The interrelation of social support, maternal adjustment, and child adjustment. *Journal of Pediatric Psychology, 17,* 725–740.

Baskin, C. H., Forehand, R., & Saylor, C. (1986). Predictors of psychological adjustment in mothers of children with cancer. *Journal of Psychosocial Oncology, 3,* 43–54.

Bazyk, S. (1989). Changes in attitudes and beliefs regarding parent participation in home programs: An update. *American Journal of Occupational Therapy, 43,* 723–728.

Beales, J. G., Keen, J. H., & Holt, P. J. L. (1983). The child's perception of the disease and the experience of pain in juvenile chronic arthritis. *Journal of Rheumatology, 10,* 61–65.

Beck, A. T., Steer, R. A., & Garbin, M. G. (1988). Psychometric properties of the Beck Depression Inventory: Twenty-five years of evaluation. *Clinical Psychology Review, 8,* 77–100.

Beck, A. T., Ward, C. H., Mendelson, M., Mock, J., & Erbaugh, J. (1961). An inventory for measuring depression. *Archives of General Psychiatry, 4,* 53–63.

Becker, M. H., Maiman, L. A., Kirscht, J. P., Haefner, D. P., Drachman, R. H., & Taylor, D. W. (1979). Patient perceptions and compliance: Recent studies of the health belief model. In R. B. Haynes, D. W. Taylor, & D. L. Sackett (Eds.), *Compliance in Health Care* (pp. 78–109). Baltimore, MD: The Johns Hopkins University Press.

Belsky, J. (1984). The determinants of parenting: A process model. *Child Development, 55,* 83–96.

Belsky, J., Lerner, R., & Spanier, G. (1984). *The child in the family.* Reading, MA: Addison-Wesley.

Belsky, J., Robins, E., & Gamble, W. (1984). The determinants of parental competence: Toward a contextual theory. In M. Lewis (Ed.), *Social connections: Beyond the dyad* (pp. 251–280). New York: Plenum.

Bender, B. G., Lerner, J. A., & Kollasch, E. (1988). Mood and memory changes in asthmatic children receiving corticosteroids. *Journal of the American Academy of Child and Adolescent Psychiatry, 27,* 720–725.

Bennett, D. S. (1994). Depression among children with chronic medical problems: A meta analysis. *Journal of Pediatric Psychology, 19*, 149–170.

Berde, C., Ablin, A., Glazer, J., Miser, A., Shapiro, B., Weisman, S., & Zeltzer, P. (1990). Report of the subcommittee on disease-related pain in childhood cancer. *Pediatrics, 86* (Suppl.), 818–825.

Berry, S. L., Hayford, J. R., Ross, C. K., Pachman, L. M., & Lavigne, J. V. (1993). Conceptions of illness by children with juvenile rheumatoid arthritis: A cognitive developmental approach. *Journal of Pediatric Psychology, 18*, 83–97.

Bibace, R., & Walsh, M. E. (1979). Developmental stages in children's conceptions of illness. In G. C. Stone, F. Cohen, & N. E. Adler (Eds.), *Health Psychology* (pp. 285–301). San Francisco: Jossey-Bass.

Bibace, R., & Walsh, M. E. (1980). Development of children's concepts of illness. *Pediatrics, 66*, 912–917.

Blanchard-Fields, F., & Irion, J. C. (1987). Coping strategies from the perspective of two developmental markers: Age and social reasoning. *Journal of Genetic Psychology, 149*, 141–151.

Bloch, A. (1986). Chronic illness and its impact on academic achievement. *Pediatrician, 13*, 128–132.

Blount, R. L., Corbin, S. M., Sturges, J. W., Wolfe, V. V., Prater, J. M., & James, L. D. (1989). The relationship between adults' behavior and child coping and distress during BMA/LP procedures: A sequential analysis. *Behavioral Therapy, 20*, 585–601.

Blount, R. L., Davis, N., Powers, S. W., & Roberts, M. C. (1991). The influence of environmental factors and coping style on children's coping and distress. *Clinical Psychology Review, 11*, 93–116.

Boat, T. F., Welsh, M. J., & Beaudet, A. L. (1989). Cystic fibrosis. In C. L. Scriver, A. L. Beaudet, W. S. Sly, & D. Valle (Eds.), *The metabolic bases of inherited disease* (pp. 2469–2680). New York: McGraw-Hill.

Bolig, R., Brown, R. T., Kuo, J. H. (1992). A comparison of never-hospitalized and previously hospitalized adolescents: Self-esteem and locus of control. *Adolescence, 27*, 227–234.

Boyle, I. R., di Sant'Agnese, P. A., Sack, S., Millican, F., & Kulczycki, L. L. (1976). Emotional adjustment of adolescents and young adults with cystic fibrosis. *Journal of Pediatrics, 88*, 318–326.

Bradburn, N. M. (1969). *The structure of psychological well-being*. Chicago: Aldine.

Breslau, N. (1985). Psychiatric disorder in children with physical disabilities. *Journal of the American Academy of Child Psychiatry, 24*, 87–94.

Breslau, N., & Marshall, I. A. (1985). Psychological disturbance in children with physical disabilities: Continuity and change in a 5-year follow-up. *Journal of Abnormal Child Psychology, 13*, 199–216.

Breslau, N., & Prabucki, K. (1987). Siblings of disabled children. *Archives of General Psychiatry, 44*, 1040–1046.

Breslau, N., Staruch, K. S., & Mortimer, E. A. (1982). Psychological distress in mothers of disabled children. *American Journal of Diseases in Childhood, 136,* 682–686.

Breslau, N., Weitzman, M., & Messenger, K. (1981). Psychologic functioning of siblings of disabled children. *Pediatrics, 67,* 344–353.

Bronfenbrenner, U. (1975). Is early intervention effective? In M. Guntag & E. Struening (Eds.), *Handbook of evaluation research* (Vol. 2, pp. 519–603). Beverly Hills, CA: Sage.

Bronfenbrenner, U. (1977). Toward an experimental ecology of human development. *American Psychologist, 32,* 513–531.

Bronfenbrenner, U. (1979). *The ecology of human development.* Cambridge, MA: Harvard University Press.

Brown, J. M., O'Keefe, J., Sanders, S. H., & Baker, B. (1986). Developmental changes in children's cognition to stressful and painful situations. *Journal of Pediatric Psychology, 11,* 343–357.

Brown, R. T., Armstrong, F. D., & Eckman, J. R. (1993). Neurocognitive aspects of pediatric sickle cell disease. *Journal of Learning Disabilities, 26,* 33–45.

Brown, R. T., Buchanan, I., Doepke, K., Eckman, J. R., Baldwin, K., Goonan, B., & Schoenherr, S. (1993). Cognitive and academic functioning in children with sickle cell disease. *Journal of Clinical Child Psychology, 22,* 207–218.

Brown, R. T., Kaslow, N. J., Doepke, K., Buchanan, I., Eckman, J., Baldwin, K., & Goonan, B. (1993). Psychosocial and family functioning in children with sickle cell syndrome and their mothers. *Journal of the American Academy of Child and Adolescent Psychiatry, 32,* 545–553.

Brown, R. T., Kaslow, N. J., Hazzard, A. P., Madan-Swain, A., Sexson, S. B., Lambert, R., & Baldwin, K. (1992). Psychiatric and family functioning in children with leukemia and their families. *Journal of the American Academy of Child and Adolescent Psychiatry, 31,* 495–502.

Brown, R. T., Kaslow, N. J., Madan-Swain, A., Doepke, K. J., Sexson, S. B., & Hill, L. (1993). Parental psychopathology and children's adjustment to leukemia. *Journal of the American Academy of Child and Adolescent Psychiatry, 32,* 554–561.

Brown, R. T., Kaslow, N. J., Sansbury, L., Meacham, L., & Culler, F. L. (1991). Internalizing and externalizing symptoms and attributional style in youth with diabetes. *Journal of American Academy of Child and Adolescent Psychiatry, 30,* 921–925.

Burbach, D. J., & Peterson, L. (1986). Children's concepts of physical illness: A review and critique of the cognitive-developmental literature. *Health Psychology, 5,* 307–325.

Bush, J. P., & Harkins, S. W. (1991). Conceptual foundations: Pain and child development. In J. P. Bush & S. W. Harkins (Eds.), *Children in pain: Clinical and research issues from a developmental perspective* (pp. 1–30). New York: Springer-Verlag.

Bush, J. P., Melamed, B. G., Sheras, P. L., & Greenbaum, P. E. (1986). Mother-child patterns of coping with anticipatory stress. *Health Psychology, 5,* 137–157.

Butler, R. W., & Copeland, D. R. (1993). Neuropsychological effects of central nervous system prophylactic treatment in childhood leukemia: Methodological considerations. *Journal of Pediatric Psychology, 18,* 319–338.

Cadman, D., Boyle, M., Szatmari, P., & Offord, D. R. (1987). Chronic illness, disability, and mental and social well-being: Findings of the Ontario Child Health Study. *Pediatrics, 79,* 805–813.

Cadman, D., Rosenbaum, P., Boyle, M., & Offord, D. R. (1991). Children with chronic illness: Family and parent demographic characteristics and psychosocial adjustment. *Pediatrics, 87,* 884–889.

Cairns, N. U., Klopovich, P., Hearne, E., & Lansky, S. B. (1982). School attendance of children with cancer. *Journal of School Health, 52,* 152–155.

Campbell, J. D. (1975). Illness is a point of view: The development of children's concepts of illness. *Child Development, 46,* 92.

Campbell, M. M., Hayden, P. W., & Davenport, S. L. (1977). Psychological adjustment of adolescents with myelodysplasia. *Journal of Youth and Adolescence, 6,* 397–407.

Carpentieri, S. C., Mulhern, R. K., Douglas, S., Hanna, S., & Fairclough, D. J. (1993). Behavioral resiliency among children surviving brain tumors: A longitudinal study. *Journal of Clinical Child Psychology, 22,* 236–246.

Catlett, A. T., Thompson, R. J., Jr., Johndrow, D. A., & Boshkoff, M. R. (1993). Risk status for dropping out of developmental follow-up for very low birthweight infants. *Public Health Reports, 108,* 589–594.

Cecalupo, A. (1994). Childhood cancers: Medical issues. In R. A. Olson, L. L. Mullins, J. B. Gillman, & J. M. Chaney (Eds.), *The sourcebook of pediatric psychology* (pp. 90–97). Boston: Allyn & Bacon.

Celano, M. P., & Geller, R. J. (1993). Learning, school performance, and children with asthma: How much at risk? *Journal of Learning Disabilities, 26,* 23–32.

Chaney, J. M., & Peterson, L. (1989). Family variables and disease management in juvenile rheumatoid arthritis. *Journal of Pediatric Psychology, 14,* 389–404.

Charache, S., Lubin, B., & Reid, C. D. (1989). *Management and therapy of sickle cell disease* (NIH Publication No. 89-2117). Washington, DC: National Institutes of Health.

Charlton, A., Larcombe, I. J., Meller, S. T., Morris-Jones, P. H., Mott, M. G., Potton, M. W., Tranmer, M. D., Walker, J. J. P. (1991). Absence from school related to cancer and other chronic conditions. *Archives of Disease in Childhood, 66,* 1217–1222.

Chasnoff, I. J. (1989). Drug use and women: Establishing a standard of care. *Annals of the New York Academy of Sciences, 562,* 208–210.

Chaves, J. F., & Brown, J. M. (1987). Spontaneous cognitive strategies in the control of pain and stress. *Journal of Behavioral Medicine, 10,* 263–276.

Chesler, M., Barbarin, O., & Lebo-Stein, J. (1984). Patterns of participation in a self-help group for parents of children with cancer. *Journal of Psychosocial Oncology, 2*, 41–63.

Chiles, L. (1987). Federal involvement in mental retardation programs: Past, present, and future directions. *American Psychologist, 42*, 792–795.

Christopherson, E. R. (1994). *Pediatric compliance: A guide for the primary care physician*. New York: Plenum Medical Book.

Cochran, M., & Brassard, J. (1979). Child development and personal social networks. *Child Development, 50*, 601–616.

Cohen, S., & Wills, T. (1985). Stress, social support and the buffering hypotheses. *Psychological Bulletin, 98*, 310–357.

Cohn, J. F., Matias, R., Tronick, E. Z., Lyons-Ruth, K., & Connell, D. (1986). Face-to-face interactions, spontaneous and structured, of mothers with depressive symptoms. In T. Field & E. Z. Tronick (Eds.), *Maternal depression and child development* (pp. 31–46). San Francisco: Jossey-Bass.

Cohn, J. F., & Tronick, E. Z. (1983). Three-month-old infants' reaction to simulated maternal depression. *Child Development, 54*, 472–505.

Coie, J. D. (1985). Fitting social skills intervention to the target group. In B. H. Schneider, K. H. Rubin, & J. E. Ledingham (Eds.), *Children's peer relations: Issues in assessment and intervention* (pp. 141–156). New York: Springer-Verlag.

Compas, B. E. (1987). Coping with stress during childhood and adolescence. *Psychological Bulletin, 101*, 393–403.

Compas, B. E., Davis, G. E., & Forsythe, C. J. (1985). Characteristics of life events during adolescence. *American Journal of Community Psychology, 13*, 677–691.

Compas, B. E., Davis, G. E., Forsythe, C. J., & Wagner, B. M. (1987). Assessment of major and daily stressful events during adolescence: The Adolescent Perceived Events Scale (1987). *Journal of Consulting and Clinical Psychology, 55*, 534–541.

Compas, B. E., Forsythe, C. J., & Wagner, B. M. (1988). Consistency and variability in causal attributions and coping with stress. *Cognitive Therapy and Research, 12*, 305–320.

Compas, B. E., Howell, D. C., Phares, V., Williams, R. A., & Ledoux, N. (1989). Parent and child stress and symptoms: An integrative analysis. *Developmental Psychology, 25*, 550–559.

Compas, B. E., Malcarne, V. L., & Fondacaro, K. M. (1988). Coping with stressful events in older children and young adolescents. *Journal of Consulting and Clinical Psychology, 56*, 405–411.

Compas, B. E., Wagner, B. M., Slavin, L. A., & Vannatta, K. (1986). A prospective study of life events, social support, and psychological symptomatology during the transition from high school to college. *American Journal of Community Psychology, 14*, 241–257.

Conger, R. D., McCarty, J. A., Yang, R. K., Lahey, B. B., & Kropp, J. P. (1984). Perception of child, child-rearing values, and emotional distress as mediating links between environmental stressors and observed maternal behavior. *Child Development, 55,* 2234–2247.

Consensus Conference. (1987). Newborn screening for sickle cell disease and other hemoglobinopathies. *Journal of the American Medical Association, 258,* 1205–1209.

Cook, B. A., Schaller, K., & Krischer, J. P. (1985). School absence among children with chronic illness. *Journal of School Health, 55,* 265–267.

Cooley, C. H. (1902). *Human nature and the social order.* New York: Charles Scribner's Sons.

Costello, A. J., Edelbrock, C., Dulcan, M. K., Kalas, R., & Klaric, S. H. (1984). *Development and Testing of the NIMH Diagnostic Interview Schedule for Children in a Clinic Population.* Rockville, MD: Center for Epidemiologic Studies, National Institute of Mental Health.

Cotton, C. R., & Range, L. M. (1990). Children's death concepts: Relationship to cognitive functioning, age, experience with death, fear of death, and helplessness. *Journal of Clinical Child Psychology, 19,* 123–127.

Cousens, P., Said, J., Waters, B., & Stevens, M. (1988). Cognitive effects of cranial irradiation in leukemia: A survey and meta-analysis. *Journal of Child Psychology and Psychiatry, 29,* 839–852.

Cousens, P., Ungerer, J. A., Crawford, J. A., & Stevens, M. (1991). Cognitive effects of childhood leukemia therapy: A case for four specific deficits. *Journal of Pediatric Psychology, 16,* 475–488.

Cowen, E. L., Pederson, A., Babigian, H., Izzo, L. D., & Trost, M. A. (1973). Long term follow-up of early detected vulnerable children. *Journal of Consulting and Clinical Psychology, 41,* 438–446.

Creer, T. L., & Gustafson, K. E. (1989). Psychological problems associated with drug therapy in childhood asthma. *Journal of Pediatrics, 115,* 850–855.

Creer, T. L., Harm, D. L., & Marion, R. J. (1988). Childhood asthma. In D. K. Routh (Ed.), *Handbook of pediatric psychology* (pp. 162–189). New York: Guilford Press.

Creer, T. L., Kotses, H., Gustafson, K. E., Wigal, J. K., Wagner, M. D., Westlund, R. E., & Trusel, C. S. (1988). A critique of studies investigating the association of theophylline to psychologic or behavioral performance. *Pediatric Asthma, Allergy, and Immunology, 2,* 169–184.

Creer, T. L., Renne, C. M., & Chai, H. (1982). The application of behavioral techniques to childhood asthma. In D. C. Russo & J. W. Varni (Eds.), *Behavioral pediatrics: Research and practice* (pp. 27–66). New York: Plenum.

Creer, T. L., & Yoches, C. (1971). The modification of an inappropriate behavioral pattern in asthmatic children. *Journal of Chronic Disease, 24,* 507–513.

Crnic, K. A., & Greenberg, M. T. (1990). Minor parenting stress with young children. *Child Development, 61,* 1628–1637.

Cystic Fibrosis Foundation. (1994). *Patient Registry 1993 annual data report.* Bethesda, MD: Author.

Dahlquist, L. M. (1989). Cognitive-behavioral treatment of pediatric cancer patients' distress during painful and invasive medical procedures. In M. C. Roberts & C. E. Walker (Eds.), *Casebook of child and pediatric psychology* (pp. 360–379). New York: Guilford Press.

Dahlquist, L. M. (1992). Coping with aversive medical treatments. In A. M. La Greca, L. J. Siegel, J. L. Wallander, & C. E. Walker (Eds.), *Stress and Coping in Child Health* (pp. 345–376). New York: Guilford Press.

Dahlquist, L. M., Czyzewski, D. I., Copeland, K. G., Jones, C. L., Taub, E., & Vaughan, J. K. (1993). Parents of children newly diagnosed with cancer: Anxiety, coping, and marital distress. *Journal of Pediatric Psychology, 18,* 365–376.

Daniels, D., Moos, R. H., Billings, A. G., & Miller, J. J., III. (1987). Psychosocial risk and resistance factors among children with chronic illness, healthy siblings, and healthy controls. *Journal of Abnormal Child Psychology, 15,* 295–308.

Davis, G. E., & Compas, B. E. (1986). Cognitive appraisal of major and daily stressful events during adolescence: A multidimensional scaling analysis. *Journal of Youth and Adolescence, 15,* 377–388.

Deaton, A. V. (1985). Adaptive noncompliance in pediatric asthma: The parent as expert. *Journal of Pediatric Psychology, 10,* 1–14.

DeLongis, A., Folkman, S., & Lazarus, R. S. (1988). The impact of daily stress on health and mood: Psychological and social resources as mediators. *Journal of Personality and Social Psychology, 54,* 486–495.

DeMaso, D. R., Beardslee, W. R., Silbert, A. R., & Flyer, D. C. (1990). Psychological functioning in children with cyanotic heart defects. *Journal of Developmental and Behavioral Pediatrics, 11,* 289–294.

Derogatis, L. R. (1975). *Scoring and procedures manual for PAIS.* Baltimore: Johns Hopkins University, Clinical Psychometric Research Unit.

Derogatis, L. R. (1977). *SCL-90-R manual.* Baltimore: Johns Hopkins University, Clinical Psychometrics Research Unit.

Derogatis, L. R. (1983). *SCL-90-R: Administration, scoring, and procedures manual II.* Baltimore: Johns Hopkins University, Clinical Psychometric Research Unit.

Derogatis, L. R., & Spencer, P. M. (1982). *The Brief Symptom Inventory: Administration, scoring, and procedures manual.* Baltimore: Johns Hopkins University, Clinical Psychometric Research Unit.

Developmental Disabilities Service and Facilitation Construction Amendments of 1970, Pub. L. No. 91-517, § 133, 84 Stat. 1318 (1971).

Developmentally Disabled Assistance and Bill of Rights Act, Pub. L. No. 94-103, § 1, 89 Stat. 486 (1977).

Diaz, C., Starfield, B., Holtzman, N., Holtzman, N., Mellits, E. D., Hankin, J., Smalky, K., & Benson, P. (1986). Ill health and use of medical care: Community-based assessment of morbidity in children. *Medical Care, 24,* 848–856.

Diggs, L. M. (1973). Anatomic lesions in sickle cell disease. In H. Abramson, J. F. Bertles, & D. L. Wethers (Eds.), *Sickle cell disease: Diagnosis, management, education, and research* (pp. 189–229). St. Louis, MO: C. V. Mosby.

Dix, T. H., & Grusec, J. E. (1985). Parent attributional processes in the sociali-zation of children. In I. E. Sigel (Ed.), *Parental belief systems: The psychological consequences for children* (pp. 201–233). Hillsdale, NJ: Erlbaum.

Dix, T. H., Ruble, D., Grusec, J. E., & Nixon, S. (1986). Social cognition in parents: Inferential and affective reactions to children of three age levels. *Child Development, 57,* 879–894.

Dix, T. H., Ruble, D. N., & Zambarano, R. J. (1989). Mothers' implicit theories of discipline: Child effects, parent effects, and the attribution process. *Child Development, 60,* 1373–1391.

Dodge, K. A., McClaskey, C. L., & Feldman, E. (1985). A situational approach to the assessment of social competence in children. *Journal of Consulting and Clinical Psychology, 53,* 344–353.

Dorland, T. D. (1977). NIAID initiatives in allergy research. *Journal of Allergy and Clinical Immunology, 49,* 323–328.

Douglas, J. W. B., & Bloomfield, J. M. (1958). *Children under five.* London: Allen & Unwin.

Drotar, D. (1981). Psychological perspectives in chronic childhood illness. *Journal of Pediatric Psychology, 6,* 211–228.

Drotar, D., & Crawford, P. (1985). Psychological adaptation of siblings of chron-ically ill children. Research and practice implications. *Journal of Developmental and Behavioral Pediatrics, 6,* 355–362.

Drotar, D., Doershuk, C. F., Stern, R. C., Boat, T. F., Boyer, W., & Matthews, L. (1981). Psychosocial functioning of children with cystic fibrosis. *Pediatrics, 67,* 338–343.

Dunbar-Jacob, J., Dunning, E. J., & Dwyer, K. (1993). Compliance research in pediatric and adolescent populations: Two decades of research. In N. P. Kras-negor, L. Epstein, S. B. Johnson, & S. J. Yaffe (Eds.), *Developmental aspects of health compliance behavior* (pp. 29–51). Hillside, NJ: Erlbaum.

Dunst, C. J., Trivette, C. M., Davis, M., & Cornwell, J. (1988). Enabling and empowering families of children with health impairments. *Children's Health Care, 17,* 71–81.

Dweck, C. S. (1975). The role of expectations and attributions in the alleviation of learned helplessness. *Journal of Personality and Social Psychology, 31,* 674–685.

Dyson, L. L. (1989). Adjustment of siblings of handicapped children: A compar-ison. *Journal of Pediatric Psychology, 14,* 215–229.

D'Zurilla, T. J., & Goldfried, M. R. (1971). Problem solving and behavior modi-fication. *Journal of Abnormal Psychology, 78,* 107–126.

Eaton, M. L., Hayes, J., Armstrong, F. D., Pegelow, C. H., & Thomas, M. (1991, May). *Relationship between painful episodes, school absenteeism, and academic performance in children with sickle cell anemia.* Paper presented at the annual meeting of the National Sickle Cell Disease Program, Mobile, AL.

Ebata, A., & Moos, R. (1991). Coping and adjustment in distressed and healthy adolescents. *Journal of Applied Developmental Psychology, 12,* 33–54.

Edelbrock, C., & Achenbach, T. M. (1984). The teacher version of the Child Behavior Profile: I. Boys aged 6–11. *Journal of Consulting and Clinical Psychology, 52,* 207–217.

Edelbrock, C., Costello, A. J., Dulcan, M. K., Conover, N. C., & Kalas, K. (1986). Parent–child agreement on child psychiatric symptoms assessed via structured interview. *Journal of Child Psychology and Psychiatry, 27,* 181–190.

Edelbrock, C., Costello, A. J., Dulcan, M. K., Kalas, R., & Conover, N. C. (1985). Age differences in the reliability of the psychiatric interview. *Child Development, 56,* 265–275.

Education Amendments of 1974, Pub. L. No. 93-380, § 101, 88 Stat. 484 (1976).

Education for All Handicapped Children Act of 1975, Pub. L. No. 94-142, § 2, 89 Stat. 773 (1977).

Education of the Handicapped Act, Pub. L. No. 91-230, § 601, 84 Stat. 175 (1971).

Education of the Handicapped Act Amendments of 1986, Pub. L. No. 99-457, § 1, 100 Stat. 1145 (1989).

Eiser, C., Havermans, T., Pancer, M., & Eiser, J. R. (1992). Adjustment to chronic disease in relation to age and gender: Mothers' and fathers' reports of their children's behavior. *Journal of Pediatric Psychology, 17,* 261–276.

Ellsworth, R. B. (1979). *CAAP Scale: The measurement of child and adolescent adjustment.* Roanoke, VA: Institute for Program Evaluation.

Engel, G. L. (1977). The need for a new medical model: A challenge for biomedicine. *Science, 196,* 129–136.

Engel, G. L. (1980). The clinical application of the biopsychosocial model. *American Journal of Psychiatry, 137,* 535–544.

English, H. B., & English, A. C. (1958). *A comprehensive dictionary of psychological and psychoanalytical terms.* New York: McKay.

Epstein, L. H., & Cluss, P. A. (1982). A behavioral medicine perspective on adherence to long-term medical regimens. *Journal of Consulting and Clinical Psychology, 50,* 950–971.

Epstein, N., Baldwin, L., & Bishop, D. (1983). The Family Assessment Device. *Journal of Marital and Family Therapy, 9,* 171–184.

Erikson, E. (1964). *Childhood and society.* New York: Norton.

Evans, C. A., Stevens, M., Cushway, D., & Houghton, J. (1992). Sibling response to childhood cancer: A new approach. *Child: Care, Health and Development, 18,* 229–244.

Evans, R., Mullally, D. I., Wilson, R. W., Gergen, P. J., Rosenberg, H. M., Grauman, J. S., Chevarley, F. M., & Feinleib, M. (1987). Prevalence, hospitalization and death from asthma over two decades: 1965–1984. *Chest, 91,* 65S–74S.

Fahrner, R. (1992). Pediatric HIV infection and AIDS. In P. L. Jackson & J. A. Vessey (Eds.), *Primary care of the child with a chronic condition* (pp. 408–425). St. Louis, MO: Mosley Year-Book.

Family and Medical Leave Act of 1993, Pub. L. No. 103-3, § 2, 107 Stat. 6 (1994).

Feldman, W. S., & Varni, J. W. (1985). Conceptualizations of health and illness by children with spina bifida. *Children's Health Care, 13*, 102–108.

Ferrari, M. (1987). The diabetic child and well sibling: Risks to the well child's self concept. *Children's Health Care, 15*, 141–148.

Field, T., Healy, B., Goldstein, S., Perry, S., Bendell, D., Schanberg, S., Zimmerman, E. A., & Kuhn, C. (1988). Infants of depressed mothers show "depressed" behavior even with nondepressed adults. *Child Development, 59*, 1569–1579.

Fiese, B. H., & Sameroff, A. J. (1992). Family context in pediatric psychology: A transactional perspective. In M. C. Roberts & J. L. Wallander (Eds.), *Family issues in pediatric psychology* (pp. 239–260). Hillsdale, NJ: Erlbaum.

Fife, B., Norton, J., & Groom, G. (1987). The family's adaptation to childhood leukemia. *Social Science and Medicine, 24*, 159–168.

Fink, D. L. (1976). Tailoring the consensual regimen. In D. L. Sackett & R. B. Haynes (Eds.), *Compliance with therapeutic regimens* (pp. 110–118). Baltimore: Johns Hopkins University Press.

Fletcher, J. M., & Copeland, D. R. (1988). Neurobehavioral effects of central nervous system prophylactic treatment of cancer in children. *Journal of Clinical and Experimental Neuropsychology, 10*, 495–538.

Fletcher, J. M., Francis, D. J., Pequegnat, W., Raudenbush, S. W., Bornstein, M. H., Schmitt, F., Browers, P., & Stover, E. (1991). Neurobehavioral outcomes in diseases of childhood: Individual change models for pediatric human immunodeficiency viruses. *American Psychologist, 46*, 1267–1277.

Folkman, S. (1984). Personal control and stress and coping processes: A theoretical analysis. *Journal of Personality and Social Psychology, 46*, 839–852.

Folkman, S., & Lazarus, R. S. (1980). An analysis of coping in a middle-aged community sample. *Journal of Health and Social Behavior, 21*, 219–239.

Forehand, R. (1993). Twenty years of research on parenting: Does it have practical implications for clinicians working with parents and children? *The Clinical Psychologist, 46*, 169–176.

Forehand, R., Lautenschlager, G. L., Faust, J., & Graziano, W. G. (1986). Parent perceptions and parent–child interaction in clinic-referred children: A preliminary investigation of the effects of maternal depressive mood. *Behavior Research and Therapy, 24*, 73–75.

Fowler, M. G., Davenport, M. G., & Garg, R. (1992). School functioning of U.S. children with asthma. *Pediatrics, 90*, 939–944.

Fowler, M. G., Johnson, M. P., & Atkinson, S. S. (1985). School achievement and absence in children with chronic health conditions. *Journal of Pediatrics, 106*, 683–687.

Friedman, A. G., & Mulhern, R. K. (1992). Psychological aspects of childhood cancer. In B. B. Lahey & A. E. Kazdin (Eds.), *Advances in clinical child psychology* (Vol. 14, pp. 165–189). New York: Plenum.

Furman, W., & Buhrmester, D. (1985). Children's perception of the qualities of sibling relationships. *Child Development, 56,* 448–461.

Futterman, E. H., & Hoffman, I. (1970). Transient school phobia in a leukemic child. *Journal of the American Academy of Child Psychiatry, 9,* 477–494.

Gaffney, A. (1993). Cognitive developmental aspects of pain in school-age children. In N. L. Schechter, C. B. Berde, & M. Yaster (Eds.), *Pain in infants, children, and adolescents* (pp. 75–85). Baltimore: Williams & Wilkins.

Gaffney, A., & Dunne, E. A. (1986). Developmental aspects of children's definitions of pain. *Pain, 26,* 105–117.

Gaffney, A., & Dunne, E. A. (1987). Children's understanding of the causality of pain. *Pain, 29,* 91–104.

Gallagher, J. J. (1989). A new policy initiative: Infants and toddlers with handicapping conditions. *American Psychologist, 44,* 387–391.

Garmezy, N. (1981). Children under stress: Perspectives on antecedents and correlates of vulnerability and resistance to psychopathology. In A. I. Rabin, J. Arnoff, A. M. Barclay, & R. A. Zucker (Eds.), *Further explorations in personality* (pp. 196–269). New York: Wiley.

Garrison, W. T., & McQuiston, S. (1989). *Chronic illness during childhood and adolescence: Psychological aspects.* London: Sage.

Garwood, S. G. (1987). Political, economic, and practical issues affecting the development of universal early intervention for handicapped infants. *Topics in Early Childhood Special Education, 7,* 6–18.

Garwood, S. G., Phillips, D., Hartman, A., & Zigler, E. F. (1989). As the pendulum swings: Federal agency programs for children. *American Psychologist, 44,* 434–440.

Gayton, W. F., Friedman, S. B., Tavormina, J. B., & Tucker, F. (1977). Children with cystic fibrosis: I. Psychological test findings of patient, siblings and parents. *Pediatrics, 59,* 888–894.

Gergen, P. J., Mullally, D. I., & Evans, R., III. (1988). National survey of prevalence of asthma among children in the United States, 1976 to 1980. *Pediatrics, 81,* 1–7.

Gil, K. M., Thompson, R. J., Jr., Keith, B. R., Tota-Faucette, M., Noll, S., & Kinney, T. R. (1993). Sickle cell disease pain in children and adolescents: Change in pain frequency and coping strategies over time. *Journal of Pediatric Psychology, 18,* 621–637.

Gil, K. M., Williams, D. A., Thompson, R. J., Jr., & Kinney, T. R. (1991). Sickle cell disease in children and adolescents: The relation of child and parent pain coping strategies to adjustment. *Journal of Pediatric Psychology, 16,* 643–663.

Glauser, T. A., & Packer, R. J. (1991). Cognitive deficits in long-term survivors of childhood brain tumors. *Child's Nervous System, 7,* 2–12.

Gonzalez, J. C., Routh, D. K., & Armstrong, F. D. (1993). Effects of maternal distraction versus reassurances on children's reactions to injections. *Journal of Pediatric Psychology, 18,* 593–604.

Gonzalez, J. C., Routh, D. K., Saab, P. G., Armstrong, F. D., Shifman, L., Guerra, E., & Fawcett, N. (1989). Effects of parent presence on children's reactions to injections: Behavioral, physiological, and subjective aspects. *Journal of Pediatric Psychology, 14,* 449–462.

Goodnow, J. J. (1984). Parents' ideas about parenting and development: A review of issues and recent work. In M. E. Lamb, A. L. Brown, & B. Rogoff (Eds.), *Advances in developmental psychology* (Vol. 3, pp. 193–242). Hillsdale, NJ: Erlbaum.

Gordon, W. A. (1982). The behavioral disorders of children with spina bifida. In A. Baum & J. E. Singer (Eds.), *Handbook of psychology and health: Vol. 2. Issues in child health and adolescent health* (pp. 213–229). Hillsdale, NJ: Erlbaum.

Gortmaker, S. L. (1985). Demography of chronic childhood diseases. In N. Hobbs & J. M. Perrin (Eds.), *Issues in the care of children with chronic illness: A sourcebook of problems, services, and policies* (pp. 135–154). San Francisco: Jossey-Bass.

Gortmaker, S. L., & Sappenfield, W. (1984). Chronic childhood disorders: Prevalence and impact. *Pediatric Clinics of North America, 31,* 3–18.

Gortmaker, S. L., Walker, D. K., Weitzman, M., & Sobol, A. M. (1990). Chronic conditions, socioeconomic risks and behavioral problems in children and adolescents. *Pediatrics, 85,* 267–276.

Graetz, B., & Shute, R. (1995). Assessment of peer relationships in children with asthma. *Journal of Pediatric Psychology, 20,* 205–216.

Greenberg, H. S., Kazak, A., & Meadows, A. T. (1989). Psychologic functioning in 8- to 18-year-old cancer survivors and their parents. *Journal of Pediatrics, 114,* 488–493.

Gross, A., Stern, R., Levin, R., Dale, J., & Wojnilower, D. (1983). The effect of mother–child separation on the behavior of children experiencing a diagnostic medical procedure. *Journal of Consulting and Clinical Psychology, 51,* 783–785.

Gross, R. T. (1990). Enhancing the outcomes of low birth weight, premature infants: A multisite, randomized trial. *Journal of the American Medical Association, 263,* 3035–3042.

Hack, M., Horbar, J. D., Malloy, M. H., Tyson, J. E., Wright, E., & Wright, L. (1991). Very low birth weight outcomes of the National Institute of Child Health and Human Development Neonatal Network. *Pediatrics, 87,* 587–597.

Haggerty, R. J. (1984). Foreword: Symposium on chronic disease in children. *Pediatric Clinics of North America, 31,* 1–2.

Haggerty, R. J. (1980). Life stress, illness, and social supports. *Developmental Medicine and Child Neurology, 22,* 391–400.

Haggerty, R. J., Roghmann, K. J., & Pless, I. B. (Eds.). (1975). *Child Health and the Community.* New York: Wiley.

Hamburg, D. A. (1974). Coping behavior in life-threatening circumstances. *Psychotherapy and Psychosomatics, 23,* 13–25.

Handicapped Children's Early Education Assistance Act, Pub. L. No. 90-538, § 2, 82 Stat. 901 (1969).

Hanson, C. L. (1990). Understanding insulin-dependent diabetes mellitus (IDDM) and treating children with IDDM and their families. In S. W. Henggeler & C. M. Borduin (Eds.), *Family therapy and beyond: A multisystemic approach to treating the behavior problems of children and adolescents* (pp. 278–323). Pacific Grove, CA: Brooks/Cole.

Hanson, C. L. (1992). Developing systematic models of the adaptation of youths with diabetes. In A. M. La Greca, L. J. Siegel, J. L. Wallander, & C. E. Walker (Eds.), *Stress and Coping in Child Health* (pp. 212–241). New York: Guilford Press.

Hanson, C. L., Cigrang, J. A., Harris, M. A., Carle, D. L., Relyea, G., & Burghen, G. A. (1989). Coping styles in youths with insulin-dependent diabetes mellitus. *Journal of Consulting and Clinical Psychology, 57*, 644–651.

Hanson, C. L., DeGuire, M. J., Schinkel, A. M., Henggeler, S. W., & Burghen, G. A. (1992). Comparing social learning and family systems correlates of adaptation in youths with IDDM. *Journal of Pediatric Psychology, 17*, 555–572.

Hanson, C. L., Henggeler, S. W., Harris, M. A., Burghen, G. A., & Moore, M. (1989). Family system variables and the health status of adolescents with insulin-dependent diabetes mellitus. *Health Psychology, 8*, 239–253.

Hanson, C. L., Henggeler, S. W., Harris, M. A., Cigrang, J. A., Schinkel, A. M., Rodrigue, J. R., & Klesges, R. C. (1992). Contributions of sibling relations to the adaptation of youths with insulin-dependent diabetes mellitus. *Journal of Consulting and Clinical Psychology, 60*, 104–112.

Hanson, C. L., Rodrigue, J. R., Henggeler, S. W., Harris, M. A., Klesges, R. C., & Carle, D. L. (1990). The perceived self-competence of adolescents with insulin-dependent diabetes mellitus: Deficit or strength? *Journal of Pediatric Psychology, 15*, 605–618.

Harbeck, C., & Peterson, L. (1992). Elephants dancing in my head: A developmental approach to children's concepts of specific pains. *Child Development, 63*, 138–149.

Harter, S. (1986). Processes underlying the construct, maintenance, and enhancement of the self-concept in children. In J. Suls & A. Greenwald (Eds.), *Psychological perspectives on the self* (Vol. 3, pp. 137–181). Hillsdale, NJ: Erlbaum.

Hartup, W. W. (1989). Social relationships and their developmental significance. *American Psychologist, 11*, 120–126.

Hauser, S., Jacobson, A., Lavori, P., Wolfsdorf, J., Herskowitz, R., Milley, J., Bliss, R., Wertlieb, D., & Stein, J. (1990). Adherence among children and adolescents with insulin-dependent diabetes mellitus over a four-year longitudinal follow-up: II. Immediate and long-term linkages with the family milieu. *Journal of Pediatric Psychology, 15*, 511–526.

Havinghurst, R. J. (1973). History of developmental psychology. In P. B. Baltes & K. W. Schaie (Eds.), *Lifespan developmental psychology: Personality and socialization* (pp. 3–24). New York: Academic Press.

Haynes, R. B. (1976). Strategies for improving compliance: A methodologic analysis and review. In D. L. Sackett and R. B. Haynes (Eds.), *Compliance with therapeutic regimens* (pp. 69–82). Baltimore: Johns Hopkins University Press.

Haynes, R. B. (1979). Strategies to improve compliance with referrals, appointments, and prescribed medical regimens. In R. B. Haynes, D. W. Taylor, & D. L. Sackett (Eds.), *Compliance in health care* (pp. 121–143). Baltimore: Johns Hopkins University Press.

Haynes, R. B., Taylor, D. W., & Sackett, D. L. (Eds.). (1979). *Compliance in health care*. Baltimore: Johns Hopkins University Press.

Hebbeler, K. M., Smith, B. J., & Black, T. L. (1991). Federal early childhood special education policy: A model for the improvement of services for children with disabilities. *Exceptional Children, 58,* 104–112.

Hixson, D. D., Stoff, E., & White, P. H. (1992). Parents of children with chronic health impairments: A new approach to advocacy training. *Children's Health Care, 21,* 111–115.

Hobbs, N., & Perrin, J. M. (Eds.). (1985). *Issues in the care of children with chronic illness*. San Francisco: Jossey-Bass.

Hodges, K., Gordon, Y., & Lennon, M. P. (1990). Parent–child agreement on symptoms assessed via a clinical research interview for children: The Child Assessment Schedule (CAS). *Journal of Child Psychology and Psychiatry, 31,* 427–436.

Hodges, K., Kline, J., Stern, L., Cytryn, L., & McKnew, D. (1982). The development of a child assessment interview for research and clinical use. *Journal of Abnormal Child Psychology, 10,* 173–189.

Horowitz, F. D., & O'Brien, M. (1989). In the interest of the nation: A reflective essay on the state of our knowledge and the challenges before us. *American Psychologist, 44,* 441–445.

Howe, G. W., Feinstein, C., Reiss, D., Molock, S., & Berger, K. (1993). Adolescent adjustment to chronic physical disorders: I. Comparing neurological and non-neurological conditions. *Journal of Child Psychology and Psychiatry, 14,* 1153–1171.

Hulka, B. (1977). Patient–clinician interactions and compliance. In R. B. Haynes, D. W. Taylor, & D. L. Sackett (Eds.), *Compliance in health care* (pp. 63–77). Baltimore: Johns Hopkins University Press.

Hunt, J. V., Cooper, B. A., & Tooley, W. H. (1988). Very low birth weight infants at 8 and 11 years of age: Role of neonatal illness and family status. *Pediatrics, 82,* 596–603.

Hurtig, A. L., Koepke, D., & Park, K. B. (1989). Relation between severity of chronic illness and adjustment in children and adolescents with sickle cell disease. *Journal of Pediatric Psychology, 14,* 117–132.

Hurtig, A. L., & White, L. S. (1986). Psychological adjustment in children and adolescents with sickle cell disease. *Journal of Pediatric Psychology, 11,* 411–427.

Iannotti, R. J., & Bush, P. J. (1993). Toward a developmental theory of compliance. In N. A. Krasneger, L. Epstein, S. B. Johnson, & S. J. Yaffe (Eds.), *Developmental aspects of health compliance behavior* (pp. 59–76). Hillsdale, NJ: Erlbaum.

Iscoe, L., & Bordelon, K. (1985). Pilot parents: Peer support for parents of handicapped children. *Children's Health Care, 14,* 103–109.

Jacobsen, P. B., Manne, S. L., Gorfinkle, K., Schorr, O., Rapkin, B., & Redd, W. H. (1990). Analysis of child and parent behavior during painful medical procedures. *Health Psychology, 9,* 559–576.

Jacobson, A. M., Hauser, S. T., Lavori, P., Wolfsdorf, Herskowitz, R. D., Milley, J. E., & Gelfand, E. (1990). Adherence among children and adolescents with insulin-dependent diabetes mellitus over a four-year longitudinal follow-up: I. The influence of patient coping and adjustment. *Journal of Pediatric Psychology, 15,* 511–526.

Jacobson, A. M., Hauser, S. T., Wertleib, D., Wolfsdorf, J. I., Orleans, J., & Vieyra, M. (1986). Psychological adjustment of children with recently diagnosed diabetes mellitus. *Diabetes Care, 9,* 323–329.

James, W. (1982). *Psychology: The briefer course.* New York: Holt, Rinehart & Winston.

Jay, S. M. (1988). Invasive medical procedures: Psychological intervention and assessment. In D. K. Routh (Ed.), *Handbook of pediatric psychology* (pp. 401–425). New York: Guilford Press.

Jay, S. M., & Elliott, C. H. (1990). A stress inoculation program for parents whose children are undergoing painful medical procedures. *Journal of Consulting and Clinical Psychology, 58,* 799–804.

Jay, S. M., Elliott, C. H., Katz, E., & Siegel, S. E. (1987). Cognitive–behavioral and pharmacologic interventions for children's distress during painful medical procedures. *Journal of Consulting and Clinical Psychology, 55,* 860–865.

Jay, S. M., Ozolens, M., Elliott, C. H., & Caldwell, S. (1983). Assessment of children's distress during painful medical procedures. *Health Psychology, 2,* 133–147.

Jessop, D. J., Riessman, C. K., & Stein, R. E. K. (1988). Chronic childhood illness and maternal mental health. *Journal of Developmental and Behavioral Pediatrics, 9,* 147–156.

Johnson, F. (1990). Role of bone marrow transplantation in childhood lymphoblastic leukemia. *Hematology/Oncology Clinics of North America, 32,* 801–810.

Johnson, S. B. (1988). Diabetes mellitus in childhood. In D. K. Routh (Ed.), *Handbook of pediatric psychology* (pp. 9–31). New York: Guilford Press.

Johnson, S. B., Pollak, T., Silverstein, J. H., Rosenbloom, A. L., Spillar, R., McCallum, M., & Harkavy, J. (1982). Cognitive and behavioral knowledge about insulin-dependent diabetes among children and parents. *Pediatrics, 69,* 708–713.

Kagan, J. (1983). Stress and coping in early development. In N. Garmezy and M. Rutter (Eds.), *Stress, coping, and development in children* (pp. 191–216). New York: McGraw-Hill.

Kaplan, R. M. (1990). Behavior as the central outcome in health care. *American Psychologist, 45*, 1211–1220.

Kaplan, R. M., & Anderson, J. P. (1988). The general health policy model: Update and application. *Health Services Research, 23*, 203–235.

Kashani, J. H., Barbero, G. J., Wilfley, D. E., Morris, D. A., & Sheppard, J. A. (1988). Psychological concomitants of cystic fibrosis in children and adolescents. *Adolescence, 23*, 873–880.

Kashani, J. H., Konig, P., Sheppard, J. A., Wilfley, D., & Morris, D. A. (1988). Psychopathology and self-concept in asthmatic children. *Journal of Pediatric Psychology, 13*, 509–520.

Katz, E. R., Rubenstein, C. L., Hubert, N. C., & Blew, A. (1988). School and social reintegration of children with cancer. *Journal of Psychosocial Oncology, 6*, 123–140.

Katz, E. R., & Varni, J. W. (1993). Social support and social cognitive problem-solving in children with newly diagnosed cancer. *Cancer, 15*, 3314–3319.

Katz, E. R., Varni, J. W., Rubenstein, C. L., Blew, A., & Hubert, N. (1992). Teacher, parent, and child evaluative ratings of school reintegration intervention for children with newly diagnosed cancer. *Children's Health Care, 21*, 69–75.

Kazak, A. (1986). Families with physically handicapped children: Social ecology and family systems. *Family Process, 25*, 265–281.

Kazak, A. E. (1989). Families of chronically ill children: A systems and social–ecological model of adaptation and challenge. *Journal of Consulting and Clinical Psychology, 57*, 25–30.

Kazak, A. (1992). The social context of coping with childhood chronic illness: Family systems and social support. In A. LaGreca, L. Siegel, J. Wallander, & C. E. Walker (Eds.), *Advances in pediatric psychology: Stress and coping with pediatric conditions* (pp. 262–278). New York: Guilford Press.

Kazak, A. E., & Meadows, A. T. (1989). Families of young adolescents who have survived cancer: Social-emotional adjustment, adaptability, and social support. *Journal of Pediatric Psychology, 14*, 175–192.

Kazak, A., Reber, M., & Carter, A. (1988). Structural and qualitative aspects of social networks in families with young chronically ill children. *Journal of Pediatric Psychology, 13*, 171–182.

Kazdin, A. E., & Heidish, I. E. (1984). Convergence of clinically derived diagnoses and parent checklists among inpatient children. *Journal of Abnormal Child Psychology, 12*, 421–436.

Kellerman, J., Zeltzer, L., Ellenberg, L., Dash, J., & Rigler, D. (1980). Psychological effects of illness in adolescence: I. Anxiety, self-esteem, and perception of control. *Journal of Pediatrics, 97*, 126–131.

Kerem, B., Rommens, J. M., Buchanan, J. A., Markiewicz, D., Cox, T. K., Chakravarti, A., Buchwald, M., & Tsui, L. (1989, September 8). Identification of the cystic fibrosis gene: Genetic analysis. *Science, 245*, 1073–1080.

Khoury, M. J., Erickson, J. D., & James, L. M. (1982). Etiologic heterogeneity of neural tube defects: Clues from epidemiology. *American Journal of Epidemiology, 115*, 538–548.

Kidwell, S., Riley, A., Finney, J., & Wilkerson, W. (1992). *Psychosocial functioning and health: Impact on social achievement and absenteeism.* Paper presented at the 100th annual convention of the American Psychological Association, Washington, DC.

Kitchen, W. H., Ryan, M. M., Rickards, A., McDougall, A. B., Billson, F. A., Keir, E. H., & Naylor, F. D. (1980). A longitudinal study of very low birth weight infants. IV: An overview of performance at eight years of age. *Developmental Medicine and Child Neurology, 22*, 172–188.

Kliewer, W. (1991). Coping in middle childhood: Relations to competence, Type A behavior, monitoring, blunting, and locus of control. *Developmental Psychology, 27*, 689–697.

Kliewer, W., & Sandler, I. N. (1992). Locus of control and self-esteem as moderators of stressor-symptom relations in children and adolescents. *Journal of Abnormal Child Psychology, 20*, 393–413.

Koch, C., & Lanng, S. (1995). Other organ systems. In M. E. Hodson & D. M. Geddes (Eds.), *Cystic Fibrosis* (pp. 295–314). London: Chapman & Hall.

Koocher, G. P. (1973). Childhood, death, and cognitive development. *Developmental Psychology, 9*, 369–375.

Koocher, G. P., Gudas, L. J., & McGrath, M. L. (1992). Behavioral aspects of cystic fibrosis. In M. Wolraich & D. K. Routh (Eds.), *Advances in developmental and behavioral pediatrics* (Vol. 10, pp. 195–220). Greenwich, CT: JAI Press.

Kovacs, M. (1980–1981). Rating scales to assess depression in school-aged children. *Acta Paedopsychiatrica, 46*, 305–315.

Kovacs, M. (1983). *The Children's Depression Inventory: A self-rated depression scale for school-aged youngsters.* Unpublished manuscript, University of Pittsburgh School of Medicine, Pittsburgh, PA.

Kovacs, M., Brent, D., Steinberg, T. F., Paulauskas, S., & Reid, J. (1986). Children's self-reports of psychological adjustment and coping strategies during first year of insulin-dependent diabetes mellitus. *Diabetes Care, 9*, 472–479.

Kovacs, M., Feinberg, T. L., Paulauskas, S., Finkelstein, R., Pollock, M., & Crouse-Novak, M. (1985). Initial coping responses and psychosocial characteristics of children with insulin-dependent diabetes mellitus. *Journal of Pediatrics, 106*, 827–834.

Kovacs, M., Iyengar, S., Goldston, D., Obrosky, D. S., Stewart, J., & Marsh, J. (1990). Psychological functioning among mothers of children with insulin-dependent diabetes mellitus: A longitudinal study. *Journal of Consulting and Clinical Psychology, 58*, 189–195.

Kovacs, M., Iyengar, S., Goldston, D., Stewart, J., Obrosky, D. S., & Marsh, J. (1990). Psychological functioning of children with insulin-dependent diabetes mellitus: A longitudinal study. *Journal of Pediatric Psychology, 15*, 619–632.

Krasnegor, N. A. (1993). Epilogue: Future research directions. In N. A. Krasnegor, L. Epstein, S. B. Johnson, & S. J. Yaffe (Eds.), *Developmental aspects of health compliance behavior* (pp. 355–358). Hillside, NJ: Erlbaum.

Kronenberger, W. G., & Thompson, R. J., Jr. (1990). Dimensions of family functioning in families with chronically ill children: A higher order factor analysis of the Family Environment Scale. *Journal of Clinical Child Psychology, 19,* 380–388.

Kronenberger, W. G., & Thompson, R. J., Jr. (1992). Medical stress, appraised stress, and the psychological adjustment of mothers of children with myelomeningocele. *Journal of Developmental and Behavioral Pediatrics, 13,* 405–411.

Kun, L. E., Mulhern, R. K., & Crisco, J. J. (1983). Quality of life in children treated for brain tumors: Intellectual, emotional, and academic function. *Journal of Neurosurgery, 58,* 1–6.

Kupst, M. J., & Schulman, J. L. (1988). Long-term coping with pediatric leukemia: A six-year follow-up study. *Journal of Pediatric Psychology, 13,* 7–23.

Kupst, M. J., Schulman, J. L., Honig, G., Maurer, H., Morgan, E., & Fochtman, D. (1982). Family coping with childhood leukemia: One year after diagnosis. *Journal of Pediatric Psychology, 7,* 157–174.

Kupst, M. J., Schulman, J. L., Maurer, H., Honig, G., Morgan, E., & Fochtman, D. (1983). Family coping with leukemia: The first six months. *Medical and Pediatric Oncology, 11,* 269–278.

Kupst, M. J., Schulman, J. L., Maurer, H., Morgan, E., Honig, G., & Fochtman, D. (1984). Coping with pediatric leukemia: A two-year follow-up. *Journal of Pediatric Psychology, 9,* 149–163.

Kupst, M. J., Tylke, L., Thomas, L., Mudd, M. E., Richardson, C. C., & Schulman, J. L. (1983). Strategies of intervention with pediatric cancer patients. *Social Work in Health Care, 8,* 31–47.

Kuttner, M. J., Delamater, A. M., & Santiago, J. V. (1990). Learned helplessness in diabetic youths. *Journal of Pediatric Psychology, 15,* 581–594.

La Greca, A. M. (1988). Adherence to prescribed medical regimens. In D. K. Routh (Ed.), *Handbook of pediatric psychology* (pp. 299–320). New York: Guilford Press.

La Greca, A. M. (1990). Social consequences of pediatric conditions: Fertile area for future investigation and intervention. *Journal of Pediatric Psychology, 15,* 285–307.

La Greca, A. M. (1992). Peer influences in pediatric chronic illness: An update. *Journal of Pediatric Psychology, 17,* 773–784.

La Greca, A. M., & Mesibov, G. B. (1979). Social skills intervention with learning disabled children: Selecting skills and implementing training. *Journal of Clinical Child Psychology, 8,* 234–241.

La Greca, A. M., & Santogrossi, D. A. (1980). Social skills training with elementary school students: A behavioral group approach. *Journal of Consulting and Clinical Psychology, 48,* 220–227.

Lansky, S. B., Cairns, N. U., & Zwartjes, W. (1983). School attendance among children with cancer: A report from two centers. *Journal of Psychosocial Oncology, 1,* 75–83.

Lansky, S. B., Lowman, J. T., Vats, T., & Gyulay, J. E. (1975). School phobia in children with malignant neoplasms. *American Journal of Diseases in Children, 129,* 42–46.

Lanzkowsky, P. (1995). *Manual of pediatric hematology and oncology.* New York: Churchill Livingstone.

Lavigne, J. V. (1983). Psychological functioning of cystic fibrosis patients. In J. Lloyd-Still (Ed.), *Textbook of cystic fibrosis* (pp. 419–432). Boston: Jolen Wright/PSG.

Lavigne, J. V., & Faier-Routman, J. (1992). Psychological adjustment to pediatric physical disorders: A meta-analytic review. *Journal of Pediatrics, 17,* 133–158.

Lavigne, J. V., & Faier-Routman, J. (1993). Correlates of psychological adjustment to pediatric physical disorders: A meta-analytic review and comparison with existing models. *Journal of Developmental and Behavioral Pediatrics, 14,* 117–123.

Lavigne, J. V., Nolan, P., & McLone, P. G. (1988). Temperament, coping, and psychological adjustment in young children with myelomeningocele. *Journal of Pediatric Psychology, 13,* 363–378.

Lavigne, J. V., Traisman, H. S., Marr, T. J., & Chasnoff, I. J. (1982). Parental perceptions of the psychosocial adjustment of children with diabetes and their siblings. *Diabetes Care, 5,* 420–426.

Lazarus, R. S., & Folkman, S. (1984). *Stress, appraisal, and coping.* New York: Springer.

Lazarus, R. S., & Launier, R. (1980). Stress-related transactions between person and environment. In L. A. Pervin & M. Lewis (Eds.), *Perspectives in interactional psychology* (pp. 287–327). New York: Plenum.

Leikin, S. L., Gallagher, D., Kinney, T. R., Sloane, D., Klug, P., & Rida, W. (1989). Mortality in children and adolescents with sickle cell disease. *Pediatrics, 84,* 500–508.

Lemanek, K. L., Moore, S. L., Gresham, F. M., Williamson, D. A., & Kelley, M. L. (1986). Psychological adjustment of children with sickle cell anemia. *Journal of Pediatric Psychology, 11,* 397–410.

Lerner, R., & Lerner, J. (1983). Temperament-intelligence reciprocities in early childhood: A contextual model. In M. Lewis (Ed.), *Origins of intelligence* (2nd ed., pp. 399–421). New York: Plenum.

Leventhal, H. (1993). Theories of compliance, and turning necessities into preferences: Application to adolescent health action. In N. A. Krasnegar, L. Epstein, S. B. Johnson, & S. J. Yaffe (Eds.), *Developmental aspects of health compliance behavior* (pp. 91–124). Hillsdale, NJ: Erlbaum.

Levitan, I. B. (1989, June 23). The basic defect in cystic fibrosis. *Science, 244,* 1423.

Lewis, C. E., Siegel, J. M., & Lewis, M. A. (1984). Feeling bad: Exploring sources of distress among pre-adolescent children. *American Journal of Public Health, 74*, 117–122.

Lewis, M., & Rosenblum, L. A. (1974). *The effect of the infant on its caregiver.* New York: Wiley.

Lewiston, N. J. (1985). Cystic fibrosis. In N. Hobbs & J. M. Perrin (Eds.), *Issues in the care of children with chronic illness* (pp. 196–213). San Francisco: Jossey-Bass.

Lipowski, A. J. (1970). Physical illness, the individual and the coping process. *Psychiatric Medicine, 1*, 91–102.

Litt, I. F., & Cuskey, W. R. (1980). Compliance with medical regimens during adolescence. *Pediatric Clinics of North America, 27*, 3–15.

Lobato, D. (1983). Siblings of handicapped children: A review. *Journal of Autism and Developmental Disorders, 13*, 347–364.

Lobato, D., Faust, D., & Spirito, A. (1988). Examining the effects of chronic disease and disability in children's sibling relationships. *Journal of Pediatric Psychology, 13*, 389–407.

Lyons-Ruth, K., Zoll, D., Conell, D., & Grunebaum, H. V. (1986). The depressed mother and her one-year-old infant: Environment, interaction, attachment, and infant development. In T. Field & E. Tronick (Eds.), *Maternal depression and infant disturbance* (pp. 61–82). San Francisco: Jossey-Bass.

Maccoby, E. E. (1983). Social-emotional development and response to stressors. In N. Garmezy & M. Rutter (Eds.), *Stress, coping, and development in children* (pp. 217–234). New York: McGraw-Hill.

MacLean, W. E., Perrin, J. M., Gortmaker, S., & Pierre, C. B. (1992). Psychological adjustment of children with asthma: Effects of illness severity and recent stressful life events. *Journal of Pediatric Psychology, 17*, 159–172.

Madan-Swain, A., & Brown, R. T. (1991). Cognitive and psychosocial sequelae for children with acute lymphocytic leukemia and their families. *Clinical Psychology Review, 11*, 267–294.

Manne, S. L., Bakeman, R., Jacobsen, P. B., Gorfinkle, K., Bernstein, D., & Redd, W. H. (1992). Adult-child interaction during invasive medical procedures. *Health Psychology, 11*, 241–249.

Manne, S. L., Jacobsen, P. B., Gorfinkle, K., Gerstein, F., & Redd, W. H. (1993). Treatment adherence difficulties among children with cancer: The role of parenting style. *Journal of Pediatric Psychology, 18*, 47–62.

Manne, S. L., Redd, W. H., Jacobsen, P. B., Gorfinkle, K., Schorr, O., & Rapkin, B. (1990). Behavioral intervention to reduce child and parent distress during venipunctures. *Journal of Consulting and Clinical Psychology, 58*, 565–572.

Masten, A. S., Morison, P., & Pellingrini, D. S. (1985). A revised class play method of peer assessment. *Developmental Psychology, 21*, 523–533.

Maternal and Child Health and Mental Retardation Planning Amendments of 1963, Pub. L. No. 88-156, § 2, 77 Stat. 273 (1964).

Matthews, L. W., & Drotar, D. (1984). Cystic fibrosis: A challenging long-term chronic disease. *Pediatric Clinics of North America, 31*, 133–152.

Mattsson, A. (1972). Long-term physical illness in childhood: A challenge to psychosocial adaptation. *Pediatrics, 50*, 801–811.

Maurer, A. C. (1979). The therapy of diabetes. *American Scientist, 67*, 422–431.

McCormick, M. C. (1989). Long-term follow-up of infants discharged from neonatal intensive care units. *Journal of the American Medical Association, 261*, 1767–1772.

McCubbin, H. I., Patterson, J. M., & Wilson, L. R. (1985). FILE: Family Inventory of Life Events and Changes. In D. H. Olson, H. I. McCubbin, H. Barnes, A. Larsen, M. Muxen, & M. Wilson (Eds.), *Family inventories: Inventories used in a national survey of families across the life cycle* (pp. 105–127). St. Paul, MN: Family Social Science, University of Minnesota.

McGrath, P. A. (1993). Psychological aspects of pain perception. In N. L. Schechter, C. B. Berde, & M. Yaster (Eds.), *Pain in infants, children and adolescents* (pp. 39–63). Baltimore: Williams and Wilkins.

McGrath, P. J., Beyer, J., Cleeland, C., Eland, J., McGrath, P. A., & Portenoy, R. (1990). Report of the subcommittee on assessment and methodologic issues in the management of pain in childhood cancer. *Pediatrics, 86*, (Suppl.), 814–817.

McGrath, P. J., Dunn-Geier, J., Cunningham, S. J., Brunette, R., D'Astoris, J., Humphreys, P., Latter, J., & Keene, D. (1986). Psychological guidelines for helping children cope with chronic benign intractable pain. *Clinical Journal of Pain, 1*, 229–233.

McGrath, P. J. & McAlpine, L. (1993). Psychologic perspectives on pediatric pain. *Journal of Pediatrics, 122*, 52–58.

McHale, S. M., & Gamble, W. C. (1989). Sibling relationships of children with disabled and nondisabled brothers and sisters. *Developmental Psychology, 25*, 421–429.

McKeever, P. (1983). Siblings of chronically ill children: A literature review with implications for research and practice. *American Journal of Orthopsychiatry, 53*, 209–218.

McLane, D. G. (1982). Results of treatment of children born with a myelomeningocele. *Clinical Neurosurgery, 30*, 407–435.

Meichenbaum, D., & Turk, D. (1987). *Facilitating treatment adherence: A practitioner's guidebook.* New York: Plenum.

Melamed, B. G., & Siegel, L. J. (1975). Reduction of anxiety in children facing hospitalization and surgery by use of filmed modeling. *Journal of Consulting and Clinical Psychology, 43*, 511–521.

Mental Retardation Facilities and Community Mental Health Centers Construction Act of 1963, Pub. L. No. 88-164, § 761, 77 Stat. 282 (1964).

Middlebrook, J. L., & Forehand, R. (1985). Maternal perceptions of deviance in child behavior as a function of stress and clinic versus nonclinic status of the child: An analogue study. *Behavior Therapy, 16*, 494–502.

Miller, S. A. (1986). Parents' beliefs about their children's cognitive abilities. *Developmental Psychology, 22*, 276–284.

Miller, S. A. (1988). Parents' beliefs about children's cognitive development. *Child Development, 59*, 259–285.

Mills, R. S. L., & Rubin, K. H. (1990). Parental beliefs about problematic social behaviors in early childhood. *Child Development, 61*, 138–151.

Monat, A., & Lazarus, R. S. (Eds.). (1977). *Stress and coping: An anthology.* New York: Columbia University Press.

Moos, R. H., Cronkite, R. C., & Finney, J. W. (1990). *Health and Daily Living* (2nd ed.). Palo Alto, CA: Center for Health Care Evaluations, Veterans Affairs and Stanford University Medical Center.

Moos, R. H., & Moos, B. S. (1981). *Family Environment Scale manual.* Palo Alto, CA: Consulting Psychologists Press.

Moos, R. H., & Tsu, U. D. (1977). The crisis of physical illness: An overview. In R. H. Moos (Ed.), *Coping with physical illness* (pp. 3–21). New York: Plenum.

Morgan, S. A., & Jackson, J. (1986). Psychological and social concomitants of sickle cell anemia in adolescents. *Journal of Pediatric Psychology, 11*, 429–440.

Morrow, G. A., Hoagland, A., & Carnrike, L. M., Jr. (1981). Social support and parental adjustment to pediatric cancer. *Journal of Consulting and Clinical Psychology, 49*, 763–765.

Mulhern, R. K., Carpentieri, S., Shema, S., Stone, P., & Fairclough, D. (1993). Factors associated with social and behavioral problems among children recently diagnosed with brain tumor. *Journal of Pediatric Psychology, 18*, 339–350.

Mulhern, R. K., Fairclough, D. L., Smith, B., & Douglas, S. M. (1992). Maternal depression, assessment methods, and physical symptoms affect estimates of depressive symptomatology among children with cancer. *Journal of Pediatric Psychology, 17*, 313–326.

Mulhern, R. K., Wasserman, A. L., Friedman, A. G., & Fairclough, D. (1989). Social competence and behavioral adjustment of children who are long-term survivors of cancer. *Pediatrics, 83*, 18–25.

Mullins, L. L., Olson, R. A., Reyer, S., Bernardy, N., Husztic, H. C., & Volk, R. J. (1991). Risk and resistance factors in the adaptation of mothers of children with cystic fibrosis. *Journal of Pediatric Psychology, 16*, 701–715.

Murch, R. L., & Cohen, L. H. (1989). Relationships among life stress, perceived family environment, and the psychological distress of spina bifida adolescents. *Journal of Pediatric Psychology, 14*, 193–214.

Myers, G. J. (1984). Myelomeningocele: The medical aspects. *Pediatric Clinics of North America, 31*, 165–175.

Nagy, S., & Ungerer, J. A. (1990). The adaptation of mothers and fathers to children with cystic fibrosis: A comparison. *Children's Health Care, 19*, 147–154.

Nassau, J. H., & Drotar, D. (1995). Social competence in children with IDDM and asthma: Child, teacher, and parent reports of children's social adjustment, social performance, and social skills. *Journal of Pediatric Psychology, 20,* 187–204.

National Center for Health Statistics. (1981). Current estimates from the National Health Interview Survey: United States, 1981. *Vital and health statistics* (PHS Publication No. 83-1569). Washington, DC: U.S. Government Printing Office.

Neufield, R. W. J., & Paterson, R. J. (1989). Issues concerning control and its implementation. In R. W. J. Neufield (Ed.), *Advances in the investigation of psychological stress* (pp. 43–67). New York: Wiley.

Newacheck, P. W., Budetti, P. P., & Haflon, N. (1986). Trend in activity-limiting chronic conditions among children. *American Journal of Public Health, 76,* 178–184.

Nolen-Hoeksema, S., Girgus, J. S., & Seligman, M. E. P. (1986). Learned helplessness in children: A longitudinal study of depression, achievement, and explanatory style. *Journal of Personality and Social Psychology, 51,* 435–442.

Noll, R. B., Bukowski, W. B., Rogosch, F. A., LeRoy, S., & Kulkarni, R. (1990). Social interactions between children with cancer and their peers: Teacher ratings. *Journal of Pediatric Psychology, 15,* 43–56.

Noll, R. B., LeRoy, S., Bukowski, W. M., Rogosch, F. A., & Kulkarni, R. (1991). Peer relationships and adjustment in children with cancer. *Journal of Pediatric Psychology, 16,* 307–326.

Noll, R. B., Ris, M. D., Davies, W. H., Bukowski, W. M., & Koontz, K. (1992). Social interactions between children with cancer or sickle cell disease and their peers: Teacher ratings. *Developmental and Behavioral Pediatrics, 13,* 187–193.

Norrish, M., Tooley, M., & Godfrey, S. (1977). Clinical, physiological, and psychological study of asthmatic children attending a hospital clinic. *Archives of Disease in Childhood, 52,* 912–917.

Olson, D. H., Portner, J., & Lavee, Y. (1985). FACES III: Family adaptability and cohesion evaluation scales. In D. H. Olson, H. I. McCubbin, H. Barnes, A. Lassen, M. Muxen, & M. Wilson (Eds.), *Family inventories: Inventories used in a national survey of families across the family life cycle* (pp. 18–42). St. Paul: Family Social Science, University of Minnesota.

Olson, D. H., Sprenkle, D., & Russell, C. S. (1979). Circumplex model of marital and family systems: I. Cohesion and adaptability dimensions, family types, and clinical applications. *Family Process, 18,* 3–28.

Orenstein, D. M., & Wachnowsky, D. M. (1985). Behavioral aspects of cystic fibrosis. *Annals of Behavioral Medicine, 7,* 17–20.

Parcel, G. S., Gilman, S. C., Nader, P. R., & Bunce, H. (1979). A comparison of absentee rates of elementary school children with asthma and nonasthmatic schoolmates. *Pediatrics, 64,* 878–881.

Parker, J. G., & Asher, S. R. (1987). Peer relations and later personal adjustment: Are low-accepted children at risk? *Psychological Bulletin, 102,* 357–389.

Parkes, K. R. (1984). Locus of control, cognitive appraisal, and coping in stressful episodes. *Journal of Personality and Social Psychology, 46,* 655–668.

Patterson, G. R. (1983). Stress: A change agent for family process. In N. Garmezy & M. Rutter (Eds.), *Stress, coping, and development in children* (pp. 235–264). New York: McGraw-Hill.

Perrin, E. C., Ayoub, C. C., & Willett, J. B. (1993). In the eyes of the beholder: Family and maternal influences on perceptions of adjustment of children with a chronic illness. *Journal of Developmental and Behavioral Pediatrics, 14,* 94–105.

Perrin, E. C., & Gerrity, P. S. (1981). There's a demon in your belly: Children's understanding of illness. *Pediatrics, 67,* 841–849.

Perrin, E. C., & Gerrity, P. S. (1984). Development of children with a chronic illness. *Pediatric Clinics of North America, 31,* 19–32.

Perrin, E. C., & Shapiro, D. (1985). Health locus of control beliefs of healthy children, children with a chronic physical illness, and their mothers. *The Journal of Pediatrics, 107,* 627–633.

Perrin, E. C., Stein, R. K., & Drotar, D. (1991). Cautions in using the Child Behavior Checklist: Observations based on research about children with a chronic illness. *Journal of Pediatric Psychology, 16,* 411–422.

Perrin, J. M. (1985). Introduction. In N. Hobbs & J. M. Perrin (Eds.), *Issues in the care of children with chronic illness: A sourcebook on problems, services, and policies* (pp. 1–10). San Francisco: Jossey-Bass.

Perrin, J. M., & Ireys, H. T. (1984). The organization of service for chronically ill children and their families. *Pediatric Clinics of North America, 31,* 235–257.

Perrin, J. M., & MacLean, W. E., Jr. (1988a). Biomedical and psychosocial dimensions of chronic illness in childhood. In P. Karoly (Ed.), *Handbook of child health assessment: Biopsychosocial perspectives* (pp. 11–28). New York: Wiley.

Perrin, J. M., & MacLean, W. E., Jr. (1988b). Children with chronic illness: The prevention of dysfunction. *Pediatric Clinics of North America, 35,* 1325–1337.

Perrin, J. M., MacLean, W. E., Jr., & Perrin, E. C. (1989). Parents' perception of health status and psychological adjustment of children with asthma. *Pediatrics, 83,* 26–30.

Peterson, C., & Seligman, M. E. P. (1984). Causal explanations as a risk factor for depression: Theory and evidence. *Psychological Review, 91,* 347–374.

Peterson, J. L., & Zill, N. (1986). Marital disruption, parent-child relationships and behavior problems in children. *Journal of Marriage and the Family, 48,* 295–307.

Pinkerton, P. (1967). Correlating physiologic with psychodynamic data in the study and management of childhood asthma. *Journal of Psychosomatic Research, 11,* 11–25.

Platt, O. S., Brambilla, D. J., Rosse, W. F., Milner, P. F., Castro, O., Steinberg, M. H., & Klue, P. P. (1994). Mortality in sickle cell disease: Life expectancy and risk factors for early death. *New England Journal of Medicine, 330,* 1639–1644.

Pless, I. B. (1984). Clinical assessment: Physical and psychological functioning. *Pediatric Clinics of North America, 31*, 33–45.

Pless, I. B., & Douglas, J. W. B. (1971). Chronic illness in childhood: Epidemiological and clinical characteristics. *Pediatrics, 47*, 405–414.

Pless, I. B., & Nolan, T. (1991). Revision, replication and neglect—research on maladjustment in chronic illness. *Journal of Child Psychology and Psychiatry and Allied Disciplines, 32*, 347–365.

Pless, I. B., & Perrin, J. M. (1985). Issues common to a variety of illnesses. In N. Hobbs & J. M. Perrin (Eds.), *Issues in the care of children with chronic illness* (pp. 41–60). San Francisco: Jossey-Bass.

Pless, I. B., & Pinkerton, P. (1975). *Chronic childhood disorders: Promoting patterns of adjustment.* Chicago: Year-Book Medical Publishers.

Pless, I. B., & Roghmann, K. J. (1971). Chronic illness and its consequences: Observations based on three epidemiologic surveys. *Journal of Pediatrics, 79*, 351–359.

Pless, I. B., Roghmann, K. J., & Haggerty, R. J. (1972). Chronic illness, family functioning, and psychological adjustment: A model for the allocation of preventive mental health services. *International Journal of Epidemiology, 1*, 271–277.

Potter, P. C., & Roberts, M. C. (1984). Children's perceptions of chronic illness: The roles of disease symptoms, cognitive development, and information. *Journal of Pediatric Psychology, 9*, 13–27.

Power, T. (1989). *Parenting Dimensions Inventory: A research manual.* Unpublished manuscript, University of Houston.

Powers, S. W., Blount, R. L., Bachanas, P. J., Cotter, M. W., & Swan, S. C. (1993). Helping preschool leukemia patients and their parents cope during injections. *Journal of Pediatric Psychology, 18*, 681–695.

Quittner, A. L., DiGirolamo, A. M., Michel, M., & Eigen, H. (1992). Parental response to cystic fibrosis: A contextual analysis of the diagnostic phase. *Journal of Pediatric Psychology, 17*, 683–704.

Radloff, L. S. (1977). The CES-D scale: A self-report depression scale for research in the general population. *Applied Psychological Measurement, 1*, 385–401.

Redpath, C. C., & Rogers, C. S. (1984). Healthy young children's concepts of hospitals, medical personnel, operations, and illness. *Journal of Pediatric Psychology, 9*, 29–40.

Rehabilitation, Comprehensive Services, and Developmental Disabilities Amendments of 1978, Pub. L. No. 95-602, § 101, 92 Stat. 2955 (1980).

Reynolds, C. R., & Richmond, B. O. (1985). *Manual for the Revised Children's Manifest Anxiety Scales.* Los Angeles: Western Psychological Services.

Roberts, M. C., Beidleman, W. B., & Wurtele, S. K. (1981). Children's perceptions of medical and psychological disorders in their peers. *Journal of Clinical Child Psychology, 10*, 76–78.

Roberts, M. C., & Wallander, J. L. (1992). Family issues in pediatric psychology: An overview. In M. C. Roberts & J. L. Wallander (Eds.), *Family issues in pediatric psychology* (pp. 1–24). Hillsdale, NJ: Erlbaum.

Rodger, S. (1985). Siblings of handicapped children: A population at risk? *The Exceptional Child, 32*, 47–56.

Rodger, S. (1986). Parents as therapists: A responsible alternative or abrogation of responsibility? *The Exceptional Child, 33*, 17–27.

Roghmann, K. J., & Haggerty, R. J. (1970). Rochester Child Health Surveys: I. Objectives, organization and methods. *Medical Care, 8*, 47–59.

Rolland, J. (1987). Chronic illness and the life cycle: A conceptual framework. *Family Process, 26*, 203–221.

Ross, D. M., & Ross, S. A. (1984). Childhood pain: The school-aged child's viewpoint. *Pain, 20*, 179–191.

Roth, S., & Cohen, L. J. (1986). Approach, avoidance, and coping with stress. *American Psychologist, 41*, 813–819.

Rothbaum, F., Weisz, J. R., & Snyder, S. S. (1982). Changing the world and changing the self: A two-process model of perceived control. *Journal of Personality and Social Psychology, 42*, 5–37.

Rotter, J. B. (1966). Generalized expectancies for internal versus external control of reinforcement. *Psychological Monographs, 80*(1, Whole No. 609).

Rovet, J. F., Ehrlich, R. M., Czuchta, D., & Akler, M. (1993). Psychoeducational characteristics of children and adolescents with insulin-dependent diabetes mellitus. *Journal of Learning Disabilities, 26*, 7–22.

Rovet, J. F., Ehrlich, R. M., & Hoppe, M. (1987). Behavior problems in children with diabetes as a function of sex and age of onset of disease. *Journal of Child Psychology and Psychiatry, 28*, 477–491.

Rubin, K. H., Mills, R. S. L., & Rose-Krasnor, L. (1989). Maternal beliefs and children's social competence. In B. H. Schneider, G. Attili, J. Nadel, & R. P. Weissberg (Eds.), *Social competence in developmental perspective* (pp. 313–331). Dordrecht, The Netherlands: Kluwer Academic.

Rutter, M. (1983). Stress, coping, and development: Some issues and some questions. In N. Garmezy & M. Rutter (Eds.), *Stress, coping, and development in children* (pp. 1–41). New York: McGraw-Hill.

Rutter, M. (1987). Psychosocial resilience and protective mechanisms. *American Journal of Orthopsychiatry, 57*, 316–331.

Rutter, M., Tizard, J., & Whitmore, K. (1970). *Education, health and behavior.* London: Longmans, Green.

Ryan, C. M., Longstreet, C., & Morrow, L. A. (1985). The effects of diabetes mellitus on the school attendance and school achievement of adolescents. *Child: Care, Health, and Development, 11*, 229–240.

Ryan, C. M., & Morrow, L. A. (1986). Self-esteem in diabetic adolescents: Relationship between age at onset and gender. *Journal of Consulting and Clinical Psychology, 54*, 730–731.

Ryan-Wenger, N. M. (1992). A taxonomy of children's coping strategies: A step toward theory development. *American Journal of Orthopsychiatry, 62,* 256–263.

Sackett, D. L., & Haynes, R. B. (1976). *Compliance with therapeutic regimens.* Baltimore: Johns Hopkins University Press.

Sackett, D. L., & Snow, J. C. (1979). The magnitude of compliance and noncompliance. In R. B. Haynes, D. W. Taylor, & D. L. Sackett (Eds.), *Compliance in health care* (pp. 11–22). Baltimore: Johns Hopkins University Press.

Sameroff, A. J., & Chandler, M. J. (1975). Reproductive risk and the continuum of caretaking causality. In F. D. Horowitz, M. Hetherington, S. Scarr-Salapatek, & G. Siegel (Eds.), *Review of child development* (Vol. 4, pp. 187–244). Chicago: University of Chicago Press.

Sanders, M. R., Rebgetz, M., Morrison, M., Bor, W., Gordon, A., Dadds, M., & Shepherd, R. (1989). Cognitive-behavioral treatment of recurrent nonspecific abdominal pain in children: An analysis of generalization, maintenance, and side effects. *Journal of Consulting and Clinical Psychology, 57,* 294–300.

Sanders, M. R., Shepherd, R. W., Cleghorn, G., & Woolford, H. (1994). The treatment of recurrent abdominal pain in children: A controlled comparison of cognitive-behavioral family intervention and standard pediatric care. *Journal of Consulting and Clinical Psychology, 62,* 306–314.

Sandler, N. (1989). *A parent's guide to asthma.* New York: Doubleday.

Sanger, M. S., Copeland, D. R., & Davidson, E. R. (1991). Psychosocial adjustment among pediatric cancer patients: A multidimensional assessment. *Journal of Pediatric Psychology, 16,* 463–474.

Sanger, M. S., Perrin, E. C., & Sandler, H. M. (1993). Development in children's causal theories of their seizure disorders. *Journal of Developmental and Behavioral Pediatrics, 14,* 88–93.

Satel, S. L. (1990). Mental status changes in children receiving glucocorticoids: Review of the literature. *Clinical Pediatrics, 29,* 383–388.

Satin, W., La Greca, A. M., Zigo, M. A., & Skyler, J. S. (1989). Diabetes in adolescence: Effects of multifamily group intervention and parent simulation of diabetes. *Journal of Pediatric Psychology, 14,* 259–275.

Sawyer, M., Crettendon, A., & Toogood, I. (1986). Psychological adjustment of families of children and adolescents treated for leukemia. *American Journal of Pediatric Hematology/Oncology, 8,* 200–207.

Schechter, N. L., Altman, A., & Weisman, S. (1990). Report of the consensus conference on the management of pain in childhood cancer. *Pediatrics, 86,* (Suppl.), 5.

Schechter, N. L., Berde, C. B., & Yaster, M. (Eds.). (1993). *Pain in infants, children, and adolescents.* Baltimore: Williams & Wilkins.

Schoenherr, S. J., Brown, R. T., Baldwin, K., & Kaslow, N. (1992). Attributional styles and psychopathology in pediatric chronic illness groups. *Journal of Clinical Child Psychology, 21,* 380–387.

Seligman, M. E. P., Peterson, C., Kaslow, N. J., Tannenbaum, R. L., Alloy, L. B., & Abramson, L. Y. (1984). Attributional style and depressive symptoms among children. *Journal of Abnormal Psychology, 93,* 235–238.

Senapati, R., & Hayes, A. (1988). Sibling relationships of handicapped children: A review of conceptual and methodological issues. *International Journal of Behavioral Development, 11,* 89–115.

Serjeant, G. R. (1985). *Sickle cell disease.* New York: Oxford University Press.

Sexson, S. B., & Madan-Swain, A. (1993). School reentry for the child with chronic illness. *Journal of Learning Disabilities, 26,* 115–125.

Shaw, E. G., & Routh, D. K. (1982). Effect of mother presence on children's reaction to invasive procedures. *Journal of Pediatric Psychology, 1,* 33–42.

Shelton, T. L., & Stepanek, J. S. (1994). *Family-centered care for children needing specialized health and developmental services.* Bethesda, MD: Association for the Care of Children's Health.

Sheppard, M. N. (1995). The pathology of cystic fibrosis. In M. E. Hodson & D. M. Geddes (Eds.), *Cystic fibrosis* (pp. 131–150). London: Chapman & Hall.

Shurtleff, D. B. (1980). Myelodysplasia: Management and treatment. *Current Problems in Pediatrics, 10,* 1–98.

Sickle Cell Disease Guideline Panel. (1993). *Sickle cell disease: Screening, diagnosis, management, and counseling in newborns and infants. Clinical Practice Guideline,* No. 6, AHCPR Pub. No. 93-0562. Rockville, MD: Agency for Health Care Policy and Research Public Health Service, U.S. Department of Health and Human Services.

Siegel, L. J., & Peterson, L. (1980). Stress reduction in young dental patients through coping skills and sensory information. *Journal of Consulting and Clinical Psychology, 48,* 785–787.

Silverstein, J. (1994). Diabetes: Medical issues. In R. A. Olson, L. L. Mullins, J. B. Gillman, & J. M. Chaney (Eds.), *The sourcebook of pediatric psychology* (pp. 111–117). Boston: Allyn & Bacon.

Simeonsson, R. J. (1992). Theories of child development. In C. F. Walker & M. C. Roberts (Eds.), *Handbook of clinical psychology* (pp. 26–46). New York: Wiley-Interscience.

Simeonsson, R. J., Buckley, L., & Monson, L. (1979). Conceptions of illness causality in hospitalized children. *Journal of Pediatric Psychology, 4,* 77–84.

Simeonsson, R. J., & McHale, S. M. (1981). Review: Research on handicapped children: Sibling relationships. *Child: Care, Health and Development, 7,* 153–171.

Simmons, R. J., Corey, M., Cowen, L., Keenan, N., Robertson, J., & Levinson, H. (1985). Emotional adjustment of early adolescents with cystic fibrosis. *Psychosomatic Medicine, 47,* 111–122.

Simmons, R. J., Corey, M., Cowen, L., Keenan, N., Robertson, J., & Levinson, H. (1987). Behavioral adjustment of latency age children with cystic fibrosis. *Psychosomatic Medicine, 49,* 291–301.

Sines, J. O., Pauker, J. D., Sines, L. K., & Owen, D. R. (1969). Identification of clinically relevant dimensions of children's behavior. *Journal of Consulting and Clinical Psychology, 33,* 728–734.

Slavin, R. (1977). *Prognosis in bronchial asthma.* Report prepared for the Asthma Committee, the Task Force on Asthma and Other Allergic Diseases, National Institute of Allergic and Infectious Disease.

Smith, S. (1990). Individualized education programs (IEPs) in special education: From intent to acquiescence. *Exceptional Children, 57,* 6–14.

Sparling, J., & Lewis, I. (1984). *Partners for learning.* Lewisville, NC: Kaplan Press.

Spaulding, B. R., & Morgan, S. B. (1986). Spina bifida children and their parents: A population prone to family dysfunction? *Journal of Pediatric Psychology, 11,* 359–374.

Spielberger, C. D. (1977). Theory and measure of anxiety status. In R. Cattel & R. Dreger (Eds.), *Handbook of modern personality theory* (pp. 239–253). Washington, DC: Hemisphere/Wiley.

Spielberger, C. D., Gorsuch, R. L., Lushene, R. E., Vagg, P. R., & Jacobs, G. A. (1970). *Manual for the State-Trait Inventory.* Palo Alto, CA: Consulting Psychologists Press.

Spirito, A., DeLawyer, D. D., & Stark, L. J. (1991). Peer relations and social adjustment of chronically ill children and adolescents. *Clinical Psychology Review, 11,* 539–564.

Spirito, A., Stark, L. J., Cobiella, C., Drigan, R., Androkites, A., & Hewett, K. (1990). Social adjustment of children successfully treated for cancer. *Journal of Pediatric Psychology, 15,* 359–371.

Spitzer, R. L., Williams, J. B., & Gibbons, M. (1987). *Structured Clinical Interview for DSM-III-R.* New York: State Psychiatric Institute.

Spivack, G., Platt, J. J., & Shure, M. B. (1976). *The problem-solving approach to adjustment.* San Francisco: Jossey-Bass.

Springer, K. (1994). Beliefs about illness causality among preschoolers with cancer: Evidence against immanent justice. *Journal of Pediatric Psychology, 19,* 91–101.

Springer, K., & Ruckel, J. (1992). Early beliefs about the cause of illness: Evidence against immanent justice. *Cognitive Development, 7,* 429–443.

Starfield, B. (1985). The state of research on chronically ill children. In N. Hobbs & J. M. Perrin (Eds.), *Issues in the care of children with chronic illness* (pp. 109–131). San Francisco: Jossey-Bass.

Stark, L. J., Spirito, A., Williams, C. A., & Guevremont, D. C. (1989). Common problems and coping strategies: I. Findings with normal adolescents. *Journal of Abnormal Child Psychology, 17,* 203–221.

Stehbens, J. A. (1988). Childhood cancer. In D. K. Routh (Ed.), *Handbook of pediatric psychology* (pp. 135–161). New York: Guilford Press.

Stehbens, J. A., Kisker, C. T., & Wilson, B. K. (1983). School behavior and attendance during the first year of treatment for childhood cancer. *Psychology in the Schools, 20,* 223–228.

Stein, R. E. K., & Jessop, D. J. (1982). A noncategorical approach to chronic childhood illness. *Public Health Reports, 97,* 354–362.

Stein, R. E. K., & Jessop, D. J. (1984). Relationship between health status and psychological adjustment among children with chronic conditions. *Pediatrics, 73,* 169–174.

Steinhausen, H., & Gobel, D. (1987). Convergence of parent checklists and child psychiatric diagnoses. *Journal of Abnormal Child Psychology, 15,* 147–151.

Stipek, D., & McCroskey, J. (1989). Investing in children: Government and workplace policies for parents. *American Psychologist, 44,* 416–423.

Straker, G., & Kuttner, M. (1980). Psychological compensation in the individual with a life-threatening illness: A study of adolescents with cystic fibrosis. *South African Medical Journal, 57,* 61–62.

Strickland, B. R. (1978). Internal–external expectancies and health-related behaviors. *Journal of Consulting and Clinical Psychology, 46,* 1192–1211.

Suess, W. M., Stump, N., Chai, H., & Kalisker, A. (1986). Mnemonic effects of asthma medication in children. *Journal of Asthma, 23,* 291–296.

Suls, J., & Fletcher, B. (1985). The relative efficacy of avoidant and nonavoidant coping strategies: A meta-analysis. *Health Psychology, 4,* 249–288.

Surwit, R. S., Feinglos, M. N., & Scovern, A. W. (1983). Diabetes and behavior: A paradigm for health psychology. *American Psychologist, 38,* 255–262.

Swift, A. V., Cohen, M. J., Hynd, G. W., Wisenbaker, J. M., McKie, K. M., Makari, G., & McKie, V. (1989). Neuropsychological impairment in children with sickle cell anemia. *Pediatrics, 84,* 1077–1085.

Tavormina, J. B., Kastner, L. S., Slater, P. M., & Watt, S. L. (1976). Chronically ill children: A psychologically and emotionally deviant population? *Journal of Abnormal Child Psychology, 4,* 99–110.

Tew, B. J., & Lawrence, K. M. (1973). Mothers, brothers and sisters of patients with spina bifida. *Developmental Medicine and Child Neurology, 15,* (Suppl. 29), 69–76.

Thompson, R. J., Jr. (1985). Coping with the stress of chronic childhood illness. In A. N. O'Quinn (Ed.), *Management of chronic disorders of childhood* (pp. 11–41). Boston: G. K. Hall.

Thompson, R. J., Jr., Cappleman, M. W., Conrad, H. H., & Jordan, W. B. (1982). Early intervention program for adolescent mothers and their infants. *Journal of Developmental and Behavioral Pediatrics, 3,* 18–21.

Thompson, R. J., Jr., Gil, K. M., Abrams, M. R., & Phillips, G. (1992). Stress, coping and psychological adjustment of adults with sickle cell disease. *Journal of Consulting and Clinical Psychology, 60,* 433–440.

Thompson, R. J., Jr., Gil, K. M., Burbach, D. J., Keith, B. R., & Kinney, T. R. (1993a). Psychological adjustment of mothers of children and adolescents with sickle cell disease: The role of stress, coping methods and family functioning. *Journal of Pediatric Psychology, 18,* 549–559.

Thompson, R. J., Jr., Gil, K. M., Burbach, D. J., Keith, B. R., & Kinney, T. R. (1993b). Role of child and maternal processes in the psychological adjustment of children with sickle cell disease. *Journal of Consulting and Clinical Psychology, 61,* 468–474.

Thompson, R. J., Gil, K. M., Gustafson, K. E., George, L. K., Keith, B. R., Spock, A., & Kinney, T. R. (1994). Stability and change in the psychological adjustment of mothers of children and adolescents with cystic fibrosis and sickle cell disease. *Journal of Pediatric Psychology, 19,* 171–188.

Thompson, R. J., Jr., Gil, K. M., Keith, B. R., Gustafson, K. E., George, L. K., & Kinney, T. R. (1994). Psychological adjustment of children with sickle cell disease: Stability and change over a 10-month period. *Journal of Consulting and Clinical Psychology, 62,* 856–860.

Thompson, R. J., Jr., Gustafson, K. E., George, L. K., & Spock, A. (1994). Change over a 12-month period in the psychological adjustment of children and adolescents with cystic fibrosis. *Journal of Pediatric Psychology, 19,* 189–203.

Thompson, R. J., Jr., Gustafson, K. E., & Gil, K. M. (1995). Psychological adjustment of adolescents with cystic fibrosis or sickle cell disease and their mothers. In J. Wallander & L. Siegel (Eds.), *Advances in pediatric psychology: II. Behavioral perspectives on adolescent health* (pp. 232–247). New York: Guilford Press.

Thompson, R. J., Jr., Gustafson, K. E., Hamlett, K. W., & Spock, A. (1992a). Psychological adjustment of children with cystic fibrosis: The role of child cognitive processes and maternal adjustment. *Journal of Pediatric Psychology, 17,* 741–755.

Thompson, R. J., Jr., Gustafson, K. E., Hamlett, K. W., & Spock, A. (1992b). Stress, coping, and family functioning in the psychological adjustment of mothers of children with cystic fibrosis. *Journal of Pediatric Psychology, 17,* 573–585.

Thompson, R. J., Jr., Hodges, K., & Hamlett, K. W. (1990). A matched comparison of adjustment in children with cystic fibrosis and psychiatrically referred and non-referred children. *Journal of Pediatric Psychology, 15,* 745–759.

Thompson, R. J., Jr., & Kronenberger, W. (1992). A heuristic review of the psychosocial aspects of myelodysplasia. In M. Wolraich & D. K. Routh (Eds.), *Advances in developmental and behavioral pediatrics* (Vol. 9, pp. 89–108). Philadelphia: Jessica Kingsley.

Thompson, R. J., Jr., Kronenberger, W., & Curry, J. F. (1989). Behavior classification system for children with developmental, psychiatric and chronic medical problems. *Journal of Pediatric Psychology, 14,* 559–575.

Thompson, R. J., Jr., Kronenberger, W. G., Johnson, D. F., & Whiting, K. (1989). The role of central nervous system functioning and family functioning in behavioral problems of children with myelodysplasia. *Developmental and Behavioral Pediatrics, 10,* 242–248.

Thompson, R. J., Jr., Merritt, K. A., Keith, B. R., Murphy, L. B., & Johndrow, D. A. (1993). The role of maternal stress and family functioning in maternal distress and mother-reported and child-reported psychological adjustment of non-referred children. *Journal of Clinical Child Psychology, 22,* 78–84.

Thompson, R. J., Jr., & O'Quinn, A. N. (1979). *Developmental disabilities: Etiologies, manifestation, diagnosis and treatment.* New York: Oxford University Press.

Thompson, R. J., Jr., Zeman, J. L., Fanurik, D., & Sirotkin-Roses, M. (1992). The role of parent stress and coping and family functioning in parent and child adjustment to Duchenne Muscular Dystrophy. *Journal of Clinical Psychology, 48,* 11–19.

Timko, C., Stovel, K. W., & Moos, R. H. (1992). Functioning among mothers and fathers of children with juvenile rheumatic disease: A longitudinal study. *Journal of Pediatric Psychology, 17,* 705–724.

Tin, L. G., & Teasdale, G. R. (1985). An observation study of the social adjustment of spina bifida children in integrated settings. *Journal of Educational Psychology, 55,* 81–83.

Tronick, E. Z. (1989). Emotions and emotional communication in infants. *American Psychologist, 44,* 112–119.

Ungerer, J. A., Horgan, B., Chaitow, J., & Champion, G. D. (1988). Psychosocial functioning in children and young adults with juvenile arthritis. *Pediatrics, 81,* 195–202.

Varni, J. W., Katz, E. R., Colegrove, R., Jr., & Dolgin, M. (1993). The impact of social skills training on the adjustment of children with newly diagnosed cancer. *Journal of Pediatric Psychology, 18,* 751–767.

Varni, J. W., Katz, E. R., Colegrove, R., & Dolgin, M. (1994). Perceived social support and adjustment of children with newly diagnosed cancer. *Journal of Developmental and Behavioral Pediatrics, 15,* 20–26.

Varni, J. W., Katz, E. R., & Dash, J. (1982). Behavioral and neurochemical aspects of pediatric pain. In D. C. Russo & J. W. Varni (Eds.), *Behavioral pediatrics: Research and practice* (pp. 177–224). New York: Plenum.

Varni, J. W., Katz, E. R., & Waldron, S. A. (1993). Cognitive-behavioral treatment interventions in childhood cancer. *The Clinical Psychologist, 46,* 192–197.

Varni, J. W., Rubenfeld, L. A., Talbot, D., & Setoguchi, Y. (1989a). Determinants of self-esteem in children with congenital/acquired limb deficiencies. *Journal of Developmental and Behavioral Pediatrics, 10,* 13–16.

Varni, J. W., Rubenfeld, L. A., Talbot, D., & Setoguchi, Y. (1989b). Family functioning, temperament, and psychologic adaptation in children with congenital or acquired limb deficiencies. *Pediatrics, 84,* 323–330.

Varni, J. W., & Setoguchi, Y. (1991). Correlates of perceived physical appearance in children with congenital/acquired limb deficiencies. *Journal of Developmental and Behavioral Pediatrics, 12,* 171–176.

Varni, J. W., & Setoguchi, Y. (1993). Effects of parental adjustment on the adaptation of children with congenital or acquired limb deficiencies. *Journal of Developmental and Behavioral Pediatrics, 14,* 13–20.

Varni, J. W., Setoguchi, Y., Rappaport, L. R., & Talbot, D. (1991). Effects of stress, social support, and self-esteem on depression in children with limb deficiencies. *Archives of Physical Medicine and Rehabilitation, 72,* 1053–1058.

Varni, J. W., Setoguchi, Y., Rappaport, L. R., & Talbot, D. (1992). Psychological adjustment and perceived social support in children with congenital acquired limb deficiencies. *Journal of Behavioral Medicine, 15,* 31–44.

Varni, J. W., Walco, G. A., & Katz, E. R. (1989). A cognitive–behavioral approach to pain associated with pediatric chronic disease. *Journal of Pain and Symptom Management, 4,* 238–241.

Varni, J. W., Walco, G. A., & Wilcox, K. T. (1990). Cognitive–biobehavioral assessment and treatment of pediatric pain. In A. M. Gross & R. S. Drabman (Eds.), *Handbook of clinical behavioral pediatrics* (pp. 83–97). New York: Plenum.

Vernon, D. T. A., Foley, J. M., & Schulman, J. L. (1967). Effect of mother-child separation and birth order on young children's responses to two potentially stressful experiences. *Journal of Personality and Social Psychology, 5,* 162–174.

Wagner, B. M., Compas, B. E., & Howell, D. C. (1988). Daily and major life events: A test of an integrative model of psychosocial stress. *American Journal of Community Psychology, 16,* 189–205.

Walco, G. A., & Dampier, C. D. (1987). Chronic pain in adolescent patients. *Journal of Pediatric Psychology, 12,* 215–225.

Walco, G. A., & Varni, J. W. (1991). Cognitive-behavioral interventions for children with chronic illnesses. In P. C. Kendall (Ed.), *Child and adolescent therapy: Cognitive–behavioral procedures* (pp. 209–244). New York: Guilford Press.

Walker, D. K. (1984). Care of chronically ill children in schools. *Pediatric Clinics of North America, 31,* 221–233.

Walker, D. K. (1987). Chronically ill children in schools: Programmatic and policy directions for the future. *Rheumatic Disease Clinics of North America, 13,* 113–121.

Walker, D. K., & Jacobs, F. H. (1985). Public school programs for chronically ill children. In N. Hobbs & J. M. Perrin (Eds.), *Issues in the care of children with chronic illness* (pp. 615–655). San Francisco: Jossey-Bass.

Walker, L. S., Ford, M. B., & Donald, W. D. (1987). Cystic fibrosis and family stress: Effects of age and severity of illness. *Pediatrics, 79,* 239–246.

Walker, L. S., Garber, J., Van Slyke, D. A., & Greene, J. W. (1995). Long-term health outcomes in patients with recurrent abdominal pain. *Journal of Pediatric Psychology, 20,* 233–245.

Walker, L. S., Green, J. W., Garber, J., Horndasch, R. L., Barnard, J., & Ghishan, F. (1993). Psychosocial factors in pediatric abdominal pain: Implications for assessment and treatment. *The Clinical Psychologist, 46,* 206–213.

Walker, L. S., Ortiz-Valdes, J. A., & Newbrough, J. R. (1989). The role of maternal employment and depression in the psychological adjustment of chronically ill mentally retarded, and well children. *Journal of Pediatric Psychology, 14,* 357–370.

Wallander, J. L. (1992). Theory-driven research in pediatric psychology: A little bit on why and how. *Journal of Pediatric Psychology, 17,* 521–535.

Wallander, J. L., Feldman, W. S., & Varni, J. W. (1989). Physical status and psychosocial adjustment in children with spina bifida. *Journal of Pediatric Psychology, 14*, 89–102.

Wallander, J. L., Hubert, N. C., & Varni, J. W. (1988). Child and maternal temperament characteristics, goodness of fit, and adjustment in physically handicapped children. *Journal of Clinical Child Psychology, 17*, 336–344.

Wallander, J. L., & Thompson, R. J., Jr. (1995). Psychosocial adjustment of children with chronic physical conditions. In M. C. Roberts (Ed.), *Handbook of pediatric psychology* (2nd ed., pp. 124–141). New York: Guilford Press.

Wallander, J. L., & Varni, J. W. (1989). Social support and adjustment in chronically ill and handicapped children. *American Journal of Community Psychology, 17*, 185–201.

Wallander, J. L., & Varni, J. W. (1992). Adjustment in children with chronic physical disorders: Programmatic research on a disability-stress-coping model. In A. M. LaGreca, L. Siegal, J. L. Wallander, & C. E. Walker (Eds.), *Stress and coping with pediatric conditions* (pp. 279–298). New York: Guilford Press.

Wallander, J. L., Varni, J. W., Babani, L., Banis, H. T., DeHaan, C. B., & Wilcox, K. T. (1989). Disability parameters: Chronic strain and adaptation of physically handicapped children and their mothers. *Journal of Pediatric Psychology, 14*, 23–42.

Wallander, J. L., Varni, J. W., Babani, L., Banis, H. T., & Wilcox, K. T. (1988). Children with chronic physical disorders: Maternal reports of their psychological adjustment. *Journal of Pediatric Psychology, 13*, 197–212.

Wallander, J. L., Varni, J. W., Babani, L., Banis, H. T., & Wilcox, K. T. (1989). Family resources as resistance factors for psychological maladjustment in chronically ill and handicapped children. *Journal of Pediatric Psychology, 14*, 157–173.

Wallander, J. L., Varni, J. W., Babani, L., DeHaan, C. B., Wilcox, K. T., & Banis, H. T. (1989). The social environment and the adaptation of mothers of physically handicapped children. *Journal of Pediatric Psychology, 14*, 371–387.

Wallston, K., & Wallston, B. (1981). Health locus of control scales. In H. Lefcourt (Ed.), *Research with the locus of control construct* (pp. 189–243). San Diego, CA: Academic Press.

Wasik, B. H. (1984). *Coping with parenting through effective problem solving: A handbook for professionals.* Chapel Hill, NC: Frank Porter Graham Child Development Center.

Wasserman, A. L., Wilimas, J. A., Fairclough, D. L., Mulhern, R. K., & Wang, W. (1991). Subtle neuropsychological deficits in children with sickle cell disease. *American Journal of Pediatric Hematology/Oncology, 13*, 14–20.

Webster-Stratton, C. (1990). Stress: A potential description of parent perceptions and family interactions. *Journal of Clinical Child Psychology, 19*, 302–312.

Weigel, C., Wertlieb, D., & Feldstein, M. (1989). Perception of control, competence, and contingency as influences on the stress–behavior symptom relation in school-age children. *Journal of Personality and Social Psychology, 56,* 456–464.

Weiss, S. M. (1987). Behavioral medicine in the trenches. In J. Blumenthal & D. McKee (Eds.), *Applications in behavioral medicine and health psychology: A clinician's source book* (pp. xvii–xxiii). Sarasota, FL: Professional Resource Exchange.

Weist, M. D., Finney, J. W., Barnar, M. U., Davis, C. D., & Ollendick, T. H. (1993). Empirical selection of psychosocial treatment targets for children and adolescents with diabetes. *Journal of Pediatric Psychology, 18,* 11–28.

Weisz, J. R. (1980). Developmental change in perceived control: Recognizing noncontingency in the laboratory and perceiving it in the world. *Developmental Psychology, 16,* 365–390.

Weisz, J. R., McCabe, M. A., & Dennig, M. D. (1994). Primary and secondary control among children undergoing medical procedures: Adjustment as a function of coping style. *Journal of Consulting and Clinical Psychology, 62,* 324–332.

Weisz, J. R., Rothbaum, F. M., & Blackburn, T. F. (1984a). Standing out and standing in: The psychology of control in America and Japan. *American Psychologist, 39,* 955–969.

Weisz, J. R., Rothbaum, F. M., & Blackburn, T. C. (1984b). Swapping recipes for control. *American Psychologist, 39,* 974–975.

Weisz, J. R., & Stipek, D. J. (1982). Competence, contingency, and the development of perceived control. *Human Development, 25,* 250–281.

Weisz, J. R., Yeates, K. O., Robertson, D., & Beckham, J. C. (1982). Perceived contingency of skill and chance events: A developmental analysis. *Developmental Psychology, 18,* 898–905.

Weitzman, M. (1986). School absence rates as outcome measures in studies of children with chronic illness. *Journal of Chronic Disease, 39,* 799–808.

Weitzman, M., Walker, D. K., & Gortmaker, S. (1986). Chronic illness, psychosocial problems, and school absences. *Clinical Pediatrics, 25,* 137–141.

Wertlieb, D., Hauser, S. T., & Jacobson, A. M. (1986). Adaptation to diabetes: Behavior symptoms and family context. *Journal of Pediatric Psychology, 11,* 463–479.

Wertlieb, D., Weigel, C., & Feldstein, M. (1987). *Stress, social support, and behavior symptoms in middle childhood. Journal of Clinical Child Psychology, 16,* 204–211.

Westbrook, L. E., Bauman, L. J., & Shinnar, S. (1992). Applying stigma theory to epilepsy: A test of a conceptual model. *Journal of Pediatric Psychology, 17,* 633–658.

Whitt, J. K., Dykstra, W., & Taylor, C. A. (1979). Children's conception of illness and cognitive development. *Clinical Pediatrics, 18,* 327–339.

Wills, K. E. (1993). Neuropsychological functioning in children with spina bifida and/or hydrocephalus. *Journal of Clinical Child Psychiatry, 22,* 247–265.

Wolraich, M. (1983). Meylomeningocele. In J. A. Blackman (Ed.), *Medical aspects of developmental disabilities in children birth to three* (pp. 159–165). Iowa City, IA: University of Iowa Press.

Wood, S. P., Walker, D. K., & Gardner, J. (1986). School health practices for children with complex medical needs. *Journal of School Health, 56,* 215–217.

Worchel, F. F., Copeland, D. R., & Barker, D. G. (1987). Control-related coping strategies in pediatric oncology patients. *Journal of Pediatric Psychology, 12,* 25–38.

Worchel, F. F., Nolan, B. F., Willson, V. L., Purser, J. S., Copeland, D. R., & Pfefferbaum, B. (1988). Assessment of depression in children with cancer. *Journal of Pediatric Psychology, 13,* 101–112.

Wysocki, T. (1993). Associations among teen–parent relationships, metabolic control, and adjustment to diabetes in adolescents. *Journal of Pediatric Psychology, 18,* 441–452.

Young, G. A. (1994). Asthma: Medical issues. In R. A. Olson, L. L. Mullins, J. B. Gillman, & J. M. Chaney (Eds.), *The sourcebook of pediatric psychology* (pp. 57–60). Boston: Allyn & Bacon.

# AUTHOR INDEX

Gerstein, F., 257

Gil, K. M., 10, 18, 59, 60, 69, 72, 78, 83, 92, 96, 100, 107, 112, 118, 119, 142, 144, 145, 158, 168, 169, 176, 282

Gilman, S. C., 128

Girqus, J. S., 210

Glauser, T. A., 127

Gobel, D., 58

Godfrey, S., 72

Goldfried, M. R., 239

Goldston, D., 66, 84, 91, 95, 99, 103, 104, 106, 107

Gonzalez, J. C., 275, 278

Goodnow, J. J., 151

Gordon, W. A., 54, 55

Gordon, Y., 59

Gorfinkle, K., 257

Gorsuch, R. L., 160

Gortmaker, S. L., 2, 3, 4, 28, 29, 30, 31, 62, 71, 102, 118, 123, 128

Graetz, B., 65, 117, 121

Graziano, W. G., 154

Greenberg, M. T., 8, 12, 65, 74, 81, 153

Greene, J. W., 283

Gresham, F. M., 77

Groom, G., 163

Gross, A., 275

Gross, R. T., 17, 243

Grunebaum, H. V., 8, 154

Grusec, J. E., 11, 152

Gudas, L. J., 48

Guevremont, D. C., 220

Gustafson, K. E., 10, 59, 69, 71, 72, 76, 81, 82, 92, 96, 100, 102, 112, 118, 119, 126, 142, 143, 144, 145, 158, 168, 169, 176

Gyulay, J. E., 129

Hack, M., 3

Haefner, D. P., 260

Haflon, N., 31

Haggerty, R. J., 2, 5, 9, 29, 32, 60

Hamburg, D. A., 137

Hamlett, K. W., 10, 59, 72, 76, 81, 102, 119, 142, 143, 158, 168

Hanson, C. L., 17, 90, 94, 98, 104, 106, 112, 174, 263

Harbeck, C., 186, 188, 190

Harkins, S. W., 187

Harm, D. L., 41

Harris, M. A., 104, 174

Harter, S., 211, 212, 213

Hartman, A., 294, 299

Hartup, W. W., 115

Hauser, S. T., 77, 259

Havermans, T., 80, 120

Havinghurst, R. J., 13

Hayden, P. W., 55

Hayes, A., 170, 171

Hayes, J., 129

Hayford, J. R., 185

Haynes, R. B., 250, 252, 254, 255, 266, 267

Hearne, E., 129

Hebbeler, K. M., 302, 305

Heidish, I. E., 58

Henggeler, S. W., 90, 94, 98, 104, 112, 174

Herbert, N. C., 93, 97, 101

Hixson, D. D., 306

Hoagland, A., 164

Hobbs, N., 297

Hodges, K., 59, 72, 111

Hoffman, I., 129

Holt, P. J. L., 193

Hoppe, M., 105

Horgan, B., 103

Horowitz, F. D., 294, 298, 306

Houghton, J., 173

Howe, G. W., 65, 79, 124

Howell, C. T., 58, 117

Howell, D. C., 202

Hubert, N. C., 16, 106, 235

Huberty, T. J., 90, 94, 98, 108

Hulka, B., 255

Hunt, J. V., 3

Hurtig, A. L., 65, 77, 81, 90, 94, 98, 102, 117, 121

Iannotti, R. J., 261

Ireys, H. T., 295, 296, 297

Irion, J. D., 219

Iscoe, L., 246

Iyengar, S., 66, 84, 91, 95, 99, 103, 104, 106, 107

Izzo, L. D., 116

Jackson, J., 67, 71, 77, 81, 116

Jacobs, F. H., 303

Jacobs, G. A., 160

Jacobsen, P. B., 257, 273, 275, 277

Jacobson, A. M., 65, 76, 77, 117, 256, 259

James, L. M., 54
James, W., 212
Jay, S. M., 274, 275, 276, 279, 286
Jessop, D. J., 4, 5, 33, 36, 89, 92, 96,
    100, 102, 103, 129, 230
Johndrow, D. A., 59, 111, 203, 263
Johnson, D. F., 68, 78, 80, 119
Johnson, F., 46
Johnson, M. P., 124
Johnson, S. B., 49, 50, 264, 265
Jordan, W. B., 242

Kagan, J., 198, 200
Kalas, R., 58, 59, 172
Kalisker, A., 126
Kaplan, R. M., 16, 231
Karem, B., 46
Kashani, J. H., 65, 66, 72, 73, 75, 81,
    116, 117
Kaslow, N. J., 64, 71, 77, 81, 211
Katz, E. R., 16, 187, 235, 236, 237, 240,
    241, 272, 279, 281, 314
Kazak, A. E., 7, 11, 66, 71, 74, 80, 81,
    148
Kazdin, A. E., 58
Keen, J. H., 193
Keith, B. R., 10, 59, 60, 72, 78, 83, 111,
    118, 142, 144, 145, 158, 169,
    203
Kellerman, J., 66, 71, 81
Kelley, M. L., 77
Kerem, B., 46
Khoury, M. J., 54
Kidwell, S., 128
Kinney, T. R., 10, 18, 59, 60, 72, 78,
    107, 142, 144, 145, 158, 169,
    282
Kirscht, J. P., 260
Kitchen, W. H., 3
Klaric, S. H., 172
Kliewer, W., 207, 208
Kline, J., 111
Klopovich, P., 129
Koch, C., 47
Koepke, D., 102
Kollasch, E., 126
Konig, P., 66, 72, 73, 80, 117
Koocher, G. P., 48, 191
Kovacs, M., 66, 72, 81, 84, 90, 95, 99,
    103, 104, 106, 107, 203
Krasnegor, N. A., 266

Krischer, J. P., 128
Kronenberger, W., 55, 68, 78, 79, 80, 81,
    119, 143, 167
Kropp, J. P., 153
Kulczycki, L. L., 63, 116
Kulkarni, R., 117, 240
Kun, L. E., 127
Kuo, J. H., 209
Kupst, M. J., 163, 164
Kuttner, M., 116
Kuttner, M. J., 91, 95, 99, 102, 210

La Greca, A. M., 66, 116, 117, 121, 237,
    238, 244, 250, 251, 252, 255,
    256, 259, 260, 264
Lahey, B. E., 153
Lanng, S., 47
Lansky, S. B., 128, 129
Lanzkowsky, P., 44, 45
Launier, R., 9
Lautenschlager, G. L., 154
Lavee, Y., 259
Lavigne, J. V., 60, 66, 75, 79, 85, 88, 89,
    91, 95, 99, 103, 105, 106, 108,
    110, 117, 185
Lawrence, K. M., 171
Lazarus, R. S., 8, 9, 135, 143, 165, 166,
    198, 199, 203, 215, 216, 219,
    220
Lebo-Stein, J., 246
Ledoux, N., 202
Leikin, S. L., 53
Lemanek, K. L., 67, 77, 80, 81
Lennon, M. P., 59
Lerner, J., 150
Lerner, J. A., 126
Lerner, R., 149, 150
LeRoy, S., 117, 240
Leventhal, H., 261, 262
Levin, R., 275
Levitan, I. B., 47
Lewis, C. E., 201
Lewis, I., 242, 244
Lewis, M., 14
Lewis, M. A., 201
Lewiston, N. J., 47
Linney, J. A., 90, 94, 98, 111, 112, 166
Lipowski, A. J., 137
Litt, I. F., 33, 251, 259
Lobato, D., 170, 173
Longstreet, C., 129
Lowman, J. T., 129

Pachman, L. M., 185
Packer, R. J., 127
Pancer, M., 80, 120
Parcel, G. S., 128
Park, K. B., 102
Parker, J. G., 116
Parkes, K. R., 208
Paterson, R. J., 205
Patterson, G. R., 8, 153
Pauker, J. D., 58, 111, 119
Paulauskas, S., 81, 106
Pederson, A., 116
Pegelow, C. H., 129
Pelligrini, D. S., 120
Perrin, E. C., 12, 13, 15, 72, 91, 95, 99,
        102, 105, 111, 112, 117, 185,
        192, 208
Perrin, J. M., 2, 4, 5, 16, 28, 29, 32, 34,
        35, 37, 71, 91, 95, 99, 102, 103,
        112, 118, 230, 231, 295, 296,
        297
Peterson, C., 209, 210
Peterson, J. L., 62
Peterson, L., 183, 186, 188, 190, 192,
        223, 258
Phares, V., 202
Phillips, D., 294, 299
Pierre, C. B., 71, 102, 118
Pinkerton, P., 4, 9, 28, 35, 36, 63, 89,
        133, 134, 135
Platt, J. J., 239
Platt, O. S., 3, 53
Pless, I. B., 4, 5, 9, 28, 29, 32, 34, 35,
        36, 37, 60, 61, 89, 104, 133, 134,
        135
Portner, J., 259
Potter, P. C., 194
Power, T., 257
Powers, S. W., 220, 278
Prabucki, K., 172

Quittner, A. L., 11, 149

Radloff, L. S., 161
Range, L. M., 191
Rappaport, L. R., 240
Redd, W. H., 257
Redpath, C. C., 193
Reid, C. D., 51
Reid, J., 81, 106
Reiss, D., 79, 124
Renne, C. M., 41

Reynolds, C. R., 203
Richmond, B. O., 203
Riessman, C. K., 5
Rigler, D., 71
Riley, A., 128
Ris, M. D., 117
Roberts, M. C., 146, 147, 186, 194, 220
Robertson, D., 206
Robins, E., 151
Rodger, S., 170, 232
Rogers, C. S., 193
Roghmann, K. J., 5, 28, 29, 32, 60, 61,
        104
Rogosch, F. A., 117, 240
Rolland, J., 14, 34, 36, 37, 39, 149
Rose-Krasnor, L., 8, 151
Rosenbaum, P., 159
Rosenblum, L. A., 14
Ross, C. K., 185, 275
Ross, D. M., 188, 275
Ross, S. A., 188
Roth, S., 215
Rothbaum, F. M., 217
Rotter, J. B., 199, 204
Routh, D. K., 275, 278
Rovet, J. F., 21, 49, 92, 96, 100, 105,
        106, 126
Rubenfeld, L. A., 103, 107, 237
Rubenstein, C. L., 235
Rubin, K. H., 8, 11, 151
Ruble, D. N., 152, 217
Ruckel, J., 186
Russell, C. S., 11, 109, 147
Rutter, M., 29, 60, 122, 123, 124, 139,
        158, 160
Ryan, C. M., 91, 95, 99, 105, 106, 129
Ryan-Wenger, N. M., 216

Sack, S., 63, 116
Sackett, D. L., 250, 251, 254, 266
Said, J., 127
Sameroff, A. J., 7, 146, 155
Sanders, M. R., 19, 284, 285
Sanders, S. M., 218
Sandler, I. N., 207, 208
Sandler, N., 43, 192
Sanger, M. S., 67, 73, 92, 96, 100, 102,
        112, 192
Sansbury, L., 71
Santiago, J. V., 102, 103, 210
Santogrossi, D. A., 238
Sappenfield, W., 2, 4, 20, 29, 30

# SUBJECT INDEX

Age-related factors. *See also*
Developmental perspective;
Developmental processes
in experience of pain, 188–190
onset of illness, 105–106
in treatment compliance, 256–257
Aggressive behavior, 238–239
Aid to Families with Dependent
Children, 296, 298
AIDS/HIV, 31
in neonates, 3
ALL. *See* Acute lymphoblastic leukemia
Allergic disorders, 29
Antibiotic therapy for cystic fibrosis, 48
Anxiety disorders
in children with cystic fibrosis, 76
risk of, secondary to chronic
childhood illness, 86
Arthritis, pediatric adherence, 253
Assessment. *See also* Classification of
chronic childhood illnesses
adherence, 250–251, 257–258
adjustment over time, 82–85, 86
child self-reports, 81
classification of chronic childhood
illnesses, 4–5
current conceptualizations, 57–60
of functional status, 103–104
in major epidemiological studies, 60
methodological problems, 72, 82
multiple informants, agreement
among, 81–82, 86
parents as informants, 58–60, 80–81,
120
premorbid profile, 134–135
psychological adjustment of mothers,
167
of psychosocial adjustment, 5, 6, 310
of social adjustment, 117–118
of social skills/social competence,
238
of social support system, 148
teachers as informants, 81, 120
Assimilation, 182
Asthma, 102
adaptive noncompliance in,
264–265
child perceptions of, as adjustment
factor, 108
and child's social adjustment, 121

clinical course, 35
clinical features, 41–42
defined, 41
epidemiology, 29, 41
etiology, 41
iatrogenic effects of medications,
126
morbidity and mortality, 41, 42
onset characteristics, 42
pediatric compliance, 253
prevalence, 29
risk of psychological maladjustment,
72–73
school absenteeism related to, 128
school functioning of children with,
123–124
severity of, as social adjustment
factor, 121
social adjustment problems
correlated with, 120
treatment, 43–44
Attention deficit hyperactivity disorder,
62
Attributional style, 209–211, 213–214
Autonomy, as developmental task, 13
Autosomal recessive disease, 32
Avoidance behaviors, 218, 220–221

Beck Depression Inventory, 161, 162, 163
Behavior Problem Index, 62
Behavior problems
assessment by multiple informants,
81–82, 86
assessment method bias, 82
assessment over time, 82–85, 86
child self-assessment, 81
in children with asthma, 72–73
in children with cancer, 73–74
in children with cystic fibrosis,
75–76, 79–80, 81, 82
in children with sickle-cell disease,
77
in children with spina bifida, 78–79
clinical studies in childhood chronic
illness, 63–70
and coping strategies, 220–222
and environmental stress, 153
as function of illness type, 79–80
meta-analyses, 85–86
methodological problems of existing
research, 71–72

social problem-solving strategies, 239

and stress-adjustment mediation, 213–214

in stress and coping models, 10

transactional model of family functioning, 155

treatment complexity as adherence factor, 264–265

understanding of disease, coping style and, 221

understanding of disease, treatment adherence and, 266–267

Compliance. *See* Adherence

Cooperative Study of Sickle-Cell Disease, 3, 53

Coping. *See* Stress and coping

Corticosteroids, 43, 126

Cost of care, 296–298

Crippled Children's Service Programs, 296, 297

Cystic fibrosis, 85, 102

as autosomal recessive disorder, 32

and child's social adjustment, 119, 121

child's stress experience in, 204

clinical course, 35

clinical features, 46–47

depression risk in children with, 86

epidemiology, 46

etiology, 46

maternal adjustment, 111–112, 168

and mother–child adaptational processes, 143–144

parent perception of child adjustment, 59, 75

parental psychological adjustment problems, 159–160, 161

perceived health locus of control in, 108

pulmonary system effects, 13

race as risk factor, 29

reproductive disorders in, 47

risk of psychosocial maladjustment, 75–76, 79–80, 81, 82

school absenteeism related to, 128–129

sibling adaptation, 171

stability of adjustment over time, 82–83

survival rate, 2, 30, 47

transactional stress and coping model, 143–144, 145

treatment, 47–48

Day care, 298

Death, children's conceptualizations of, 191

Depression

in children with cancer, 73–74

in children with chronic illness, 85–86

in children with cystic fibrosis, 76

in children with diabetes, 86, 104

in children with sickle-cell disease, 77

and coping methods, 220–221

explanatory style associated with, 210, 211

maternal, 12, 111, 153–154, 161

and perceived social support in school, 237

in siblings, 172

Developmental Disabilities Service and Facilities Construction Amendments of 1970, 300

Developmental disorders

in AIDS-infected infants, 3

public policy, 299–302

Developmental perspective

assessment issues, 58–59

asthma life-course, 42

and classification of chronic disorders, 40

duration of illness as adjustment factor, 104

explanation of illness to child, 195

intervention goals, 227, 234

life crisis model of adaptation, 135–139

living with insulin-dependent diabetes, 51

onset of disease, 34–35

pain response, 286

parental functioning in, 150–153

perceptions of control, 205–207, 209

risk and resiliency model of adaptation, 139–140

role of siblings, 173–174

self-concept in, 198, 212–213

socialization experiences, 115–116, 152

correlated with school performance, 123
defined, 230
public policy, 299–305
risk for psychiatric disorder, 61–62
Disability–stress–coping model, 10, 140–142
Duration of illness
correlated with compliance, 255
correlated with psychological adjustment, 104
in definition of chronic illness, 28
and risk for adjustment problems, 5

Education for the Handicapped Act Amendments of 1986, 302, 304
Education for All Handicapped Children Act of 1975, 20, 31–32, 232, 302–303
Education of the Handicapped Act, 302
Educational/informational interventions
for asthma management, 43–44
with complex treatment regimen, 264–265
developmental considerations in explanation of illness, 195
impact on child conceptualizations of illness, 194
to improve compliance, 266–267
to reduce stress of invasive treatment, 273–274, 279–281
sickle-cell disease, 54
Empowerment, 233–234
Epidemiology. *See also* Incidence of chronic childhood illness; Prevalence of chronic childhood illness
asthma, 41
cancer, 44
cognitive impairment secondary to chronic illness, 234
cystic fibrosis, 46
data sources, 28–29, 31, 60–63
as dimension of disease classification, 34–35
insulin-dependent diabetes mellitus, 48
psychological maladjustment secondary to chronic illness, 60–63
sickle-cell disease, 51
spina bifida, 54

terminology, 28
trends, 29–32
Epilepsy, 108, 120
pediatric compliance research, 253
Etiology
acute lymphoblastic leukemia, 44
asthma, 41
autosomal recessive disorders, 32
cystic fibrosis, 46
genetics, 32
insulin-dependent diabetes mellitus, 48
sex-linked disorders, 32
sickle-cell disease, 51
Expectations
appraisal of stress, 199
of control in children with chronic illness, 208–209
perceptions of control, 205–207
self-efficacy, 205
and stress mediation, 207
in transactional stress and coping model of adaptation, 143

Families. *See also* Family functioning
as coping resource, 142
multifamily intervention for children with diabetes, 244–245
parameters correlated with psychological adjustment, 108–109
structural trends, 298
Family Adaptability and Cohesion Evaluation Scale, 259
Family and Medical Leave Act, 299
Family Assessment Device, 159
Family Environment Scale, 110, 259
Family functioning. *See also* Families
adaptability in, 147, 148
as adjustment factor, 5, 109–110
cohesion, 110, 147, 148, 259
developmental models of chronic illness, 13–14
duration of illness as adjustment factor, 104
as factor in child's social adjustment, 121
family systems theories, 11–12, 146–148
and patient compliance, 17, 257–259, 263

Interpersonal Cognitive Problem-Solving
Model, 239
Interventions
attributional style, implications of,
211
biopsychosocial framework, 16, 230
child conceptualizations of cures and
illness, 184–185
child's developmental
conceptualizations, implications
of, 194–195
cognitive and stress processing
model of parenting, 154–155
collaborative approach, 233,
246–247, 267–268, 313–314
conceptual basis, 227, 230–232
conceptual development, 232–234
to cope with chronic pain, 281–286
family interaction patterns, 146, 147
family role in, 233
to foster cognitive and social
development, 242–244
to foster normalization, 16
goodness-of-fit considerations, 208
to improve adherence, 266–268
integrated model of adaptation,
134–135
life crisis model of adaptation,
138–139
maternal adjustment, 163, 176
and models of adaptation, 156
multidisciplinary approach, 231–232
multifamily group for children with
diabetes, 244–245
outcome classification, 231
parenting skills training, 241–242
parents as target of, conceptual basis
for, 241, 313
parents' role, 232, 246
to reduce stress of invasive
treatment, 273–281
research needs, 21, 314
school-focused, rationale for, 245
in schools, 16, 238–239
self-concept issues, 213
self-control coping skills, 223
social–cognitive problem solving,
239–241
social skills training, 16, 238–239
support for parental participation,
246
targets for, 312–314

transactional model of family
functioning, implications of, 155
See also Medical management;
Preventive interventions;
Treatment goals
Isle of Wight study, 29, 60, 122, 158, 234

Learned helplessness, 210–211, 214
Leukemia, 120. See also Acute
lymphoblastic leukemia
coping strategies, effectiveness of,
222
iatrogenic effects of treatment, 127
parental psychological adjustment,
162–163, 164
Life crisis model of adaptation, 33,
135–139
Limb deficiencies, 107–108
Locus of control
and categories of coping, 217
in children with chronic illness
experience, 208–209
coping strategies related to perceived
control, 219, 221–222
correlated with adjustment, 108
developmental conceptualizations of
children, 184–185
developmental context, 205–207
goodness-of-fit model, 208
of mothers of children with chronic
illness, 208
and self-worth concepts, 212–213
significance of, 204–205
stress mediation, 207
treatment implications, 194–195,
208
Low birth weight infants
cognitive development intervention,
243–244
long-term outcomes, 3
survival rate trends, 3

Marital functioning, 110
circumplex model, 147–148
correlated with maternal adjustment,
165–166
as determinant of parental
functioning, 151
Mast-cell stabilizer medications, 43
Maternal and Child Health and Mental
Retardation Planning
Amendments, 300

as cancer complication, 45
epidemiological trends, 31
iatrogenic effects of treatment, 126
prevalence, 29
as sequelae of childhood chronic
illness, 125–126
social adjustment problems
correlated with, 119

Obesity, 119
Onset of disorder
asthma, 42
diabetes, and neurocognitive
sequelae, 126
impact of disorder and, 34–35, 105–
106
insulin-dependent diabetes mellitus,
49
in psychosocial topology of chronic
childhood illness, 36–37
Ontario Child Health Study, 61, 123,
159
Oppositional disorders, 76, 78
Organ transplantation in cystic fibrosis,
48
Otitis media, 253

Pain
acute, 187
adaptive value, 187
attributing meaning to, 287
behavior modification for coping
with, 282–286
biopsychosocial model, 186
chronic/recurrent, 187, 281–286
classification, 18, 187–188, 272
defined, 186
developmental conceptualizations,
186, 188–190, 286
experience of, 286–287
guidelines for coping with, 286–287
of invasive procedures, interventions
to ameliorate, 273–279, 286
multicomponent
cognitive–behavioral intervention
to reduce, 279–281
pharmacotherapy, 272
psychological management models,
18–19, 228
regulating perception of, 281–282
response component, 186, 272

sensory component, 186, 272
in sickle-cell disease, 53–54
Palliative–emotion-focused coping, 9
Parenting Dimensions Inventory, 257
Parents/parenting. *See also* Fathers;
Mothers
adjustment of, as child adjustment
factor, 111–112
as assessment informants, 58–60,
80–81, 120
behavioral adjustment intervention,
241–242
child influences on, 150
in child pain-coping interventions,
283–285
and child social development, 152
cognitive and social development
intervention, 242–244
cognitive processing in, 151–153
cognitive and stress processing
model, 154–155
correlates of psychological
adjustment, 164–166, 312
family systems theories of
adaptation, 11–12
information-processing model, 152–
153
in interventions to reduce
treatment-related stress, 275–280,
286
marital adjustment, 110
in pain management programs,
18–19
and patient compliance, 257–258,
260
process model, 149–151
psychological adjustment as function
of child's illness type, 162
psychological adjustment over time,
162–164
psychological adjustment problems
experienced by, 158–162
psychological adjustment research,
157–158
public policies, 291, 298–299, 306
risk for adjustment difficulties, 5–6,
311
role in treatment, 232, 246
role stress, 149
sickle-cell disease education, 54

of children with insulin-dependent
diabetes, 76–77
of children with sickle-cell disease,
77–78, 80, 81, 82
of children with spina bifida, 78–79
and children's stress experience,
203–204
clinical literature review, 63–70
cognitive responses to stress,
198–200
and coping style, 134, 135
current conceptualizations, 310–311
determinants of stress response, 138
and family functioning, 175–176
integrated model of adaptation,
133–135
major epidemiological studies, 60–61
maternal assessment, 167
methodological problems of existing
research, 71–72
mother–child adaptational processes
in, 143–144
parental, as function of child's illness
type, 162
parental, correlates of, 164–166
parenting as determinant of, 149
problems experienced by parents,
158–162
research on parents, 157–158
risk of maladjustment secondary to
chronic illness, 61–63
in school, 129
self-concept in, 134, 135
of siblings, 170–175
transactional model, 133
transactional stress and coping
model, 143–144
and treatment compliance, 256–257
types of problems, 63
Psychosocial adaptation. *See also* Peer
relationships; Psychological
adjustment; Social adjustment
adaptive tasks in chronic illness,
136–137
and age at onset, 34–35
age-related factors, 105–106
assessment of, 5, 6
basis for interventional programs,
15–16, 230–232
change over time, 63, 82–85, 133

child coping methods as factor in,
106–107
child parameters correlated with,
105, 113, 142, 311
in children with brain-involved
conditions, 102
child's functional status correlated
with, 103–104
cognitive processes correlated with,
107–108
components of, 87
condition characteristics correlated
with, 89–102, 142, 311
defined, 32
developmental models of illness,
13–14
as dimension of disease classification,
33, 34, 36–37
direct relationship to chronic illness,
87
disability–stress–coping model, 10,
140–142
duration of illness correlated with,
104
family functioning as factor in,
109–110, 311
family systems models, 146–147
in family systems theories, 11–12
gender as factor in, 105
individual temperament correlated
with, 106
interaction among correlated factors,
110
life crisis model, 33, 135–139
and medical adherence in diabetes,
17
need for theoretical model, 131
and onset of disease, 36
organizational matrix for analysis of
correlates of, 88–89
parental, as child adjustment factor,
111–112
parental cognitive functioning as
child adjustment factor, 112–113
parents' marital adjustment as factor
in, 110
process determinants, 6
research needs, 20–21, 311–312
risk and resiliency model of,
139–140, 156

# ABOUT THE AUTHORS

**Robert J. Thompson, Jr.,** is Professor and Head of the Division of Medical Psychology in the Department of Psychiatry and Behavioral Sciences and Professor of Psychology in the Department of Psychology: Social and Health Sciences at Duke University. Thompson is a Fellow of the Division of Clinical Psychology of the American Psychological Association and a Fellow of the International Academy for Research and Learning Disabilities. He holds the Diplomate in Clinical Psychology of the American Board of Professional Psychology. He has served on the editorial board of the *Journal of Developmental and Behavioral Pediatrics* and the *Journal of Clinical Psychology in Medical Settings* and serves as a consulting editor for the *Journal of Pediatric Psychology*. Thompson received the Distinguished Researchers Award (1993) of the Association of Medical School Professors of Psychology and the Distinguished Teacher Award (1985–1986) from the Division of Medical Psychology at Duke University. With Aglaia O'Quinn, he wrote *Developmental Disabilities: Etiologies, Manifestations, Diagnoses, and Treatments* (1979). He also was the author of the monograph *Behavior Problems in Children with Developmental and Learning Disabilities* (1986) and was one of the authors of *Introduction to Behavioral Science and Medicine* (1983). In addition, he has written numerous journal articles and book chapters about how biological and psychosocial processes act together in the development and adjustment of children with developmental and medical problems.

**Kathryn E. Gustafson** is Assistant Professor of Medical Psychology in the Department of Psychiatry and Behavioral Sciences and Assistant Professor of Psychology in the Department of Psychology: Social and

Health Sciences at Duke University. She received her PhD in clinical psychology from Ohio University and completed a clinical child/pediatric internship at the Medical University of South Carolina. Subsequently, she completed a pediatric psychology fellowship at Duke University Medical Center. Her research and clinical interests are in the areas of child and family adaptation to chronic childhood illness, and ethical issues in clinical psychology. She has been a co-investigator and coordinator of federally funded clinical research grants with infants of very low birth weight and with children with cystic fibrosis and sickle-cell disease. Gustafson has also been the coordinator of the Pediatric Psychology Laboratory and Consultation Service at Duke University Medical Center. A particular area of clinical focus has been children with brain tumors, and Gustafson serves as the psychologist on the multidisciplinary Pediatric Neuro-Oncology team at Duke. Gustafson has also served on the editorial board of the *Journal of Developmental and Behavioral Pediatrics*. She has authored or coauthored articles that have appeared in journals such as *Journal of Pediatric Psychology*, *Journal of Consulting and Clinical Psychology*, *Journal of Developmental and Behavioral Pediatrics*, and *Professional Psychology: Research and Practice*.